The ACE Programmer's Guide

The ACE Programmer's Guide

Practical Design Patterns for Network and Systems Programming

Stephen D. Huston
James CE Johnson
Umar Syyid

✦✦ Addison-Wesley

Boston • San Francisco • New York • Toronto • Montreal
London • Munich • Paris • Madrid
Capetown • Sydney • Tokyo • Singapore • Mexico City

Many of the designations used by manufacturers and sellers to distinguish their products are claimed as trademarks. Where those designations appear in this book, and Addison-Wesley was aware of a trademark claim, the designations have been printed with initial capital letters or all capitals.

The authors and publisher have taken care in the preparation of this book, but make no expressed or implied warranty of any kind and assume no responsibility for errors or omissions. No liability is assumed for incidental or consequential damages in connection with or arising out of the use of the information or programs contained herein.

Figures 7.1, 7.2, 7.3, and 8.1 originally published in Schmidt/Huston, *C++ Network Programming, Volume 2: Systematic Reuse with ACE and Frameworks*, Copyright © 2003 by Pearson Education, Inc. Reprinted with permission of Pearson Education, Inc.

The publisher offers discounts on this book when ordered in quantity for bulk purchases and special sales. For more information, please contact:

U.S. Corporate and Government Sales
(800) 382-3419
corpsales@pearsontechgroup.com

For sales outside of the U.S., please contact:

International Sales
(317) 581-3793
international@pearsontechgroup.com

Visit Addison-Wesley on the Web: www.awprofessional.com

Library of Congress Cataloging-in-Publication Data

Huston, Stephen D.
    The ACE programmer's guide : practical design patterns for network and systems
programming / Stephen D. Huston, James CE Johnson and Umar Syyid.
        p.   cm.
    ISBN 0-201-69971-0 (pbk. : alk. paper)
    1. Computer software—Development. 2. Object-oriented programming (Computer science)
3. Software patterns. I. Johnson, James C. E. II. Syyid, Umar. III. Title.

QA76.76.D47H89 2003
005.1'17—dc21   2003014046

Copyright © 2004 by Pearson Education, Inc.

ISBN 0-201-69971-0
Text printed on recycled paper.
1 2 3 4 5 6 7 8 9 10—CRS—0706050403
First printing, November 2003

Contents

Illustrations. xi
Tables xiii
Foreword xv
Preface xix

Part I: ACE Basics   **1**

1. Introduction to ACE. 3
    1.1   A History of ACE 3
    1.2   ACE's Benefits 5
    1.3   ACE's Organization 6
    1.4   Patterns, Class Libraries, and Frameworks. 7
    1.5   Porting Your Code to Multiple Operating Systems 8
    1.6   Smoothing the Differences among C++ Compilers 11
    1.7   Using Both Narrow and Wide Characters 19
    1.8   Where to Find More Information and Support. 21
    1.9   Summary. 23

2. How to Build and Use ACE in Your Programs 25
    2.1   A Note about ACE Versions. 25
    2.2   Guide to the ACE Distribution 26

2.3   How to Build ACE 27
2.4   How to Include ACE in Your Applications 30
2.5   How to Build Your Applications 31
2.6   Summary 36

3. Using the ACE Logging Facility 37

3.1   Basic Logging and Tracing 38
3.2   Enabling and Disabling Logging Severities 43
3.3   Customizing the ACE Logging Macros 47
3.4   Redirecting Logging Output 55
3.5   Using Callbacks 60
3.6   The Logging Client and Server Daemons 64
3.7   The LogManager Class 70
3.8   Runtime Configuration with the ACE Logging Strategy 73
3.9   Summary 75

4. Collecting Runtime Information 77

4.1   Command Line Arguments and ACE_Get_Opt 78
4.2   Accessing Configuration Information 83
4.3   Building Argument Vectors 85
4.4   Summary 86

5. ACE Containers 87

5.1   Container Concepts 88
5.2   Sequence Containers 90
5.3   Associative Containers 103
5.4   Allocators 115
5.5   Summary 119

Part II: Interprocess Communication   121

6. Basic TCP/IP Socket Use 123

6.1   A Simple Client 124
6.2   Adding Robustness to a Client 129
6.3   Building a Server 135
6.4   Summary 140

7. Handling Events and Multiple I/O Streams 141

7.1   Overview of the Reactor Framework 142
7.2   Handling Multiple I/O Sources 142

7.3   Signals 155
7.4   Notifications 158
7.5   Timers 160
7.6   Using the Acceptor-Connector Framework 168
7.7   Reactor Implementations 181
7.8   Summary. 185

8. Asynchronous I/O and the ACE Proactor Framework 187

8.1   Why Use Asynchronous I/O? 188
8.2   How to Send and Receive Data 189
8.3   Establishing Connections 197
8.4   The ACE_Proactor Completion Demultiplexer 201
8.5   Using Timers 202
8.6   Other I/O Factory Classes. 202
8.7   Combining the Reactor and Proactor Frameworks. 203
8.8   Summary. 205

9. Other IPC Types 207

9.1   Interhost IPC with UDP/IP 207
9.2   Intrahost Communication 213
9.3   Summary. 215

Part III: Process and Thread Management   217

10. Process Management 219

10.1   Spawning a New Process 219
10.2   Using the ACE_Process_Manager 226
10.3   Synchronization Using ACE_Process_Mutex 231
10.4   Summary. 234

11. Signals 235

11.1   Using Wrappers 236
11.2   Event Handlers 239
11.3   Guarding Critical Sections 246
11.4   Signal Management with the Reactor. 247
11.5   Summary. 248

12. Basic Multithreaded Programming 249

12.1   Getting Started 250
12.2   Basic Thread Safety 251

12.3   Intertask Communication 257
12.4   Summary. 266

13. Thread Management 267

13.1   Types of Threads. 267
13.2   Priorities and Scheduling Classes. 271
13.3   Thread Pools. 275
13.4   Thread Management Using ACE_Thread_Manager 276
13.5   Signals 279
13.6   Thread Start-Up Hooks. 283
13.7   Cancellation 284
13.8   Summary. 288

14. Thread Safety and Synchronization 289

14.1   Protection Primitives 289
14.2   Thread Synchronization 301
14.3   Thread-Specific Storage 309
14.4   Summary. 311

15. Active Objects 313

15.1   The Pattern 314
15.2   Using the Pattern. 316
15.3   Summary. 324

16. Thread Pools. 325

16.1   Understanding Thread Pools 325
16.2   Half-Sync/Half-Async Model. 326
16.3   Leader/Followers Model. 338
16.4   Thread Pools and the Reactor. 343
16.5   Summary. 346

Part IV: Advanced ACE   347

17. Shared Memory 349

17.1   ACE_Malloc and ACE_Allocator 350
17.2   Persistence with ACE_Malloc 352
17.3   Position-Independent Allocation 356
17.4   ACE_Malloc for Containers. 359
17.5   Wrappers. 374
17.6   Summary. 376

18. ACE Streams Framework 377

18.1   Overview 377
18.2   Using a One-Way Stream 378
18.3   A Bidirectional Stream 397
18.4   Summary 417

19. ACE Service Configurator Framework 419

19.1   Overview 420
19.2   Configuring Static Services 420
19.3   Setting Up Dynamic Services 427
19.4   Setting Up Streams 430
19.5   Reconfiguring Services During Execution 431
19.6   Using XML to Configure Services and Streams 433
19.7   Configuring Services without svc.conf 434
19.8   Singletons and Services 434
19.9   Summary 435

20. Timers 437

20.1   Timer Concepts 437
20.2   Timer Queues 439
20.3   Prebuilt Dispatchers 447
20.4   Managing Event Handlers 450
20.5   Summary 455

21. ACE Naming Service 457

21.1   The ACE_Naming_Context 457
21.2   A Single-Process Naming Context: PROC_LOCAL 459
21.3   Sharing a Naming Context on One Node: NODE_LOCAL 468
21.4   Sharing a Naming Context across the Network: NET_LOCAL 476
21.5   Summary 478

Bibliography 479
Index 481

Illustrations

7.1   Acceptor-Connector framework classes 169

7.2   Steps in `ACE_Acceptor` connection acceptance. 172

7.3   Reactive shutdown of an `ACE_Svc_Handler` 176

8.1   Classes in the Proactor framework 190

8.2   Sequence diagram for asynchronous data echo example 196

12.1   Using a queue for communication 261

13.1   Kernel- and User-Level Threads. 269

15.1   Asynchronous `log()` method 314

15.2   Active Object pattern participants 315

15.3   Active Object collaborations 317

15.4   Active Object pattern applied to example. .319

18.1   Diagram of an `ACE_Stream` 379

18.2   Logical structure of the command stream .397

20.1   Timer queue class hierarchy 438

20.2   Timer dispatcher example class diagram 441

20.3   Timer dispatcher example sequence diagram. 442

20.4   Timer queue template classes 451

20.5   Upcall handler sequence diagram. 452

Tables

1.1	Data Types Defined by ACE	15
1.2	ACE Memory Allocation Macros	20
1.3	Macros Related to Character Width	20
2.1	Configuration Files for Popular ACE Platforms	29
2.2	GNU make Options	30
2.3	ACE Library File Names for Visual C++	35
3.1	ACE_Log_Msg Logging Severity Levels	39
3.2	ACE Logging Format Directives	41
3.3	ACE Logging Macros	44
3.4	Commonly Used ACE_Log_Msg Methods	48
3.5	Valid ACE_Log_Msg Flags Values	56
3.6	Mapping ACE Logging Severity to Windows Event Log Severity	58
3.7	ACE_Log_Record Attributes	65
3.8	ACE Logging Strategy Configuration Options	75
5.1	Allocators Available in ACE	116
7.1	Meaning of Event Handler Callback Return Values	149
12.1	ACE Guard Classes	256
12.2	Various Queue Types	266

13.1   Thread Creation Flags 268

13.2   Thread Priority Macros..................................272

14.1   Protection Primitives in ACE.............................290

14.2   ACE Synchronization Primitives 302

17.1   Memory Pool Types 351

17.2   Memory Pool Macro Names..............................352

17.3   `ACE_MMAP_Memory_Pool_Options` Attributes 360

19.1   Service Configurator Command Line Options.................427

20.1   Timer Storage Structures and Relative Performance 439

21.1   Name Options Attributes 458

Foreword

I started programming computers in the mid-1980s. Then, like today, computing and communication systems were heterogeneous; that is, there were many different programming languages, operating systems, and networking protocols. Moreover, due to the accidental complexities of programming with low-level and nonportable application programming interfaces (APIs), the types of networked applications available to software developers and end users were relatively primitive, consisting largely of e-mail, remote login, and file transfer. As a result, many applications were either centralized on mainframes and minicomputers or localized on a single stand-alone PC or workstation.

There have been significant advances in information technology (IT) for computing and communication during the intervening two decades. Languages, programming environments, operating systems, networking protocols, and middleware are more mature and standardized. For example, C++ has become an ISO/ANSI standard and is being used in a broad range of application domains. Likewise, the UNIX, Windows, and TCP/IP standards have also become ubiquitous. Even distributed computing middleware standards, such as CORBA, .NET, and J2EE, are becoming widely embraced by the IT industry and end users.

Even with all these advances, however, there is still a layer of the networked software design space—host infrastructure middleware for performance-driven, multiplatform, networked and/or concurrent software systems—that is not well served by standard solutions at other levels of abstraction. Host infrastructure middleware encapsulates native operating system (OS) concurrency and interprocess communication (IPC) mechanisms to alleviate many tedious, error-prone, and nonportable activities associated with developing networked applications via native OS APIs, such as Sockets or POSIX threads (Pthreads). Performance-driven systems also have stringent quality of service (QoS) requirements.

Providing host infrastructure middleware for today's popular computing environments is particularly important for (1) high-performance computing systems, such as those that support scientific visualization, distributed database servers, and online financial trading systems; (2) distributed real-time and embedded systems that monitor and control real-world artifacts, such as avionics mission- and flight-control software, supervisory control and data acquisition systems, and automotive braking systems; and (3) multiplatform applications that must run portably across local- and wide-area networks. These types of systems are increasingly subject to the following trends:

- *The need to access native OS mechanisms to meet QoS requirements.* For example, multimedia applications that require long-duration, bidirectional bytestream communication services are poorly suited to the synchronous request/response model provided by conventional distribution middleware. Likewise, many distribution middleware implementations incur significant overhead and lack sufficient hooks to manipulate other QoS-related properties, such as latency, throughput, and jitter.

- *Severe cost and time-to-market pressures.* Global competition and market deregulation are shrinking budgets for the in-house development and quality assurance (QA) of software, particularly for the OS and middleware infrastructure. Moreover, performance-driven users are often unable or less willing to pay for specialized proprietary infrastructure software.

- *The demand for user-specific customization.* Because performance-intensive software often pushes the limits of technology, it must be optimized for particular runtime contexts and application requirements. General-purpose, one-size-fits-all software solutions often have unacceptable performance.

As these trends continue to accelerate, they present many challenges to developers of tomorrow's networked software systems. In particular, to succeed in today's competitive, fast-paced computing industry, successful middleware and application software must exhibit the following eight characteristics:

1. Affordability, to ensure that the total ownership costs of software acquisition and evolution aren't prohibitively high

2. Extensibility, to support successions of quick updates and additions to address new requirements and take advantage of emerging markets

3. Flexibility, to support a growing range of data types, traffic flows, and end-to-end QoS requirements

4. Portability, to reduce the effort required to support applications on heterogeneous OS platforms and compilers

5. Predictability and efficiency, to provide low latency to delay-sensitive real-time applications, high performance to bandwidth-intensive applications, and usability over low-bandwidth networks, such as wireless links

6. Reliability, to ensure that applications are robust and tolerant of faults

7. Scalability, to enable applications to handle many users simultaneously

8. Trustworthiness, to ensure integrity, confidentiality, and availability in inter-networked systems

I've encountered all these challenges while working on scores of research and production performance-driven software systems during the past two decades. In 1992, I began creating a software toolkit called the ADAPTIVE Communication Environment (ACE) to address concurrent network programming challenges. ACE is portable object-oriented host infrastructure middleware written in C++. ACE was designed to solve a very pragmatic problem—to save time implementing my doctoral dissertation project on parallel protocol processing engines in both SunOS 4.x and SunOS 5.x operating systems. Having worked on free software projects for many years, I recognized immediately that making ACE available in open-source form would help to galvanize a community whereby other developers and users could assist with the QA, documentation, and support activities needed to transform ACE into a high-quality production software toolkit.

Over the next decade, a core group of around 30 developers and I teamed up with more than 1,700 contributors from around the world to evolve ACE so it encapsulates and augments a wide range of native OS capabilities that are essential to support performance-driven software systems. The core frameworks and wrapper facades in ACE provide an integrated collection of reusable object-oriented classes that simplify and automate connection establishment, event demultiplexing, secure and efficient interprocess communication, (de)marshaling, dynamic configuration of application components, concurrency, and synchronization. Most important, the ACE frameworks can be customized readily to support a wide range of runtime contexts and application requirements.

Today, ACE runs on dozens of hardware and OS platforms, including most versions of Windows and UNIX, as well as many real-time and embedded operating systems. Due to its maturity, efficiency, and scope, ACE is being used by thousands of development teams, ranging from large Fortune 500 companies to small start-ups to advanced research projects at universities and industry labs. Its open-source development model and highly knowledgeable user community is similar in spirit, enthusiasm, and productivity to that driving the Linux operating system, the Apache web server, and the GNU compiler collection.

For many years, however, the only way to learn ACE was to read the source code and example applications, technical papers that described its patterns and the design of its frameworks, and online tutorials. Although a surprisingly large number of ACE users managed to master ACE via this process, the learning curve was time consuming and error prone. In 2002 and 2003, I teamed up with Steve Huston to write a pair of books on C++ Network Programming (C++NP), which cover the motivation, design, implementation, and use of the most popular wrapper facade classes and frameworks in ACE.

The ACE Programmer's Guide takes a different tack from the C++NP books, explaining quickly and directly how to make the best use of ACE. In addition to its nuts-and-bolts approach to explaining key ACE capabilities, this book addresses important topics not covered in the C++NP books, including how to build ACE and your programs that use ACE, ACE's OS and compiler portability features, the ACE logging facility, command line options processing, container classes, signal handling, and shared memory. The book also covers certain material in greater depth than the C++NP books, including concurrency models, bidirectional streams, and asynchronous I/O. Throughout this book, many examples using ACE show how key patterns and design principles can be applied to develop object-oriented networked software successfully. By learning the material in this book, you'll be better able to design and implement performance-driven networked software that can't be bought off-the-shelf, thereby staying ahead of your competition.

We are fortunate that Steve, James, and Umar have found time in their hectic schedules to write this book. If you're designing software and systems that must be portable, flexible, extensible, predictable, reliable, and affordable, this book and the ACE toolkit will enable you to be more effective in all these areas. Even after spending more than a decade developing ACE and using it to build networked software applications, I find that I've learned a great deal from this book, and I'm confident that you will too.

—Douglas C. Schmidt
Professor of Electrical Engineering and Computer Science at
Vanderbilt University and Inventor of ACE
Nashville, Tennessee

Preface

ACE (the ADAPTIVE Communication Environment) is a powerful C++ toolkit that helps you develop portable, high-performance applications, especially networked and/or multithreaded applications, more easily and more quickly with more flexibility and fewer errors. And, because of ACE's design and frameworks, you can do all this with much less code than with other development approaches. We've been using ACE for years and have found it exceedingly helpful and well worth any price. What's better is that it's available for free! The historical price many developers have paid to use ACE is a steep learning curve. It's a big toolkit with a large set of capabilities. Until recently, the best documentation has been the source code, which is, of course, freely available, and a set of academic papers born of the research that produced ACE, approachable only by advanced professionals and upper-level students. This barrier to learning has kept ACE's power and easy-to-use elegance one of the best-kept secrets in software development. That's why we're very excited to write this book! It flattens out ACE's learning curve, bringing ACE's power, elegance, and capabilities to all.

This book teaches you about ACE: a bit of its history and approach to development, how it's organized, how to begin using it, and also how to use some of its more advanced capabilities. We teach you how to do things the ACE way in this book, but we could not possibly fit in a complete reference. Use this book to get started with ACE and to begin using it in your work. If you've been using ACE for a while, there are probably descriptions of some capabilities you haven't seen before, so the book is useful for experienced ACE users as well.

Who Should Read This Book

This book is meant to serve as both an introductory guide for ACE beginners and a quickly accessible review for experienced ACE users. If you are an ACE beginner, we recommend starting at the beginning and proceeding through the chapters in order. If you are experienced and know what you want to read about, you can quickly find that part of the book and do not need to read the previous sections.

This book is written for C++ programmers who have been exposed to some of the more advanced C++ features, such as virtual inheritance and class templates. You should also have been exposed to basic operating system facilities you plan to use in your work. For example, if you plan to write programs that use TCP/IP sockets, you should at least be familiar with the general way sockets are created, connections are established, and data is transferred.

This book is also an excellent source of material for those who teach others: in either a commercial or an academic setting. ACE is an excellent example of how to design object-oriented software and use C++ to design and write high-performance, easily maintained software systems.

Organization

This book is a hands-on, how-to guide to using ACE effectively. The many source code examples illustrate proper use of the pieces of ACE being described. The source code examples are kept fairly short and to the point. Sometimes, the example source is abridged in order to focus attention on a topic. The complete source code to all examples is on the included CD-ROM and is also available on Riverace Corporation's web site. The included CD-ROM also includes a copy of ACE's source kit, installable versions of ACE prebuilt for a number of popular platforms, and complete reference documentation for all the classes in ACE.

The book begins with basic areas of functionality that many ACE users need and then proceeds to build on the foundations, describing the higher-level features that abstract behavior out into powerful patterns.

- Part I introduces ACE and provides some generally useful information about the facilities ACE provides. Part I also explains how to configure and build ACE, as well as how to build your applications that use ACE. Widely used programming aids, such as logging and tracing, command line processing and configuration access, and ACE's container classes, are also described.

- Part II discusses ACE's facilities for interprocess communication (IPC), beginning with basic, low-level TCP/IP Sockets wrapper classes and proceeding to show how to handle multiple sockets, as well as other events, such as timers and signals, simultaneously using ACE's Reactor and Proactor frameworks. Part II also describes ACE's Acceptor-Connector framework and then ends with a discussion of some of the other IPC wrapper classes ACE offers, many of which are substitutable for TCP/IP wrapper classes in the covered frameworks.

- Part III covers a wide range of topics related to process and thread management using ACE. This part explains how to use ACE's process management classes and then covers signals, followed by three chapters about multi-threaded programming, thread management, and the critical areas of thread safety and synchronization. Part III ends with discussions of Active Objects and various ways to use thread pools in ACE—critical topics for effective use of multithreading in high-performance applications.

- Part IV covers advanced ACE topics: shared memory, the ACE Streams framework for assembling modular data-processing streams, and how to make your applications more flexible and configurable by using the ACE Service Configurator framework. Part IV concludes with an in-depth discussion of ACE's timer management classes and the ACE Naming Service, one of ACE's network services components to assist with often needed networked application programming tasks.

The book concludes with a bibliography and an extensive subject index.

Conventions Used in This Book

All ACE classes begin with ACE_. When we refer to patterns instead of the classes they implement, we omit the prefix. For example, the Reactor pattern is implemented by the ACE_Reactor class.

All class member variables are suffixed with '_'. This convention is used in the ACE sources, and we carry it through to the examples in this book as well.

C++ code and file names are set in this font. Command lines are set in **this font**.

Acknowledgments

We are indebted to the review team that read and commented on the entire manuscript. Craig L. Ching, Dave Mercer, Johnny Willemsen, and Steven P. Witten provided insightful and helpful feedback and ideas that improved the book greatly.

We are also grateful to the members of the ACE user community worldwide who volunteered their free time to review a number of manuscript drafts and provide helpful corrections and advice. Like the many contributors to ACE itself, these individuals show the cooperative nature of many Open-Source developer/user communities, and the ACE users in particular: Bill Cassanova, Ufuk Çoban, Todd Cooper, Ning Cui, Alain Decamps, John Fowler, Chris D. Gill, Kelly F. Hickel, Don Hinton, Robert Kindred, Michael Kleck, Franz Klein, Sven Köster, Dieter Knüppel, Theo Landman, Mark Levan, Alexander Libman, John Lilley, Stephen McDonald, Mike Mullen, Mats Nilsson, Jaroslaw Nozderko, Rick Ohnemus, Wojtek Pilorz, Sunanda C. Prasad, Dietrich Quehl, Irma Rastegayeva, Michael Searles, Rich Siebel, Chris Smith, Scott Smith, Edward Thompson, Alain Totouom, Bill Trudell, and Lothar Werzinger.

Our editorial team at Addison-Wesley was very helpful and encouraging during this long process as well. Thanks to our editors: Marina Lang, Debbie Lafferty, Peter Gordon, and Bernie Gaffney. Thank you to our copy editor, Evelyn Pyle, who did a marvelous job molding our differing approaches and styles into a unified whole. Many, many thanks to our production coordinator, Elizabeth Ryan, who has now ushered all three ACE-related books through production with great skill, grace, and patience.

Steve's Acknowledgments

As in all my work, I am deeply indebted to my wonderful wife, Jane, for her abiding love, constant support, and much-needed help during the long process of writing this book. You sacrificed much more than anyone should ever have to and are truly God's gift to me—thank you! As wise Solomon once said, "Of making many books there is no end, and much study wearies the body" (Ecclesiastes 12:12, NIV). I'm a bit weary and thankful to God for the energy to complete this work. I'm also grateful to my late mother, Karen L. Anderson, who would be pleased with the lessons I've finally learned.

James's Acknowledgments

I would like to thank my wife, Karla, and my son, Riley, who was born half-way through this four-year process, for their patience and understanding every time I disappeared into the basement office for hours on end. Without their constant support and encouragement, I don't think I would have ever made it to this point. I would also like to thank my parents for always encouraging me to put forth my best effort and to never settle for second best. And, finally, thanks to Doug Schmidt for creating ACE in the first place and giving us all the opportunity to create this text.

Umar's Acknowledgments

First of all I would like to thank my wife, Ambreen, and my son, Hassan. If it weren't for them, I might not leave the computer at all for a few days; thanks for calling me home. Ambreen deserves my special thanks for enduring my constant babble over the years. Without her support, I would not have written a single page. I would also like to thank my mother for her courage and support during the more difficult times in my life. In addition, I would like to thank my father for making me want to show him that I could. Finally, thanks to Doug Schmidt for driving down to the University of Illinois to provide a graduate seminar that first taught me about a framework called ACE.

Concluding Remarks

This book is a true coauthorship, with each of us writing equal amounts of the text. Therefore, we all share equally in the blame for any problems you may find in the text. Please report anything you do find to either the ACE users mailing list (`ace-users@cs.wustl.edu`) or to us at `ace-tutorial@tragus.org`. Writing a book on a topic as broad as ACE is a very difficult task. The fact that we had a team of authors made the task considerably easier. In addition, the help available from the DOC group and the ACE user community has proved invaluable.

Steve Huston
James CE Johnson
Umar Syyid

Part I

ACE Basics

Chapter 1
Introduction to ACE

ACE is a rich and powerful toolkit with a distinctively nontraditional history. To help you get a feel for where ACE comes from, this chapter gives a brief history of ACE's development. Before going into programming details, we cover some foundational concepts: class libraries, patterns, and frameworks. Then we cover one of ACE's less glamorous but equally useful aspects: its facilities for smoothing out the differences among operating systems, hardware architectures, C++ compilers, and C++ runtime support environments. It is important to understand these aspects of ACE before we dive into the rest of ACE's capabilities.

1.1 A History of ACE

ACE (the ADAPTIVE—A Dynamically Assembled Protocol Transformation, Integration, and eValuation Environment—Communication Environment) grew out of the research and development activities of Dr. Douglas C. Schmidt at the University of California at Irvine. Doug's work was focused on design patterns, implementation, and experimental analysis of object-oriented techniques that facilitate the development of high-performance, real-time distributed object computing frameworks. As is so often the case, that work began on a small handful of hardware and OS (operating system) platforms and expanded over time. Doug ran into the following problems that still vex developers today.

- Trying to rearrange code to try out new combinations of processes, threads, and communications mechanisms is very tedious. The process of ripping code apart, rearranging it, and getting it working again is very boring and error prone.
- Working at the OS API (application programming interface) level adds accidental complexity. Identifying the subtle programming quirks and resolving these issues takes an inordinate amount of time in development schedules.
- Successful projects need to be ported to new platforms and platform versions. Standards notwithstanding, no two platforms or versions are the same, and the complexities begin again.

Doug, being the smart guy he is, came up with a plan. He invented a set of C++ classes that worked together, allowing him to create templates and strategize his way around the bumps inherent in rearranging the pieces of his programs. Moreover, these classes implemented some very useful design patterns for isolating the changes in the various computing platforms he kept getting, making it easy for his programs to run on all the new systems his advisors and colleagues could throw at him. Life was good. And thus was born ACE.

At this point, Doug could have grabbed his Ph.D. and some venture funding and taken the world of class libraries by storm. We'd all be paying serious money for the use of ACE today. Fortunately for the world's C++ developers, Doug decided to pursue further research in this area. He created the large and successful Distributed Object Computing group at Washington University in St. Louis. ACE was released as Open Source,[1] and its development continued with the aid of more than US$7 million funding from visionary commercial sponsors.

Today, most of the research-related work on ACE is carried out at the Institute for Software Integrated Systems (ISIS) at Vanderbilt University, where Doug is now a professor and still heavily involved in ACE's day-to-day development. ACE is increasingly popular in commercial development as well. It enjoys a reputation for solving the cross-platform issues that face all high-performance networked application and systems developers. Additionally, commercial-level technical support for ACE is now available worldwide.

ACE is freely available for any use, including commercial, without onerous licensing requirements. For complete details, see the COPYING file in the top-level directory of the ACE source kit. Another interesting file in the top-level

---

1. If you'd like more information on Open Source Software in general, please visit the Open Source Initiative page on the web at http://www.opensource.org/.

directory is THANKS. It lists all the people who have contributed to ACE over the years—more than 1,700 at the time of this writing! If you contribute improvements or additions to ACE, you too can get your name listed.

1.2 ACE's Benefits

The accidental complexity and development issues that led to ACE reflect lessons learned by all of us who've written networking programs, especially portable, high-performance networking programs.

- Multiplatform source code is difficult to write. The many and varied standards notwithstanding, each new port introduces a new set of problems. To remain flexible and adaptive to new technology and business conditions, software must be able to quickly change to take advantage of new operating systems and hardware. One of the best ways to remain that flexible is to take advantage of libraries and middleware that absorb the differences for you, allowing your code to remain above the fray. ACE has been ported to a wide range of systems—from handheld to supercomputer—running a variety of operating systems and using many of the available C++ compilers.

- Networked applications are difficult to write. Introducing a network into your design introduces a large set of challenges and issues throughout the development process. Network latency, byte ordering, data structure layout, network instability and performance, and handling multiple connections smoothly are a few typical problems that you must be concerned with when developing networked applications. ACE makes dozens of frameworks and design pattern implementations available to you, so you can take advantage of solutions that many other smart people have already come up with.

- Most system-provided APIs are written in terms of C API bindings because C is so common and the API is usable from a variety of languages. If you're considering working with ACE, you've already committed to using C++, though, and the little tricks that seemed so slick with C, such as overlaying the `sockaddr` structure with `sockaddr_in`, `sockaddr_un`, and friends, are just big opportunities for errors. Low-level APIs have many subtle requirements, which sometimes change from standard to standard—as in the series of drafts leading to POSIX 1004.1c Pthreads—and are sometimes poorly documented and difficult to use. (Remember when you first figured out that the `socket()`, `bind()`, `listen()`, and `accept()` functions were all related?) ACE provides a well-organized, coherent set of abstractions to make IPC, shared memory, threads, synchronization mechanisms, and more easy to use.

1.3 ACE's Organization

ACE is more than a class library. It is a powerful, object-oriented application toolkit. Although it is not apparent from a quick look at the source or reference pages, the ACE toolkit is designed using a layered architecture composed of the following layers:

- *OS adaptation layer.* The OS adaptation layer provides wrapper functions for most common system-level operations. This layer provides a common base of system functions across all the platforms ACE has been ported to. Where the native platform does not provide a desired function, it is emulated, if possible. If the function is available natively, the calls are usually inlined to maximize performance.

- *Wrapper facade layer.* A wrapper facade consists of one or more classes that encapsulate functions and data within a type-safe, object-oriented interface [5]. ACE's wrapper facade layer makes up nearly half of its source base. This layer provides much of the same capability available natively and via the OS adaptation layer but in an easier-to-use, type-safe form. Applications make use of the wrapper facade classes by selectively inheriting, aggregating, and/or instantiating them.

- *Framework layer.* A framework is an integrated collection of components that collaborate to produce a reusable architecture for a family of related applications [4] [7]. Frameworks emphasize the integration and collaboration of application-specific and application-independent components. By doing this, frameworks enable larger-scale reuse of software rather than simply reusing individual classes or stand-alone functions. ACE's frameworks integrate wrapper facade classes and implement canonical control flows and class collaborations to provide semicomplete applications. It is very easy to build applications by supplying application-specific behavior to a framework.

- *Networked services layer.* The networked services layer provides some complete, reusable services, including the distributed logging service we'll see in Chapter 3.

Each layer reuses classes in lower layers, abstracting out more common functionality. This means that any given task in ACE can usually be done in more than one way, depending on your needs and design constraints. Although we sometimes approach a problem "bottom up" because existing knowledge helps transition smoothly to ACE programming techniques, we generally cover the higher-level ways rather than the lower-level ways to approach problems in more depth. It is relatively easy, however, to find the lower-level classes and interfaces for your use when needed. The ACE reference documentation on the included CD-ROM can be used to find all class relationships and complete programming references.

1.4　Patterns, Class Libraries, and Frameworks

Computing power and network bandwidth have increased dramatically over the past decade. However, the design and implementation of complex software remains expensive and error prone. Much of the cost and effort stem from the continuous rediscovery and reinvention of core concepts and components across the software industry. In particular, the growing heterogeneity of hardware architectures and diversity of operating system and communication platforms make it difficult to build correct, portable, efficient, and inexpensive applications from scratch. Patterns, class libraries, and frameworks are three tools the software industry is using to reduce the complexity and cost of developing software.

Patterns represent recurring solutions to software development problems within a particular context. Patterns and frameworks both facilitate reuse by capturing successful software development strategies. The primary difference is that frameworks focus on reuse of concrete designs, algorithms, and implementations in a particular programming language. In contrast, patterns focus on reuse of abstract designs and software microarchitectures.

Frameworks can be viewed as a concrete implementation of families of design patterns that are targeted for a particular application domain. Likewise, design patterns can be viewed as more abstract microarchitectural framework elements that document and motivate the semantics of frameworks in an effective way. When patterns are used to structure and document frameworks, nearly every class in the framework plays a well-defined role and collaborates effectively with other classes in the framework.

Like frameworks, class libraries are implementations of useful, reusable software artifacts. Frameworks extend the benefits of OO (object-oriented) class libraries in the following ways.

- *Frameworks define "semicomplete" applications that embody domain-specific object structures and functionality.* Components in a framework work together to provide a generic architectural skeleton for a family of related applications. Complete applications are composed by inheriting from and/or instantiating framework components. In contrast, class libraries are less domain specific and provide a smaller scope of reuse. For instance, class library components, such as classes for strings, complex numbers, arrays, and bitsets, are relatively low level and ubiquitous across many application domains.

- *Frameworks are active and exhibit "inversion of control" at runtime.* Class libraries are typically passive; that is, they are directed to perform work by other application objects, in the same thread of control as those application objects. In contrast, frameworks are active; that is, they direct the flow of control within an application via event dispatching patterns, such as Reactor and Observer. The "inversion of control" in the runtime architecture of a framework is often referred to as the Hollywood Principle: "Don't call us; we'll call you."

In practice, frameworks and class libraries are complementary technologies. For instance, frameworks typically use class libraries internally to simplify the development of the framework. (Certainly, ACE's frameworks reuse other parts of the ACE class library.) Likewise, application-specific code invoked by framework event handlers can use class libraries to perform such basic tasks as string processing, file management, and numerical analysis.

So, to summarize, ACE is a toolkit packaged as a class library. The toolkit contains many useful classes. Many of those classes are related and combined into frameworks, such as the Reactor and Event Handler, that embody semicomplete applications. In its classes and frameworks, ACE implements many useful design patterns.

1.5 Porting Your Code to Multiple Operating Systems

Many software systems must be designed to work correctly on a range of computing platforms. Competitive forces and changing technology combine to make it a nearly universal requirement that today's software systems be able to run on a range of platforms, sometimes changing targets during development. Networked systems have a stronger need to be portable, owing to the inherent mix of computing environments needed to build and configure competitive systems in today's marketplace. Standards provide some framework for portability; however, marketing messages notwithstanding, standards do not guarantee portability across systems. As Andrew Tanenbaum said, "The nice thing about standards is that there are so many to choose from" [3]. And rest assured, vendors often choose to implement different standards at different times. Standards also change and evolve, so it's very unlikely that you'll work on more than one platform that implements all the same standards in the same way.

In addition to operating system APIs and their associated standards, compiling and linking your programs and libraries is another area that differs among operating systems and compilers. The ACE developers over the years have developed an effective system of building ACE based on the GNU Make tool. Even on systems for which a make utility is supplied by the vendor, not all makes are created equal. GNU Make provides a common, powerful tool around which ACE has its build facility. This allows ACE to be built on systems that don't supply native make utilities but to which GNU Make has been ported. Don't worry if you're a Windows programmer using Microsoft or Borland compilers and don't have GNU Make. The native Microsoft and Borland build utilities are supported as well.

Data type differences are a common area of porting difficulty that experienced multiplatform developers have found numerous ways to engineer around. ACE provides a set of data types it uses internally, and you are encouraged to use them as well. These are described later, in the discussion of compilers.

ACE's OS adaptation layer provides the lowest level of functionality and forms the basis of ACE's wide range of portability. This layer uses the Wrapper Facade [4] and Façade [3] patterns to shield you from platform differences. The Wrapper pattern forms a relatively simple wrapper around a function, and ACE uses this pattern to unify the programming interfaces for common system functions where small differences in APIs and semantics are smoothed over. The Façade pattern presents a single interface to what may, on some platforms, be a complicated set of systems calls. For example, the `ACE_OS::thr_create()` method creates a new thread with a caller-specified set of attributes: scheduling policy, priority, state, and so on. The native system calls to do all that's required during thread creation vary widely among platforms in form, semantics, and the combination and order of calls needed. The Façade pattern allows the presentation of one consistent interface across all platforms to which ACE has been ported.

For relatively complex and obviously nonportable actions, such as creating a thread, you would of course think to use the `ACE_OS` methods—well, at least until you read about the higher-level ACE classes and frameworks later in the

book. But what about other functions that are often taken for granted, such as
`printf()` and `fseek()`? Even when you need to perform a basic function, it is
safest to use the `ACE_OS` methods rather than native APIs. This usage guarantees
that you won't be surprised by a small change in arguments to the native calls
when you compile your code on a different platform.

The ACE OS adaptation layer is implemented in the `ACE_OS` class. The
methods in this class are all static. You may wonder why a separate namespace
wasn't used instead of a class, as that's basically what the class achieves. As we'll
soon see, one of ACE's strengths is that it works with a wide variety of old and
new C++ compilers, some of which do not support namespaces at all. We are not
going to list all the supplied functions here. You won't often use these functions
directly. They are still at a very low level, not all that much different from writing
in C. Rather, you'll more often use high-level classes that themselves call
`ACE_OS` methods to perform the requested actions. Therefore, we're going to
leave a detailed list of these methods to the `ACE_OS` reference pages.

As you might imagine, ACE contains quite a lot of conditionally compiled
code, especially in the OS adaptation layer. ACE does not make heavy use of
vendor-supplied compiler macros for this, for a couple of reasons. First, a number
of the settings deal with features that are missing or broken in the native platform
or compiler. The missing or broken features may change over time; for instance,
the OS is fixed or the compiler is updated. Rather than try to find a vendor-
supplied macro for each possible item and use those macros in many places in
ACE, any setting and vendor-supplied macro checking is done in one place and
the result remembered for simple use within ACE. The second reason that vendor-
supplied macros are not used extensively is that they may either not exist or may
conflict with another vendor's macros. Rather than use a complicated combination
of ACE-defined and vendor-supplied macros, a set of ACE-defined macros is used
extensively and is sometimes augmented by vendor-supplied macros, although
this is relatively rare.

The setting of all the ACE-defined compile-time macros is done in one file,
`ace/config.h`, which we'll look at in Chapter 2. Many varieties of this configuration file are supplied with ACE, matching all the platforms ACE has been
ported to. If you obtain a prebuilt version of ACE for installation in your environment, you most likely will never need to read or change this file. But sometime
when you're up for some adventure, read through it anyway for a sampling of the
range of features and issues ACE handles for you.

1.6   Smoothing the Differences among C++ Compilers

You're probably wondering why it's so important to smooth over the differences among compilers, as the C++ standard has finally settled down. There are a number of reasons.

- Compiler vendors are at various levels of conformance to the standard.
- ACE works with a range of C++ compilers, many of which are still at relatively early drafts of the C++ standard.
- Some compilers are simply broken, and ACE works around the problems.

Many items of compiler capability and disability adjustment are used to build ACE properly, but from a usage point of view, ACE helps you work with or around four primary areas of compiler differences:

1. Templates, both use and instantiation
2. Data types, both hardware and compiler
3. Runtime initialization and shutdown
4. Allocating heap memory

1.6.1   Templates

C++ templates are a powerful form of generic programming, and ACE makes heavy use of them, allowing you to combine and customize functionality in powerful ways. This brief discussion introduces you to class templates. If templates are a new feature to you, we suggest that you also read an in-depth discussion of their use in a good C++ book, such as Bjarne Stroustrup's *The C++ Programming Language, 3rd Edition* [11] or *C++ Templates: The Complete Guide* by David Vandevoorde and Nicolai M. Josuttis [14]. As you're reading, keep in mind that the dialect of C++ described in your book and that implemented by your compiler may be different. Check your compiler documentation for details, and stick to the guidelines documented in this book to be sure that your code continues to build and run properly when you change compilers.

C++'s template facility allows you to generically define a class or function, and have the compiler apply your template to a given set of data types at compile time. This increases code reuse in your project and enables you to reuse code across projects. For example, let's say that you need to design a class that remembers the largest value of a set of values you specify over time. Your system may have multiple uses for such a class—for example, to track integers, floating-point numbers, text strings, and even other classes that are part of your system. Rather than write a separate class for each possible type you want to track, you could write a class template:

```
template <class T> class max_tracker {
public:
  void track_this (const T val);
private:
  T max_val_;
};

template <class T>
void max_tracker::track_this (const T val)
{
  if (val > this->max_val_)
    this->max_val_ = val;
  return;
}
```

Then when you want to track the maximum temperature of your home in integer degrees, you declare and use one of these objects:

```
max_tracker<int>  temperature_tracker;

// Get a new temperature reading and track it
int temp_now = Thermometer.get_temp ();
temperature_tracker.track_this (temp_now);
```

The use of the template class would cause the compiler to generate code for the `max_tracker` class, substituting the `int` type for `T` in the class template. You could also declare a `max_tracker<float>` object, and the compiler would instantiate another set of code to use floating-point values. This magic of instantiating class template code brings us to the first area ACE helps you with—getting the needed classes instantiated correctly.

Template Instantiation

Many modern C++ compilers automatically "remember" which template instantiations your code needs and generate them as a part of the final link phase. In these cases, you're all set and don't need to do anything else. For one or more of the following reasons, however, you may need to take further steps regarding instantiation.

- You need to port your system to another platform on which the compiler isn't so accommodating.

- Your compiler is really slow when doing its magical template autoinstantiation, and you'd like to control it yourself, speeding up the build process.

Compilers provide a variety of directives and methods to specify template instantiation. Although the intricacies of preprocessors and compilers make it extremely difficult to provide one simple statement for specifying instantiation, ACE provides a boilerplate set of source lines you should use to control explicit template instantiation. The best way to explain it is to show its use. In the preceding example code, the following code would be added at the end of the source file:

```
#if defined (ACE_HAS_EXPLICIT_TEMPLATE_INSTANTIATION)
template class max_tracker<int>;
#elif defined (ACE_HAS_TEMPLATE_INSTANTIATION_PRAGMA)
#pragma instantiate max_tracker<int>
#endif /* ACE_HAS_EXPLICIT_TEMPLATE_INSTANTIATION */
```

This code will successfully build on all compilers that correctly handle automatic instantiation, as well as all compilers ACE has been ported to that customarily use explicit template instantiation for one reason or another. If you have more than one class to instantiate, you add more `template class` and `#pragma instantiate` lines to cover them.

Be careful when deciding to explicitly instantiate templates in projects that use the standard C++ library. The templates in the standard library often use other, not so obvious, templates, and it's easy to end up in a maze of instantiation statements that change between compilers. It's much safer to let the compiler automatically instantiate template classes whenever possible.

Use of Types Defined in Classes That Are Template Arguments

A number of ACE classes define types as traits of that class. For example, the `ACE_SOCK_Stream` class defines `ACE_INET_Addr` as the `PEER_ADDR` type. The other stream-abstracting classes also define a `PEER_ADDR` type internally to define the type of addressing information needed for that class. This use of traits will be seen in more detail in Section 7.6 when using the `ACE_Svc_Handler` class and in Chapter 17 when discussing `ACE_Malloc`. For now, though, view the use of traits as an example of this problem: If a template class can be used with one of these trait-defining classes as a template argument, the template class may need to know and use the trait type.

You'd think that the template argument class could be accessed as if the class were used by itself. But not so; some older compilers disallow that. ACE works around the limitation and keeps your code compiler neutral by defining a set of macros for the cases in ACE when the information is required together. In the case of the `ACE_SOCK_Stream` class's usage, when the addressing trait is also needed, ACE defines `ACE_SOCK_STREAM`, which expands to include the addressing type for compilers that don't support typedefs in classes used as template arguments. It expands to `ACE_SOCK_Stream` for compilers that do support it. The many uses of this tactic in ACE will be noted for you at the points in the book where their use comes up.

1.6.2 Data Types

Programs you must port to multiple platforms need a way to avoid implicit reliance on the hardware size of compiler types and the relationships between them. For example, on some hardware/compiler combinations, an `int` is 16 bits; in others, it is 32 bits.[2] On some platforms, a `long int` is the same as an `int`, which is the same length as a pointer; on others, they're all different sizes. ACE provides a set of type definitions for use when the size of a data value really matters and must be the same on all platforms your code runs on. They are listed in Table 1.1, with some other definitions that are useful in multiple-platform development. If you use these types, your code will use properly sized types on all ACE-supported platforms.

1.6.3 Runtime Initialization and Rundown

One particular area of platform difference and incompatibility is runtime initialization of objects and the associated destruction of those objects at program rundown. This difference is particularly true when multiple threads are involved, as there is no compiler-added access serialization to the time-honored method of automatic initialization and destruction of runtime data: static objects. So remember this ACE saying: *Statics are evil!* Fortunately, ACE provides a portable solution to this problem in the form of three related classes:

- `ACE_Object_Manager`. As its name implies, this class manages objects. The ACE library contains a single instance of this class, which when initialized instantiates a set of ACE objects that are needed to properly support the ACE internals and also destroys them at rundown time. ACE programs can

---

2. It wouldn't surprise us if there were also other possible values, such as 8 bits or 64 bits. The point is: Don't count on a particular size.

Table 1.1. Data Types Defined by ACE

Type	Meaning
ACE_INT16, ACE_UINT16	16-bit integer, signed and unsigned
ACE_INT32, ACE_UINT32	32-bit integer, signed and unsigned
ACE_UINT64	64-bit unsigned integer; on platforms without native 64-bit integer support, ACE provides a class to emulate it
ACE_SIZEOF_CHAR	Number of bytes in a character
ACE_SIZEOF_WCHAR	Number of bytes in a wide character
ACE_SIZEOF_SHORT	Number of bytes in a short int
ACE_SIZEOF_INT	Number of bytes in an int
ACE_SIZEOF_LONG	Number of bytes in a long int
ACE_SIZEOF_LONG_LONG	Number of bytes in a long long int; on platforms without native long long support, this is 8, and ACE_UINT64 is ACE_U_LongLong
ACE_SIZEOF_VOID_P	Number of bytes in a pointer
ACE_SIZEOF_FLOAT	Number of bytes in a float
ACE_SIZEOF_DOUBLE	Number of bytes in a double
ACE_SIZEOF_LONG_DOUBLE	Number of bytes in a long double
ACE_BYTE_ORDER	Has a value of either ACE_BIG_ENDIAN or ACE_LITTLE_ENDIAN

make use of the Object Manager by registering objects that must be destroyed. The Object Manager destroys all the objects registered with it at rundown time, in reverse order of their registration.

- ACE_Cleanup. ACE_Object_Manager uses this class's interface to manage object life cycles. Each object to be registered with the Object Manager must be derived from ACE_Cleanup.
- ACE_Singleton. The Singleton pattern [3] is used to provide a single instance of an object to a program and provide a global way to access it. This object instance is similar to a global object in that it's not hidden from any part of the program. However, the instantiation and deletion of the object is under control of your program, not the platform's runtime environment. ACE's

singleton class also adds thread safety to the basic Singleton pattern by using the Double-Checked Locking Optimization pattern [5]. The double-checked lock ensures that only one thread initializes the object in a multithreaded system.

The two most common ways to be sure that your objects are properly cleaned up at program rundown are described next. Which one you use depends on the situation. If you want to create a number of objects of the same class and be sure that each is cleaned up, use the ACE_Cleanup method. If you want one instance of your object accessible using the Singleton pattern, use the ACE_Singleton method.

- ACE_Cleanup method. To be able to create a number of objects of a class and have them be cleaned up by the ACE Object Manager, derive your class from ACE_Cleanup, which has a cleanup() method that the Object Manager calls to do the cleanup. To tell the Object Manager about your object—so it knows to clean it up—you make one simple call, probably from your object's constructor:

```
ACE_Object_Manager::at_exit (this);
```

- ACE_Singleton method. Use the ACE_Singleton class to create one and only one instance of your object. This class uses the Adapter pattern [3] to turn any ordinary class into a singleton optimized with the Double-Checked Locking Optimization pattern. ACE_Singleton is a template class with this definition:

```
template <class TYPE, class ACE_LOCK>
class ACE_Singleton : public ACE_Cleanup
```

TYPE is name of the class you are turning into a singleton. ACE_LOCK is the type of lock the Double-Checked Locking Optimization pattern implementation uses to serialize checking when the object needs to be created. For code that operates in a multithreaded environment, use ACE_Recursive_Thread_Mutex. If you are writing code without threads, you should use ACE_Null_Mutex, which provides the proper interface but does not lock anything. This would be useful if your main factor in choosing the Singleton pattern is to provide its "instantiate when needed" semantics, as well as have the Object Manager clean up the object. As an example, assume that you have a class named SystemController and that you want a single instance of it. You would define your class and then

```
typedef ACE_Singleton<SystemController,
ACE_Recursive_Thread_Mutex> TheSystemController;
```

When you need access to the instance of that object, you get a pointer to it from anywhere in your system by calling its `instance()` method. For example:

`SystemController *s = TheSystemController::instance();`

As we've seen, the ACE Object Manager is quite a useful and powerful object. You need to remember only two rules in order to successfully make use of this facility.

1. Never call `exit()` directly.

2. Make sure that the Object Manager is initialized successfully.

The first is easy. Remember all the registrations with the Object Manager to request proper cleanup at rundown time? If you call `exit()`, your program will terminate directly, without the Object Manager's having a chance to clean anything up. Instead, have your `main()` function simply do a `return` to end. If your program encounters a fatal condition inside a function call tree, either return, passing error indications, or throw an exception that your `main()` function will catch so it can cleanly return after cleaning up. In a pinch, you may call `ACE_OS::exit()` instead of the "naked" `exit()`. That will ensure that the Object Manager gets a chance to clean up.

Object Manager initialization is an important concept to understand. Once you understand it, you can often forget about it for a number of platforms. The Object Manager is, effectively, a Singleton. Because it is created before any code has a chance to create threads, the Object Manager doesn't need the same protection that Singletons generally require. And, what object would the Object Manager register with for cleanup? The cleanup chain has to end somewhere, and this is where. As we said, statics are generally evil.

However, on some platforms, statics are not completely evil, and the Object Manager is in fact a static object, initialized and destroyed properly by the platform's runtime environment, even when used in combination with shared libraries, some of which are possibly loaded and unloaded dynamically. On these platforms,[3] you can usually ignore the rule for properly initializing the Object Manager.[4] On the others, however, the Object Manager needs to be initialized and terminated explicitly. For use cases in which you are writing a regular C++ application that has the standard `int main (int argc, char *argv[])` entry point or the wide-character-enabled `ACE_TMAIN` entry point shown in

---

3. The `config.h` file for these does *not* define ACE_HAS_NONSTATIC_OBJECT_MANAGER.

4. No, Windows is definitely not one of those platforms.

Section 1.7, ACE magically redefines your `main()` function and inserts its own, which instantiates the Object Manager on the runtime stack and then calls your `main()` function. When your `main()` function returns, the Object Manager is run down as well. (This is an example of why your code should not call `exit()`: You'd bypass the Object Manager cleanup.)

If your application does not have a standard `main()` function but needs to initialize and run down the Object Manager, you need to call two functions:

1. `ACE::init()` to initialize the Object Manager before any other ACE operations are performed.

2. `ACE::fini()` to run down the Object Manager after all your ACE operations are complete. This call will trigger the cleanup of all objects registered with the Object Manager.

This may be necessary for Windows programs that have a `WinMain()` function rather than the standard `main()` function and for libraries that make use of ACE but the users of the library do not. For libraries, it is advantageous to add initialize and finalize functions to the library's API and have those functions call `ACE::init()` and `ACE::fini()`, respectively. In case you're writing a Windows DLL (dynamic link library) and thinking you can make the calls from `DllMain()`, don't go there. It's been tried.

You can also build ACE on Windows with

```
#define ACE_HAS_NONSTATIC_OBJECT_MANAGER 0
```

in your `config.h` file before including `ace/config-win32.h`. (Chapter 2 describes ACE's configuration.) This removes the need to explicitly call `ACE::init()` and `ACE::fini()` but may cause problems when using dynamic services.

1.6.4 Allocating Heap Memory

Dynamic memory allocation from the runtime heap is a common need in most programs. If you've used memory allocation functions from C, you've certainly written code like this:

```
char *c = (char *)malloc (64);
if (c == 0)
  exit(1);      /* Out of memory! */
```

When transitioning to C++, this sort of code was replaced by:

```
char *c = new char[64];
if (c == 0)
  exit(1);      /* Out of memory! */
```

Straightforward stuff—until the C++ standard settled down. Now `operator new()` throws an exception if the memory allocation request fails. However, you probably need to develop code to run in some C++ runtime environments that return a 0 and some that throw an exception on failure. ACE also supports a mix of these environments, so it uses a set of macros that adapt to the compiler's model to what ACE expects. Because it was built in the days when a failed allocation returned a 0 pointer, ACE uses that model internally and adapts the new exception throwing model to it. With the macros, the preceding code example becomes:

```
char *c;
ACE_NEW_NORETURN (c, char[64]);
if (c == 0)
  exit(1);      /* Out of memory! */
```

The complete set of ACE memory allocation macros is listed in Table 1.2.

1.7 Using Both Narrow and Wide Characters

Developers outside the United States are acutely aware that many character sets in use today require more than one byte, or octet, to represent each character. Characters that require more than one octet are referred to as "wide characters." The most popular wide-character standard is ISO/IEC 10646, the Universal Multiple-Octet Coded Character Set (UCS). Unicode is a separate standard but can be thought of as a restricted UCS subset that uses two octets for each character (UCS-2). Many Windows programmers are familiar with Unicode.

C++ represents wide characters with the `wchar_t` type, which enables methods to offer multiple signatures that are differentiated by their character type. Wide characters have a separate set of C string manipulation functions, however, and existing C++ code, such as string literals, requires change for wide-character usage. As a result, programming applications to use wide-character strings can become expensive, especially when applications written initially for U.S. markets must be internationalized for other countries. To improve portability and ease of use, ACE uses C++ method overloading and the macros described in Table 1.3 to use different character types without changing APIs.

For applications to use wide characters, ACE must be built with the `ACE_HAS_WCHAR` configuration setting, which most modern platforms are

Table 1.2. ACE Memory Allocation Macros

Macro	Action
`ACE_NEW(p, c)`	Allocate memory by using constructor `c` and assign pointer to `p`. On failure, `p` is 0 and `return;`
`ACE_NEW_RETURN(p, c, r)`	Allocate memory by using constructor `c` and assign pointer to `p`. On failure, `p` is 0 and `return r;`
`ACE_NEW_NORETURN(p, c)`	Allocate memory by using constructor `c` and assign pointer to `p`. On failure, `p` is 0 and control continues at next statement.

Table 1.3. Macros Related to Character Width

Macro	Purpose
`ACE_HAS_WCHAR`	Configuration setting that enables ACE's wide-character methods
`ACE_USES_WCHAR`	Configuration setting that directs ACE to use wide characters internally
`ACE_TCHAR`	Matches ACE's internal character width; defined as either `char` or `wchar_t`, depending on the lack or presence of `ACE_USES_WCHAR`
`ACE_TMAIN`	Properly defines program's main entry point for command line argument type, based on `ACE_USES_WCHAR`
`ACE_TEXT(str)`	Defines the string literal `str` correctly, based on `ACE_USES_WCHAR`
`ACE_TEXT_CHAR_TO_TCHAR(str)`	Converts a `char *` string to `ACE_TCHAR` format, if needed
`ACE_TEXT_WCHAR_TO_TCHAR(str)`	Converts a `wchar_t *` string to `ACE_TCHAR` format, if needed
`ACE_TEXT_ALWAYS_CHAR(str)`	Converts an `ACE_TCHAR` string to `char *` format, if needed

capable of. Moreover, ACE must be built with the `ACE_USES_WCHAR` setting if ACE should also use wide characters internally. The `ACE_TCHAR` and `ACE_TEXT` macros are illustrated in examples throughout this book.

ACE also supplies two string classes—`ACE_CString` and `ACE_WString`—that hold narrow and wide characters, respectively. These classes are analogous to the standard C++ `string` class but can be configured to use custom memory allocators and are more portable. `ACE_TString` is a typedef for one of the two string types depending on the `ACE_USES_WCHAR` configuration setting.

1.8 Where to Find More Information and Support

As you're aware by the number and scope of items ACE helps with—from compiling to runtime—and from a perusal of the Contents—not to mention the size of this book!—you may be starting to wonder where you can find more information about ACE, how to use all its features, and where to get more help. A number of resources are available: ACE reference documentation, ACE kits, user forums, and technical support.

The ACE reference documentation is generated from specially tagged comments in the source code itself, using a tool called Doxygen.[5] That reference documentation is available in the following places:

- On the CD-ROM included with this book

- At Riverace's web site: `http://www.riverace.com/docs/`

- At the DOC group's web site, which includes the reference documentation for ACE and TAO (The ACE ORB) for the most recent stable version, the most recent beta version, and the nightly development snapshot: `http://www.dre.vanderbilt.edu/Doxygen/`

ACE is, of course, freely available in a number of forms from the following locations.

- The complete ACE 5.3b source and prebuilt kits for selected platforms are on the included CD-ROM.

---

5. For more information on Doxygen, please see `http://www.doxygen.org/`.

- The source and kits that are on the CD-ROM are also available, along with older versions, at Riverace's web site: `http://www.riverace.com`.
- Complete sources for the current release, current BFO (bug fix only) beta, and the most recent beta versions of ACE are available from the DOC group's web site: `http://deuce.doc.wustl.edu/Download.html`. The various types of kits are explained in Section 2.1.

A number of ACE developer forums are available via e-mail and Usenet news. The authors and the ACE developers monitor traffic to these forums. These people, along with the ACE user community at large, are very helpful with questions and problems. If you post a question or a problem to any of the following forums, please include the information in the `PROBLEM-REPORT-FORM` file located in the top-level directory of the ACE source kit:

- `comp.soft-sys.ace` newsgroup.
- `ace-users@cs.wustl.edu` mailing list. To join this list, send a request to `ace-users-request@cs.wustl.edu`. Include the following command in the body of the e-mail:

```
subscribe ace-users [emailaddress@domain]
```

You must supply `emailaddress@domain` only if your message's `From` address is not the address you wish to subscribe. If you use this alternative address method, the list server will require an extra authorization step before allowing you to join the list.

Messages posted to the `ace-users` list are forwarded to the `comp.soft-sys.ace` newsgroup, but not vice versa. You can search an archive of the `comp.soft-sys.ace` newsgroup at `http://groups.google.com`.

Although the level of friendly assistance on the ACE user forums is extraordinary, it is all on a best-effort, volunteer basis. If you're developing commercial projects with ACE, you may benefit greatly from the technical support services that are available. Using technical support allows you and your development team to stay focused on your project instead of needing to learn all about ACE's internals and to get involved in toolkit maintenance.

Riverace Corporation is the premier support provider for the ACE toolkit. You can learn all about Riverace's services at `http://www.riverace.com`. A number of other companies have recently begun providing support services for ACE and TAO worldwide. A current list is available at `http://www.cs.wustl.edu/~schmidt/commercial-support.html`.

1.9 Summary

This chapter introduced the ACE toolkit's organization and described some foundational concepts and techniques that you'll need to work with ACE. The chapter covered some helpful macros and facilities provided to smooth out the differences among C++ compilers and runtime environments, showed how to take advantage of both narrow and wide characters, and, finally, listed some sources of further information about ACE and the available services to help you make the most of ACE.

Chapter 2
How to Build and Use ACE in Your Programs

Traditional, closed-source libraries and toolkits are often packaged as shared libraries (DLLs), often without source code. Although ACE is available in install-able packages for some popular platforms, its open-source nature means that you can not only see the source but also change it to suit your needs and rebuild it. Thus, it is very useful to know how to build it from sources.

You will also, of course, need to build your own applications. This chapter shows how to include ACE in your application's source code and build it.

2.1 A Note about ACE Versions

ACE kits are released periodically as either of two types:

1. Release—two numbers, such as 5.3. These versions are stable and well tested. You should use release versions for product development unless you need to add a new feature to ACE in support of your project.

2. Beta—three numbers, such as 5.3.4. These versions are development snap-shots: the "bleeding edge." They may contain bug fixes above the previous release, but they may also contain more bugs or new features whose effects and interactions have not yet been well tested.

The first beta kit following each release—for example, 5.3.1—is traditionally reserved for bug fixes to the release and usually doesn't contain any new features or API changes. This is sometimes referred to as a BFO (bug fix only) version. However, it doesn't go through all the same aggressive testing that a release does.

Riverace Corporation also releases "Fix Kits": fixes made to a release version and labeled with the release version number followed by a letter that increases with each Fix Kit, such as 5.3c. Riverace maintains a separate stream of fixes for each ACE release and generates Fix Kits separately from the main ACE development stream. For this book's purposes, Fix Kits are treated the same as release versions. This book's descriptions and examples are based on ACE 5.3.

2.2 Guide to the ACE Distribution

The ACE distribution is arranged in a directory tree. This tree structure is the same whether you obtain ACE as part of a prebuilt kit or as sources only. The top-level directory in the ACE distribution is named `ACE_wrappers`, but it may be located in different places, depending on what type of kit you have.

- If you installed a prebuilt kit, ask your system administrator where the kit was installed to.
- If you have a source kit, it is probably a Gzip-compressed tar file. Copy the distribution file, which we'll assume is named `ACE-5.3.tar.gz`, to an empty directory. If on a UNIX system, use the following commands to unpack the kit:

```
$ gunzip ACE-5.3.tar.gz
$ tar xf ACE-5.3.tar
```

If on Windows, the WinZip utility is a good tool for unpacking the distribution. It works for either a Gzip'd tar file or a zip file.

In both cases, you'll have a directory named `ACE_wrappers` that contains the ACE sources and a lot of other useful files and information. Some useful and interesting files in `ACE_wrappers` are:

- `VERSION`—Identifies what version of ACE you have.
- `PROBLEM-REPORT-FORM`—Provides the information you'll need to report when asking for help or advice from Riverace or on the ACE user groups.
- `ChangeLog`—Provides a detailed list in reverse chronological order of all changes made to ACE. The `ChangeLog` file gets very long over time, so it's periodically moved to the `ChangeLogs` directory and a new `ChangeLog` started. For each new ACE version, Riverace writes release notes that summa-

rize the more noteworthy changes and additions to ACE, but if you're curious about details, they're all in the `ChangeLog`.

- `THANKS`—Lists all the people who have contributed to ACE over the years. It is an impressive list, for sure. If you are so inspired to contribute new code or fixes to ACE, your name will be added too.

The following directories are located below `ACE_wrappers`:

- `ace` contains the source code for the ACE toolkit.
- `bin` contains a number of useful utilities, which we'll describe as their use comes up in this book.
- `apps` contains a number of ACE-based application programs, such as the JAWS web server and the Gateway message router. These programs are often useful in and of themselves; however, they also contain great examples of how to use ACE in various scenarios.
- `docs` contains information related to various aspects of ACE, such as its coding guidelines. (Should you wish to contribute code, it should follow these guidelines.)
- `examples` contains many examples of how to use ACE classes and frameworks. The examples are arranged by category to make it easier to find what you need.
- `include/makeinclude` contains all the ACE build system files.
- `tests` contains ACE's regression test suite. If you build ACE, it's a good idea to build and run the tests as well, using the `run_test.pl` Perl script. Even if you don't need to run the tests, these programs also contain many examples of ACE usage.

You should define an environment variable named `ACE_ROOT` to reference the full path to the top-level `ACE_wrappers` directory. You'll need this environment variable when building both ACE and your applications.

2.3 How to Build ACE

Why would you want to (re)build ACE?

- ACE has been ported to many platforms, but a prebuilt kit may not be available for yours.
- You've fixed a bug or obtained a source patch.

- You've added a new feature.
- You've changed a configuration setting.

Many open-source projects use the GNU Autotools to assist in configuring a build for a particular platform. ACE doesn't use GNU Autotools, because when ACE's build scheme was developed, GNU Autotools wasn't mature enough to handle ACE's requirements on the required platforms. Future versions of ACE will use the GNU Autotools, however.

ACE has its own build scheme that uses GNU Make (version 3.79 or newer is required) and two configuration files.

1. `config.h` contains platform-specific settings used to select OS features and adapt ACE to the platform's compilation environment.

2. `platform_macros.GNU` contains commands and command options used to build ACE. This file allows selection of debugging capabilities, to build with threads or not, and so on. This file is not used with Microsoft Visual C++, as all command, feature, and option settings are contained in the Visual C++ project files.

Platform-specific versions of each of these files are included in the ACE source distribution.

The procedure for building ACE follows.

1. If you don't already have it, obtain the ACE source kit. See Section 1.8 for information on where to find ACE kits.

2. The kit comes in a few formats, most commonly a Gzip-compressed `tar` file. Use gunzip and tar—or WinZip on Windows—to unpack the kit into a new, empty directory.

3. (You can skip this step if using Microsoft Visual C++.) If you haven't already set the `ACE_ROOT` environment variable, set it to the full pathname of the top-level `ACE_wrappers` directory: for example, **ACE_ROOT=/home/ mydir/ace/ACE_wrappers; export ACE_ROOT**

4. Create the `config.h` file in `$ACE_ROOT/ace/config.h`. The file must include one of the platform-specific configuration files supplied by ACE. For example, the following is for building ACE on Windows:

```
#include "ace/config-win32.h"
```

Table 2.1 lists the platform-specific configuration files for popular platforms. The full set of files is contained in `$ACE_ROOT/ace`.

Table 2.1. Configuration Files for Popular ACE Platforms

OS/Compiler	`config.h` File	`platform_macros.GNU` File
AIX 4/Visual Age C++	`config-aix-4.x.h`	`platform_aix_ibm.GNU`
HP-UX 11/aC++	`config-hpux-11.00.h`	`platform_hpux_aCC.GNU`
Linux	`config-linux.h`	`platform_linux.GNU`
Solaris 8/Forte C++	`config-sunos5.8.h`	`platform_sunos5_sunc++.GNU`
Windows	`config-win32.h`	—

5. (Skip this step if using Microsoft Visual C++.) Create the
   `platform_macros.GNU` file in `$ACE_ROOT/include/makein-`
   `clude/platform_macros.GNU`. The file must include one of the platform-specific files supplied by ACE. For example, the following could be used
   for building on Linux:

   `include $(ACE_ROOT)/include/makeinclude/platform_linux.GNU`

   Note that this is a GNU Make directive, not a C++ preprocessor directive, so
   there's no leading '`#`', and use of an environment variable is legal.

   Table 2.1 lists the platform-specific macros files for popular platforms. The
   full set of files is contained in `$ACE_ROOT/include/makeinclude`.

6. Build ACE. The method depends on your compiler.

   - Microsoft Visual C++ 6: Start Visual C++ and open the workspace file
     `$ACE_ROOT/ace/ace.dsw`, select the desired configuration, and build.

   - Microsoft Visual C++ .NET: Start Visual C++ and open the solution file
     `$ACE_ROOT/ace/ace.sln`, select the desired configuration, and build.

   - Borland C++Builder: Set your current directory to `$ACE_ROOT\ace`, set
     the BCCHOME environment variable to the home directory where
     C++Builder is installed; use the C++Builder make command. For example:
     make -i -f Makefile.bor -DDEBUG=1 all

   - All others: Set your current directory to `$ACE_ROOT/ace`, and use the
     GNU make command: **make [options]**. Table 2.2 lists the options,

Table 2.2. GNU make Options

Option	Description
debug=1|0	Enable or disable debugging in the built library or program. Default is enabled (1).
optimize=1|0	Turn compiler optimization on or off. Default is off (0).
buildbits=*bits*	Explicitly select, for example, 32-bit or 64-bit build target. Default is the compiler's default for the build machine. This option works for AIX, Solaris, and HP-UX.
exceptions=1|0	Enable or disable exception handling. Default is platform specific but usually enabled (1).
inline=1|0	Enable or disable inlining of many of ACE's methods. Default is platform specific but usually enabled (1).
templates=*model*	Specify how templates are instantiated. Most common values for *model* are **automatic**, the default for compilers that support it well, and **explicit**, requiring source code directives to explicitly instantiate needed templates (see Section 1.6.1).
static_libs=1|0	Build and use static libraries. Default is to not build static libraries (0).

which can also be placed in the `platform_macros.GNU` file before including the platform-specific file.

2.4 How to Include ACE in Your Applications

This book describes many things you can do with ACE and how to do them. Including ACE in your programs has two practical requirements.

1. Include the necessary ACE header files in your sources. For example, to include the basic OS adaptation layer methods, add this to your source:

```
#include "ace/OS.h"
```

You should always specify the `ace` directory with the file to avoid confusion with choosing a file from somewhere in the include path other than the ACE sources. To be sure that the ACE header files are located correctly, you must include `$ACE_ROOT` in the compiler's include search path, usually done by using the `-I` or `/I` option.

You should include the necessary ACE header files before including your own headers or system-provided headers. ACE's header files can set preprocessor macros that affect system headers and feature tests, so it is important to include ACE files first. This is especially important for Windows but is good practice to follow on all platforms.

2. Link the ACE library with your application or library. For POSIX platforms, this involves adding -lACE to the compiler link command. If your ACE version was installed from a prebuilt kit, the ACE library was probably installed to a location that the compiler/linker searches by default. If you built ACE yourself, the ACE library is in $ACE_ROOT/ace. You must include this location in the compiler/linker's library search path, usually by using the -L option.

2.5   How to Build Your Applications

The scheme used to build ACE can also be used to build your applications. The advantage to using the supplied scheme is that you take advantage of the built-in knowledge about how to compile and link both libraries and executable programs properly in your environment. One important aspect of that knowledge is having the correct compile and link options to properly include ACE and the necessary vendor-supplied libraries in each step of your build. Even if you don't use the ACE build scheme, you should read about how the compile and link options are set for your platform to be sure that you do compatible things in your application's build scheme.

This is a small example of how easy it is to use the GNU Make-based system. Microsoft Visual C++ users will not need this information and can safely skip to Section 2.5.1.

If you have a program called hello_ace that has one source file named hello_ace.cpp, the Makefile to build it would be:

```
BIN   = hello_ace
BUILD = $(VBIN)
SRC = $(addsuffix .cpp,$(BIN))
LIBS = -lMyOtherLib
LDFLAGS = -L$(PROJ_ROOT)/lib
#----------------------------------------------------
#Include macros and targets
#----------------------------------------------------
include $(ACE_ROOT)/include/makeinclude/wrapper_macros.GNU
```

```
include $(ACE_ROOT)/include/makeinclude/macros.GNU
include $(ACE_ROOT)/include/makeinclude/rules.common.GNU
include $(ACE_ROOT)/include/makeinclude/rules.nonested.GNU
include $(ACE_ROOT)/include/makeinclude/rules.bin.GNU
include $(ACE_ROOT)/include/makeinclude/rules.local.GNU
```

That Makefile would take care of compiling the source code and linking it with
ACE and would work on each ACE platform that uses the GNU Make-based
scheme. The LIBS = -lMyOtherLib line specifies that, when linking the
program, -lMyOtherLib will be added to the link command; the specified
LDFLAGS value will as well. This allows you to include libraries from another
part of your project or from a third-party product. The ACE make scheme will
automatically add the options to include the ACE library when the program is
linked. Building an executable program from multiple source files would be
similar:

```
BIN = hello_ace
FILES = Piece2 Piece3
SRC= $(addsuffix .cpp,$(FILES))
OBJ= $(addsuffix .o,$(FILES))
BUILD   = $(VBIN)
#---------------------------------------------------------
# Include macros and targets
#---------------------------------------------------------
include$(ACE_ROOT)/include/makeinclude/wrapper_macros.GNU
include$(ACE_ROOT)/include/makeinclude/macros.GNU
include$(ACE_ROOT)/include/makeinclude/rules.common.GNU
include$(ACE_ROOT)/include/makeinclude/rules.nonested.GNU
include$(ACE_ROOT)/include/makeinclude/rules.bin.GNU
include$(ACE_ROOT)/include/makeinclude/rules.local.GNU
```

This Makefile would add Piece2.cpp and Piece3.cpp to the hello_ace
program, first compiling the new files and then linking all the object files together
to form the hello_ace program.

The following example shows how to build a shared library from a set of
source files:

```
SHLIB   = libSLD.$(SOEXT)
FILES   = Source1 Source2 Source3
LSRC    = $(addsuffix .cpp,$(FILES))
LIBS   += $(ACELIB)
BUILD   = $(VSHLIB)
#---------------------------------------------------------
```

```
#       Include macros and targets
#----------------------------------------------------------
include $(ACE_ROOT)/include/makeinclude/wrapper_macros.GNU
include $(ACE_ROOT)/include/makeinclude/macros.GNU
include $(ACE_ROOT)/include/makeinclude/rules.common.GNU
include $(ACE_ROOT)/include/makeinclude/rules.nonested.GNU
include $(ACE_ROOT)/include/makeinclude/rules.lib.GNU
include $(ACE_ROOT)/include/makeinclude/rules.local.GNU

#----------------------------------------------------------
#       Local targets
#----------------------------------------------------------
ifeq ($(shared_libs),1)
ifneq ($(SHLIB),)
CPPFLAGS      += -DSLD_BUILD_DLL
endif
endif
```

This Makefile builds `libSLD.so`—the suffix will automatically be the correct one for shared libraries on the build platform—by compiling `Source1.cpp`, `Source2.cpp`, and `Source3.cpp` and then linking them by using the appropriate commands for the build platform.

The last section of the previous Makefile example conditionally adds a preprocessor macro named `SLD_BUILD_DLL` when building a shared library. This is related to the need to declare library functions as "exported" and is needed mostly on Windows. The next section discusses this further.

2.5.1 Import/Export Declarations and DLLs

Windows has specific rules for explicitly importing and exporting symbols in DLLs. Developers with a UNIX background may not have encountered these rules in the past, but they are important for managing symbol usage in DLLs on Windows. The rules follow.

- When building a DLL, each symbol that should be visible from outside the DLL must have the declaration `__declspec(dllexport)` to specify that the symbol or class members are to be exported from the DLL for use by other programs or DLLs.
- When declaring the use of a symbol that your code is importing from another DLL, your declaration of the symbol or class must include `__declspec(dllimport)`.

Thus, depending on whether a particular symbol or class is being imported from a DLL or being built into a DLL for export to other users, the declaration of the symbol must be different. When symbol declarations reside in header files, as is most often the case, a scheme is needed to declare the symbol correctly in either case.

ACE makes it easy to conform to these rules by supplying a script that generates the necessary import/export declarations and a set of guidelines for using them successfully. To ease porting, the following procedure can be used on all platforms that ACE runs on.

1. Select a concise mnemonic for each DLL to be built.

2. Run the `$ACE_ROOT/bin/generate_export_file.pl` Perl script, specifying the DLL's mnemonic on the command line. The script will generate a platform-independent header file and write it to the standard output. Redirect the output to a file named *mnemonic*`_export.h`.

3. Include the generated file in each DLL source file that declares a globally visible class or symbol.

4. To use in a class declaration, insert the keyword *mnemonic*`_Export` between the `class` keyword and the class name.

5. When compiling the source code for the DLL, define the macro `mnemonic_BUILD_DLL` (`SLD_BUILD_DLL` in the previous example).

Following this procedure results in the following behavior on Windows.

- Symbols decorated using the preceding guidelines will be declared using `__declspec (dllexport)` when built in their DLL.

- When referenced from components outside the DLL, the symbols will be declared `__declspec (dllimport)`.

If you choose a separate mnemonic for each DLL and use them consistently, it will be straightforward to build and use DLLs across all OS platforms.

2.5.2 Important Notes for Microsoft Visual C++ Users

As mentioned, the GNU Make scheme is not used with Microsoft Visual C++. All needed settings are recorded in Visual C++'s project files. Because there's no common "include" file that a project can reuse settings from, each project must define the correct settings for each build configuration: debug versus release, DLL versus LIB, MFC versus non-MFC. Settings important for proper ACE usage

Table 2.3. ACE Library File Names for Visual C++

Configuration	File Name
DLL debug	`aced`
DLL release	`ace`
Static library debug	`acesd`
Static library release	`aces`
MFC DLL debug	`acemfcd`
MFC DLL release	`acemfc`

follow. These descriptions are valid for Visual C++ version 6, and are all accessible via the Project>Settings... menu.

- C/C++ tab
  - Code Generation category: Choose a multithreaded version of the runtime library.
  - Preprocessor category: You should include `$(ACE_ROOT)` in the "Additional include directories" field. Some users choose to include `$(ACE_ROOT)` in the Tools>Options... menu on the Directories tab. This is acceptable if you always use one version of ACE for all projects. It is more flexible, however, to specify the ACE include path in each project.
- Link tab
  - Input category: Include the proper ACE library file in the "Object/library modules" field. Unlike the POSIX platforms, the name of the ACE library is different for various build configurations. Table 2.3 lists the ACE library file names. Select the desired name and append `.lib` to it to get the file name to add to the "Object/library modules" field. When building a debug configuration of your project, you should choose one of the debug ACE files as well—similarly, choose a release ACE file for a release build of your project—or you may get errors at link time.
  - Input category: Include the path to the ACE library link file in the "Additional library path" field. This will generally be `$(ACE_ROOT)/ace`. If you're linking with an ACE DLL, the export library file (`.LIB`) is in `$(ACE_ROOT)/ace`, and the matching DLL your program will access at runtime is in `$(ACE_ROOT)/bin`; it has the same base name but a `.DLL`

suffix. Do not include $(ACE_ROOT)/bin in the "Additional library path" field. Instead, either include %ACE_ROOT%/bin in your PATH environment variable, or copy the needed DLL file to a location that is part of the PATH.

2.6 Summary

In this chapter, we learned about ACE kits and version types, how to build ACE, and why you might need to. We also learned how to build both an executable program and a shared library (DLL) that use ACE. Finally, we learned some details about building and using shared libraries on Windows platforms.

Next, we look at one of the most basic developer needs—a flexible way to log runtime information and trace program execution—and how to use the facilities ACE provides to meet those needs.

Chapter 3
Using the ACE Logging Facility

Every program needs to display diagnostics: error messages, debugging output, and so on. Traditionally, we might use a number of `printf()` calls or `cerr` statements in our application in order to help trace execution paths or display helpful runtime information. ACE's logging facility provides us with ways to do these things while at the same time giving us great control over how much of the information is printed and where it is directed.

It is important to have a convenient way to create debug statements. In this modern age of graphical source-level debuggers, it might seem strange to pepper your application with the equivalent of a bunch of print statements. However, diagnostic statements are useful both during development and long after an application is considered to be bug free.

- They can record information while the program is running and a debugger isn't available or practical, such as with a server.
- They can record output during testing for regression analysis, as the ACE test suite does.

The ACE mechanisms allow us to enable and disable these statements at compile time. When compiled in, they can also be enabled and disabled at will at runtime. Thus, you don't have to pay for the overhead—in either CPU cycles or disk space—under normal conditions. But if a problem arises, you can easily cause copious amounts of debugging information to be recorded to assist you in finding and fixing it. It is an unfortunate fact that many bugs will never appear until the program is in the hands of the end user.

In this chapter, we cover how to

- Use basic logging and tracing techniques
- Enable and disable display of various logging message severities
- Customize the logging mechanics
- Direct the output messages to various logging sinks
- Capture log messages before they're output
- Use the distributed ACE logging service
- Combine various logging facility features
- Dynamically configure logging sinks and severity levels

3.1 Basic Logging and Tracing

Three macros are commonly used to display diagnostic output from your code: ACE_DEBUG, ACE_ERROR, and ACE_TRACE. The arguments to the first two are the same; their operation is nearly identical, so for our purposes now, we'll treat them the same. They both take a severity indicator as one of the arguments, so you can display any message using either; however, the convention is to use ACE_DEBUG for your own debugging statements and ACE_ERROR for warnings and errors. The use of these macros is the same:

```
ACE_DEBUG ((severity, formatting-args));

ACE_ERROR ((severity, formatting-args));
```

The *severity* parameter specifies the severity level of your message. The most common levels are LM_DEBUG and LM_ERROR. All the valid severity values are listed in Table 3.1.

The *formatting-args* parameter is a printf()-like set of format conversion operators and formatting arguments for insertion into the output. The complete set of formatting directives is described in Table 3.2. One might wonder why printf()-like formatting was chosen instead of the more natural—to C++ coders—C++ iostream-style formatting. In some cases, it would have been easier to correctly log certain types of information with type-safe insertion operators. However, an important factor in the logging facility's design is the ability to effectively "no-op" the logging statements at compile time. Note that the ACE_DEBUG

Table 3.1. `ACE_Log_Msg` Logging Severity Levels

Severity Level	Meaning
LM_TRACE	Messages indicating function-calling sequence
LM_DEBUG	Debugging information
LM_INFO	Messages that contain information normally of use only when debugging a program
LM_NOTICE	Conditions that are not error conditions but that may require special handling
LM_WARNING	Warning messages
LM_ERROR	Error messages
LM_CRITICAL	Critical conditions, such as hard device errors
LM_ALERT	A condition that should be corrected immediately, such as a corrupted system database
LM_EMERGENCY	A panic condition, normally broadcast to all users

and `ACE_ERROR` invocations require two sets of parentheses. The outer set delimits the single macro argument. This single argument comprises all the arguments, and their enclosing parentheses, needed for a method call. If the preprocessor macro `ACE_NDEBUG` is defined, the `ACE_DEBUG` macro will expand to a blank line, ignoring the content of the inner set of parentheses. Achieving this same optimization with insertion operators would have resulted in a rather odd usage:

```
ACE_DEBUG ((debug_info << "Hi Mom" << endl));
```

Similarly, many of the formatting tokens, such as `%I`, would have been awkward to implement and overly verbose to use:

```
ACE_DEBUG((debug_info<<ACE_Log_Msg::nested_indent<<"Hi
Mom"<<endl));
```

One could argue away the compile-time optimization by causing `ACE_NDEBUG` to put the debug output stream object into a no-op mode. That may be sufficient for some platforms, but for others, such as embedded real-time systems, you really *do* want the code to simply not exist.

Unlike `ACE_DEBUG` and `ACE_ERROR`, which cause output where the macro is placed, `ACE_TRACE` causes one line of debug information to be printed at the point of the `ACE_TRACE` statement and another when its enclosing scope is exited. Therefore, placing an `ACE_TRACE` statement at the beginning of a function or method provides a trace of when that function or method is entered and exited. The `ACE_TRACE` macro accepts a single character string rather than a set of formatting directives. Because C++ doesn't have a handy way to dump a stack trace, this can be very useful indeed.

Let's take a look at a simple application:

```
#include "ace/Log_Msg.h"

void foo (void);

int ACE_TMAIN (int, ACE_TCHAR *[])
{
  ACE_TRACE(ACE_TEXT ("main"));

  ACE_DEBUG ((LM_INFO, ACE_TEXT ("%IHi Mom\n")));
  foo();
  ACE_DEBUG ((LM_INFO, ACE_TEXT ("%IGoodnight\n")));

  return 0;
}

void foo (void)
{
  ACE_TRACE (ACE_TEXT ("foo"));

  ACE_DEBUG ((LM_INFO, ACE_TEXT ("%IHowdy Pardner\n")));
}
```

Our first step is always to include the `Log_Msg.h` header file. It defines many helpful macros, including `ACE_DEBUG` and `ACE_ERROR`, to make your life easier. The full set of output-producing macros is listed in Table 3.3.

You can use `ACE_DEBUG` to print just about any arbitrary string you want, and the many format directives listed in Table 3.2 can also be modified with `printf()`-style modifiers for length, precision, and fill adjustments. (See a `printf()` reference for details on the modifiers.) In the preceding example, we've used `%I` so that the `ACE_DEBUG` messages are nicely indented along with the `ACE_TRACE` messages.

If you compile and execute the preceding code, you should get something like this:

Table 3.2. ACE Logging Format Directives

Code	Argument Type	Displays
A	ACE_timer_t	Floating-point number; long decimal number if platform doesn't support floating point
a	—	Aborts the program after displaying output
c	char	Single character
C	char*	Character string (narrow characters)
i,d	int	Decimal number
I	—	Indents output according to the nesting depth, obtained from ACE_Trace::get_nesting_indent()
e,E, f,F, g,G	double	Double-precision floating-point number
l	—	Line number where logging macro appears
M	—	Text form of the message severity level
m	—	Message corresponding to errno value, as done by strerror(), for example
N	—	File name where logging macro appears
n	—	Program name given to ACE_Log_Msg::open()
o	int	Octal number
P	—	Current process ID
p	ACE_TCHAR*	Specified character string, followed by the appropriate errno message, that is, as done by perror()
Q	ACE_UINT64	Decimal number
r	void (*)()	Nothing; calls the specified function
R	int	Decimal number
S	int	Signal name of the numbered signal
s	ACE_TCHAR*	Character string: narrow or wide, according to ACE_TCHAR type
T	—	Current time as hour:minute:sec.usec
D	—	Timestamp as month/day/year hour:minute:sec.usec
t	—	Calling thread's ID (1 if single threaded)

Table 3.2. ACE Logging Format Directives (Continued)

Code	Argument Type	Displays
u	int	Unsigned decimal number
w	wchar_t	Single wide character
W	wchar_t*	Wide-character string
x,X	int	Hexadecimal number
@	void*	Pointer value in hexadecimal
%	N/A	Single percent sign: "%"

```
(1024) calling main in file `Simple1.cpp' on line 7
   Hi Mom
   (1024) calling foo in file `Simple1.cpp' on line 18
      Howdy Pardner
   (1024) leaving foo
   Goodnight
(1024) leaving main
```

The compile-time values of three configuration settings control whether the logging macros produce logging method calls: ACE_NTRACE, ACE_NDEBUG, and ACE_NLOGGING. These macros are all interpreted as "not." For example, ACE_NTRACE is "not tracing" when its value is 1. To enable the configuration area, set the macro to 0. ACE_NTRACE usually defaults to 1 (disabled), and the others default to 0 (enabled). Table 3.3 shows which configuration setting controls each logging macro. This allows you to sprinkle your code with as little or as much debug information as you want and then turn it on or off when compiling.

When deciding which features to enable, be aware that ACE_TRACE output is conditional on both the ACE_NTRACE and ACE_NDEBUG configuration settings. The reason is that the ACE_TRACE macro, when enabled, expands to instantiate an ACE_Trace object. The ACE_Trace class's constructor and destructor use ACE_DEBUG to log the entry and exit messages. They're logged at the LM_TRACE severity level, so that level also must be enabled at runtime to show any tracing output; it is enabled by default.

3.2 **Enabling and Disabling Logging Severities**

Consider this slightly modified code:

```
#include "ace/Log_Msg.h"

void foo(void);

int ACE_TMAIN (int, ACE_TCHAR *[])
{
  ACE_TRACE (ACE_TEXT ("main"));

  ACE_LOG_MSG->priority_mask (LM_DEBUG | LM_NOTICE,
                              ACE_Log_Msg::PROCESS);
  ACE_DEBUG ((LM_INFO, ACE_TEXT ("%IHi Mom\n")));
  foo ();
  ACE_DEBUG ((LM_DEBUG, ACE_TEXT ("%IGoodnight\n")));

  return 0;
}

void foo(void)
{
  ACE_TRACE (ACE_TEXT ("foo"));

  ACE_DEBUG ((LM_NOTICE, ACE_TEXT ("%IHowdy Pardner\n")));
}
```

The following output is produced:

```
(1024) calling main in file `Simple2.cpp' on line 7
    Howdy Pardner
  Goodnight
```

In this example, we changed the logging level at runtime so that only messages logged with LM_DEBUG and LM_NOTICE priority are displayed; all others are ignored. The LM_INFO "Hi Mom" message is not displayed, and there is no ACE_TRACE output.

We've also revealed a little more about how ACE's logging facility works. The ACE_Log_Msg class implements the log message formatting capabilities in ACE. ACE automatically maintains a thread-specific singleton instance of the ACE_Log_Msg class for each spawned thread, as well as the main thread. ACE_LOG_MSG is a shortcut for obtaining the pointer to the thread's singleton

Table 3.3. ACE Logging Macros

Macro	Function	Disabled by
ACE_ASSERT(test)	Much like the assert() library call. If the test fails, an assertion message including the file name and line number, along with the test itself, will be printed and the application aborted.	ACE_NDEBUG
ACE_HEX_DUMP ((level, buffer, size [,text]))	Dumps the buffer as a string of hex digits. If provided, the optional text parameter will be printed prior to the hex string. The op_status[a] is set to 0.	ACE_NLOGGING
ACE_RETURN(value)	No message is printed, the calling function returns with value; op_status is set to value.	ACE_NLOGGING
ACE_ERROR_RETURN ((level, string, ...), value)	Logs the string at the requested level. The calling function then returns with value; op_status is set to value.	ACE_NLOGGING
ACE_ERROR((level, string, ...))	Sets the op_status to −1 and logs the string at the requested level.	ACE_NLOGGING
ACE_DEBUG((level, string, ...))	Sets the op_status to 0 and logs the string at the requested level.	ACE_NLOGGING
ACE_ERROR_INIT(value, flags)	Sets the op_status to value and the logger's option flags to flags. Valid flags values are defined in Table 3.5.	ACE_NLOGGING
ACE_ERROR_BREAK ((level, string, ...))	Invokes ACE_ERROR() followed by a break. Use this to display an error message and exit a while or for loop, for instance.	ACE_NLOGGING

Table 3.3. ACE Logging Macros (Continued)

Macro	Function	Disabled by
`ACE_TRACE(string)`	Displays the file name, line number, and `string` where `ACE_TRACE` appears. Displays "Leaving 'string'" when the `ACE_TRACE`-enclosing scope exits.	`ACE_NTRACE`

a. Many of the macros in this table refer to `op_status`. This internal variable is used to keep the logging framework aware of the program state, that is, the "operation status." By convention, a value of 0 indicates good. Anything else is considered an error or exception state. Also see Table 3.4.

instance. All the ACE logging macros use `ACE_LOG_MSG` to make method calls on the correct `ACE_Log_Msg` instance. There is seldom a reason to instantiate an `ACE_Log_Msg` object directly. ACE automatically creates a new instance for each thread spawned, keeping each thread's logging output separate.

We can use the `ACE_Log_Msg::priority_mask()` method to set the logging severity levels we desire output to be produced for: All the available logging levels are listed in Table 3.1. Each level is represented by a mask, so the levels can be combined. Let's look at the complete signature of the `priority_mask()` methods:

```
/// Get the current ACE_Log_Priority mask.
u_long priority_mask (MASK_TYPE = THREAD);

/// Set the ACE_Log_Priority mask, returns original mask.
u_long priority_mask (u_long, MASK_TYPE = THREAD);
```

The first version is used to read the severity mask; the second changes it and returns the original mask so it can be restored later. The second argument must be one of two values, reflecting two different scopes of severity mask setting:

1. `ACE_Log_Msg::PROCESS`: Specifying `PROCESS` retrieves or sets the processwide mask affecting logging severity for all `ACE_Log_Msg` instances.

2. `ACE_Log_Msg::THREAD`: Each `ACE_Log_Msg` instance also has its own severity mask, and this value retrieves or sets it. `THREAD` is technically a misnomer, as it refers to the `ACE_Log_Msg` instance the method is invoked on, and you can create `ACE_Log_Msg` instances in addition to those that

ACE creates for each thread. However, that is a relatively rare thing to do, so we usually simply refer to ACE_Log_Msg instances as thread specific.

When evaluating a log message's severity, ACE_Log_Msg examines both the processwide and per instance severity masks. If either of them has the message's severity enabled, the message is logged. By default, all bits are set at the process level and none at the instance level, so all message severities are logged. To make each thread decide for itself which severity levels will be logged, set the process-wide mask to 0 and allow each thread set its own per instance mask. For example, the following code disables all logging severities at the process level and enables LM_DEBUG and LM_NOTICE severities in the current thread only:

```
ACE_LOG_MSG->priority_mask (0, ACE_Log_Msg::PROCESS);
ACE_LOG_MSG->priority_mask (LM_DEBUG | LM_NOTICE,
                            ACE_Log_Msg::THREAD);
```

A third mask maintained by ACE_Log_Msg is important when you start setting individual severity masks on ACE_Log_Msg instances. The per instance default mask is used to initialize each ACE_Log_Msg instance's severity mask. The per instance default mask is initially 0 (no severities are enabled). Because each ACE_Log_Msg instance's severity mask is set from the default value when the instance is created, you can change the default for groups of threads before spawning them. This puts the logging policy into the thread-spawning part of your application, alleviating the need for the threads to set their own level, although each thread can change its ACE_Log_Msg instance's mask at any time. Consider this example:

```
ACE_LOG_MSG->priority_mask (0, ACE_Log_Msg::PROCESS);
ACE_Log_Msg::enable_debug_messages ();
ACE_Thread_Manager::instance ()->spawn (service);
ACE_Log_Msg::disable_debug_messages ();
ACE_Thread_Manager::instance ()->spawn_n (3, worker);
```

We'll learn about thread management in Chapter 13. For now, all you need to know is that ACE_Thread_Manager::spawn() spawns one thread and that ACE_Thread_Manager::spawn_n() spawns multiple threads. In the preceding example, the processwide severity mask is set to 0 (all disabled). This means that each ACE_Log_Msg instance's mask controls its enabled severities totally. The thread executing the service() function will have the LM_DEBUG severity enabled, but the threads executing the worker() function will not.

The complete method signatures for changing the per instance default mask are:

```
static void disable_debug_messages
    (ACE_Log_Priority priority = LM_DEBUG);

static void enable_debug_messages
    (ACE_Log_Priority priority = LM_DEBUG);
```

Our example used the default argument, LM_DEBUG, in both cases. Even though the method names imply that LM_DEBUG is the only severity that can be changed, you can also supply any set of legal severity masks to either method. Unlike the priority_mask() method, which replaces the specified mask, the enable_debug_messages() and disable_debug_messages() methods add and subtract, respectively, the specified severity bits in both the calling thread's per instance mask and the per instance default severity mask.

Of course, you can use any message severity level at any time. However, take care to specify a reasonable level for each of your messages; then at runtime, you can use the priority_mask() method to enable or disable messages you're interested in. This allows you to easily overinstrument your code and then enable only the things that are useful at any particular time.

ACE_Log_Msg has a rich set of methods for recording the current state of your application. Table 3.4 summarizes the more commonly used functions. Most methods have both accessor and mutator signatures. For example, there are two op_status() methods:

```
int op_status(void);
void op_status(int status));
```

Although the method calls are most often made indirectly via the ACE logging macros, they are also available for direct use.

3.3 Customizing the ACE Logging Macros

In most cases, people will use the standard ACE tracing and logging macros shown in Table 3.3. Sometimes, however, their behavior may need to be customized. Or you might want to create wrapper macros in anticipation of future customization.

Table 3.4. Commonly Used `ACE_Log_Msg` Methods

Method	Purpose
`op_status`	The return value of the current function. By convention, −1 indicates an error condition.
`errnum`	The current `errno` value.
`linenum`	The line number on which the message was generated.
`file`	File name in which the message was generated.
`msg`	A message to be sent to the log output target.
`inc`	Increments nesting depth. Returns the previous value.
`dec`	Decrements the nesting depth. Returns the new value.
`trace_depth`	The current nesting depth.

`start_tracing`
`stop_tracing`
`tracing_enabled`
	Enable/disable/query the tracing status for the current `ACE_Log_Msg` instance. The tracing status of a thread's `ACE_LOG_MSG` singleton determines whether an `ACE_Trace` object generates log messages.

`priority_mask`	Get/set the set of severity levels—at instance or process level—for which messages will be logged.
`log_priority_enabled`	Return non-zero if the requested priority is enabled.
`set`	Sets the line number, file name, `op_status`, and several other characteristics all at once.
`conditional_set`	Sets the line number, file name, `op_status`, and `errnum` values for the next log message; however, they take effect only if the next logging message's severity level is enabled.

3.3.1 Wrapping ACE_DEBUG

Perhaps you want to ensure that all your `LM_DEBUG` messages contain a particular text string so that you can easily grep for them in your output file. Or maybe you want to ensure that every one of them is prefixed with the handy "%I" directive so they indent properly. If you lay the groundwork at the beginning of your project and encourage your coders to use your macros, it will be easy to implement these kinds of things in the future.

The following macro definitions wrap the `ACE_DEBUG` macro in a handy way. Note how we've guaranteed that every message will be properly indented,

and we've prefixed each message to make searching for specific strings in the
output easier.

```
#define DEBUG_PREFIX        ACE_TEXT ("DEBUG%I")
#define INFO_PREFIX         ACE_TEXT ("INFO%I")
#define NOTICE_PREFIX       ACE_TEXT ("NOTICE%I")
#define WARNING_PREFIX      ACE_TEXT ("WARNING%I")
#define ERROR_PREFIX        ACE_TEXT ("ERROR%I")
#define CRITICAL_PREFIX     ACE_TEXT ("CRITICAL%I")
#define ALERT_PREFIX        ACE_TEXT ("ALERT%I")
#define EMERGENCY_PREFIX    ACE_TEXT ("EMERGENCY%I")
#define MY_DEBUG(FMT, ...)       \
        ACE_DEBUG(( LM_DEBUG,  \
                    DEBUG_PREFIX FMT \
                    __VA_ARGS__ ))
#define MY_INFO(FMT, ...)        \
        ACE_DEBUG(( LM_INFO,  \
                    INFO_PREFIX FMT \
                    __VA_ARGS__ ))
#define MY_NOTICE(FMT, ...)         \
        ACE_DEBUG(( LM_NOTICE,  \
                    NOTICE_PREFIX FMT \
                    __VA_ARGS__ ))
#define MY_WARNING(FMT, ...)        \
        ACE_DEBUG(( LM_WARNING,  \
                    WARNING_PREFIX FMT \
                    __VA_ARGS__ ))
#define MY_ERROR(FMT, ...)        \
        ACE_DEBUG(( LM_ERROR,  \
                    ERROR_PREFIX FMT \
                    __VA_ARGS__ ))
#define MY_CRITICAL(FMT, ...)        \
        ACE_DEBUG(( LM_CRITICAL,  \
                    CRITICAL_PREFIX FMT \
                    __VA_ARGS__ ))
#define MY_ALERT(FMT, ...)        \
        ACE_DEBUG(( LM_ALERT,  \
                    ALERT_PREFIX FMT \
                    __VA_ARGS__ ))
#define MY_EMERGENCY(FMT, ...)        \
        ACE_DEBUG(( LM_EMERGENCY,  \
                    EMERGENCY_PREFIX FMT \
                    __VA_ARGS__ ))
```

Of course, it would be more useful if each of our prefixes were surrounded by an #ifdef to allow them to be overridden, but we leave that as an exercise to the reader.

Using these macros instead of the usual ACE_DEBUG macros is, as expected, easy to do:

```
#include "Trace.h"

void foo (void);

int ACE_TMAIN (int, ACE_TCHAR *[])
{
  ACE_TRACE (ACE_TEXT ("main"));
  MY_DEBUG (ACE_TEXT ("Hi Mom\n"));
  foo ();
  MY_DEBUG (ACE_TEXT ("Goodnight\n"));
  return 0;
}

void foo (void)
{
  ACE_TRACE (ACE_TEXT ("foo"));
  MY_DEBUG (ACE_TEXT ("Howdy Pardner\n"));
}
```

Our output is nicely indented and prefixed as requested:

```
(1024) calling main in file `Wrap_Macros.cpp' on line 11
DEBUG   Hi Mom
   (1024) calling foo in file `Wrap_Macros.cpp' on line 20
DEBUG       Howdy Pardner
   (1024) leaving foo
DEBUG   Goodnight
(1024) leaving main
```

The __VA_ARGS__ trick works fine for recent versions of the GNU C/C++ preprocessor but may not be available everywhere else, so be sure to read your compiler's documentation before committing yourself to this particular approach. If something similar isn't available to you, you can use a slightly less elegant approach:

```
#define MY_DEBUG      LM_DEBUG,      ACE_TEXT ("DEBUG%I")
#define MY_INFO       LM_INFO,       ACE_TEXT ("INFO%I")
#define MY_NOTICE     LM_NOTICE,     ACE_TEXT ("NOTICE%I")
#define MY_WARNING    LM_WARNING,    ACE_TEXT ("WARNING%I")
#define MY_ERROR      LM_ERROR,      ACE_TEXT ("ERROR%I")
#define MY_CRITICAL   LM_CRITICAL,   ACE_TEXT ("CRITICAL%I")
#define MY_ALERT      LM_ALERT,      ACE_TEXT ("ALERT%I")
#define MY_EMERGENCY  LM_EMERGENCY,  ACE_TEXT ("EMERGENCY%I")
```

This approach could be used something like this:

```
ACE_DEBUG ((MY_DEBUG ACE_TEXT ("Hi Mom\n")));

ACE_DEBUG ((MY_DEBUG ACE_TEXT ("Goodnight\n")));
```

It produces exactly the same output at the expense of slightly less attractive code.

3.3.2 ACE_Trace

We will now create an ACE_TRACE variant that will display the line number at which a function exits. The default ACE_Trace object implementation doesn't do this and doesn't provide an easy way for us to extend it, so, unfortunately, we have to create our own object from scratch. However, we can cut and paste from the ACE_Trace implementation in order to give ourselves a head start.

Consider this simple class:

```
class Trace
{
public:
  Trace (const ACE_TCHAR *prefix,
         const ACE_TCHAR *name,
         int line,
         const ACE_TCHAR *file)
    {
      this->prefix_ = prefix;
      this->name_   = name;
      this->line_   = line;
      this->file_   = file;

      ACE_Log_Msg *lm = ACE_LOG_MSG;
      if (lm->tracing_enabled ()
          && lm->trace_active () == 0)
        {
```

```
          lm->trace_active (1);
          ACE_DEBUG
            ((LM_TRACE,
              ACE_TEXT ("%s%*s(%t) calling %s in file `%s'")
              ACE_TEXT (" on line %d\n"),
              this->prefix_,
              Trace::nesting_indent_ * lm->inc (),
              ACE_TEXT (""),
              this->name_,
              this->file_,
              this->line_));
          lm->trace_active (0);
        }
    }

  void setLine (int line)
    {
      this->line_ = line;
    }

  ~Trace (void)
    {
      ACE_Log_Msg *lm = ACE_LOG_MSG;
      if (lm->tracing_enabled ()
          && lm->trace_active () == 0)
        {
          lm->trace_active (1);
          ACE_DEBUG
            ((LM_TRACE,
              ACE_TEXT ("%s%*s(%t) leaving %s in file `%s'")
              ACE_TEXT (" on line %d\n"),
              this->prefix_,
              Trace::nesting_indent_ * lm->dec (),
              ACE_TEXT (""),
              this->name_,
              this->file_,
              this->line_));
          lm->trace_active (0);
        }
    }

private:
  enum { nesting_indent_ = 3 };

  const ACE_TCHAR *prefix_;
```

```
    const ACE_TCHAR *name_;
    const ACE_TCHAR *file_;
    int line_;
};
```

Trace is a simplified version of ACE_Trace. Because our focus is printing
a modified function exit message, we chose to leave out some of the more esoteric
ACE_Trace functionality. We did, however, include a prefix parameter to the
constructor so that each entry/exit message can be prefixed (before indentation), if
you want. In an ideal world, you would simply use the following method to select
the messages you're interested in: ACE_Log_Msg::priority_mask(). On
the other hand, if you're asked to do a postmortem analysis of a massive, all-
debug-enabled log file, the prefixes can be quite handy.

With our new Trace class available to us, we can now create a set of simple
macros that will use this new class to implement function tracing in our code:

```
#define TRACE_PREFIX        ACE_TEXT ("TRACE ")

#if (ACE_NTRACE == 1)
#    define TRACE(X)
#    define TRACE_RETURN(V)
#    define TRACE_RETURN_VOID()
#else
#    define TRACE(X)                              \
            Trace ____ (TRACE_PREFIX,             \
                    ACE_TEXT (X),                 \
                    __LINE__,                     \
                    ACE_TEXT (__FILE__))

#    define TRACE_RETURN(V)                       \
            do { ____.setLine(__LINE__); return V; } while (0)

#    define TRACE_RETURN_VOID()                   \
            do { ____.setLine(__LINE__); } while (0)
#endif
```

The addition of the TRACE_RETURN and TRACE_RETURN_VOID macros is
how our Trace object's destructor will know to print the line number at which
the function exits. Each of these macros uses the convenient setLine() method
to set the current line number before allowing the Trace instance to go out of
scope, destruct, and print our message.

This is a simple example using our new object:

```
#include "Trace.h"

void foo (void);

int ACE_TMAIN (int, ACE_TCHAR *[])
{
  TRACE (ACE_TEXT ("main"));

  MY_DEBUG (ACE_TEXT ("Hi Mom\n"));
  foo ();
  MY_DEBUG (ACE_TEXT ("Goodnight\n"));

  TRACE_RETURN (0);
}

void foo (void)
{
  TRACE (ACE_TEXT ("foo"));
  MY_DEBUG (ACE_TEXT ("Howdy Pardner\n"));
  TRACE_RETURN_VOID ();
}
```

It produces the following output:

```
TRACE (1024) calling main in file `Trace_Return.cpp' on line 11
DEBUG    Hi Mom
TRACE     (1024) calling foo in file `Trace_Return.cpp' on line 22
DEBUG       Howdy Pardner
TRACE     (1024) leaving foo in file `Trace_Return.cpp' on line 24
DEBUG    Goodnight
TRACE (1024) leaving main in file `Trace_Return.cpp' on line 17
```

Although the output is a bit wordy, we succeeded in our original intent of printing the line number at which each function returns. Although that may seem like a small thing for a trivial program, consider the fact that few useful programs are trivial. If you are trying to understand the flow of a legacy application, it may well be worth your time to liberally instrument it with TRACE and TRACE_RETURN macros to get a feel for the paths taken. Of course, training yourself to use TRACE_RETURN may take some time, but in the end, you will have a much better idea of how the code flows.

3.4 Redirecting Logging Output

As our previous examples have shown, the default logging sink for ACE's logging facility is the standard error stream. In this section, we discuss output to the standard error stream, as well as two other common and useful targets:

- The system logger (UNIX syslog or NT Event Log)
- A programmer-specified output stream, such as a file

3.4.1 Standard Error Stream

Output to the standard error stream (STDERR) is so common that it is, in fact, the default sink for all ACE logging messages. Our examples so far have taken advantage of this. Sometimes, you may want to direct your output not only to STDERR but also to one of the other targets available to you. In these cases, you will have to explicitly include STDERR in your choices:

```
int ACE_TMAIN (int, ACE_TCHAR *argv[])
{
  // open() requires the name of the application
  // (e.g. -- argv[0]) because the underlying
  // implementation may use it in the log output.
  ACE_LOG_MSG->open (argv[0], ACE_Log_Msg::STDERR);
```

or

```
ACE_DEBUG ((LM_DEBUG, ACE_TEXT ("%IHi Mom\n")));
ACE_LOG_MSG->set_flags (ACE_Log_Msg::STDERR);
foo ();
```

If you choose the second approach, it may be necessary to invoke `clr_flags()` to disable any other output destinations. Everything after the `set_flags()` will be directed to STDERR until you invoke `clr_flags()` to prevent it. The complete signatures of these methods are:

```
// Enable the bits in the logger's options flags.
void set_flags (unsigned long f);
```

```
// Disable the bits in the logger's options flags.
void clr_flags (unsigned long f);
```

The set of defined flag values are listed in Table 3.5.

Table 3.5. Valid `ACE_Log_Msg` Flags Values

Flag	Meaning
STDERR	Write messages to STDERR
LOGGER	Write messages to the local client logger daemon (see Section 3.6)
OSTREAM	Write messages to the assigned output stream
MSG_CALLBACK	Write messages to the callback object (see Section 3.5)
VERBOSE	Prepends program name, timestamp, host name, process ID, and message priority to each message
VERBOSE_LITE	Prepends timestamp and message priority to each message
SILENT	Do not print messages at all
SYSLOG	Write messages to the system's event log
CUSTOM	Write messages to the user-provided back end: an advanced usage topic not discussed in this book

3.4.2 System Logger

Most modern operating systems support the notion of a system logger. The implementation details range from a library of function calls to a network daemon. The general idea is that all applications direct their logging activity to the system logger, which will, in turn, direct it to the correct file(s) or other configurable destination(s). For example, UNIX system administrators can configure the UNIX syslog facility so that different classes and levels of logging get directed to different destinations. Such an approach provides a good combination of scalability and configurability.

To use the system logger, you would do something like this:

```
int ACE_TMAIN (int, ACE_TCHAR *argv[])
{
  ACE_LOG_MSG->open
    (argv[0], ACE_Log_Msg::SYSLOG, ACE_TEXT ("syslogTest"));
```

Although one would think that we could use the `set_flags()` method to enable syslog output after the `ACE_Log_Msg` instance has been opened, that isn't the case, unfortunately. Likewise, if you want to quit sending output to syslog, a simple `clr_flags()` won't do the trick.

In order to communicate with the system logger, `ACE_Log_Msg` must perform a set of initialization procedures that are done only in the `open()` method. Part of the initialization requires the program name that will be recorded in syslog: (the third argument). If we don't do this when our program starts, we will have to do it later, in order to get the behavior we expect from invoking `set_flags()`. Similarly, the `open()` method will properly close down any existing connection to the system logger if invoked without the `ACE_Log_Msg::SYSLOG` flag:

```
#include "ace/Log_Msg.h"

void foo (void);

int ACE_TMAIN (int, ACE_TCHAR *argv[])
{
  // This will be directed to stderr (the default ACE_Log_Msg
  // behavior).
  ACE_TRACE (ACE_TEXT ("main"));

  ACE_DEBUG ((LM_DEBUG, ACE_TEXT ("%IHi Mom\n")));

  // Everything from foo() will be directed to the system logger
  ACE_LOG_MSG->open
    (argv[0], ACE_Log_Msg::SYSLOG, ACE_TEXT ("syslogTest"));
  foo ();

  // Now we reset the log output to default (stderr)
  ACE_LOG_MSG->open (argv[0]);
  ACE_DEBUG ((LM_INFO, ACE_TEXT ("%IGoodnight\n")));

  return 0;
}

void foo (void)
{
  ACE_TRACE (ACE_TEXT ("foo"));

  ACE_DEBUG ((LM_INFO, ACE_TEXT ("%IHowdy Pardner\n")));
}
```

Although it may seem strange to invoke `ACE_LOG_MSG->open()` more than once in your application, nothing is wrong with it. Think of it as more of a reopen. Before we end this chapter, we will create a simple `LogManager` class to help hide some of these kinds of details.

Directing logging output to `SYSLOG` means different things on different platforms, according to what the platform's native "system logger" is and what it is capable of. If the runtime platform doesn't support any type of system logger, directing output to `SYSLOG` has no effect. The following platforms have `SYSLOG` support in ACE:

- Windows NT 4 and newer, such as Windows 2000 and XP: ACE directs `SYSLOG` output to the system's Event Log. The third argument to `ACE_Log_Msg::open()` is an `ACE_TCHAR*` character string. It is optional; if supplied, it replaces the program name as the event source name for recording events in the system's event log. The ACE message severities are mapped to Event Log severities, as shown in Table 3.6.

- UNIX/Linux: ACE directs `SYSLOG` output to the syslog facility. The syslog facility has its own associated configuration details about logging facilities, which are different from ACE's logging severity levels. ACE's syslog back end specifies the `LOG_USER` syslog facility by default. This value can be changed at compile time by changing the `config.h` setting `ACE_DEFAULT_SYSLOG_FACILITY`. Please consult the syslog man page for details on how to configure the logging destination for the specified facility.

Table 3.6. Mapping ACE Logging Severity to Windows Event Log Severity

ACE Severity	Event Log Severity
LM_STARTUP LM_SHUTDOWN LM_TRACE LM_DEBUG LM_INFO	EVENTLOG_INFORMATION_TYPE
LM_NOTICE LM_WARNING	EVENTLOG_WARNING_TYPE
LM_ERROR LM_CRITICAL LM_ALERT LM_EMERGENCY	EVENTLOG_ERROR_TYPE

3.4.3 **Output Streams**

The preferred way to handle output to files and other targets in C++ is output streams (C++ `ostream` objects). They provide enhanced functionality over the `printf()` family of functions and usually result in more readable code. The `ACE_Log_Msg::msg_ostream()` method lets us provide an output stream on which the logger will write our information:

```
ACE_OSTREAM_TYPE *output =
  new std::ofstream ("ostream.output.test");
ACE_LOG_MSG->msg_ostream (output, 1);
ACE_LOG_MSG->set_flags (ACE_Log_Msg::OSTREAM);
ACE_LOG_MSG->clr_flags (ACE_Log_Msg::STDERR);
```

Note that it's perfectly safe to select `OSTREAM` as output—via either `open()` or `set_flags()`—and then generate logging output before you invoke `msg_ostream()`. If you do so, the output will simply disappear, because no `ostream` is assigned. Also note that we have used the two-argument version of `msg_ostream()`. This not only sets the `ostream` for the `ACE_Log_Msg` instance to use but also tells `ACE_Log_Msg` that it should assume ownership and delete the `ostream` instance when the `ACE_Log_Msg` object is deleted. The single-argument version of `msg_ostream()` doesn't specify its default behavior with regard to ownership, so it pays to be explicit in your wishes.

You may wonder why the stream type is `ACE_OSTREAM_TYPE` instead of simply `std::ostream`. This is another aspect of ACE that helps its portability to platforms of all sizes and capabilities. `ACE_OSTREAM_TYPE` can be defined with or without the `std` namespace declaration, and it can also be defined as `FILE` for platforms without any C++ iostream support at all, such as some embedded environments.

3.4.4 **Combined Techniques**

We can now easily combine all these techniques and distribute our logging information among all three choices:

```
#include "ace/Log_Msg.h"
#include "ace/streams.h"

int ACE_TMAIN (int, ACE_TCHAR *argv[])
{
  // Output to default destination (stderr)
  ACE_LOG_MSG->open (argv[0]);
```

```
ACE_TRACE (ACE_TEXT ("main"));

ACE_OSTREAM_TYPE *output =
      new std::ofstream ("ostream.output.test");

ACE_DEBUG ((LM_DEBUG, ACE_TEXT ("%IThis will go to STDERR\n")));

ACE_LOG_MSG->open
   (argv[0], ACE_Log_Msg::SYSLOG, ACE_TEXT ("syslogTest"));
ACE_LOG_MSG->set_flags (ACE_Log_Msg::STDERR);
ACE_DEBUG
   ((LM_DEBUG, ACE_TEXT ("%IThis goes to STDERR & syslog\n")));

ACE_LOG_MSG->msg_ostream (output, 0);
ACE_LOG_MSG->set_flags (ACE_Log_Msg::OSTREAM);
ACE_DEBUG ((LM_DEBUG,
            ACE_TEXT ("%IThis will go to STDERR, ")
            ACE_TEXT ("syslog & an ostream\n")));

ACE_LOG_MSG->clr_flags (ACE_Log_Msg::OSTREAM);
delete output;

return 0;
}
```

Beware of a subtle bug waiting to get you when you use an ostream. Note that before we deleted the ostream instance output, we first cleared the OSTREAM flag on the ACE_Log_Msg instance. Remember that the ACE_TRACE for main still has to write its final message when the trace instance goes out of scope at the end of main(). If we delete the ostream without removing the OSTREAM flag, ACE_Log_Msg will dutifully attempt to write that final message on a deleted ostream instance, and your program will most likely crash.

3.5 Using Callbacks

To this point, we've been content to give our logging output to ACE_Log_Msg, which formatted the messages and directed them to the configured logging sinks. For most cases, that will be fine. What if, though, we want to do something with that output ourselves? Can we inspect or even modify the logging output before it reaches its final destination? Of course. That's where `ACE_Log_Msg_Callback` comes in.

Using a callback object is quite easy. Follow these steps:

1. Derive a callback class from `ACE_Log_Msg_Callback`, and reimplement the following method:

```
virtual void log (ACE_Log_Record &log_record);
```

2. Create an object of your new callback type.

3. To register the callback object with an `ACE_Log_Msg` instance, pass a pointer to your callback object to the `ACE_Log_Msg::msg_callback()` method.

4. Call `ACE_Log_Msg::set_flags()` to enable output to your callback object.

Once registered and enabled, your callback object's `log()` method will be invoked with an `ACE_Log_Record` object any time `ACE_Log_Msg::log()` is invoked. As it turns out, that is exactly what happens when an output-producing ACE logging macro is used.

Some important caveats to remember when using the callback approach are documented on the `ACE_Log_Msg_Callback` reference page. They bear repeating here.

- Callback registration and enabling are specific to each `ACE_Log_Msg` instance. Therefore, a callback set up in one thread won't be used by any other thread in your application.

- Callback objects are not inherited by the `ACE_Log_Msg` instances created for any threads you create. So if you're going to be using callback objects with multithreaded applications, you need to take special care that each thread is given an appropriate callback instance. It is possible to use a single object safely: see the description of `ACE_Singleton` in Section 1.6.3.

- As with the `OSTREAM` caveat, be sure that you don't delete a callback instance that might still be used by the `ACE_Log_Msg` instance it's registered with.

A simple callback implementation follows:

```
#include "ace/streams.h"
#include "ace/Log_Msg.h"
#include "ace/Log_Msg_Callback.h"
#include "ace/Log_Record.h"

class Callback : public ACE_Log_Msg_Callback
{
```

```
public:
  void log (ACE_Log_Record &log_record) {
    log_record.print (ACE_TEXT (""), 0, cerr);
    log_record.print (ACE_TEXT (""), ACE_Log_Msg::VERBOSE, cerr);
  }
};
```

The program that uses it follows:

```
#include "ace/Log_Msg.h"
#include "Callback.h"

int ACE_TMAIN (int, ACE_TCHAR *[])
{
  Callback *callback = new Callback;

  ACE_LOG_MSG->set_flags (ACE_Log_Msg::MSG_CALLBACK);
  ACE_LOG_MSG->clr_flags (ACE_Log_Msg::STDERR);
  ACE_LOG_MSG->msg_callback (callback);

  ACE_TRACE (ACE_TEXT ("main"));

  ACE_DEBUG ((LM_DEBUG, ACE_TEXT ("%IHi Mom\n")));
  ACE_DEBUG ((LM_INFO, ACE_TEXT ("%IGoodnight\n")));

  return 0;
}
```

The program creates this output:

```
(1024) calling main in file `Use_Callback.cpp' on line 12
Sep 24 12:35:02.829 2003@@22396@LM_TRACE@(1024) calling main in fi
le `Use_Callback.cpp' on line 12
   Hi Mom
Sep 24 12:35:02.830 2003@@22396@LM_DEBUG@   Hi Mom
   Goodnight
Sep 24 12:35:02.830 2003@@22396@LM_INFO@   Goodnight
(1024) leaving main
Sep 24 12:35:02.830 2003@@22396@LM_TRACE@(1024) leaving main
```

The first `log_record.print()` simply prints the message we've always seen. The second, however, uses the VERBOSE flag to provide much more information. Both direct their output to the standard error stream.

Once you have access to the ACE_Log_Record instance, you have control to do anything you want. Let's take a look at a bit more of the information contained in ACE_Log_Record:

```cpp
#include "ace/streams.h"
#include "ace/Log_Msg_Callback.h"
#include "ace/Log_Record.h"
#include "ace/SString.h"

class Callback : public ACE_Log_Msg_Callback
{
public:
  void log (ACE_Log_Record &log_record)
    {
      cerr << "Log Message Received:" << endl;
      unsigned long msg_severity = log_record.type ();
      ACE_Log_Priority prio =
        ACE_static_cast (ACE_Log_Priority, msg_severity);
      const ACE_TCHAR *prio_name =
        ACE_Log_Record::priority_name (prio);
      cerr << "\tType:          "
           << ACE_TEXT_ALWAYS_CHAR (prio_name)
           << endl;

      cerr << "\tLength:        " << log_record.length () << endl;

      const time_t epoch = log_record.time_stamp ().sec ();
      cerr << "\tTime_Stamp:    "
           << ACE_TEXT_ALWAYS_CHAR (ACE_OS::ctime (&epoch))
           << flush;

      cerr << "\tPid:           " << log_record.pid () << endl;

      ACE_CString data (">> ");
      data += ACE_TEXT_ALWAYS_CHAR (log_record.msg_data ());

      cerr << "\tMsgData:       " << data.c_str () << endl;
    }
};
```

The following output is created:

```
Log Message Received:
        Type:           LM_TRACE
        Length:         88
        Time_Stamp:     Wed Sep 24 12:35:09 2003
        Pid:            22411
        MsgData:        >> (1024) calling main in file `Use_Callback2
.cpp' on line 12

Log Message Received:
        Type:           LM_DEBUG
        Length:         40
        Time_Stamp:     Wed Sep 24 12:35:09 2003
        Pid:            22411
        MsgData:        >>    Hi Mom

Log Message Received:
        Type:           LM_INFO
        Length:         40
        Time_Stamp:     Wed Sep 24 12:35:09 2003
        Pid:            22411
        MsgData:        >>    Goodnight

Log Message Received:
        Type:           LM_TRACE
        Length:         48
        Time_Stamp:     Wed Sep 24 12:35:09 2003
        Pid:            22411
        MsgData:        >> (1024) leaving main
```

As you can see, we have quite a bit of access to the `ACE_Log_Record` internals. We're not limited to changing only the message text. We can, in fact, change any of the values we want. Whether that makes any sense is up to your application. Table 3.7 lists the attributes of `ACE_Log_Record` and what they mean.

3.6 The Logging Client and Server Daemons

Put simply, the ACE Logging Service is a configurable two-tier replacement for UNIX syslog. Both syslog and the Windows Event Logger are pretty good at what they do and can even be used to capture messages from remote hosts. But if you have a mixed environment, they simply aren't sufficient.

Table 3.7. `ACE_Log_Record` Attributes

Attribute	Description
`type`	The log record type from Table 3.1
`priority`	Synonym for *type*
`priority_name`	The log record's priority name
`length`	The length of the log record, set by the creator of the log record
`time_stamp`	The timestamp—generally, creation time—of the log record; set by the creator of the log record
`pid`	ID of the process that created the log record instance
`msg_data`	The textual message of the log record
`msg_data_len`	Length of the `msg_data` attribute

The ACE netsvcs logging framework has a client/server design. On one host in the network, you run the logging server that will accept logging requests from any other host. On that and every host in the network where you want to use the distributed logger, you invoke the logging client. The client acts somewhat like a proxy by accepting logging requests from clients on the local system and forwarding them to the server. This may seem to be a bit of an odd design, but it helps prevent pounding the server with a huge number of client connections, many of which may be transient. By using the proxy approach, the proxy on each host absorbs a little bit of the pounding, and everyone is better off.

To configure our server and client proxy, we will use the ACE Service Configurator framework. The Service Configurator is an advanced topic that is covered in Chapter 19. We will show you just enough here to get things off the ground. Feel free to jump ahead and read a bit more about the Service Configurator now, or wait and read it later.

To start the server, you need to first create a file `server.conf` with the following content:

```
dynamic Logger Service_Object * ACE:_make_ACE_Logging_Strategy() "
-s foobar -f STDERR|OSTREAM|VERBOSE"

dynamic Server_Logging_Service Service_Object * netsvcs:_make_ACE_
Server_Logging_Acceptor() active "-p 20009"
```

Note these lines are wrapped for readability. Your `server.conf` should contain only two lines, each beginning with the word `dynamic`. The first line defines the *logging strategy* to write the log output to standard error and the output stream attached to a file named `foobar`. This line also requests verbose log messages instead of a more terse format. (Section 3.8 discusses more ways to use this service.) The second line of `server.conf` causes the server to listen for client connections at TCP (Transmission Control Protocol) port 20009[1] on all network interfaces available on your computer. You can now start the server with:

```
$ACE_ROOT/netsvcs/servers/main -f server.conf
```

The next step is to create the configuration file for the client proxy and start the proxy. The file could be named `client.conf` and should look something like this:

```
dynamic Client_Logging_Service Service_Object * netsvcs:_make_ACE_
Client_Logging_Acceptor() active "-p 20009 -h localhost"
```

Again, that's all on one line. The important parts are `-p 20009`, which tells the proxy which TCP port the server will be listening to—this should match the `-p` value in your `server.conf`—and `-h localhost`, which sets the host name where the logging server is executing. For our simple test, we are executing both client and server on the same system. In the real world, you will most likely have to change `localhost` to the name of your real logging server.

Although we provide the port on which the server is listening, we did not provide a port value for clients of the proxy. This value is known as the *logger key*, and its form and value change, depending on the capabilities of the platform the client logger is built on. On some platforms, it's a pipe; where that's not possible, it's a loopback TCP socket at address `localhost:20012`. If you want your client proxy to listen at a different address, you can specify that with the `-k` parameter in `client.conf`.

You can now start the client logger with:

```
$ACE_ROOT/netsvcs/servers/main -f client.conf
```

Using the logging service in one of our previous examples is trivial:

---

1. Although nothing is particularly magic about the port 20009, a standard set of ports is typically used by the ACE examples and tests. Throughout this text, we have tried to maintain consistency with that set.

```
#include "ace/Log_Msg.h"

int ACE_TMAIN (int, ACE_TCHAR *argv[])
{
  ACE_LOG_MSG->open (argv[0],
                     ACE_Log_Msg::LOGGER,
                     ACE_DEFAULT_LOGGER_KEY);

  ACE_TRACE (ACE_TEXT ("main"));

  ACE_DEBUG ((LM_DEBUG, ACE_TEXT ("%IHi Mom\n")));
  ACE_DEBUG ((LM_INFO, ACE_TEXT ("%IGoodnight\n")));

  return 0;
}
```

As with the syslog example, we must use the open() method when we want to use the logging service; set_flags() isn't sufficient. Note also the open() parameter ACE_DEFAULT_LOGGER_KEY. This has to be the same logger key that the client logger is listening at; if you changed it with the -k option in client.conf, you must specify the new value to open().

To summarize: On every machine on which you want to use the logging service, you must execute an instance of the client logger. Each instance is configured to connect to a single instance of the logging server somewhere on your network. Then, of course, you execute that server instance on the appropriate system.

For the truly adventurous, your application can communicate directly with the logging server instance. This approach has two problems:

1. Your program is now more complicated because of the connection and logging logic.
2. You run the risk of overloading the server instance because you've removed the scaling afforded by the client proxies.

However, if you still want your application to talk directly to the logging server, here's a way to do so:

```
#include "ace/Log_Msg.h"
#include "Callback-3.h"

int ACE_TMAIN (int, ACE_TCHAR *[])
{
  Callback *callback = new Callback;
```

```
ACE_LOG_MSG->set_flags (ACE_Log_Msg::MSG_CALLBACK);
ACE_LOG_MSG->clr_flags (ACE_Log_Msg::STDERR);
ACE_LOG_MSG->msg_callback (callback);

ACE_TRACE (ACE_TEXT ("main"));

ACE_DEBUG ((LM_DEBUG, ACE_TEXT ("%IHi Mom\n")));
ACE_DEBUG ((LM_INFO, ACE_TEXT ("%IGoodnight\n")));

return 0;
}
```

This looks very much like our previous callback example. We use the callback
hook to capture the ACE_Log_Record instance that contains our message. Our
new Callback object then sends that to the logging server:

```
#include "ace/streams.h"
#include "ace/Log_Msg.h"
#include "ace/Log_Msg_Callback.h"
#include "ace/Log_Record.h"
#include "ace/SOCK_Stream.h"
#include "ace/SOCK_Connector.h"
#include "ace/INET_Addr.h"

#define LOGGER_PORT 20009

class Callback : public ACE_Log_Msg_Callback
{
public:
  Callback ()
    {
      this->logger_ = new ACE_SOCK_Stream;
      ACE_SOCK_Connector connector;
      ACE_INET_Addr addr (LOGGER_PORT, ACE_DEFAULT_SERVER_HOST);

      if (connector.connect (*(this->logger_), addr) == -1)
        {
          delete this->logger_;
          this->logger_ = 0;
        }
    }

  virtual ~Callback ()
    {
```

```
          if (this->logger_)
            {
              this->logger_->close ();
            }
          delete this->logger_;
        }

    void log (ACE_Log_Record &log_record)
      {
        if (!this->logger_)
          {
            log_record.print
              (ACE_TEXT (""), ACE_Log_Msg::VERBOSE, cerr);
            return;
          }

        size_t len = log_record.length ();
        log_record.encode ();

        if (this->logger_->send_n ((char *) &log_record, len) == -1)
          {
            delete this->logger_;
            this->logger_ = 0;
          }
      }

private:
  ACE_SOCK_Stream *logger_;
};
```

We've introduced some things here that you won't read about for a bit. The gist of what we're doing is that the callback object's constructor opens a socket to the logging service. The `log()` method then sends the `ACE_Log_Record` instance to the server via the socket. Because several of the `ACE_Log_Record` attributes are numeric, we must use the `encode()` method to ensure that they are in a network-neutral format before sending them. Doing so will prevent much confusion if the byte ordering of the host executing your application is different from that of the host executing your logging server.

3.7 The LogManager Class

The preceding sections explained how to direct the logging output to several
places. We noted that you can change your mind at runtime and direct the logging
output somewhere else. Unfortunately, what you need to do when you change
your mind isn't always consistent. Let's take a look at a simple class that attempts
to hide some of those details:

```
class LogManager
{
public:
  LogManager ();
  ~LogManager ();

  void redirectToDaemon
    (const ACE_TCHAR *prog_name = ACE_TEXT (""));
  void redirectToSyslog
    (const ACE_TCHAR *prog_name = ACE_TEXT (""));
  void redirectToOStream (ACE_OSTREAM_TYPE *output);
  void redirectToFile (const char *filename);
  void redirectToStderr (void);
  ACE_Log_Msg_Callback * redirectToCallback
    (ACE_Log_Msg_Callback *callback);

  // ...
};
```

The idea is pretty simple: An application will use the `redirect*` methods at
any time to select the output destination:

```
void foo (void);

int ACE_TMAIN (int, ACE_TCHAR *[])
{
  LOG_MANAGER->redirectToStderr ();
  ACE_TRACE (ACE_TEXT ("main"));
  LOG_MANAGER->redirectToSyslog ();
  ACE_DEBUG ((LM_INFO, ACE_TEXT ("%IHi Mom\n")));
  foo ();
  LOG_MANAGER->redirectToDaemon ();
  ACE_DEBUG ((LM_INFO, ACE_TEXT ("%IGoodnight\n")));

  return 0;
}
```

```
void foo (void)
{
  ACE_TRACE (ACE_TEXT ("foo"));
  LOG_MANAGER->redirectToFile ("output.test");
  ACE_DEBUG ((LM_INFO, ACE_TEXT ("%IHowdy Pardner\n")));
}
```

"But wait," you say. "Where did LOG_MANAGER come from?" This is an example of the ACE_Singleton template, mentioned in Section 1.6.3. That's what we're using behind LOG_MANAGER. ACE_Singleton simply ensures that we create one single instance of the LogManager class at runtime, even if multiple threads all try to create one at the same time. Using a singleton gives you quick access to a single instance of an object anywhere in your application. To declare our singleton, we add the following to our header file:

```
typedef ACE_Singleton<LogManager, ACE_Null_Mutex>
        LogManagerSingleton;
#define LOG_MANAGER LogManagerSingleton::instance()
```

To deal with compilers that don't do automatic template instantiation, we must add the following to our .cpp file:

```
#if defined (ACE_HAS_EXPLICIT_TEMPLATE_INSTANTIATION)
 template class ACE_Singleton<LogManager, ACE_Null_Mutex>;
#elif defined (ACE_HAS_TEMPLATE_INSTANTIATION_PRAGMA)
#pragma instantiate ACE_Singleton<LogManager, ACE_Null_Mutex>
#elif defined (__GNUC__) && (defined (_AIX) || defined (__hpux))
template ACE_Singleton<LogManager, ACE_Null_Mutex> *
  ACE_Singleton<LogManager, ACE_Null_Mutex>::singleton_;
#endif /* ACE_HAS_EXPLICIT_TEMPLATE_INSTANTIATION */
```

Our LogManager implementation is a straightforward application of the things discussed earlier in this chapter:

```
LogManager::LogManager ()
  : log_stream_ (0), output_stream_ (0)
{ }

LogManager::~LogManager ()
{
  if (log_stream_)
    log_stream_->close ();
  delete log_stream_;
}
```

```
void LogManager::redirectToSyslog (const ACE_TCHAR *prog_name)
{
  ACE_LOG_MSG->open (prog_name, ACE_Log_Msg::SYSLOG, prog_name);
}

void LogManager::redirectToDaemon (const ACE_TCHAR *prog_name)
{
  ACE_LOG_MSG->open (prog_name, ACE_Log_Msg::LOGGER,
                     ACE_DEFAULT_LOGGER_KEY);
}

void LogManager::redirectToOStream (ACE_OSTREAM_TYPE *output)
{
  output_stream_ = output;
  ACE_LOG_MSG->msg_ostream (this->output_stream_);
  ACE_LOG_MSG->clr_flags
    (ACE_Log_Msg::STDERR | ACE_Log_Msg::LOGGER);
  ACE_LOG_MSG->set_flags (ACE_Log_Msg::OSTREAM);
}

void LogManager::redirectToFile (const char *filename)
{
  log_stream_ = new std::ofstream ();
  log_stream_->open (filename, ios::out | ios::app);
  this->redirectToOStream (log_stream_);
}

void LogManager::redirectToStderr (void)
{
  ACE_LOG_MSG->clr_flags
    (ACE_Log_Msg::OSTREAM | ACE_Log_Msg::LOGGER);
  ACE_LOG_MSG->set_flags (ACE_Log_Msg::STDERR);
}

ACE_Log_Msg_Callback *
LogManager::redirectToCallback (ACE_Log_Msg_Callback * callback)
{
  ACE_Log_Msg_Callback *previous =
    ACE_LOG_MSG->msg_callback (callback);
  if (callback == 0)
    ACE_LOG_MSG->clr_flags (ACE_Log_Msg::MSG_CALLBACK);
  else
    ACE_LOG_MSG->set_flags (ACE_Log_Msg::MSG_CALLBACK);
  return previous;
}
```

The primary limitation of the `LogManager` class is the assumption that output will go to only one place at a time. For our trivial examples, that may be sufficient but could be a problem for a real application. Modifying the `LogManager` class to overcome this should be a fairly easy task, and we leave that to the reader.

3.8 Runtime Configuration with the ACE Logging Strategy

Thus far, all our decisions about what to log and where to send the output have been determined at compile time. In many cases, it is unreasonable to require a recompile to change the logging options. We could, of course, provide parameters or a configuration file to our application, but we would have to spend valuable time writing and debugging that code. Fortunately, ACE has already provided us with a convenient solution in the form of the `ACE_Logging_Strategy` object.

Consider the following file:

```
dynamic Logger Service_Object * ACE:_make_ACE_Logging_Strategy()
"-s log.out -f STDERR|OSTREAM -p INFO"
```

We've seen this kind of thing before when we were talking about the distributed logging service. In this case, we're instructing the ACE Service Configurator to create and configure a logging strategy instance just like the distributed logging server. Again, the Service Configurator is an advanced topic with many exciting features[2] and is covered in Chapter 19.

The following sample application uses the preceding file:

```
int ACE_TMAIN (int argc, ACE_TCHAR *argv[])
{
  if (ACE_Service_Config::open (argc,
                                argv,
                                ACE_DEFAULT_LOGGER_KEY,
                                1,
                                0,
                                1) < 0)
```

---

2. One of the most exciting is the ability to reconfigure the service object while the application is running. In the context of our logging strategy, this means that you can change the -p value to reconfigure the logging level without stopping and restarting your application!

```
ACE_ERROR_RETURN ((LM_ERROR, ACE_TEXT ("%p\n"),
                   ACE_TEXT ("Service Config open")),
                  1);
ACE_TRACE (ACE_TEXT ("main"));
ACE_DEBUG ((LM_NOTICE, ACE_TEXT ("%t%IHowdy Pardner\n")));
ACE_DEBUG ((LM_INFO, ACE_TEXT ("%t%IGoodnight\n")));

return 0;
}
```

The key is the call to ACE_Service_Config::open(), which is given our command line parameters. By default it will open a file named svc.conf, but we can specify an alternative by specifying **-f someFile**. In either case, the file's content would be something like the preceding, which tells the logging service to direct the output to both STDERR and the file log.out.

Be careful that you call ACE_Service_Config::open() as shown rather than with the default parameters. If the final parameter is not 1, the open() method will restore the logging flags to their preopen values. Because the logging service loads its configuration and sets the logging flags from within the service configuration's open(), you will be unpleasantly surprised to find that the logging strategy had no effect on the priority mask once open() completes.

Recall that, by default, all logging severity levels are enabled at a processwide level. If you specify -p INFO in your config file, you will probably be surprised when you get other logging levels also; they were already enabled by default. To get what you want, be sure to use the disable flags, such as ~INFO, as well; these are listed in Table 3.8.

One of the most powerful features of the logging strategy is the ability to rotate the application's log files when they reach a specified size. Use the -m parameter to set the size and the -N parameter to set the maximum number of files to keep. Authors of long-running applications will appreciate this, as it will go a long way toward preventing rampant disk space consumption.

Table 3.8 lists all the ACE Logging Strategy options that can be specified and their values. The possible values for -p and -t are the same as those listed in Table 3.1, but without the LM_ prefix. Any value can be prefixed with ~ to omit that log level from the output. Multiple flags can be OR'd (|) together as needed.

Table 3.8. ACE Logging Strategy Configuration Options

Option	Arguments and Meaning
-f	Specify ACE_Log_Msg flags (OSTREAM, STDERR, LOGGER, VERBOSE, SILENT, VERBOSE_LITE) used to control logging.
-i	The interval, in seconds, at which the log file size is sampled (default is 0; do not sample by default).
-k	Specify the rendezvous point for the client logger.
-m	The maximum log file size in Kbytes.
-n	Set the program name for the %n format specifier.
-N	The maximum number of log files to create.
-o	Request the standard log file ordering (keeps multiple log files in numbered order). Default is not to order log files.
-p	Pass in the processwide priorities to either enable (DEBUG, INFO, WARNING, NOTICE, ERROR, CRITICAL, ALERT, EMERGENCY) or to disable (~DEBUG, ~INFO, ~WARNING, ~NOTICE, ~ERROR, ~CRITICAL, ~ALERT, ~EMERGENCY).
-s	Specify the file name used when OSTREAM is specified as an output target.
-t	Pass in the per instance priorities to either enable (DEBUG, INFO, WARNING, NOTICE, ERROR, CRITICAL, ALERT, EMERGENCY) or to disable (~DEBUG, ~INFO, ~WARNING, ~NOTICE, ~ERROR, ~CRITICAL, ~ALERT, ~EMERGENCY).
-w	Cause the log file to be wiped out on both start-up and reconfiguration.

3.9 Summary

Every program needs to have a good logging mechanism. ACE provides you with more than one way to handle such things. Consider your application and how you expect it to grow over time. Your choices range from the simple ACE_DEBUG macros to the highly flexible logging service. You can run "out of the box" or customize things to fit your specific environment. Take the time to try out several approaches before settling on one. With ACE, changing your mind is easy.

Chapter 4
Collecting Runtime Information

Most applications offer ways for users to direct or alter runtime behavior. Two of the most common approaches are

- *Accepting command line arguments and options.* This approach is often used for information that can reasonably change on each application invocation. For example, the host name to connect to during an FTP (file transfer protocol) or TELNET session is usually different each time the command is run.

- *Reading configuration files.* Configuration files usually hold site- or user-specific information that doesn't often change or that should be remembered between application invocations. For example, an installation script may store file system locations to read from or record log files to. The configuration information may indicate which TCP or UDP (user datagram protocol) ports a server should listen on or whether to enable various logging severity levels.

Any information that can reasonably change at runtime should be made available to an application at runtime, not built into the application itself. This allows the information to change without having to rebuild and redistribute the application. In this chapter, we look at the following ACE classes that help in this effort:

- `ACE_Get_Opt`: to access command line arguments and options
- `ACE_Configuration`: to manipulate configuration information on all platforms using the `ACE_Configuration_Heap` class and, for the Windows registry, the `ACE_Configuration_Win32Registry` class

4.1 Command Line Arguments and ACE_Get_Opt

ACE_Get_Opt is ACE's primary class for command line argument processing. This class is an iterator for parsing a counted vector of arguments, such as those passed on a program's command line via argc/argv. POSIX developers will recognize ACE_Get_Opt's functionality because it is a C++ wrapper facade for the standard POSIX getopt() function. Unlike getopt(), however, each instance of ACE_Get_Opt maintains its own state, so it can be used reentrantly. In addition, ACE_Get_Opt is easier to use than getopt(), as the option definition string and argument vector are passed only once to the constructor rather than to each iterator call.

ACE_Get_Opt can parse two kinds of options:

1. Short, single-character options, which begin with a single dash ('-')

2. Long options, which begin with a double dash ('--')

For example, the following code implements command line handling for a program that offers command line option **-f**, which takes an argument—the name of a configuration file—and an equivalent long option **--config**:

```
static const ACE_TCHAR options[] = ACE_TEXT (":f:");
ACE_Get_Opt cmd_opts (argc, argv, options);
if (cmd_opts.long_option
    (ACE_TEXT ("config"), 'f', ACE_Get_Opt::ARG_REQUIRED) == -1)
  return -1;
int option;
ACE_TCHAR config_file[MAXPATHLEN];
ACE_OS_String::strcpy (config_file, ACE_TEXT ("HAStatus.conf"));
while ((option = cmd_opts ()) != EOF)
  switch (option) {
  case 'f':
    ACE_OS_String::strncpy (config_file,
                            cmd_opts.opt_arg (),
                            MAXPATHLEN);
    break;
  case ':':
    ACE_ERROR_RETURN
      ((LM_ERROR, ACE_TEXT ("-%c requires an argument\n"),
        cmd_opts.opt_opt ()), -1);
  default:
    ACE_ERROR_RETURN
      ((LM_ERROR, ACE_TEXT ("Parse error.\n")), -1);
  }
```

This example uses the `cmd_opts` object to extract the command line arguments. This example illustrates what you must do to process a command line.

- *Define the valid options.* To define short options, build a character string containing all valid option letters. A colon following an option letter means that the option requires an argument. In the preceding example, **-f** requires an argument. Use a double colon if the argument is optional. To add equivalent long options, use the `long_option()` method to equate a long option string with one of the short options. Our example equates the **--config** option with **-f**.

- *Use `operator()` to iterate through the command line options.* It returns the short option character when located and the short option equivalent when a long option is processed. The option's argument is accessed via the `opt_arg()` method. The `operator()` method returns EOF when all the options have been processed.

`ACE_Get_Opt` keeps track of where in the argument vector it is when processing the `argv` elements. When it finds an option that takes an argument, `ACE_Get_Opt` takes the option's argument from the remaining characters of the current `argv` element or the next `argv` element as needed. Optional arguments, however, must be in the same element as the option character. The behavior when a required argument is missing depends on the first character of the short options definition string. If it is a ' : ', as in our example, `operator()` returns a ' : ' when a required argument is missing. Otherwise, it returns ' ? '.

Short options that don't take arguments can be grouped together on the command line after the leading **-**, but in that case, only the last short option in the group can take an argument. A ' ? ' is returned if the short option is not recognized.

Because short options are defined as integers, long options that wouldn't normally have a meaningful short option equivalent can designate nonalphanumeric values for the corresponding short option. These nonalphanumerics cannot appear in the argument list or in short options definition string but can be returned and processed efficiently in a `switch` statement. The following two lines of code could be added to the previous example. They illustrate two ways to register a long option without a corresponding short option:

```
cmd_opts.long_option (ACE_TEXT ("cool_option"));
cmd_opts.long_option (ACE_TEXT ("the_answer"), 42);
```

The first call to `long_option()` adds a long option **--cool_option** that will cause a 0 to be returned from `operator()` if **--cool_option** is specified on the command line. The second is similar but specifies that the integer value 42 will be returned from `operator()` when **--the_answer** is found on the command line. The following shows the additions that would be made to the switch block in the example on page 78:

```
case 0:
  ACE_DEBUG ((LM_DEBUG, ACE_TEXT ("Yes, very cool.\n")));
  break;

case 42:
  ACE_DEBUG ((LM_DEBUG, ACE_TEXT ("the_answer is 42\n")));
  break;
```

When the user supplies long options on the command line, each one can be abbreviated as long it is unambiguous. Therefore, **--cool_option** could be abbreviated as short as **--coo**. (Anything shorter would also match **--config**.)

An `argv` element of **--** signifies the end of the option section, and `operator()` returns EOF. If the `opt_ind()` method returns a value that's less than the number of command line elements (`argc`), some elements haven't been parsed.

That's the basic use case; however, ACE_Get_Opt can do a lot more.

4.1.1 Altering ACE_Get_Opt's Behavior

The `ACE_Get_Opt` class's extended capabilities are accessed by specifying values for the defaulted arguments in the constructor. The complete signature for the constructor is:

```
ACE_Get_Opt (int argc,
             ACE_TCHAR **argv,
             const ACE_TCHAR *optstring,
             int skip_args = 1,
             int report_errors = 0,
             int ordering = PERMUTE_ARGS,
             int long_only = 0);
```

Start Parsing at an Arbitrary Index

`ACE_Get_Opt` can be directed to start processing the argument vector at an arbitrary point specified by the `skip_args` parameter. The default value is 1, which causes ACE_Get_Opt to skip argv[0]—traditionally, the program name—when parsing a command line passed to main(). When ACE_Get_Opt is used to parse options received when initializing a dynamic service (see Chapter 19), skip_args is often specified as 0, because arguments passed to services initialized via the ACE Service Configurator framework start in argv[0]. The skip_args parameter can also be set to any other value that's less than the value of argc to skip previously processed arguments or arguments that are already known.

Report Errors while Parsing

By default, ACE_Get_Opt is silent about parsing errors; it simply returns the appropriate value from operator(), allowing your application to handle and report errors in the most sensible way. If, however, you'd rather have ACE_Get_Opt display an error message when it detects an error in the specified argument vector, the constructor's report_errors argument should be nonzero. In this case, ACE_Get_Opt will use ACE_ERROR with the LM_ERROR severity to report the error. See Chapter 3 for a discussion of ACE's logging facility, including the ACE_ERROR macro.

Alternative Long Option Specification

If "W;" is included in the options definitions string, ACE_Get_Opt treats -W as if the next command line element is preceded by --. For example, -W foo will be parsed the same as --foo. This can be useful when manipulating argument vectors to change parameters into long options by inserting an element with -W instead of inserting -- on an existing element.

Long Options Only

If the long_only parameter to the ACE_Get_Opt constructor is nonzero, command line tokens that begin with a single - are checked as long options. For example, in the program on page 78, if the long_only argument were set to 1, the user could type either --config or -config.

4.1.2 Understanding Argument Ordering

Some applications require you to specify all options at the beginning of the command line, whereas others allow you to mix options and other nonoption tokens, such as file names. ACE_Get_Opt supports selection of use cases defined by enumerators defined in ACE_Get_Opt. One of these values can be passed as the constructor's `ordering` parameter, which accepts the following values:

- `ACE_Get_Opt::PERMUTE_ARGS`. As the argument vector is parsed, the elements are dynamically rearranged so that those with valid options—and their arguments—appear at the front of the argument vector, in their original relative ordering. Nonoption elements, placed after the option elements, can be processed by another part of your system or as known nonoptions, such as file names. When `operator()` returns EOF to indicate the end of options, `opt_ind()` returns the index to the first nonoption element in the argument vector. This is the default ordering mode.

- `ACE_Get_Opt::REQUIRE_ORDER`. The argument vector is not reordered, and all options and their arguments must be at the front of the argument vector. If a nonoption element is encountered, `operator()` returns EOF; `opt_ind()` returns the index of the nonoption element.

- `ACE_Get_Opt::RETURN_IN_ORDER`. The argument vector is not reordered. Any nonoption element causes `operator()` to return 1, and the actual element is accessible via the `opt_arg()` method. This mode is useful for situations in which options and other arguments can be specified in any order and in which the relative ordering makes a difference. In this situation, it may be useful to parse options, examine nonoptions, and continue parsing after the nonoptions, using the `skip_args` argument to specify the new starting point.

As mentioned, the argument ordering can be changed by specifying an enumerator for the `ACE_Get_Opt` constructor's `ordering` parameter. However, the argument ordering can also be changed by using two other mechanisms. Specifying a value for the constructor takes least precedence. The other two methods both override the constructor value and are listed here in increasing order of precedence.

1. If the `POSIXLY_CORRECT` environment variable is set, the ordering mode is set to `REQUIRE_ORDER`.

2. A + or - character is at the beginning of the options string. A + changes the ordering mode to `REQUIRE_ORDER`; - changes it to `RETURN_IN_ORDER`. If both are at the start of the options string, the last one is used.

4.2 Accessing Configuration Information

Many applications are installed via installation scripts that store collected information in a file that the application reads at runtime. On modern versions of Microsoft Windows, this information is often stored in the Windows registry; in earlier versions, a file was used. Most other platforms use files as well. The `ACE_Configuration` class defines the configuration interface for the following two classes available for accessing and manipulating configuration information.

1. `ACE_Configuration_Heap`, available on all platforms, keeps all information in memory. The memory allocation can be customized to use a persistent backing store, but the most common use is with dynamically allocated heap memory; hence its name.

2. `ACE_Configuration_Win32Registry`, available only on Windows, implements the `ACE_Configuration` interface to access and manipulate information in the Windows registry.

In both cases, configuration values are stored in hierarchically related sections. Each section has a name and zero or more settings. Each setting has a name and a typed data value. Even though the configuration information can be both read and modified, resist the temptation to use it as a database, with frequent updates. It's not designed for that.

The following example shows how the Home Automation system uses ACE's configuration facility to configure each subsystem's TCP port number. The configuration uses one section per subsystem, with settings in each section used to configure an aspect of that subsystem. Thus, the configuration for the entire system is managed in a central location. The example uses the `config_file` command line argument read in the example on page 78. After importing the configuration data, the program looks up the `ListenPort` value in the `HAStatus` section to find out where it should listen for status requests:

```
ACE_Configuration_Heap config;
if (config.open () == -1)
  ACE_ERROR_RETURN
    ((LM_ERROR, ACE_TEXT ("%p\n"), ACE_TEXT ("config")), -1);
ACE_Registry_ImpExp config_importer (config);
if (config_importer.import_config (config_file) == -1)
  ACE_ERROR_RETURN
    ((LM_ERROR, ACE_TEXT ("%p\n"), config_file), -1);

ACE_Configuration_Section_Key status_section;
```

```
if (config.open_section (config.root_section (),
                         ACE_TEXT ("HAStatus"),
                         0,
                         status_section) == -1)
  ACE_ERROR_RETURN ((LM_ERROR, ACE_TEXT ("%p\n"),
                     ACE_TEXT ("Can't open HAStatus section")),
                     -1);

u_int status_port;
if (config.get_integer_value (status_section,
                              ACE_TEXT ("ListenPort"),
                              status_port) == -1)
  ACE_ERROR_RETURN
    ((LM_ERROR,
      ACE_TEXT ("HAStatus ListenPort does not exist\n")),
     -1);
this->listen_addr_.set (ACE_static_cast (u_short, status_port));
```

To remain portable across all ACE platforms, this example uses the
ACE_Configuration_Heap class to access the configuration data. Whereas
the ACE_Configuration_Win32Registry class operates directly on the
Windows registry, the contents of each ACE_Configuration_Heap object
persist only as long as the object itself. Therefore, the data needs to be imported
from the configuration file. We'll look at configuration storage in Section 4.2.2.

Because our example application keeps the settings for each subsystem in a
separate section, it opens the HAStatus section. The ListenPort value is
read and used to set the TCP port number in the listen_addr_ member variable.

4.2.1 Configuration Sections

Configuration data is organized hierarchically in sections, analogous to a file
system directory tree. Each configuration object contains a *root section* that has no
name, similar to the file system root in UNIX. All other sections are created hierarchically beneath the root section and are named by the application. Sections can
be nested to an arbitrary depth.

4.2.2 Configuration Backing Stores

The ACE_Configuration_Win32Registry class accesses the Windows
registry directly, and therefore acts as a wrapper around the Windows API. Thus,

Windows manages the data and all access to it. Although it is possible to use a memory-mapped allocation strategy with `ACE_Configuration_Heap`, the resultant file contents are the in-memory format of the configuration and not a human-readable form. Therefore, configuration information is usually saved in a file. ACE offers two classes for importing data from and exporting data to a file.

1. `ACE_Registry_ImpExp` uses a text format that includes type information with each value. This allows type information to be preserved across export/import, even on machines with different byte orders. This is the class used in the previous example to import configuration data from the configuration file specified on the program's command line.

2. `ACE_Ini_ImpExp` uses the older Windows "INI" file format, which does not have type information associated with the values. Therefore, configuration data exported using `ACE_Ini_ImpExp` is always imported as string data, regardless of the original type.

Both classes use text files; however, they are not interchangeable. Therefore, you should choose a format and use it consistently. It is usually best to use `ACE_Registry_ImpExp` when possible because it retains type information. `ACE_Ini_ImpExp` is most useful when your application must read existing `.INI` files over which you have no control.

4.3 Building Argument Vectors

Section 4.1 showed how to process an argument vector, such as the `argc/argv` passed to a main program. Sometimes, however, it is necessary to parse options from a single long string containing tokens similar to a command line. For example, a set of options may be read as a string from a configuration file. In this case, it is helpful to convert the string to an argument vector in order to use `ACE_Get_Opt`. `ACE_ARGV` is a good class for this use.

Let's say that a program that obtains its options from a string wants to parse the string by using `ACE_Get_Opt`. The following code converts the `cmdline` string into an argument vector and instantiates the `cmd_opts` object to parse it:

```
#include "ace/ARGV.h"
#include "ace/Get_Opt.h"

int ACE_TMAIN (int, ACE_TCHAR *[])
{
  static const ACE_TCHAR options[] = ACE_TEXT (":f:h:");
```

```
static const ACE_TCHAR cmdline[] =
  ACE_TEXT ("-f /home/managed.cfg -h $HOSTNAME");
ACE_ARGV cmdline_args (cmdline);
ACE_Get_Opt cmd_opts (cmdline_args.argc (),
                      cmdline_args.argv (),
                      options,
                      0);            // Don't skip any args
```

Note that the `ace/ARGV.h` header needs to be included to use the
`ACE_ARGV` class. Another useful feature of `ACE_ARGV` is its ability to substitute
environment variable names while building the argument vector. In the example,
the value of the `HOSTNAME` environment variable is substituted where `$HOST-`
`NAME` appears in the input string. This feature can be disabled by supplying a 0
value to the second argument on the `ACE_ARGV` constructor; by default, it is 1,
resulting in environment variable substitution.

Note that the environment variable reference uses the POSIX-like leading $,
even on platforms such as Windows, where environment variable references do
not normally use a $ delimiter. This keeps the feature usable on all platforms that
support the use of environment variables. One shortcoming in this feature,
however, is that it substitutes only when an environment variable name is present
by itself in a token. For example, if the `cmdline` literal in the previous example
contained "`-f $HOME/managed.cfg`", the value of the `HOME` environment
variable would not be substituted, because it is not in a token by itself.

The preceding example also uses the `skip_args` parameter on the
`ACE_Get_Opt` constructor. Whereas the argument vector passed to the `main()`
program entry point includes the command name in `argv[0]`, our built vector
starts in the first element. Supplying a 0 forces `ACE_Get_Opt` to start parsing at
the first token in the argument vector.

4.4 Summary

Collecting runtime information is a basic part of many applications. Developing
code to parse command lines and collect configuration information can be very
time consuming and platform dependent. This chapter showed ACE's facilities for
collecting and processing runtime information in a portable, customizable, and
easy-to-use way.

Chapter 5
ACE Containers

Robust container classes are one of the most useful tools one can obtain from a toolkit. Although the standard template library (STL), with its powerful containers and generic programming constructs, has been standardized by the C++ committee, some compilers and platforms continue to lack support for it. On some platforms, container classes remain unavailable.

ACE initially bundled an implementation of the STL with the ACE source distribution. Unfortunately, many compilers on which ACE ran did not support the C++ constructs used by the STL, so it was dropped from the ACE distribution. In its place, the ACE developers created a separate set of containers that are used internally by the library and are also exported for client development use. Although not as elegant as the STL containers, ACE's containers provide high performance and in many cases have a footprint much smaller than that of the standard C++ containers.

That being said, the standard C++ containers are recommended for application development when you are using ACE. However, the ACE containers are very useful and are recommended in any of the following situations.

- The standard C++ containers are not available.

- Standard C++ containers cannot be used, owing to footprint issues.

- You need to use ACE's special-purpose memory allocators (described in Chapter 17), owing to performance or predictability issues.

This chapter briefly reviews container concepts and then discusses the various template-based containers available in ACE, including both sequence-type containers and associative containers. We end the chapter by discussing some of the allocators that are available with ACE and that plug right into the containers.

5.1 Container Concepts

Let's first review a few container concepts that are applicable to C++. General-purpose containers can be designed and built using various design styles. What is available usually depends on the programming language and the design paradigms supported. For example, Java programmers will find object-based containers available, whereas C programmers will find libraries that support typeless (void*-based) containers.

C++ is a language that supports multiple design paradigms and can therefore support a variety of design methods when it comes to containers. In particular, template-based containers, object-based containers, and typeless containers can be built. ACE supports two of these categories of containers: template-based type-safe containers and object-based containers.

5.1.1 Template-Based Containers

Template-based containers use the C++ templates facility, which allows you to create a "type-specific" container at compile time. For example, if you wanted to store information about all the people in a household, you could create a People list that would allow insertion of only People objects into the list.

This is in sharp contrast to the C way of creating reusable lists of typeless pointers—that is, lists of void*—or the general object-oriented way of creating lists of object pointers or any common base type. An object container allows operations on a single base type; in Java, for example, the java.lang.Object type is often used. An object container allows you to insert any subtype into the container. Therefore, you could conceptually have a single list that included both People and Car objects, which is probably not desired and can occur accidentally. Such errors are usually determined at runtime when you use object containers. Typeless containers offer even less error protection, as any type can usually be added to the container. On the other hand, when a template container is instantiated, you explicitly specify what types of objects are allowed in the container.

We briefly discussed templates and explicit template instantiation in Section 1.6.1. If you are unfamiliar with these concepts and have not gone over them in this book, it might be a good idea to read that section.

One important facet of templates that we skipped in Chapter 1 is specialization. C++ allows you to specialize template classes. That is, it allows you to create special versions for certain template parameters of a class template. For example, we can write special code for an optimized `Dynamic_Array<void*>` class independent of the `Dynamic_Array<T>` class template. A user who requests `Dynamic_Array<void*>` will pick up the special optimized definition and will not instantiate a new class using the `Dynamic_Array<T>` class template. ACE uses this C++ feature to specialize several useful functors for the `ACE_Hash` and `ACE_Equal_To` class templates, which you will find in `$ACE_ROOT/ace/Functor.h`. You will get to see several examples of this as we progress through this chapter.

5.1.2 Object-Based Containers

Object-based containers support insertion and deletion of a class of object types. If you have programmed with Java or Smalltalk, you will recognize these containers as supporting insertion of the generic `object` type. ACE has a few containers of this type, built for specific uses, such as the `ACE_Message_Queue` class. We will not be discussing these in this chapter but instead will defer the discussion until their specific use comes up.

5.1.3 Iterators

Another important concept to keep in mind is the iterator. Iterators can be thought of as a generalization of the pointer concept in C. Iterators point to a particular location in a container and can be moved to the next or previous location. They can also be dereferenced to obtain the value they are pointing to and subsquently can be used to modify the underlying value in the container. The method of supported iteration and dereferencing semantics is dependent on the type of container and iterator. Some iterators allow only forward iteration; others allow bidirectional iteration. Similarly, constant iterators allow only read access to values. On many containers, ACE provides two iterator APIs: one that to a certain degree follows the C++ standard and a second that is an older ACE proprietary API.

The standard C++ library includes a set of algorithms that operate using the standard iterator types. If ACE containers supported the standard C++ iterator concept, you could use the standard C++ template algorithms with an ACE-based container. Unfortunately, very few ACE containers support enough of the standard C++ API to be used directly with the the standard algorithms.

5.2 Sequence Containers

A sequence is a container whose elements are arranged sequentially in a linear order. The ordering will not change, owing to iteration within the container. Lists, stacks, queues, arrays, and sets are all examples of sequences represented by ACE classes.

5.2.1 Doubly Linked List

Doubly linked lists maintain both forward and reverse links within the sequence, allowing efficient forward and reverse traversal within the sequence. However, you cannot randomly access elements. Therefore, you will find the iterator concept handy. The following example illustrates these features as they are provided by the doubly linked list in ACE, ACE_DLList.

ACE_DLList is a template-based container, so we need to specify in advance what element type is allowed in our list. For this purpose, we have created a simple type that wraps an int called DataElement:

```
// A simple data element class.
class DataElement
{
  friend class DataElementEx;

public:
  DataElement () { count_++; }

  DataElement (int data) : data_(data) { count_++; }

  DataElement (const DataElement& e)
  {
    data_ = e.getData ();
    count_++;
  }
```

```
DataElement & operator= (const DataElement& e)
{
  data_ = e.getData ();
  return *this;
}

bool operator== (const DataElement& e)
{ return this->data_ == e.data_; }

~DataElement () { count_--; }

int getData (void) const { return data_; }

void setData (int val) { data_ = val; }

static int numOfActiveObjects (void) { return count_; }
private:
  int data_;
  static int count_;
};
```

One nice feature of the `DataElement` class is that it remembers how many instances of it currently exist. We will use this feature to illustrate the lifetime of these elements as they are put inside and then taken out of various container types.

To make things easy, let's start by creating a convenient type definition to represent our doubly linked list of `DataElement` objects:

```
#include "ace/Containers.h"
#include "DataElement.h"

// Create a new type of list that can store only DataElements.
typedef ACE_DLList<DataElement> MyList;
```

Next, we get to our test class:

```
class ListTest
{
public:
  int run (void);
  void displayList (MyList & list); // Display all elements.
  void destroyList (MyList& list);  // Destroy all elements.
};
```

This simple test will create a list and perform insertion, deletion, and iteration operations on it when the public `run()` method is called:

```cpp
int
ListTest::run (void)
{
  ACE_TRACE (ACE_TEXT ("ListTest::run"));

  // Create a list and insert 100 elements.
  MyList list1;

  for (int i = 0; i < 100; i++)
    {
      DataElement *element;
      ACE_NEW_RETURN (element, DataElement (i), -1);
      list1.insert_tail (element);
    }

  // Iterate through and display to output.
  this->displayList (list1);

  // Create a copy of list1.
  MyList list2;
  list2 = list1;

  // Iterate over the copy and display it to output.
  this->displayList(list2);

  // Get rid of the copy list and all its elements.
  // Since both lists had the *same* elements
  // this will cause list1 to contain pointers that
  // point to data elements that have already been destroyed!
  this->destroyList (list2);

  ACE_DEBUG ((LM_DEBUG, ACE_TEXT ("# of live objects: %d\n"),
             DataElement::numOfActiveObjects()));

  // The lists themselves are destroyed here. Note that the
  // list destructor will destroy copies of whatever data the
  // list contained. Since in this case the list contained
  // copies of pointers to the data elements these are the
  // only thing that gets destroyed here.
  return 0;
}
```

This method first creates list1 and populates it with 100 data elements. Note how data population is done here. Even though we created the template type as ACE_DLList<DataElement>, we are inserting pointers to the elements instead of the elements themselves. That is, the values are not stored in the container; only pointers to the values are.

Those of you who have worked with standard C++ containers will find this behavior unexpected. This means that when the list goes out of scope, the data elements will still exist on the heap, and it is your responsiblity to ensure that you delete them, or you will have a leak.

Such a container is commonly refered to as a reference container, as it stores only pointers to the values that you insert in it. Standard C++ containers are mostly value containers. That is, they store copies of whatever value you store in them. Most ACE containers are also value containers. ACE_DLList is an exception rather than the rule.

After populating the list, we use the list assignment operator to create a copy, called list2, of list1. We iterate through list2 to make sure that everything is correctly copied over from list1. Remember, both containers contain only pointers to the data elements. To illustrate this, we destroy all the data elements by passing list2 to the destroyList() method. As expected, because both list1 and list2 pointed to the same data elements, both lists will now contain invalid pointers. We use our DataElement::numOfActiveObjects() method to determine the number of active data elements, and it dutifully reports that there are no active elements.

Let's look at the displayList() method, where we have used iterators to go through a provided list:

```
void
ListTest::displayList (MyList& list)
{
  ACE_TRACE (ACE_TEXT ("ListTest::displayList"));

  ACE_DEBUG ((LM_DEBUG, ACE_TEXT ("Forward iteration\n")));
  ACE_DLList_Iterator<DataElement> iter (list);
  while (!iter.done ())
    {
      ACE_DEBUG
        ((LM_DEBUG, ACE_TEXT ("%d:"), iter.next ()->getData ()));
      iter++;
    }
  ACE_DEBUG ((LM_DEBUG, ACE_TEXT ("\n")));

  ACE_DEBUG ((LM_DEBUG, ACE_TEXT ("Reverse Iteration \n")));
```

```
ACE_DLList_Reverse_Iterator<DataElement> riter (list);
while (!riter.done ())
  {
    ACE_DEBUG
      ((LM_DEBUG, ACE_TEXT ("%d:"), riter.next()->getData()));
    riter++;
  }
ACE_DEBUG ((LM_DEBUG, ACE_TEXT ("\n")));
}
```

Here, we get our first taste of an iterator class. Remember that you can think of iterators as generalizations of the C++ pointer concept. In this case, we use an iterator that starts from the beginning of the list and displays each element one by one. The ACE iterator has methods that let us advance forward in the sequence (operator++), get the current element we are pointing to (next ()), and determine that we have reached the end of the sequence (done ()). The example also uses a reverse iterator that starts from the end and goes backward to the beginning of the sequence. You will notice that not all containers support both reverse and forward iteration. For example, it makes sense to have a forward iterator in a stack or queue, but reverse iteration should not be, and isn't, possible.

The iterators in ACE do not support the same interface as the standard C++ iterators, although this is one of the things on ACE's to-do list. Unfortunately, we will see that ACE iterators are not as consistent as we would want and support slightly different APIs. Both of these issues make it impossible for you to use the ACE container types with the standard C++ generic algorithms. You will also notice that although some containers do offer nested type definitions for their available iterators—some of them are even like standard C++—many do not.

5.2.2 Stacks

Stacks are LIFO (last in first out) sequences. That is, the last element inserted—pushed—is always the first one that is extracted, or popped. ACE provides both dynamic and static stacks. Static stacks have a fixed size and are therefore cheaper to use. Two stacks of this type are provided: ACE_Bounded_Stack and ACE_Fixed_Stack. Dynamic stacks allocate memory on every insertion and release this memory on every extraction. ACE_Unbounded_Stack is of this variety.

The following example exercises each one of these stack types, starting with an ACE_Bounded_Stack, which is bound to a fixed number of elements when it is created. Internally, an `ACE_Bounded_Stack` is implemented as a dynamically allocated array of elements. Insertions are *O(1)*, and the constant value here is very small, especially if copying the element is a cheap operation, such as when you are pushing pointers onto the stack:

```
int StackExample::runBoundedStack (void)
{
  ACE_TRACE (ACE_TEXT ("StackExample::runBoundedStack"));
  ACE_DEBUG ((LM_DEBUG, ACE_TEXT ("Using a bounded stack\n")));

  ACE_Bounded_Stack<DataElement> bstack1 (100);

  // The element array is constrained to this scope.
  {
    DataElement elem[100];
    for (int i = 0; i < 100; i++)
      {
        elem[i].setData(i);
        // Push the element on the stack.
        bstack1.push (elem[i]);
      }
  }

  ACE_Bounded_Stack<DataElement> bstack2 (100);

  // Make a copy!
  bstack2 = bstack1;
  for (int j = 0; j < 100; j++)
    {
      DataElement elem;
      bstack2.pop (elem);
      ACE_DEBUG ((LM_DEBUG, ACE_TEXT ("%d:"), elem.getData ()));
    }

  return 0;
}
```

A bounded stack is fixed in size at runtime by passing the size as an argument to the constructor of the stack. Here, we create a stack that can contain at most 100 data elements. We then create on the stack 100 data elements that are then copied into `bstack1`. Note that the `ACE_Bounded_Stack` template is more standardlike than the previous sequence we looked at. Here, when we specify that the stack will contain `DataElement` values, that is exactly what the stack expects.

The stack creates a copy of each element that we insert into it; that is, it is a value container. If we had created an ACE_Bounded_Stack<DataElement*>, only the pointers would be copied on insertion.

Next, we use the assignment operator to copy bstack1 elements into another bounded stack, bstack2. Note that even though the elem[] array and its elements are destroyed once we leave the marked scope, bstack1 still has copies of all the destroyed elements.

We then pop and remove all elements from bstack2. Note that because bstack2 contains a copy of bstack1, another copy of the elements exists in bstack1. However, these elements are released when the destructor for bstack1 is called on exit from this function.

Now let's take a quick look at fixed and unbounded stacks:

```
int StackExample::runFixedStack (void)
{
  ACE_TRACE (ACE_TEXT ("StackExample::runFixedStack"));
  ACE_DEBUG ((LM_DEBUG, ACE_TEXT ("Using a fixed stack\n")));

  ACE_Fixed_Stack<DataElement*, 100> fstack;
  for (int k = 0; k < 100; k++)
    {
      DataElement* elem;
      ACE_NEW_RETURN(elem, DataElement (k), -1);
      fstack.push (elem);    // Push the element on the stack.
    }

  for (int l = 0; l < 100; l++)
    {
      DataElement* elem;
      fstack.pop (elem);
      ACE_DEBUG ((LM_DEBUG, ACE_TEXT ("%d:"), elem->getData ()));
      delete elem;
    }

  return 0;
}

int StackExample::runUnboundedStack (void)
{
  ACE_TRACE (ACE_TEXT ("StackExample::runUnboundedStack"));
  ACE_DEBUG ((LM_DEBUG, ACE_TEXT ("Using an unbounded stack\n")));

  ACE_Unbounded_Stack<DataElement*> ustack;
  for (int m = 0; m < 100; m++)
```

```
  {
    DataElement *elem;
    ACE_NEW_RETURN(elem, DataElement (m), -1);
    // Push the element on both stacks.
    ustack.push (elem);
    privateStack_.push (elem);
  }

// Oddly enough, you can actually iterate through an
// unbounded stack! This is because underneath the covers
// the unbounded stack is a linked list.

// This will cause the elements in the private stack to
// also disappear!
ACE_Unbounded_Stack_Iterator<DataElement*> iter (ustack);
for (iter.first (); !iter.done (); iter.advance ())
  {
    DataElement** elem;
    iter.next (elem);
    ACE_DEBUG ((LM_DEBUG, ACE_TEXT ("%d:"),
                (*elem)->getData ()));
    delete (*elem);
  }

  return 0;
}
```

The first method is similar to the previous but uses a fixed stack whose size was predetermined at compile time. Internally, the fixed stack uses an array whose size is fixed to be the value of the second template parameter of ACE_Fixed_Stack. This preempts the initial heap allocation that is required with a bounded stack.

To make things a little interesting, this method inserts pointers to the elements instead of the elements themselves. This makes the copies less expensive, as copying a pointer typically requires a single machine instruction.

Finally, we come to the ACE_Unbounded_Stack class. When you use ACE_Unbounded_Stack, you do not have to have a predetermined notion of the stack's maximum size. Internally, ACE_Unbounded_Stack uses a linked list representation, and both push and pop operations are $O(1)$. An interesting side effect of the implementation is that an unbounded stack allows you to iterate through it, although you probably should not be using the iterators.

5.2.3 Queues

Queues are FIFO (first in first out) sequences. That is, they allow element insertion at the tail of the sequence, but elements are removed from the head. ACE's
ACE_Unbounded_Queue class provides this functionality. The ACE queue
implementation allows insertion at both the head and the tail of the queue,
although elements are always extracted from the head.

The next two examples illustrate creating elements on the stack and the heap
and then putting them on our queue by value and by reference, respectively. Let's
start by looking at value insertions on the stack:

```
int QueueExample::runStackUnboundedQueue (void)
{
  ACE_TRACE (ACE_TEXT ("QueueExample::runStackUnboundedQueue"));

  ACE_Unbounded_Queue<DataElement> queue;
  int i;
  for (i = 0; i < 10; i++)
    {
      DataElement elem[10];
      elem[i].setData (9-i);
      queue.enqueue_head (elem[i]);
    }

  for (i = 0; i< 10; i++)
    {
      DataElement elem[10];
      elem[i].setData (i+10);
      queue.enqueue_tail (elem[i]);
    }

  for (ACE_Unbounded_Queue_Iterator<DataElement> iter (queue);
       !iter.done ();
       iter.advance ())
    {
      DataElement *elem;
      iter.next (elem);
      ACE_DEBUG ((LM_DEBUG, ACE_TEXT ("%d:"), elem->getData ()));
    }

  return 0;
}
```

This is fairly similar to the previous example. First, we insert a couple of elements on the front of the queue and then another few on the tail of the queue. Note that most queue implementations allow insertion only at the tail end and not on both ends. Insertion on either the head or the tail of the queue is an *O(1)* operation. After completing the insertions, we iterate through the queue with an iterator. Because both the queue and the elements are created on the stack, they will all be released when the method returns. Although we don't illustrate it here, you can dequeue elements from the queue head only by using the `dequeue_head()` method.

The next example illustrates how to create elements on the heap and enqueue them by reference:

```
int QueueExample::runHeapUnboundedQueue (void)
{
  ACE_TRACE (ACE_TEXT ("QueueExample::runHeapUnboundedQueue"));

  ACE_Unbounded_Queue<DataElement*> queue;
  for (int i = 0; i < 20; i++)
    {
      DataElement *elem;
      ACE_NEW_RETURN(elem, DataElement (i), -1);
      queue.enqueue_head (elem);
    }

  for (ACE_Unbounded_Queue_Iterator<DataElement*> iter
        = queue.begin ();
       !iter.done ();
       iter.advance ())
    {
      DataElement **elem;
      iter.next(elem);
      ACE_DEBUG
        ((LM_DEBUG, ACE_TEXT ("%d:"), (*elem)->getData ()));
      delete (*elem);
    }

  return 0;
}
```

In this case, the elements are allocated on the heap, and we keep only pointers to these elements within the queue container. As we iterate through the array for display, we also delete these elements. Note that we have not dequeued them from the queue; the unbounded queue contains invalid pointers at this point. We use the dequeue_head() method to remove these pointers from the queue. This also illustrates that queues, like stacks and the standard C++ library containers, always copy whatever you pass into them. In this example, pointers are copied into the container and are not released, even though the actual elements are destroyed.

5.2.4 Arrays

Although arrays are not sequences and are supported directly by the C++ language, ACE provides a safe wrapper type that performs checked access and offers useful features, such as copy and comparison semantics. The following simple example illustrates the use of the ACE_Array class and its features:

```
#include "ace/Containers.h"
#include "DataElement.h"

int ACE_TMAIN (int, ACE_TCHAR *[])
{
  ACE_Array<DataElement*> arr (10);
  DataElement *elem = 0;
  // Allocate and insert elements.
  for (int i = 0; i < 10; i++)
    {
      ACE_NEW_RETURN (elem, DataElement (i), -1);
      arr[i] = elem;
    }

  // Checked access.
  ACE_ASSERT (arr.set (elem, 11) == -1);
  ACE_ASSERT (arr.get (elem, 11) == -1);

  // Make a copy and compare to the original.
  ACE_Array<DataElement*> copy = arr;
  ACE_ASSERT (copy == arr);

  ACE_Array<DataElement*>::ITERATOR iter (arr);
  while (!iter.done ())
    {
      DataElement** data;
      iter.next (data);
      ACE_DEBUG ((LM_DEBUG,
                  ACE_TEXT ("%d\n"), (*data)->getData ()));
      delete (*data);
```

```
            iter.advance ();
        }
    return 0;
}
```

Note that we used a trait in this example. `ACE_Array::ITERATOR` defines the type used to iterate through an `ACE_Array` object.

5.2.5 Sets

A set is a sequence that does not allow duplicate entries. ACE includes two types of sets: a bounded set and an unbounded set. The bounded set is fixed in size, whereas the unbounded set is a dynamic structure that will grow as you add elements to it. To determine whether two elements are equal, the set collection uses the equality operator on the elements that are inserted into it. If you are inserting pointers into the collection, this will work automatically (remember, though, the pointer values will be compared; not the elements pointed to); otherwise, you must provide an equality comparison operator for the type you are inserting into the set.

The following example illustrates the use of both a bounded and an unbounded set. We start by creating a bounded set of `DataElement` objects on the stack in the `runBoundedSet()` method. One hundred objects are created and then copied into `bset` by value. That is, the collection stores copies of the `DataElement` objects. After this, we do a `find()` on two random elements, remove two elements, and then try to find them:

```
int SetExample::runBoundedSet ()
{
  ACE_TRACE (ACE_TEXT ("SetExample::runBoundedSet"));
  ACE_DEBUG ((LM_DEBUG, ACE_TEXT ("Using a bounded set\n")));
  ACE_Bounded_Set<DataElement> bset (100);

  DataElement elem[100];
  for (int i = 0; i < 100; i++)
    {
      elem[i].setData (i);

      // Inserting two copies of the same element isn't allowed.
      bset.insert (elem[i]);
      if (bset.insert (elem[i]) == -1)
        {
          ACE_DEBUG ((LM_ERROR, ACE_TEXT ("%p\n"),
```

```
                                 ACE_TEXT ("insert set")));
                }
        }
    ACE_DEBUG ((LM_DEBUG, ACE_TEXT ("%d\n"),
                DataElement::numOfActiveObjects ()));

    DataElement elem1 (10), elem2 (99);
    if (!bset.find (elem1) && !bset.find (elem2))
      {
        ACE_DEBUG ((LM_INFO,
                    ACE_TEXT ("The elements %d and %d are ")
                    ACE_TEXT ("in the set!\n"),
                    elem1.getData (), elem2.getData ()));
      }

    for (int j = 0; j < 50; j++)
      {
        bset.remove (elem[j]);   // Remove the element from the set.
        ACE_DEBUG
          ((LM_DEBUG, ACE_TEXT ("%d:"), elem[j].getData ()));
      }

    if ((bset.find (elem[0]) == -1) && (bset.find (elem[49]) == -1))
      {
        ACE_DEBUG ((LM_INFO,
                    ACE_TEXT ("The elements %d and %d are ")
                    ACE_TEXT ("NOT in the set!\n"),
                    elem[0].getData (), elem[99].getData ()));
      }

    return 0;
}
```

The unbounded set is used in the `runUnboundedSet()` method. We start by creating an unbounded set of `DataElement*`; that is, the set will keep copies of the pointers instead of copies of the elements. We then insert 100 elements that we create on the heap, find two of them randomly, iterate through the collection, and delete all the elements from the heap. We do not remove the pointers from the unbounded set. Because the set itself is on the stack, its destructor will remove the copies of the pointers that it has created. Note that we are using the iterator to walk through the collection and delete the elements from the heap, not to remove the entries from the set, which would be incorrect, as the iterator is invalid once the contents of the underlying collection change:

```
int SetExample::runUnboundedSet ()
{
  ACE_TRACE (ACE_TEXT ("SetExample::runUnboundedSet"));
  ACE_DEBUG ((LM_DEBUG, ACE_TEXT ("Using an unbounded set.\n")));
  ACE_Unbounded_Set<DataElement*> uset;
  for (int m = 0; m < 100; m++)
    {
      DataElement *elem;
      ACE_NEW_RETURN (elem, DataElement (m), -1);
      uset.insert (elem);
    }
  DataElement deBegin (0), deEnd (99);
  if (!uset.find (&deBegin) && !uset.find (&deEnd))
    {
      ACE_DEBUG ((LM_DEBUG, ACE_TEXT ("Found the elements\n")));
    }

  // Iterate and destroy the elements in the set.
  ACE_DEBUG ((LM_DEBUG, ACE_TEXT ("Deleting the elements\n")));
  ACE_Unbounded_Set_Iterator<DataElement*> iter (uset);
  for (iter = uset.begin (); iter != uset.end (); iter++)
    {
      DataElement* elem = (*iter);
      ACE_DEBUG ((LM_DEBUG, ACE_TEXT ("%d:"), elem->getData ()));
      delete elem;
    }

  return 0;
}
```

5.3   Associative Containers

Associative containers support efficient retrieval of elements, based on keys
instead of positions within the container. Examples of associative containers are
maps and binary trees. Associative containers support insertion and retrieval
based on keys and do not provide a mechanism to insert an element at a particular
position within the container.

5.3.1 Map Manager

ACE supports a simple map type via the ACE_Map_Manager class template. This class maps a key type to a value type. Therefore, the template takes the key and value types as parameters, and insertions require two parameters of these types: a key and the value that is to be associated with that key. Later retrievals require the key and return the value that was associated with the key.

The ACE_Map_Manager is implemented as a dynamic array of entries. Each entry constitutes a key/value pair. Once the dynamic array is full, new memory is allocated, and the size of the array is increased. When an element is removed from the map, the corresponding entry in the dynamic array is marked empty and added to a free list. All new insertions are done using the free list. If the free list happens to be empty, meaning that there is no space for the new entry, a new allocation takes place, and all elements are copied into the new array. The point at which copying takes place is controlled with the ACE_HAS_LAZY_MAP_MANAGER configuration setting. If this flag is set, the movement of free elements in the dynamic array to the free list is deferred until the free list is empty. This allows deletion of elements through an iterator. That is, elements can be deleted during iteration in lazy map managers.

So what does all this mean to you? Insertions in ACE_Map_Manager have a best-case time complexity of $O(1)$; however, in the worst case, it can be $O(n)$. Retrievals are always a linear $O(n)$ operation; for faster operations with an average-case retrieval complexity of $O(1)$, the ACE_Hash_Map_Manager class template is provided.

ACE_Map_Manager requires that the key, or external, element be comparable. Therefore, the equality operator must be defined on the keys that are being inserted into the map. This requirement can be relaxed by using template specialization.

The following example illustrates the fundamental operations on a map with key type KeyType (external type) and value type DataElement. We define KeyType::operator==() per the requirements of ACE_Map_Manager:

```
// Forward declaration.
class KeyType;
bool operator == (const KeyType&, const KeyType&);

class KeyType
{
public:
  friend bool operator == (const KeyType&, const KeyType&);
```

```
    KeyType () {}
    KeyType (int i) : val_(i) {}
    KeyType (const KeyType& kt) { this->val_ = kt.val_; };
    operator int() { return val_; };

private:
  int val_;
};

bool operator == (const KeyType& a, const KeyType& b)
{
  return (a.val_ == b.val_);
}
```

We start in the `MapExample::run()` method by creating 100 bindings of new records in a map. Each `bind()` call will cause a new `KeyType` object and `DataElement` to be created on the stack and then passed by reference into the `ACE_Map_Manager`, which creates and stores copies of the objects. After performing the binding, we use `find()` to locate the objects by key and display them, once again creating the required keys on the stack. The value is returned by reference. Note that this is a reference to the copy that is maintained by the map. We then iterate through the collection in the forward and reverse directions, remove all the elements, and then iterate again, showing that no elements are left:

```
int Map_Example::run (void)
{
  ACE_TRACE (ACE_TEXT ("Map_Example::run"));

  // Corresponding KeyType objects are created on the fly.
  for (int i = 0; i < 100; i++)
    {
      map_.bind (i, DataElement (i));
    }

  ACE_DEBUG ((LM_DEBUG, ACE_TEXT ("Map has \n")));
  for (int j = 0; j < 100; j++)
    {
      DataElement d;
      map_.find (j,d);
      ACE_DEBUG ((LM_DEBUG, ACE_TEXT ("%d:"), d.getData ()));
    }
  ACE_DEBUG ((LM_DEBUG, ACE_TEXT ("\n")));

  // Iterate in the forward direction.
```

```
this->iterate_forward ();

// Iterate in the other direction.
this->iterate_reverse ();

// Remove all elements from the map.
this->remove_all ();

// Iterate in the forward direction.
this->iterate_forward ();

return 0;
}
```

The iteration itself is straightforward. Note that the map supports standard-style nested type defintions for `iterator` and `reverse_iterator`. The map also supports the standard-style `begin()` and `end()` methods that return iterators to the begining and ending of the map. The only thing to note here is that when you dereference the iterator, you get an `ACE_Map_Manager<EXT_ID, INT_ID, ACE_Lock>::ENTRY`, which is type defined to be an `ACE_Map_Entry<EXT_ID, INT_ID>`. If you look at this in the header file (`Map_Manager.h`), you will see that each entry has an `int_id_` and `ext_id_` attribute that you can use to get to the actual values. In the example, we are using `int_id_` to show the values that are stored in the map:

```
void Map_Example::iterate_forward (void)
{
  ACE_TRACE (ACE_TEXT ("Map_Example::iterate_forward"));

  ACE_DEBUG ((LM_DEBUG, ACE_TEXT ("Forward iteration\n")));
  for (ACE_Map_Manager<KeyType,
                       DataElement,
                       ACE_Null_Mutex>::iterator
       iter = map_.begin ();
       iter != map_.end ();
       iter++)
    {
      ACE_DEBUG ((LM_DEBUG, ACE_TEXT ("%d:"),
                  (*iter).int_id_.getData ()));
    }
  ACE_DEBUG ((LM_DEBUG, ACE_TEXT ("\n")));
}
```

```
void Map_Example::iterate_reverse (void)
{
  ACE_TRACE (ACE_TEXT ("Map_Example::iterate_reverse"));
  ACE_DEBUG ((LM_DEBUG, ACE_TEXT ("Reverse iteration\n")));
  for (ACE_Map_Manager<KeyType,
                       DataElement,
                       ACE_Null_Mutex>::reverse_iterator
       iter = map_.rbegin ();
       iter != map_.end ();
       iter++)
    {
      ACE_DEBUG ((LM_DEBUG, ACE_TEXT ("%d:"),
                 (*iter).int_id_.getData ()));
    }
  ACE_DEBUG ((LM_DEBUG, ACE_TEXT ("\n")));
}
```

Note that we do not use the iterators to go through the map when we are removing elements. The reason is that changing the collection—by removing or adding elements—invalidates the iterator, thus making it impossible to iterate and remove or add at the same time. However, as we mentioned earlier, if the map is specified to be of type ACE_HAS_LAZY_MAP_MANAGER, this behavior is supported. That is, deletions can occur during iteration. In the example, however, we choose to use the convenient unbind_all () method to remove all entries in the map:

```
void Map_Example::remove_all (void)
{
  ACE_TRACE (ACE_TEXT ("Map_Example::remove_all"));

  // Note that we can't use the iterators here as they
  // are invalidated after deletions or insertions.
  map_.unbind_all ();
}
```

Using Specialization

Besides overloading the equality operator to satisfy the ACE_Map_Manager's requirement for comparable key types, you can also use template specialization. In this case, you can specialize the ACE_Map_Manager::equal() method to provide for the required comparision by the key type. This looks something like the following:

```
class KeyType
{
public:
  KeyType () : val_(0) {}

  KeyType (int i) : val_(i) {}

  KeyType (const KeyType& kt) { this->val_ = kt.val_; };

  operator int () const { return val_; };

private:
  int val_;
};

ACE_TEMPLATE_SPECIALIZATION
int
ACE_Map_Manager<KeyType, DataElement, ACE_Null_Mutex>::equal
(const KeyType& r1, const KeyType &r2)
{
  return (r1 == r2);
}
```

Locking

In the discussion so far, we have glossed over the third argument to the
ACE_Map_Manager template, the lock type. ACE_Map_Manager supports
thread-safe operations on it. If multiple threads will be accessing your map, you
should serialize access to it by using an ACE_Thread_Mutex instead of an
ACE_Null_Mutex, as used in the preceding example. Note that thread safety in
this sense means that the internal data structure itself will remain consistent.

But in most cases, this is not the only guarantee you need. For example, if two
threads were able to bind the same entry—an entry with the same key—without
any other synchronization, you would never be sure what entry existed in the map.
In most cases, you will find a need for coarser-grained locking than the fine-
grained locking used within the map's methods. In these cases, you may want to
use an ACE_Recursive_Thread_Mutex. You can then obtain a reference to
the lock using the mutex() method, acquire the lock, and hold it across the
appropriate operations for your use case.

5.3.2 Hash Maps

The `ACE_Hash_Map_Manager` is an implementation of a hash map data structure. This allows for best-case insertions and removals of *O(1)* and a worst case of *O(n)*. The performance of the data structure is dependent on the hashing function and the number of buckets you create for the hash, both of which are tunable in this implementation. Note that the hash map is a value container. That is, it will create copies of each key and value that you bind into it. Therefore, both types must have a valid copy constructor (`T(const T&)`) to be used with `ACE_Hash_Map_Manager`.

To illustrate, let's build a simple map between integer keys and `DataElement` values. The hashing function is specified as the third template parameter to the map, in the form of a functor. The fourth parameter is an equality functor, and the final parameter is the lock type that the map will use to ensure consistency. ACE comes with several useful hash functors that are predefined on different data types. In this case, we use `ACE_Hash<int>` as the hash functor and `ACE_Equal_To<int>` as the equality functor, both of which are predefined in `Functor.h`. To make things a little easier and more succint, we create a new template class that leaves out the key and data types but plugs everything else in:

```
// Little helper class.
template<class EXT_ID, class INT_ID>
class Hash_Map :
    public ACE_Hash_Map_Manager_Ex<EXT_ID, INT_ID,
    ACE_Hash<EXT_ID>, ACE_Equal_To<EXT_ID>, ACE_Null_Mutex>
{};
```

Next, you want to specify a bucket size that makes sense for your map. This can be a difficult decision because you want to balance creating a map that is too big and will remain mostly empty with having a map that is too small, degrading the find operation to *O(n)*. In our contrived example, we know that we will have only 100 unique keys, and our hash function is perfect; you will always get a different hash value for each key. We open our map with exactly 100 entries, knowing that we will have *O(1)* performance:

```
Hash_Map_Example::Hash_Map_Example()
{
  ACE_TRACE (ACE_TEXT ("Hash_Map_Example::Hash_Map_Example"));

  map_.open (100);
}
```

The rest of the example is similar to the previous one—we insert elements, find them, and then iterate through them using the provided iterators—and is not something we need to go over again. (Remember that dereferencing an iterator will return an ACE_Hash_Map_Entry<>.) The ACE_Hash_Map_Manager and ACE_Map_Manager support an interface that is very similar although they are not type interchangeable.

To use the ACE_Hash_Map_Manager effectively, you must in most cases define your own hashing function for your key types. (Remember, the efficiency of your searches is directly related to the ability of your hash function to ensure that all your items go into different buckets.) This can be done by specializing the ACE_Hash functor. We change our previous example by using KeyType as the external identifier for the map. We then specialize the ACE_Hash<> functor for the KeyType, in this case simply returning the underlying integer value to provide a nice distribution:

```cpp
// Key type that we are going to use.
class KeyType
{
public:
  KeyType () : val_(0) {}

  KeyType (int i) : val_(i) {}

  KeyType (const KeyType& kt) { this->val_ = kt.val_; }

  operator int (void) const { return val_; }

private:
  int val_;
};

// Specialize the hash functor.
ACE_TEMPLATE_SPECIALIZATION
class ACE_Hash<KeyType>
{
public:
  u_long operator() (const KeyType kt) const
  {
    int val = kt;
    return (u_long)val;
  }
};
```

```
// Specialize the equality functor.
ACE_TEMPLATE_SPECIALIZATION
class ACE_Equal_To<KeyType>
{
public:
  int operator() (const KeyType& kt1,
                  const KeyType& kt2) const
  {
    int val1 = kt1;
    int val2 = kt2;
    return (val1 == val2);
  }
};
```

The ACE_TEMPLATE_SPECIALIZATION macro expands out correctly for
your compiler; if it supports standard template specialization, the macro will
expand to template<> and otherwise will expand out to nothing.

5.3.3 Self-Adjusting Binary Tree

A self-adjusting binary tree provides for an average- and worst-case complexity
for lookups of $O(lg\ N)$, thus providing a better worst-case search time than a hash
map, which in the worst case is $O(N)$. Insertions and deletions also have an $O(lg\ N)$ time complexity, which is worse than the hash map. ACE provides an object
oriented implementation of the procedural Red Black Tree [2], a type of self-
adjusting binary search tree, that keeps an extra "color" attribute for each tree
node.

The ACE implemention of the tree, called ACE_RB_Tree, conforms to the
same interface that we have previously seen for the map classes in ACE. Thus, it is
relatively simple to substitute one ACE map class with another, based on how they
perform with particular data sets. This implementation is a value container; that is,
it will create copies of each element that you bind into it; copy semantics should
be valid on the copied-in entity.

The following example illustrates the use of ACE_RB_Tree in a manner
similar to what we have seen previously. We start by creating a little helper class
that derives from ACE_RB_Tree and specifies the binary ordering functor
ACE_Less_Than—more on this later—and the concurrency requirements for
our tree, using ACE_Null_Mutex:

```
#include "ace/RB_Tree.h"

// Little helper class.
template<class EXT_ID, class INT_ID>
class Tree :  public ACE_RB_Tree<EXT_ID, INT_ID,
                                 ACE_Less_Than<EXT_ID>,
                                 ACE_Null_Mutex>
{};
```

Items are inserted, found, iterated over in both directions, removed, and then
once again iterated over. Once again, we cannot use the iterator to remove
elements, as the tree does not allow you to delete the element you are iterating
over during iteration; that is, the iterator is invalidated. However, the tree does
allow you to perform additions and deletions on the collection, as long as you
don't delete the current item the iterator is pointing to:

```
int Tree_Example::run (void)
{
  ACE_TRACE (ACE_TEXT ("Tree_Example::run"));

  DataElement *d  = 0;
  for (int i = 0; i < 100; i++)
    {
      ACE_NEW_RETURN (d, DataElement (i), -1);
      int result = tree_.bind (i, d);
      if (result!= 0)
        {
          ACE_ERROR_RETURN ((LM_ERROR, ACE_TEXT ("%p\n"),
                             ACE_TEXT ("Bind")),
                            -1);
        }
    }

  ACE_DEBUG ((LM_DEBUG, ACE_TEXT ("Using find: \n")));
  for (int j = 0; j < 100; j++)
    {
      tree_.find (j, d);
      ACE_DEBUG ((LM_DEBUG, ACE_TEXT ("%d:"), d->getData ()));
    }
  ACE_DEBUG ((LM_DEBUG, ACE_TEXT ("\n")));

  // Use the forward iterator.
  this->iterate_forward ();
```

```cpp
  // Use the reverse iterator.
  this->iterate_reverse ();

  // Remove all elements from the tree.
  ACE_ASSERT (this->remove_all ()!= -1);

  // Iterate through once again.
  this->iterate_forward ();

  return 0;
}

void Tree_Example::iterate_forward (void)
{
  ACE_TRACE (ACE_TEXT ("Tree_Example::iterate_forward"));

  ACE_DEBUG ((LM_DEBUG, ACE_TEXT ("Forward Iteration: \n")));
  for (Tree<int, DataElement*>::iterator iter = tree_.begin ();
       iter != tree_.end (); iter++)
    {
      ACE_DEBUG ((LM_DEBUG, ACE_TEXT ("%d:"),
                  (*iter).item ()->getData ()));
    }
  ACE_DEBUG ((LM_DEBUG, ACE_TEXT ("\n")));
}

void Tree_Example::iterate_reverse (void)
{
  ACE_TRACE (ACE_TEXT ("Tree_Example::iterate_reverse"));

  ACE_DEBUG ((LM_DEBUG, ACE_TEXT ("Reverse Iteration: \n")));
  for (Tree<int, DataElement*>::reverse_iterator iter
          = tree_.rbegin (),
       iter != tree_.rend (); iter++)
    {
      ACE_DEBUG ((LM_DEBUG, ACE_TEXT ("%d:"),
                  (*iter).item ()->getData ()));
    }
  ACE_DEBUG ((LM_DEBUG, ACE_TEXT ("\n")));
}

int Tree_Example::remove_all (void)
{
  ACE_TRACE (ACE_TEXT ("Tree_Example::remove_all"));
  ACE_DEBUG ((LM_DEBUG, ACE_TEXT ("Removing elements\n")));
```

```
// Note that we can't use the iterators here as they are
// invalidated after deletions or insertions.
for (int i = 0; i < 100; i++)
  {
    DataElement * d = 0;
    int result = tree_.unbind (i, d);
    if (result != 0)
      {
        ACE_ERROR_RETURN ((LM_ERROR, ACE_TEXT ("%p\n"),
                            ACE_TEXT ("Unbind")),
                          -1);
      }
    ACE_ASSERT (d!= 0);
    delete d;
  }

  return 0;
}
```

In this example, unlike the previous ones, we are keeping pointers in the collection instead of the complete values. This makes it neccessary for us to delete the items before we unbind them; we can't simply use the `unbind_all()` method. ACE provides a nice `unbind()` method, which returns the value to the caller as the unbind happens. We use this method to remove the elements from the map and then delete them.

The `ACE_RB_Tree` class uses the `ACE_Less_Than` functor to provide a binary ordering between key elements that are inserted into the tree. ACE provides several specializations for this functor; however, in most cases, you will create your own specialization. For example, for the `KeyType` class, the `ACE_Less_Than` functor would be specialized as:

```
// Same key type.
class KeyType
{
public:
  KeyType () : val_(0) {}
  KeyType (int i) : val_ (i) {}
  KeyType (const KeyType& kt) { this->val_ = kt.val_; }
  operator int() const { return val_; };

private:
  int val_;
};
```

```
ACE_TEMPLATE_SPECIALIZATION
class ACE_Less_Than<KeyType>
{
public:
  int operator() (const KeyType k1, const KeyType k2)
  { return k1 < k2; }
};
```

5.4 Allocators

As in most container libraries, ACE allows you to specify an allocator class that encapsulates the memory allocation routines the container will use to manage memory. This allows fine-grained control over how you want to manage this memory.

You can either build your own custom allocator or use one of the allocators provided by ACE. All allocators must support the ACE_Allocator interface and are usually provided to the container during construction or during the open() call on the container. In most cases, it is advisable to use the open() call instead of the constructors, as open() returns error codes that can be used in the absence of exceptions.

If you are familiar with allocators in the standard C++ library, you will notice two significant differences in the way allocators work in ACE.

1. Allocators are passed in during object instantiation, not as a type when you instantiate the template. A reference to the provided allocator object is then kept within in the container. The container uses this reference to get to the allocator object. This causes problems if you want allocation to occur in shared memory.

2. The ACE allocators operate on raw untyped memory in the same way that C's malloc() does. They are not type aware. This is in sharp contrast to the standard C++ library's allocators, which are instantiated with supplied types and are type aware. An exception to this rule is ACE_Cached_Allocator, which is strongly typed.

Table 5.1. Allocators Available in ACE

Allocator	Description
ACE_New_Allocator	Allocates memory by using the new operator directly from the heap.
ACE_Static_Allocator	Preallocates a fixed-size pool and then allocates memory from this pool in an optimized fashion. Memory is never deallocated.
ACE_Cached_Allocator	A fixed-size strongly typed allocator that allocates a well-defined number of strongly typed fixed-sized blocks of memory. These blocks are returned on allocation and returned to a free list on deallocation.
ACE_Dynamic_Cached_Allocator	A cached-allocator version that allows you to specify the size and number of the cached blocks at runtime instead of at compile time. Unlike the ACE_Cached_Allocator, these blocks are not strongly typed.

5.4.1 ACE_Allocator

The ACE_Allocator interface is the one that all ACE containers require an allocator to support. This is a true C++ interface, with all methods being pure virtual functions. ACE provides several allocator implementations, which are described in Table 5.1.

Let's change one of our previous stack examples and make it use the cached allocator instead of the default allocator. This allocator will preallocate a specified number of fixed-size blocks of memory that are handed out on subsequent allocation calls. For example, if we were to create a cached allocator with 10 blocks of 1,024 bytes each and then do a malloc() call for 4 bytes, we would get a complete 1K block in response. You have to be careful when using this special purpose allocator; never ask for more than a block's worth of memory in a single malloc() call, and be careful that the allocator hasn't run out of memory. Cached allocators come in handy when you have a predictable memory allocation scenario in which you know what the upper bounds are on memory usage and need predictable high-speed allocation.

To have our stack use a cached allocator instead of the heap, all we have to do is choose the allocator we want to use; create it, specifying the appropriate block size and number of blocks; and then pass it to the stack during construction:

```
int StackExample::run (void)
{
  ACE_TRACE (ACE_TEXT ("StackUser::run"));

  ACE_Allocator *allocator = 0;
  size_t block_size = sizeof(ACE_Node<DataElement>);
  ACE_NEW_RETURN
    (allocator,
     ACE_Dynamic_Cached_Allocator<ACE_Null_Mutex>
       (100 + 1, block_size),
     -1);

  ACE_DEBUG ((LM_DEBUG, ACE_TEXT ("\n# of live objects %d\n"),
              DataElement::numOfActiveObjects ()));

  ACE_ASSERT (this->runUnboundedStack (allocator) != -1);

  ACE_DEBUG ((LM_DEBUG, ACE_TEXT ("\n# of live objects %d\n"),
              DataElement::numOfActiveObjects ()));

  delete allocator;
  return 0;
}
```

Here, we first determine the size of the blocks that we want to add to the cached allocator. We know that the stack is a circular list of ACE_Node<T>; thus, each time we push an element on the stack, the container allocates an ACE_Node<DataElement>. Thus, our block size should be equal to or greater than this size. Second, we know that we will be pushing at most 100 elements on the stack, so the allocator must have at least that many blocks, plus one for the head element, which is allocated as soon as the container is constructed:

```
int StackExample::runUnboundedStack (ACE_Allocator* allocator)
{
  ACE_TRACE (ACE_TEXT ("StackExample::runUnboundedStack"));

  // Pass in an allocator during construction.
  ACE_Unbounded_Stack<DataElement> ustack (allocator);

  for (int m = 0; m < 100; m++)
```

```
          {
            DataElement elem (m);
            int result = ustack.push (elem);
            if (result == -1)
              ACE_ERROR_RETURN
                ((LM_ERROR, ACE_TEXT ("%p\n"),
                  ACE_TEXT ("Push Next Element")),
                 -1);
          }

      void* furtherMemory = 0;
      furtherMemory = allocator->malloc
        (sizeof(ACE_Node<DataElement>));
      ACE_ASSERT (furtherMemory == 0);

      // No memory left..
      ACE_DEBUG ((LM_DEBUG, ACE_TEXT ("%p\n"),
                  ACE_TEXT ("No memory..")));

      // Free up some memory in the allocator.
      DataElement e;
      for (int n = 0; n < 10; n++)
        {
          ustack.pop (e);
        }

      furtherMemory =
        allocator->malloc (sizeof (ACE_Node<DataElement>));
      ACE_ASSERT (furtherMemory != 0);

      return 0;
    }
```

Next, we pass our new allocator to the stack during construction. We proceed to push 100 elements onto the stack. At this point, no more memory should be left in our allocator. To confirm this, we try to allocate another node from it. As expected, no more memory is allocated. We then use pop () on a few elements and find that the allocator once again has memory to hand out.

5.4.2 ACE_Malloc

Besides ACE_Allocator, ACE also has a general-purpose allocator interface called ACE_Malloc. This allocator is much fancier than ACE_Allocator and allows you to allocate memory by using such techniques as System V shared memory or memory-mapped files, such as mmap() -based allocation. If you want to allocate your containers using these techniques, you can use an adapter (ACE_Allocator_Adapter) to adapt the ACE_Malloc template class to the ACE_Allocator interface. We will talk about ACE_Malloc in detail in our discussion of shared memory (Chapter 17).

5.5 Summary

ACE provides a rich set of efficient, platform-independent containers that you can use in your own applications. Most of these containers are used within ACE to build out further features, so if you are going to be reading through the source, an understanding of these types is neccesary.

Although the recommended application-level containers are the standard C++ library containers, which can coexist with the ACE framework, the ACE containers come in handy not only when a complete standard C++ library is not available but also when you need to fine-tune such features as memory allocation and synchronization. Many of the ACE containers provide standardlike features, making it easier for you to switch between container types easily.

Part II

Interprocess Communication

Chapter 6
Basic TCP/IP Socket Use

This chapter introduces you to basic TCP/IP programming using the ACE toolkit. We begin by creating simple clients and then move on to explore simple servers. After reading this chapter, you will be able to create simple yet robust client/server applications.

The ACE toolkit has a rich set of wrapper facades encapsulating many forms of interprocess communication (IPC). Where possible, those wrappers present a common API, allowing you to interchange one for another without restructuring your entire application. This is an application of the Strategy pattern [3], which allows you to change your "strategy" without making large changes to your implementation. To facilitate changing one set of IPC wrappers for another, ACE's IPC wrappers are related in sets:

- Connector: Actively establishes a connection
- Acceptor: Passively establishes a connection
- Stream: Transfers data
- Address: Defines the means for addressing endpoints

    For TCP/IP programming, we use ACE's Sockets-wrapping family of classes:

- `ACE_SOCK_Connector`
- `ACE_SOCK_Acceptor`
- `ACE_SOCK_Stream`
- `ACE_INET_Addr`

Each class abstracts a bit of the low-level mess of traditional socket programming. All together, the classes create an easy-to-use type-safe mechanism for creating distributed applications. We won't show you everything they can do, but what we do show covers about 80 percent of the things you'll normally need to do.

The basic handling of TCP/IP sockets is foundational to most networked applications, so it's important that you understand the material in this chapter. Be aware that most of the time, you can—and probably should—use higher-level framework classes to simplify your application. We'll look more at these higher-level classes in Section 7.6.

6.1 A Simple Client

In BSD (Berkeley Software Distribution) Sockets programming, you have probably used a number of low-level operating system calls, such as `socket()`, `connect()`, and so forth. Programming directly to the Sockets API is troublesome because of such *accidental complexities* [6] as

- *Error-prone APIs.* For example, the Sockets API uses weakly typed integer or pointer types for socket handles, and there's no compile-time validation that a handle is being used correctly. For instance, the compiler can't detect that a passively listening handle is being passed to the `send()` or `recv()` function.

- *Overly complex APIs.* The Sockets API supports many communication families and modes of communication. Again, the compiler can offer no help in diagnosing improper use.

- *Nonportable and nonuniform APIs.* Despite its near ubiquity, the Sockets API is not completely portable. Furthermore, on many platforms, it is possible to mix Sockets-defined functions with OS system calls, such as `read()` and `write()`, but this is not portable to all platforms.

With ACE, you can take an object-oriented approach that is easier to use, more consistent, and portable.

Borrowing a page from Stevens's venerable *UNIX Network Programming* [10], we start by creating a simple client with a few lines of code. Our first task is to fill out a `sockaddr_in` structure. For purposes of our example, we'll connect to the Home Automation Status Server on our local computer:

```
struct sockaddr_in srvr;

memset (&srvr, 0, sizeof(srvr));
srvr.sin_family      = AF_INET;
srvr.sin_addr.s_addr = inet_addr ("127.0.0.1");
srvr.sin_port        = htons (50000);
```

Next, we use the `socket()` function to get a file descriptor on which we will communicate and the `connect()` function to connect that file descriptor to the server process:

```
fd = socket (AF_INET, SOCK_STREAM, 0);

assert (fd >= 0);

assert(
  connect (fd,
           (struct sockaddr *)&srvr,
           sizeof(srvr)) == 0);
```

Now, we can send a query to the server and read the response:

```
write (fd, "uptime\n", 7);
bc = read (fd, buf, sizeof(buf));

write (1, buf, bc);

close (fd);
```

That's pretty simple and you're probably asking yourself why we are discussing it. This code has some problems with portability. The most obvious one is that it will not run on Windows. In fact, it probably won't even compile. We're now going to show you The ACE Way of solving this same problem, and we wanted you to have the traditional solution fresh in your mind.

First, we'll create the equivalent of a `sockaddr_in` structure:

```
ACE_INET_Addr srvr (50000, ACE_LOCALHOST);
```

`ACE_INET_Addr` is a member of the `ACE_Addr` family of objects. Some, but not all, classes in that family are `ACE_UNIX_Addr`, `ACE_SPIPE_Addr`, and `ACE_FILE_Addr`. Each of these objects represents a concrete implementation of the `ACE_Addr` base class, and each knows how to handle the details of

addressing in its domain. We showed the most commonly used constructor of
`ACE_INET_Addr`, which takes an `unsigned short` port number and a
`char[]` host name and internally creates the appropriate `sockaddr_in`—or
`sockaddr_in6`, for IPv6—structure.

A number of other useful `ACE_INET_Addr` constructors are defined in
`ace/INET_Addr.h`. Reading through the `ACE_INET_Addr` documentation,
you will very likely find one or more that are useful to your application.

Once you have the `ACE_INET_Addr` constructed appropriately, it's time to
use that address to get your socket connected. ACE represents a connected TCP
socket with the `ACE_SOCK_Stream` object, so named because a TCP connection
tion represents a virtual connection, or "stream" of bytes, as opposed to the
connectionless datagrams you get with UDP sockets. In order to actively connect
an `ACE_SOCK_Stream` to a server, we use an `ACE_SOCK_Connector` and
the `ACE_INET_Addr` already constructed:

```
ACE_SOCK_Connector connector;
ACE_SOCK_Stream peer;

if (-1 == connector.connect (peer, srvr))
  ACE_ERROR_RETURN ((LM_ERROR,
                     ACE_TEXT ("%p\n"),
                     ACE_TEXT ("connect")), 1);
```

The `connect()` method is provided with the stream object to connect and the
address to which it should be connected. The method then attempts to establish
that relationship. If successful, the `ACE_SOCK_Stream` is placed into a
connected state, and we can use it to communicate with the server. At this point,
we can begin communicating:[1]

```
peer.send_n ("uptime\n", 7);
bc = peer.recv (buf, sizeof(buf));
write (1, buf, bc);
peer.close ();
```

---

1. The `write(1,...)` should send the output to the standard output, such as the console, for
   your operating system. However, that may mean something completely different for an
   embedded application. The point? Beware of portability issues at all times, and try to avoid
   things like `write(1,...)`.

ACE_SOCK_Stream inherits from a number of classes that are part of ACE's design to properly abstract behavior away in layers. Although send_n() is a method defined on ACE_SOCK_Stream, you should also read the reference pages for the classes ACE_SOCK_Stream inherits from—these are also depicted on the ACE_SOCK_Stream reference page—to find all the available data transfer methods—and there are a lot. We first use the send_n() method to send exactly 7 bytes of data—our "uptime" request—to the server.

In your own network programming, you have probably experienced "short writes." That is, you attempt to write a number of bytes to the remote but because of network buffer overflow or congestion or any number of other reasons, not all your bytes are transmitted. You must then move your data pointer and send the rest. You continue doing this until all the original bytes are sent. This happens so often that ACE provides you with the send_n() method call. It simply internalizes all these retries so that it doesn't return to you until it has either sent everything or failed while trying.

The recv() method we've used here is the simplest available. It will read up to *n* bytes from the peer and put them into the designated buffer. Of course, if you know exactly how many bytes to expect, you're going to have to deal with "short reads." ACE has solved this for you with the recv_n() method call. As with send_n(), you tell it exactly how much to expect, and it will take care of ensuring that they all are read before control is returned to your application.

Other send and receive methods allow you to set a timeout or change the socket I/O (input/output) flags. Other methods do various interesting things for you, such as allocate a read buffer on your behalf or even use overlapped I/O on Windows.

Here, back to back, are both the traditional and the ACE versions in their entirety:

```
#include <stdlib.h>
#include <string.h>
#include <stdio.h>
#include <assert.h>
#include <unistd.h>
#include <netinet/in.h>
#include <sys/types.h>
#include <sys/socket.h>
#include <arpa/inet.h>

int main (int argc, char * argv [])
{
  int fd;
```

```
    struct sockaddr_in srvr;

    memset (&srvr, 0, sizeof(srvr));
    srvr.sin_family     = AF_INET;
    srvr.sin_addr.s_addr = inet_addr ("127.0.0.1");
    srvr.sin_port       = htons (50000);

    fd = socket (AF_INET, SOCK_STREAM, 0);

    assert (fd >= 0);

    assert(
      connect (fd,
               (struct sockaddr *)&srvr,
               sizeof(srvr)) == 0);

    int bc;
    char buf[64];
    memset (buf, 0, sizeof(buf));

    write (fd, "uptime\n", 7);
    bc = read (fd, buf, sizeof(buf));

    write (1, buf, bc);

    close (fd);

    exit (0);
}


#include "ace/INET_Addr.h"
#include "ace/SOCK_Stream.h"
#include "ace/SOCK_Connector.h"
#include "ace/Log_Msg.h"

int ACE_TMAIN (int, ACE_TCHAR *[])
{
  ACE_INET_Addr srvr (50000, ACE_LOCALHOST);

  ACE_SOCK_Connector connector;
  ACE_SOCK_Stream peer;

  if (-1 == connector.connect (peer, srvr))
```

```
                ACE_ERROR_RETURN ((LM_ERROR,
                                   ACE_TEXT ("%p\n"),
                                   ACE_TEXT ("connect")), 1);

        int bc;
        char buf[64];

        peer.send_n ("uptime\n", 7);
        bc = peer.recv (buf, sizeof(buf));
        write (1, buf, bc);
        peer.close ();

        return (0);
    }
```

6.2 Adding Robustness to a Client

Let's consider a new client that will query our Home Automation Server for some basic status information and forward that to a logging service. Our first task is, of course, to figure out how to address these services. This time, we'll introduce the default constructor and one of the set() methods of ACE_INET_Addr:

```
ACE_INET_Addr addr;
...
addr.set ("HAStatus", ACE_LOCALHOST);
...
addr.set ("HALog", ACE_LOCALHOST);
```

The set() method is as flexible as the constructors. In fact, the various constructors simply invoke one of the appropriate set() method signatures. You'll find this frequently in ACE when a constructor appears to do something nontrivial. By creating only one address object and reusing it, we can save a few bytes of space. That probably isn't important to most applications, but if you find yourself working on an embedded project where memory is scarce, you may be grateful for it. The return value from set() is more widely used. If set() returns –1, it failed, and ACE_OS::last_error() should be used to check the error code. ACE_OS::last_error() simply returns errno on UNIX and UNIX-like systems. For Windows, however, it uses the GetLastError()

function. To increase portability of your application, you should get in the habit of using ACE_OS::last_error().

Now let's turn our attention to ACE_SOCK_Connector. The first thing we should probably worry about is checking the result of the connect() attempt. As with most ACE method calls, connect() returns 0 for success and –1 to indicate a failure. Even if your application will exit when a connection fails, it should at least provide some sort of warning to the user before doing so. In some cases, you may even choose to pause and attempt the connection later. For instance, if connect() returns –1 and errno has the value ECONNREFUSED, it simply means that the server wasn't available to answer your connect request. We're all familiar with heavily loaded web servers. Sometimes, waiting a few seconds before reattempting the connection will allow the connection to succeed.

If you look at the documentation for ACE_SOCK_Connector, you will find quite a few constructors available for your use. In fact, you can use the constructor and avoid the connect() method call altogether. That can be pretty useful, and you'll probably impress your friends, but be absolutely certain that you check for errors after constructing the connector, or you will have one nasty bug to track down:

```
ACE_SOCK_Stream status;
ACE_OS::last_error(0);
ACE_SOCK_Connector statusConnector (status, addr);
if (ACE_OS::last_error())
  ACE_ERROR_RETURN ((LM_ERROR,
                     ACE_TEXT ("%p\n"),
                     ACE_TEXT ("status")), 100);
```

In this example, we explicitly set the last error value to 0 before invoking the ACE_SOCK_Connector constructor. System functions do not generally reset errno to 0 on successful calls, so a previous error value may be noticed here as a false failure.

Don't fret if you don't want to use the active constructors but do like the functionality they provide. There are just as many connect() methods as there are constructors to let you do whatever you need. For instance, if you think that the server may be slow to respond, you may want to time out your connection attempt and either retry or exit:

```
ACE_SOCK_Connector logConnector;
ACE_Time_Value timeout (10);
ACE_SOCK_Stream log;
if (logConnector.connect (log, addr, &timeout) == -1)
```

```
  {
    if (ACE_OS::last_error() == ETIME)
      {
        ACE_DEBUG ((LM_DEBUG,
                    ACE_TEXT ("(%P|%t) Timeout while ")
                    ACE_TEXT ("connecting to log server\n")));
      }
    else
      {
        ACE_ERROR ((LM_ERROR,
                    ACE_TEXT ("%p\n"),
                    ACE_TEXT ("log")));
      }
    return (101);
  }
```

In most client applications, you will let the operating system choose your local port. ACE represents this value as `ACE_Addr::sap_any`. In some cases, however, you may want to choose your own port value. A peer-to-peer application, for instance, may behave this way. As always, ACE provides a way. Simply create your `ACE_INET_Addr` and provide it as the fourth parameter to `connect()`. If another process is or might be listening on that port, give a nonzero value to the fifth parameter, and the "reuse" socket option will be invoked for you:

```
ACE_SOCK_Connector logConnector;
ACE_INET_Addr local (4200, ACE_LOCALHOST);
if (logConnector.connect (log, addr, 0, local) == -1)
  {
    ...
```

Here, we've chosen to set the port value of our local endpoint to 4200 and "bind" to the loopback network interface. Some server applications—rsh, for example—look at the port value of the client that has connected to them and will refuse the connection if it is not in a specified range. This is a somewhat insecure way of securing an application but can be useful in preventing spoofs if combined with other techniques.

Still more you want the connector to handle for you? Reading through the `ACE_SOCK_Connector` documentation again, we find that you can set quality-of-service parameters on your connection or even begin a nonblocking connection operation. You can find many examples using this class in the example code supplied in the ACE kit.

Finally, we come to `ACE_SOCK_Stream`. We've already talked about the basic send and receive functionality. As you might suspect, both support the ability to time out long-running operations. As with the `connect()` method of `ACE_SOCK_Connector`, we simply need to provide an `ACE_Time_Value` with our desired timeout. The following waits up to 5 microseconds to complete sending all seven characters:

```
ACE_Time_Value sendTimeout (0, 5);
if (status.send_n ("uptime\n", 7, &sendTimeout) == -1)
  {
    if (ACE_OS::last_error() == ETIME)
      {
        ACE_DEBUG ((LM_DEBUG,
                    ACE_TEXT ("(%P|%t) Timeout while sending ")
                    ACE_TEXT ("query to status server\n")));
      }
  }
```

And, of course, we want to find out what the status server has to say in return. This example (very impatiently) gives the server only 1 microsecond to respond:

```
ssize_t bc ;
ACE_Time_Value recvTimeout (0, 1);
if ((bc = status.recv (buf, sizeof(buf), &recvTimeout)) == -1)
  {
    ACE_ERROR ((LM_ERROR,
                ACE_TEXT ("%p\n"),
                ACE_TEXT ("recv")));
    return (103);
  }

log.send_n (buf, bc);
```

If you've worked with the low-level socket API, you may have come across the `readv()` and `writev()` system calls. When you use the `read()` and `write()`, you have to work with contiguous data areas. With `readv()` and `writev()`, you can use an array of `iovec` structures. The `iovec` structures and the `writev()`/`readv()` system calls, introduced in the BSD 4.3 operating system, are most commonly used when you need to send data from or receive data into noncontiguous buffers. The common example is sending a header and associated data that is already in separate buffers. With a standard `write()` system call, you would have to use two calls to send each buffer individually. This is unacceptable if you want both to be written together atomically or if you need to avoid Nagle's algorithm [6] [9]. Alternatively, you could copy both into a single, larger buffer and use one call, but this has drawbacks both in the amount of memory used and in the time required. The `writev()` call—and thus the `ACE_SOCK_Stream::sendv()` method—will atomically send all entries of the `iovec` array. The `readv()` call simply does the reverse of `writev()` by filling each buffer in turn before moving on to the next. Here again, we see how ACE will make your transition from traditional network programming to object-oriented network programming much smoother.

If we wanted to use an `iovec` to send our original "uptime" query to the server, it might look something like this:

```
iovec send[4];
send[0].iov_base = ACE_const_cast (ACE_TCHAR *, "up");
send[0].iov_len  = 2;
send[1].iov_base = ACE_const_cast (ACE_TCHAR *, "time");
send[1].iov_len  = 4;
send[2].iov_base = ACE_const_cast (ACE_TCHAR *, "\n");
send[2].iov_len  = 1;

peer.sendv (send, 3);
```

Of course, this is a contrived and not very realistic example. Your real `iovec` array wouldn't likely be created this way at all.

Consider the case if you have a table of commands to send to a remote server. You could construct a "sentence" of requests by a cleverly built `iovec` array.

```
iovec query[3];
addCommand (query, UPTIME);
addCommand (query, HUMIDITY);
addCommand (query, TEMPERATURE);
peer.sendv (query, 3);
```

Imagine that `addCommand()` populates the query array appropriately from a global set of commands indexed by the `UPTIME`, `HUMIDITY`, and `TEMPERA-TURE` constants. You've now done a couple of very interesting things: You are no longer coding the command strings into the body of your application, and you've begun the process of defining macros that will allow you to have a more robust conversation with the status server.

Receiving data with an `iovec` is pretty straightforward as well. Simply create your array of `iovec` structures in whatever manner makes the most sense to your application. We'll take the easy route here and allocate some space. You might choose to point to an area of a memory-mapped file or a shared-memory segment or some other interesting place:

```
iovec receive[2];
receive[0].iov_base = new char [32];
receive[0].iov_len  = 32;
receive[1].iov_base = new char [64];
receive[1].iov_len  = 64;

bc = peer.recvv (receive, 2);
```

Still, regardless of where the `iov_base` pointers point to, you have to do something with the data that gets stuffed into them:

```
for (int i = 0; i < 2 && bc > 0; ++i)
  {
    size_t wc = receive[i].iov_len;
    if (ACE_static_cast (size_t, bc) < wc)
      wc = ACE_static_cast (size_t, bc);
    write (1, receive[i].iov_base, wc);
    bc -= receive[i].iov_len;
    delete []
      (ACE_reinterpret_cast (char *, receive[i].iov_base));
  }
```

We'd like to show you one more thing with the `iovec` approach. If you want, you can let the `recvv()` method allocate the receiving data buffer for you, filling in the `iovec` with the pointer and length. It will figure out how much data is available and allocate a buffer just that big. This can be quite handy when you're not sure how much data the remote is going to send you but are pretty sure that it will all fit into a reasonably sized space, which you'd like to be contiguous. You're still responsible for freeing the memory to prevent leaks:[2]

---

2. *Note*: Although ACE requires you to use `delete []` to free the allocated memory, this can cause heap problems on Windows if ACE allocates from one heap and your application frees it to another. Be very careful to use the same C/C++ runtime library as the one your ACE program links with.

```
peer.send_n ("uptime\n", 7);
iovec response;
peer.recvv (&response);
write (1, response.iov_base, response.iov_len);
delete [] ACE_reinterpret_cast (char *, response.iov_base);
```

6.3 **Building a Server**

Creating a server is generally considered to be more difficult than building a
client. When you consider all the many things a server must do, that's probably
true. However, when you consider only the networking bits, you'll find that the
two efforts are practically equal. Much of the difficulty in creating a server centers
on such issues as concurrency and resource handling. Those things are beyond the
scope of this chapter, but we'll come back to them in Part III.

To create a basic server, you first have to create an `ACE_INET_Addr` that
defines the port on which you want to listen for connections. You then use an
`ACE_SOCK_Acceptor` object to open a listener on that port:

```
ACE_INET_Addr port_to_listen ("HAStatus");
ACE_SOCK_Acceptor acceptor;

if (acceptor.open (port_to_listen, 1) == -1)
  ACE_ERROR_RETURN ((LM_ERROR,
                     ACE_TEXT ("%p\n"),
                     ACE_TEXT ("acceptor.open")),
                    100);
```

The acceptor takes care of the underlying details, such as `bind()` and
`accept()`. To make error handling a bit easier, we've chosen to go with the
default constructor and `open()` method in our example. If you want, however,
you can use the active constructors that take the same parameters as `open()`. The
basic `open()` method looks like this:

```
int open (const ACE_Addr &local_sap,
          int reuse_addr = 0,
          int protocol_family = PF_UNSPEC,
          int backlog = ACE_DEFAULT_BACKLOG,
           int protocol = 0);
```

This method creates a basic BSD-style socket. The most common usage will be as shown in the preceding example, where we provide an address at which to listen and the `reuse_addr` flag. The `reuse_addr` flag is generally encouraged so that your server can accept connections on the desired port even if that port was used for a recent connection. If your server is not likely to service new connection requests rapidly, you may also want to adjust the `backlog` parameter.

Once you have an address defined and have opened the acceptor to listen for new connections, you want to wait for those connection requests to arrive. This is done with the `accept()` method, which closely mirrors the `accept()` function:

```
if (acceptor.accept (peer) == -1)
  ACE_ERROR_RETURN ((LM_ERROR,
                     ACE_TEXT ("(%P|%t) Failed to accept ")
                     ACE_TEXT ("client connection\n")),
                     100);
```

This use will block until a connection attempt is made. To limit the wait time, supply a timeout:

```
if (acceptor.accept (peer, &peer_addr, &timeout, 0) == -1)
  {
    if (ACE_OS::last_error() == EINTR)
      ACE_DEBUG ((LM_DEBUG,
                  ACE_TEXT ("(%P|%t) Interrupted while ")
                  ACE_TEXT ("waiting for connection\n")));
    else
      if (ACE_OS::last_error() == ETIMEDOUT)
        ACE_DEBUG ((LM_DEBUG,
                    ACE_TEXT ("(%P|%t) Timeout while ")
                    ACE_TEXT ("waiting for connection\n")));
  }
```

If no client connects in the specified time, you can at least print a message to let the administrator know that your application is still open for business. As we learned in Chapter 3, we can easily turn those things off if they become a nuisance.

Regardless of which approach you take, a successful return will provide you a valid peer object initialized and representing a connection to the client. It is worth noting that by default, the `accept()` method will restart itself if it is interrupted by a UNIX signal, such as `SIGALRM`. That may or may not be appropriate for your application. In the preceding example, we have chosen to pass 0 as the fourth parameter (`restart`) of the `accept()` method. This will cause `accept()` to return –1 and `ACE_OS::last_error()` to return `EINTR` if the action is interrupted. Because we specified `peer_address` in the preceding example, `accept()` will fill in the address of the peer that connects—if the `accept()` succeeds.

Another handy thing we can do with `ACE_INET_Addr` is extract a string for its address. Using this method, we can easily display the new peer's address:

```
else
  {
    ACE_TCHAR peer_name[MAXHOSTNAMELEN];
    peer_addr.addr_to_string (peer_name, MAXHOSTNAMELEN);
    ACE_DEBUG ((LM_DEBUG,
                ACE_TEXT ("(%P|%t) Connection from %s\n"),
                peer_name));
```

The `addr_to_string()` method requires a buffer in which to place the string and the size of that buffer. This method takes an optional third parameter, specifying the format of the string it creates. Your options are (0) ip-name:port-number and (1) ip-number:port-number. If the buffer is large enough for the result, it will be filled and null terminated appropriately, and the method will return 0. If the buffer is too small, the method will return –1, indicating an error.

Now that we have accepted the client connection, we can begin to work with it. At this point, the distinction between client and server begins to blur because you simply start sending and receiving data. In some applications, the server will send first; in others, the client will do so. How your application behaves depends on your requirements and protocol specification. For our purposes, we will assume that the client is going to send a request that the server will simply echo back:

```
char buffer[4096];
ssize_t bytes_received;

while ((bytes_received =
          peer.recv (buffer, sizeof(buffer))) != -1)
  {
    peer.send_n (buffer, bytes_received);
  }

peer.close ();
```

As our examples become more robust in future chapters, we will begin to process those requests into useful actions.

As the server is written, it will process only one request on one client connection and then exit. If we wrap a simple `while` loop around everything following the `accept()`, we can service multiple clients but only one at a time:

```cpp
#include "ace/INET_Addr.h"
#include "ace/SOCK_Stream.h"
#include "ace/SOCK_Acceptor.h"
#include "ace/Log_Msg.h"

int ACE_TMAIN (int, ACE_TCHAR *[])
{
  ACE_INET_Addr port_to_listen ("HAStatus");
  ACE_SOCK_Acceptor acceptor;

  if (acceptor.open (port_to_listen, 1) == -1)
    ACE_ERROR_RETURN ((LM_ERROR,
                       ACE_TEXT ("%p\n"),
                       ACE_TEXT ("acceptor.open")),
                      100);

  /*
   * The complete open signature:
   *
   int open (const ACE_Addr &local_sap,
             int reuse_addr = 0,
             int protocol_family = PF_INET,
             int backlog = ACE_DEFAULT_BACKLOG,
             int protocol = 0);
   *
   */

  while (1)
    {
      ACE_SOCK_Stream peer;
      ACE_INET_Addr peer_addr;
      ACE_Time_Value timeout (10, 0);

      /*
       * Basic acceptor usage
       */
#if 0
      if (acceptor.accept (peer) == -1)
        ACE_ERROR_RETURN ((LM_ERROR,
```

```
                                              ACE_TEXT ("(%P|%t) Failed to accept ")
                                              ACE_TEXT ("client connection\n")),
                                              100);
#endif /* 0 */

       if (acceptor.accept (peer, &peer_addr, &timeout, 0) == -1)
         {
           if (ACE_OS::last_error() == EINTR)
             ACE_DEBUG ((LM_DEBUG,
                            ACE_TEXT ("(%P|%t) Interrupted while ")
                            ACE_TEXT ("waiting for connection\n")));
           else
             if (ACE_OS::last_error() == ETIMEDOUT)
               ACE_DEBUG ((LM_DEBUG,
                              ACE_TEXT ("(%P|%t) Timeout while ")
                              ACE_TEXT ("waiting for connection\n")));
         }
       else
         {
           ACE_TCHAR peer_name[MAXHOSTNAMELEN];
           peer_addr.addr_to_string (peer_name, MAXHOSTNAMELEN);
           ACE_DEBUG ((LM_DEBUG,
                        ACE_TEXT ("(%P|%t) Connection from %s\n"),
                        peer_name));
           char buffer[4096];
           ssize_t bytes_received;

           while ((bytes_received =
                       peer.recv (buffer, sizeof(buffer))) != -1)
             {
               peer.send_n (buffer, bytes_received);
             }

           peer.close ();
         }
     }

   return (0);
}
```

Such a server isn't very realistic, but it's important that you see the entire example. We will return to this simple server in Chapter 7 to enhance it with the ability to handle multiple, concurrent clients.

If you've worked with the Sockets API directly, you may have noticed something surprising about our examples. We have not once referenced a handle value. If you haven't worked with the Sockets API before, a handle is an opaque chunk of native data representing the socket. Direct handle use is a continual source of accidental complexity and, thus, errors, when using the native system functions. However, ACE's class design properly encapsulates handles, so you will almost never care what the value is, and you will never have to use a handle value directly to perform any I/O operation.

6.4 Summary

The ACE TCP/IP socket wrappers provide you with a powerful yet easy-to-use set of tools for creating client/server applications. Using what you've learned in this chapter, you will be able to convert nearly all your traditionally coded, error prone, nonportable networked applications to true C++ object-oriented, portable implementations.

By using the ACE objects, you can create more maintainable and portable applications. Because you're working at a higher level of abstraction, you no longer have to deal with the mundane details of network programming, such as remembering to zero out those `sockaddr_in` structures and when and what to cast them to. Your application becomes more type safe, which allows you to avoid more errors. Furthermore, when there are errors, they're much more likely to be caught at compile time than at runtime.

Chapter 7
Handling Events and Multiple I/O Streams

Many applications, such as the server example in Chapter 6, can benefit greatly from a simple way to handle multiple events easily and efficiently. Event handling often takes the form of an *event loop* that continually waits for events to occur, decides what actions need to be taken, and dispatches control to other functions or methods appropriate to handle the event(s). In many networked application projects, the event-handling code is often the first piece of the system to be developed, and it's often developed over and over for each new project, greatly adding to the time and cost for many projects.

The ACE Reactor framework was designed to implement a flexible event-handling mechanism in such a way that applications need never write the central, platform-dependent code for their event-handling needs. Using the Reactor framework, applications need do only three things to implement their event handling.

1. Derive one or more classes from `ACE_Event_Handler` and add application-specific event-handling behavior to virtual *callback methods*.

2. Register the application's event-handling objects with the `ACE_Reactor` class and associate each with the event(s) of interest.

3. Run the `ACE_Reactor` event loop.

After we see how easy it is to handle events, we'll look at ways ACE's Acceptor-Connector framework simplifies and enables implementation of services. The examples here are much easier, even, than the ones we saw in Chapter 6.

7.1 Overview of the Reactor Framework

Many traditional applications handle multiple I/O sources, such as network connections, by creating new processes—a process-per-connection model—or new threads—a thread-per-connection model. This is particularly popular in servers needing to handle multiple simultaneous network connections. Although these models work well in many circumstances, the overhead of process or thread creation and maintenance can be unacceptable in others. Moreover, the added code complexity for thread or process management and control can be much more trouble than it's worth in many applications.

The approach we discuss in this chapter is called the *reactive model*, which is based on the use of an event demultiplexer, such as the select(), poll(), or WaitForMultipleObjects() system functions. These excellent alternatives allow us to handle many events with only one process or thread. Writing portable applications that use these can be quite challenging, however, and that's where the ACE Reactor framework helps us out. It insulates us from the myriad details we would otherwise have to know to write a portable application capable of responding to I/O events, timers, signals, and Windows waitable handles.

The classes we visit in this chapter are

- ACE_Reactor
- ACE_Event_Handler
- ACE_Time_Value
- ACE_Sig_Set
- ACE_Acceptor
- ACE_Connector
- ACE_Svc_Handler

7.2 Handling Multiple I/O Sources

One of the most common uses of the Reactor framework is to handle I/O from various sources. Any program—client, server, peer to peer, or anything that needs to perform I/O and has other things to do at the same time—is a good candidate for using the Reactor. An excellent example is simple server in Chapter 6, on page 138, which could handle only one request on one connection. We'll restructure that server to illustrate how simple it is to take advantage of the Reactor framework's power and how little code we need to write to do so.

A simple server scenario usually requires two event handler classes: one to process incoming connection requests and one to process a client connection. When designed this way, your application will have $N + 1$ event handlers registered with the Reactor at any one time, where N is the number of currently connected clients. This approach allows your application to easily and efficiently handle many connected clients while consuming minimal system resources.

7.2.1 Accepting Connections

The first thing a server must be able to do is accept a connection request from a potential client. In Section 6.3, we used an `ACE_SOCK_Acceptor` instance to accept a connection. We'll be using that again here, but this time it will be wrapped in an event handler. By doing this, we can accept any number of connections *and* simultaneously process client requests on all open client connections.

First, we'll see the declaration of our connection-accepting event handler:

```
#include "ace/Auto_Ptr.h"
#include "ace/Log_Msg.h"
#include "ace/INET_Addr.h"
#include "ace/SOCK_Acceptor.h"
#include "ace/Reactor.h"

class ClientAcceptor : public ACE_Event_Handler
{
public:
  virtual ~ClientAcceptor ();

  int open (const ACE_INET_Addr &listen_addr);

  // Get this handler's I/O handle.
  virtual ACE_HANDLE get_handle (void) const
    { return this->acceptor_.get_handle (); }

  // Called when a connection is ready to accept.
  virtual int handle_input (ACE_HANDLE fd = ACE_INVALID_HANDLE);

  // Called when this handler is removed from the ACE_Reactor.
  virtual int handle_close (ACE_HANDLE handle,
                            ACE_Reactor_Mask close_mask);
```

```
protected:
  ACE_SOCK_Acceptor acceptor_;
};
```

Each class that will handle Reactor events of any type must be derived from `ACE_Event_Handler`. Although we could come up with a scheme in which one class controlled the connection acceptance and all the client connections, we've chosen to create separate classes for accepting and servicing connections.

- It's a better encapsulation of data and behavior. This class accepts connections from clients, and that's all it does.

- The client-representing class will service a client connection.

This class arrangement best represents what is happening in the server. It listens for connections and services each one. It is a natural way to think about this sort of application. Because it is so common, `ACE_Event_Handler` is oriented toward it. When registering an event handler with a reactor for I/O events, the reactor associates an `ACE_Event_Handler` pointer with a *handle* and the type(s) of I/O events the handler is interested in.

At the end of Chapter 6, we emphasized that ACE hides from you the concept of a handle. At some point when dealing with event demultiplexing based on I/O handles, a handle has to show up. It's here in `ACE_Event_Handler` because I/O events are associated with a handler and a handle. However, ACE encapsulates the handle so that it rarely needs to be manipulated directly by the application classes. The `get_handle()` method is the hook method `ACE_Reactor` uses to get access to the needed handle value. We'll see how it's used shortly.

The other two methods are `handle_input()` and `handle_close()`. These are two of the virtual callback methods that are inherited from `ACE_Event_Handler`. They're targets of callbacks from `ACE_Reactor` when it is dispatching events from the event loop.

Let's first look at the `open()` method. You'll recognize its code:

```
int
ClientAcceptor::open (const ACE_INET_Addr &listen_addr)
{
  if (this->acceptor_.open (listen_addr, 1) == -1)
    ACE_ERROR_RETURN ((LM_ERROR, ACE_TEXT ("%p\n"),
                       ACE_TEXT ("acceptor.open")),
```

```
                              -1);
  return this->reactor ()->register_handler
    (this, ACE_Event_Handler::ACCEPT_MASK);
}
```

As before, we open the `ACE_SOCK_Acceptor` to begin listening at the requested listen address. However, we don't do a blocking `accept()` call this time. Instead, we call `ACE_Reactor::register_handler()`, which tells the reactor to watch for ACCEPT events on the acceptor's handle. Whenever those events occur, call back to this object. But we didn't specify the handle value, so how does the Reactor know what handle to watch? If the handle isn't specified on the `register_handler()` call, the Reactor calls back to the `get_handle()` method of the object being registered. As we saw earlier, our `get_handle()` method returns the `ACE_SOCK_Acceptor`'s handle value.

In addition to the address at which we hope to receive connection requests, we've also given the acceptor's `open()` method a `reuse_addr` flag (the second argument) set to 1. Setting the flag this way will allow our acceptor to open even if some sockets are already connected at our designated listen port, probably left over from a previous execution of the server. This is generally what you want to do, because even sockets in the FIN_WAIT state can prevent an acceptor from opening successfully.

So now all this event readiness is set up. How do the event detection, demultiplexing, and dispatching occur? So far, all we've seen is class methods. Let's look at the entire main program for our new Reactor-based server:

```
int ACE_TMAIN (int, ACE_TCHAR *[])
{
  ACE_INET_Addr port_to_listen ("HAStatus");
  ClientAcceptor acceptor;
  acceptor.reactor (ACE_Reactor::instance ());
  if (acceptor.open (port_to_listen) == -1)
    return 1;

  ACE_Reactor::instance ()->run_reactor_event_loop ();

  return (0);
}
```

As in our other server examples, we set up the `ACE_INET_Addr` object for the address at which to listen for connections. We instantiate a `ClientAc-ceptor` object to represent our connection acceptor. Next is a line we haven't seen yet. `ACE_Reactor::instance()` obtains a pointer to a singleton `ACE_Reactor` instance. The vast majority of the time, this type of program uses one `ACE_Reactor` object to register all event handlers with and processes all the program's events. Because this is so common, ACE provides a singleton access to an instance that ACE manages. When it's first needed, it is created and is automatically shut down when the program finishes. It's taken care of as part of the `ACE_Object_Manager`, described in Section 1.6.3.

Because so much of what `ACE_Event_Handler` objects are used for is associated with `ACE_Reactor`, `ACE_Event_Handler` includes an `ACE_Reactor` pointer to conveniently refer to the reactor it's using. This prevents building in assumptions or hard-coded references in your code to a particular `ACE_Reactor` instance that could cause maintenance problems in the future. Our example is implemented in a main program, and using the `ACE_Reactor` singleton is usually the best thing to do in this case. However, if this code was all included in a shared library, we would probably not want to hijack the use of the singleton, because it might interfere with a program using the shared library. We set the `ACE_Reactor` we want to use right at the start, and you'll note that none of our classes refer directly to any `ACE_Reactor` instance directly. It's all done via the `ACE_Event_Handler::reactor()` methods.

After establishing the `ACE_Reactor` to use, we call the `acceptor` object's `open()` method. Recall that it will begin listening and register with the reactor for callbacks when new connections are ready to be accepted. The main program then simply enters the reactor event loop, `run_reactor_event_loop()`, which will continually handle events until an error occurs that prevents its further processing or a call is made to `end_reactor_event_loop()`. So, reactor based programs can spend quite a lot of their time waiting for something to do.

When a client connects to our server's listening port, the `ACE_Reactor` will detect an `ACCEPT` event and call back to the registered `ClientAcceptor`'s `handle_input()` method:[1]

```
int
ClientAcceptor::handle_input (ACE_HANDLE)
{
  ClientService *client;
  ACE_NEW_RETURN (client, ClientService, -1);
```

---

1. Why `handle_input()` and not something like `handle_accept()`? This is a historical artifact based on the fact that in the BSD `select()` function, listening sockets that receive a connection request are selected as readable; there is no such thing as "acceptable" in `select()`.

```
    auto_ptr<ClientService> p (client);

    if (this->acceptor_.accept (client->peer ()) == -1)
      ACE_ERROR_RETURN ((LM_ERROR,
                         ACE_TEXT ("(%P|%t) %p\n"),
                         ACE_TEXT ("Failed to accept ")
                         ACE_TEXT ("client connection")),
                        -1);
    p.release ();
    client->reactor (this->reactor ());
    if (client->open () == -1)
      client->handle_close (ACE_INVALID_HANDLE, 0);
    return 0;
}
```

Although it is usually much more straightforward to associate a single I/O handle with each handler, there's no restriction about that. An I/O handler can be registered for multiple I/O handles. The particular handle that triggered the callback is passed to `handle_input()`. Our example is concerned only with one `ACE_SOCK_Acceptor`; therefore, we ignore the `ACE_HANDLE` parameter of our `handle_input()` method.

The first thing our `handle_input()` method does is create a `Client-Service` instance. Because we made a decision to use a separate service handler object for each connection, each new connection acceptance gets a new `Client-Service` instance.

In our non-reactor-based server in Section 6.3, we saw how to use the `accept()` method of `ACE_SOCK_Acceptor` to accept an incoming connection request. Our event handler approach must do the same thing. However, we don't have an `ACE_SOCK_Stream` to pass to `accept()`. We have wrapped the `ACE_SOCK_Stream` in our `ClientService` class, but we need access to it. Therefore, `ClientService` offers a `peer()` method that returns a reference to its `ACE_SOCK_Stream` object.

Being an astute developer, you may have noticed a potential maintenance issue here. We've created a data type couple between `ClientService` and `ClientAcceptor`. As they're both based on ACE's TCP/IP socket wrappers, they know too much about each other. But ACE has already resolved the problem, and we'll see the solution in all its elegance in Section 7.6.

If we succeed in our attempt to accept the client's connection, we will pass our `ACE_Reactor` pointer along to the new event handler in case it needs it and then notify the `ClientService` that it should get ready to do some work. This is done through the `open()` method. Our example's `open()` method registers the new `ClientService` instance with the reactor:

```
int
ClientService::open (void)
{
  ACE_TCHAR peer_name[MAXHOSTNAMELEN];
  ACE_INET_Addr peer_addr;
  if (this->sock_.get_remote_addr (peer_addr) == 0 &&
      peer_addr.addr_to_string (peer_name, MAXHOSTNAMELEN) == 0)
    ACE_DEBUG ((LM_DEBUG,
                ACE_TEXT ("(%P|%t) Connection from %s\n"),
                peer_name));
  return this->reactor ()->register_handler
    (this, ACE_Event_Handler::READ_MASK);
}
```

We try to print a log message stating which host connected, then call `ACE_Reactor::register_handler()` to register for input events with the reactor. We return the return value of `register_handler()`, which is 0 for success and –1 for failure. This value is passed back to the `ClientAcceptor::handle_input()` method, and `handle_input()` also will return –1 for error and 0 for success. In fact, the return value from any event handler callback function is centrally important to correct Reactor framework programming. The meaning of event handler callback values is listed in Table 7.1. If `ClientAcceptor::handle_input()` returns –1, therefore, the following method will be called:

```
int
ClientAcceptor::handle_close (ACE_HANDLE, ACE_Reactor_Mask)
{
  if (this->acceptor_.get_handle () != ACE_INVALID_HANDLE)
    {
      ACE_Reactor_Mask m = ACE_Event_Handler::ACCEPT_MASK |
                           ACE_Event_Handler::DONT_CALL;
      this->reactor ()->remove_handler (this, m);
      this->acceptor_.close ();
    }
  return 0;
}
```

If, as according to Table 7.1, this `handle_close()` is called from the reactor when it's removing this handler from processing, why does

Table 7.1. Meaning of Event Handler Callback Return Values

Value	Meaning
== -1	The reactor should stop detecting the particular event type that was dispatched on the given handle (if it's an I/O ~~~~~~~~~~~~~~~~~~tor will call the handler's handle_close() hook meth~ ~and the event type of the event being rem~
== 0	The reactor will continue to detect the di~ handle just dispatched.
> 0	Like value 0; the reactor continues to det~ just dispatched. However, the reactor wil~ method with the same handle value *befo~* useful when you know that more I/O is ~ other handlers) to return to the reactor a~

[handwritten annotation:] EVENT_ UNREGISTER = -1 EVENT_ HANDLED = 0 EVENT_ LOCKED = 1

handle_close() call ACE_Reactor::remove_handler() to remove the handle and handler association from the reactor? If it's the reactor removing the handler, it's not needed and will do nothing. However, recall from the main program that ClientAcceptor is instantiated on the stack. Thus, it will go out of scope when the program returns from main(). However, unless there were errors, it's still registered with the reactor. To ensure that there's no dangling reactor registration, the ClientAcceptor destructor removes it:

```
ClientAcceptor::~ClientAcceptor ()
{
  this->handle_close (ACE_INVALID_HANDLE, 0);
}
```

7.2.2 Processing Input

In the previous section, ClientAcceptor creates an instance of the mysterious ClientService class. To properly encapsulate the servicing of a single client connection in ClientService, it includes an ACE_SOCK_Stream object. Let's see the declaration of ClientService:

```
#include "ace/Message_Block.h"
#include "ace/Message_Queue.h"
#include "ace/SOCK_Stream.h"
```

```
class ClientService : public ACE_Event_Handler
{
public:
  ACE_SOCK_Stream &peer (void) { return this->sock_; }

  int open (void);

  // Get this handler's I/O handle.
  virtual ACE_HANDLE get_handle (void) const
    { return this->sock_.get_handle (); }

  // Called when input is available from the client.
  virtual int handle_input (ACE_HANDLE fd = ACE_INVALID_HANDLE);

  // Called when output is possible.
  virtual int handle_output (ACE_HANDLE fd = ACE_INVALID_HANDLE);

  // Called when this handler is removed from the ACE_Reactor.
  virtual int handle_close (ACE_HANDLE handle,
                            ACE_Reactor_Mask close_mask);

protected:
  ACE_SOCK_Stream sock_;
  ACE_Message_Queue<ACE_NULL_SYNCH> output_queue_;
};
```

Previously, we looked at the reason for the peer() method and discussed the open() method. The get_handle() method is essentially the same as for ClientAcceptor: feeding the ACE_SOCK_Stream handle to the reactor when open() registers this object for input events. So, let's move right on to the handle_input() method:

```
int
ClientService::handle_input (ACE_HANDLE)
{
  const size_t INPUT_SIZE = 4096;
  char buffer[INPUT_SIZE];
  ssize_t recv_cnt, send_cnt;

  if ((recv_cnt = this->sock_.recv (buffer, sizeof(buffer))) <= 0)
    {
      ACE_DEBUG ((LM_DEBUG,
                  ACE_TEXT ("(%P|%t) Connection closed\n")));
      return -1;
    }
```

```
send_cnt =
  this->sock_.send (buffer, ACE_static_cast (size_t, recv_cnt));
if (send_cnt == recv_cnt)
  return 0;
if (send_cnt == -1 && ACE_OS::last_error () != EWOULDBLOCK)
  ACE_ERROR_RETURN ((LM_ERROR,
                     ACE_TEXT ("(%P|%t) %p\n"),
                     ACE_TEXT ("send")),
                    0);
if (send_cnt == -1)
  send_cnt = 0;
ACE_Message_Block *mb;
size_t remaining =
  ACE_static_cast (size_t, (recv_cnt - send_cnt));
ACE_NEW_RETURN
  (mb, ACE_Message_Block (&buffer[send_cnt], remaining), -1);
int output_off = this->output_queue_.is_empty ();
ACE_Time_Value nowait (ACE_OS::gettimeofday ());
if (this->output_queue_.enqueue_tail (mb, &nowait) == -1)
  {
    ACE_ERROR ((LM_ERROR,
                ACE_TEXT ("(%P|%t) %p; discarding data\n"),
                ACE_TEXT ("enqueue failed")));
    mb->release ();
    return 0;
  }
if (output_off)
  return this->reactor ()->register_handler
    (this, ACE_Event_Handler::WRITE_MASK);
return 0;
}
```

You're probably thinking that you *thought* we said that using the reactor was so easy, yet there's much more code here than there was in the example in Chapter 6. The reasons for the additional code follow.

- Previously, we handled one request on one connection, but now we handle requests until the peer closes on, potentially, many connections simultaneously. Therefore, blocking I/O operations are bad because they block all connection processing. Remember, all this work is happening in one thread.

- We added a lot of flow control and queueing that isn't needed when you can do blocking I/O. We're being thorough. Also, we can illustrate some useful ACE features for you.

To start, we receive whatever data is available on the socket. If zero bytes are received, the peer has closed its end of the socket, and that's our cue to close our end as well. Simply return –1 to tell the reactor we're done. If the `recv()` returns –1 for an error, we also give up on the socket. We can do this without checking `errno`, because we're in a single thread of execution. If we were using multiple threads, it's possible that another thread could have already handled the available data, and we'd be aborting this connection unnecessarily. In that case, we'd have added a check for `errno == EWOULDBLOCK` and simply returned 0 from `handle_input()` to wait for more input.

If input is received, we simply send it back, as in the nonreactor example. If the input is all sent successfully, we're done; return 0 to wait for more input.

Therefore, all the rest of the code is to handle the situation in which we can't send all the data back at once. If there was an error other than not being able to send data right now (`EWOULDBLOCK`), it is simply noted, the received data thrown away, and a return made to await more input. Why not return –1? If a real error on the socket makes it unusable, it will also become readable, and the reactor will dispatch to `handle_input()` again, at which time the `recv()` will fail, and the normal cleanup path is taken. It always pays to consolidate and simplify error handling and cleanup.

So, if still executing `handle_input()`, we have data to send, but some or all of it couldn't be sent, probably owing to flow control or buffering issues. In the nonreactor example, we used `send_n()` to keep trying to send for as long as it took. However, we can't block here waiting, because that would block processing on all connections and that's bad; it appears to hang the program and could, conceivably, cause a deadlock between this program and the peer. Therefore, we need a way to come back and try to write the remaining data later, when whatever prevented all data from being sent has been resolved.

To implement queueing of the data to be sent, `ClientService` has a member `ACE_Message_Queue` object. We'll see a full discussion of `ACE_Message_Queue` in Chapter 12; in addition, *C++ Network Programming, Volume 2* [7] contains a lengthy discussion of `ACE_Message_Queue`'s design and capabilities. When we need to queue data to be sent later, we allocate an `ACE_Message_Block` to hold it and then queue it for later. If we can't even queue it, we simply give up and discard the data.

If the output queue was empty before we tried to queue the remaining data to it, we do another reactor registration for this handler, this time for `WRITE` events. We'll explore the details of this in the next section.

7.2.3 **Handling Output**

As with input handling, the reactor can call us back when it's possible to write
data on the socket. It isn't so simple as it might seem to program this correctly,
because of a difference in behavior in the demultiplexers underlying different
reactor implementations (see Section 7.7 for more details on reactor implementations). In a nutshell, the difference is in how and when the output event is triggered and emanates from the underlying demultiplexer's behavior and
capabilities.

- The `select()` function is a *level-triggered* mechanism. The event is triggered based on the level, or state, of the desired state. If a socket is writable,
  `select()` will always note it as writable until it's not writable.

- `WaitForMultipleObjects()` is an *edge-triggered* mechanism. The
  event is triggered when it changes, not based on a current state. The writable
  event is noted when the socket changes from not writable to writable. Once
  noted, it's not noted again until the state changes again. Socket input is
  similar, but doing a `recv()` resets the state so it's signaled again, even before
  more data arrives, so this issue isn't so pronounced for receiving data.

Thus, it's a little tricky to get the output handling done correctly in a portable
fashion until you've seen it a few times; then it becomes natural.

As we saw in `ClientService::handle_input()`, the registration for
`WRITE` events isn't done unless the `output_queue_` was empty. Let's see why
by looking at the `handle_output()` method. The reactor will call this method
when the socket is writable:

```
int
ClientService::handle_output (ACE_HANDLE)
{
  ACE_Message_Block *mb;
  ACE_Time_Value nowait (ACE_OS::gettimeofday ());
  while (0 == this->output_queue_.dequeue_head
                            (mb, &nowait))
    {
      ssize_t send_cnt =
        this->sock_.send (mb->rd_ptr (), mb->length ());
      if (send_cnt == -1)
        ACE_ERROR ((LM_ERROR,
                    ACE_TEXT ("(%P|%t) %p\n"),
                    ACE_TEXT ("send")));
      else
        mb->rd_ptr (ACE_static_cast (size_t, send_cnt));
      if (mb->length () > 0)
```

```
          {
            this->output_queue_.enqueue_head (mb);
            break;
          }
        mb->release ();
      }
    return (this->output_queue_.is_empty ()) ? -1 : 0;
}
```

As with `handle_input()`, the reactor passes the handle that's now writable. And, once again, as we are using only one handle, we ignore the argument. The `handle_output()` method goes into a loop dequeueing the `ACE_Message_Block` objects that `handle_input()` queued. For each dequeued block, `handle_output()` tries to send all the data. If any is sent, the block's read pointer is updated, using `rd_ptr()`, to reflect the sent data. If there is still unsent data in the block, the block is put back on the head of the queue to be retried later. If the whole block has been sent, it's released, freeing the memory. This continues, sending blocks until either everything on the queue is sent or we encounter a situation in which we can't send all the data. If it's all sent, we don't need to be called back again for more `WRITE` events, so return −1 to tell the reactor that we don't need this event type any more. If more data is left on the queue, return 0 to be called back when the socket is again writable.

The `handle_output()` method shows that not all −1 returns from a callback are for errors. In `handle_output()`, we returned −1 to say "all done." The `handle_close()` method illustrates how to tell the difference between an error and simply being done with output events for now:

```
int
ClientService::handle_close (ACE_HANDLE, ACE_Reactor_Mask mask)
{
  if (mask == ACE_Event_Handler::WRITE_MASK)
    return 0;
  mask = ACE_Event_Handler::ALL_EVENTS_MASK |
         ACE_Event_Handler::DONT_CALL;
  this->reactor ()->remove_handler (this, mask);
  this->sock_.close ();
  this->output_queue_.flush ();
  delete this;
  return 0;
}
```

Recall that the reactor passes in the mask type that's being removed when it calls `handle_close()`. We know that `handle_output()` returns –1 to say that it's all done for now, so we simply return 0. If it's not the `WRITE_MASK`, we need to clean up this client handler. In essence, we undo what `open()` did. Call `remove_handler()` to remove this handler and handle from the reactor on all events. (We could have specified `READ_MASK` and `WRITE_MASK`, but this is quicker and more thorough if more events are registered in the future.) Note that we also added `DONT_CALL`. This mask bit tells the reactor not to call `handle_close()` for the removed event type(s), which it would normally do. Because we're already in `handle_close()`, asking for another callback is useless. After removing the events, we close the `ACE_SOCK_Stream` and flush the `ACE_Message_Queue` to release any `ACE_Message_Block` objects that were still waiting to be sent, to ensure that there are no resource leaks.

This time, we did a `delete this` from `handle_close()`—and the destructor does nothing—whereas in `ClientAcceptor`, the destructor called `handle_close()`. This is a result of the fact that `ClientAcceptor` was allocated on the stack, not dynamically, and all `ClientService` objects are allocated dynamically by `ClientAcceptor`. Dynamic allocation is usually the preferred method to make cleanup easier. In this case, what would happen if the reactor event loop somehow ended, the `ClientAcceptor` in the main program went out of scope, and `main()` returned? There would still be potentially many `ClientService` objects in existence, all registered with the reactor and all still holding an open socket. Recall that ACE will shut down the singleton `ACE_Reactor` at program rundown time. The `ACE_Reactor` will, during its shutdown, automatically unregister and remove all handlers that are still registered, calling their `handle_close()` callback methods. In our case, all the `ClientService` objects will correctly be closed, the sockets all neatly closed, and all resources correctly released: all neat and tidy, and all a nice benefit of the Reactor framework's design. You simply need to carefully follow the rules and not try to come up with a scheme on your own.

7.3 Signals

Responding to signals on POSIX systems traditionally involves providing the `signal()` system function with the numeric value of the signal you want to catch and a pointer to a function that will be invoked when the signal is received. The newer POSIX set of signal-handling functions (`sigaction()` and friends) are somewhat more flexible than the tried-and-true `signal()` function, but getting everything right can be a bit tricky. If you're trying to write something portable among various versions of UNIX, you then have to account for subtle and sometimes surprising differences.

As always, ACE provides us with a nice, clean API portable across dozens of operating systems. Handling signals is as simple as defining a class derived from `ACE_Event_Handler` with your code in it the new handler class's `handle_signal()` method and then registering an instance of your object with one of the two appropriate `register_handler()` methods.

7.3.1 Catching One Signal

Suppose that we need a way to shut down our reactor-based server from Section 7.2. Recall that the main program simply runs the event loop by calling `ACE_Reactor::run_reactor_event_loop()` but that there's no way to tell it to stop. Let's implement a way to catch the `SIGINT` signal and stop the event loop:

```
class LoopStopper : public ACE_Event_Handler
{
public:
  LoopStopper (int signum = SIGINT);

  // Called when object is signaled by OS.
  virtual int handle_signal (int signum,
                             siginfo_t * = 0,
                             ucontext_t * = 0);
};

LoopStopper::LoopStopper (int signum)
{
  ACE_Reactor::instance ()->register_handler (signum, this);
}

int
LoopStopper::handle_signal (int, siginfo_t *, ucontext_t *)
{
  ACE_Reactor::instance ()->end_reactor_event_loop ();
  return 0;
}
```

The `LoopStopper` class registers the single specified signal with the reactor singleton. When the signal is caught, the reactor calls the `handle_signal()` callback method, which simply calls the `end_reactor_event_loop()` method on the reactor singleton. On return to the event loop, the event loop will end. If we instantiate one of these objects in the server's main program, we will quickly and easily add the ability to shut the server down cleanly by sending it a `SIGINT` signal.

7.3.2 Catching Multiple Signals with One Event Handler

We could register many signals using the same technique as in `LoopStopper`. However, calling `register_handler()` once for each signal can start getting ugly pretty quickly. Another `register_handler()` method takes an entire set of signals instead of only one. We will explore that as we extend our server to be able to turn ACE's logging message output on and off with signals:

```
class LogSwitcher : public ACE_Event_Handler
{
public:
  LogSwitcher (int on_sig, int off_sig);

  // Called when object is signaled by OS.
  virtual int handle_signal (int signum,
                             siginfo_t * = 0,
                             ucontext_t * = 0);

  // Called when an exceptional event occurs.
  virtual int handle_exception (ACE_HANDLE fd = ACE_INVALID_HANDLE
);

private:
  LogSwitcher () {}

  int on_sig_;        // Signal to turn logging on
  int off_sig_;       // Signal to turn logging off
  int on_off_;        // 1 == turn on, 0 == turn off
};

LogSwitcher::LogSwitcher (int on_sig, int off_sig)
  : on_sig_ (on_sig), off_sig_ (off_sig)
{
  ACE_Sig_Set sigs;
```

```
    sigs.sig_add (on_sig);
    sigs.sig_add (off_sig);
    ACE_Reactor::instance ()->register_handler (sigs, this);
}
```

This initially looks very similar to the `LoopStopper` class but with some added data to be able to say which signal turns logging on and which one turns it off. We show the `register_handler()` variant that registers a whole set of signals at once.

The advantages of using `ACE_Sig_Set` instead of multiple calls to `register_handle()` may not be immediately apparent, but it is generally easier to work with a set, or collection, of things than with a number of individual items. For instance, you can create the signal set in an initialization routine, pass it around for a while, and then feed it to the reactor.

Routines in addition to `ACE_Sig_Set::sig_add()` are

- `sig_del()` to remove a signal from the set
- `is_member()` to determine whether a signal is in the set
- `empty_set()` to remove all signals from the set
- `fill_set()` to fill the set with all known signals

7.4 Notifications

Let's go back and examine the rest of our `LogSwitcher` class, which turns logging on and off using signals. The `handle_signal()` method follows:

```
int
LogSwitcher::handle_signal (int signum, siginfo_t *, ucontext_t *)
{
  if (signum == this->on_sig_ || signum == this->off_sig_)
    {
      this->on_off_ = signum == this->on_sig_;
      ACE_Reactor::instance ()->notify (this);
    }
  return 0;
}
```

As you can see, `handle_signal()` did not do anything related to `ACE_Log_Msg`, so how do we turn logging output on and off? We didn't—yet.

You need to keep in mind a subtle issue when handling signals. When in
handle_signal(), your code is not in the normal execution flow but rather at
signal state, and on most platforms, you're restricted from doing many things in
signal state. Check your OS documentation for details to be sure whether you
need to do work at this point, but the safest thing to do is usually set some state
information and find a way to transfer control back to normal execution context.
One particularly useful way to do this is by using the reactor's notification mechanism.

The reactor notification mechanism gives you a way to queue a callback event
of a type you choose to a handler you choose. The queueing of this event will
wake the reactor up if it's currently waiting on its internal event demultiplexer,
such as select() or WaitForMultipleObjects(). In fact, the reactor
code uses this mechanism internally to make a waiting reactor thread wake up and
recheck its records of what events and handles to wait for events on, which is why
you can register and unregister handlers from multiple threads while the reactor
event loop is running.

Our handle_signal() method checks whether it should turn logging on
or off and then calls notify() to queue a callback to its own
handle_exception() method. (EXCEPT_MASK is the default event type;
because we wanted that one, we left the argument off the notify() call.) After
returning to the reactor, the reactor will complete its handling of signals and return
to waiting for events. Shortly thereafter, it will notice the queued notification event
and dispatch control to handle_exception():

```
int
LogSwitcher::handle_exception (ACE_HANDLE)
{
  if (this->on_off_)
    ACE_LOG_MSG->clr_flags (ACE_Log_Msg::SILENT),
  else
    ACE_LOG_MSG->set_flags (ACE_Log_Msg::SILENT);
  return 0;
}
```

The handle_exception() method examines the saved state to see what
action it should take and sets or clears the SILENT flag.

7.5 **Timers**

Sometimes, your application needs to perform a periodic task. A traditional
approach would likely create a dedicated thread or process with appropriate
`sleep()` calls. A process-based implementation might define a `timerTask()`
function as follows:

```
pid_t timerTask (int initialDelay,
                 int interval,
                 timerTask_t task)
{
  if (initialDelay < 1 && interval < 1)
    return -1;

  pid_t pid = fork ();

  if (pid < 0)
    return -1;

  if (pid > 0)
    return pid;

  if (initialDelay > 0)
    sleep (initialDelay);

  if (interval < 1)
    return 0;

  while (1)
    {
      (*task) ();
      sleep (interval);
    }

  return 0;
}
```

The `timerTask()` function will create a child process and return its ID to
the calling function for later cleanup. Within the child process, we simply invoke
the task function pointer at the specified interval. An optional initial delay is available. One-shot operation can be achieved by providing a nonzero initial delay and
zero or negative interval:

```
int main (int, char *[])
{
  pid_t timerId = timerTask (3, 5, foo);
  programMainLoop ();
  kill (timerId, SIGINT);
  return 0;
}
```

Our `main()` function creates the timer-handling process with an initial delay of 3 seconds and an interval of 5 seconds. Thus, the `foo()` function will be invoked 3 seconds after `timerTask()` is called and every 5 seconds thereafter. Then `main()` does everything else your application requires. When done, it cleans up the timer by simply killing the process:

```
void foo ()
{
  time_t now = time (0);
  cerr << "The time is " << ctime (&now) << endl;
}
```

The `foo()` function isn't very complicated. For sake of illustration, we simply print the current time at each invocation.

As you might surmise, this approach has some problems.

- It is inherently nonportable. Using the low-level `fork()` and `kill()` calls won't work on every operating system or platform.

- It is resource intensive if you have more than a few timers. Each `timer-Task()` invocation creates a new process or thread, if you choose that implementation. If your application requires many timers, you will quickly run into limitations.

- There is no control over the timer task after its creation other than to kill it. The timer cannot be suspended or resumed, and the timing interval cannot be altered.

7.5.1 Scheduling Timers with the Reactor

Our alternative is to use an `ACE_Event_Handler` derivative to handle timeout events from the `ACE_Reactor`. This easily addresses the three obvious shortcomings.

To use the reactor in this way, we first create an event handler with more or less the functionality of the previous example's `foo()` function:

```
class MyTimerHandler : public ACE_Event_Handler
{
public:
  int handle_timeout (const ACE_Time_Value &current_time,
                      const void * = 0)
  {
    time_t epoch = ((timespec_t)current_time).tv_sec;
    ACE_DEBUG ((LM_INFO,
                ACE_TEXT ("handle_timeout: %s\n"),
                ACE_OS::ctime (&epoch)));
    return 0;
  }
};
```

We know that all handlers registered with the reactor share the same process/thread. As such, the time at which `handle_timeout()` is invoked might not be the time at which the timer expired. That is, the interval timer for a handler may expire while another event handler is in the middle of one of its callback methods. The `current_time` parameter is the time that our event handler was selected for dispatching rather than the current system time.[2]

Registering your timer handler with the reactor is straightforward:

```
MyTimerHandler * timer = new MyTimerHandler ();
ACE_Time_Value initialDelay (3);
ACE_Time_Value interval (5);
ACE_Reactor::instance()->schedule_timer (timer,
                                         0,
                                         initialDelay,
                                         interval);
```

As with our non-ACE example, we've set an initial delay of 3 seconds and an interval of 5 seconds. To create a one-shot timer, simply omit the `interval` parameter.

---

2. If you use the thread-pool reactor (`ACE_TP_Reactor`), the handlers share a pool of threads rather than just one. The `current_time` is still important, however, because you will likely register more handlers than the number of threads in the pool. Because of this shared nature, if you have timers that must be handled at exactly the timeout interval, a dedicated thread or process might be your only option.

7.5.2 State Data

The second parameter to the handle_timeout() method can be used to pass
state data into your event handler. Consider a timeout handler used for monitoring
temperature sensors. For purposes of illustration, let's assume that our design
requires us to use a single handler to monitor multiple sensors, possibly at
different intervals.

We begin by defining a TemperatureSensor object to represent each
physical sensor we wish to query:

```
class TemperatureSensor
{
public:
  TemperatureSensor (const char *location)
    : location_(location),
      count_(0),
      temperature_(0.0)
    // ...
  { }

  const char *location () const
  {
    return this->location_;
  }

  int querySensor (void)
  {
    // ...
    return ++this->count_;
  }

  float temperature (void) const
  {
    return this->temperature_;
  }

private:
  const char *location_;
  int count_;
  float temperature_;
  // ...
};
```

The details have been omitted, as we're more interested in talking about the reactor than in communicating with remote sensors. The primary method of this class, `querySensor()`, will contact the sensor to get current temperature information and store that in the member variable `temperature_`.

Our design requires us to use a single event handler to query all the sensors. To accommodate this, the `handle_timeout()` method will expect its second parameter to be a pointer to a `TemperatureSensor` instance[3]:

```
class TemperatureQueryHandler : public ACE_Event_Handler
{
public:
  TemperatureQueryHandler ()
    : ACE_Event_Handler (),
      counter_ (0),
      averageTemperature_ (0.0)
  // ...
  { }

  int handle_timeout (const ACE_Time_Value &current_time,
                      const void *arg)
  {
    time_t epoch = ((timespec_t) current_time) .tv_sec;

    const TemperatureSensor *const_sensor =
      ACE_reinterpret_cast (const TemperatureSensor *, arg);
    TemperatureSensor *sensor =
      ACE_const_cast (TemperatureSensor *, const_sensor);

    int queryCount = sensor->querySensor ();
    this->updateAverageTemperature (sensor);

    ACE_DEBUG ((LM_INFO,
                ACE_TEXT ("%s\t")
                ACE_TEXT ("%d/%d\t")
                ACE_TEXT ("%.2f/%.2f\t")
                ACE_TEXT ("%s\n"),
                sensor->location (),
                ++this->counter_,
```

---

3. If our design allowed us to use a handler instance per sensor, the handler would likely have a `TemperatureSensor` member variable. Part of the reason for the one-handler design, however, is to make it easy to maintain an average temperature. Of course, the primary reason for our design is to illustrate the use the second parameter to `handle_timeout()`.

```
                        queryCount,
                        this->averageTemperature_,
                        sensor->temperature (),
                        ACE_OS::ctime(&epoch))));
        return 0;
    }

private:
    void updateAverageTemperature (TemperatureSensor *sensor)
    {
      // ...
    }

    int counter_;
    float averageTemperature_;
};
```

Our new `handle_timeout()` method begins by casting the opaque `arg` parameter to a `TemperatureSensor` pointer. Once we have the `TemperatureSensor` pointer, we can use the instance's `querySensor()` method to query the physical device. Before printing out some interesting information about the sensor and the event handler, we update the average-temperature value.

As you can see, customizing the event handler to expect state data in the `handle_timeout()` method is quite easy. Registering the handler with state data is likewise easily done. First, of course, we must create the handler:

```
TemperatureQueryHandler *temperatureMonitor =
    new TemperatureQueryHandler ();
```

Next, we can register the handler to monitor the kitchen temperature:

```
TemperatureSensor *sensorOne =
    new TemperatureSensor ("Kitchen");
    ACE_Reactor::instance ()->schedule_timer (temperatureMonitor,
                                              sensorOne,
                                              initialDelay,
                                              intervalOne);
```

We can then register the same handler instance with another `Temperature-Sensor` instance to monitor the foyer:

```
TemperatureSensor *sensorTwo =
  new TemperatureSensor ("Foyer");
  ACE_Reactor::instance ()->schedule_timer (temperatureMonitor,
                                            sensorTwo,
                                            initialDelay,
                                            intervalTwo);
```

7.5.3   Using the Timer ID

The return value of schedule_timer() is an opaque value known as the timer
ID. With this value, you can reset the timer's interval or cancel a timer altogether.
In our interval-reset example, we have created a signal handler that, when
invoked, will increase the timer's interval:

```
class SigintHandler : public ACE_Event_Handler
{
public:
  SigintHandler (long timerId, int currentInterval)
    : ACE_Event_Handler(),
      timerId_(timerId),
      currentInterval_(currentInterval)
  { }

  int handle_signal (int,
                     siginfo_t * = 0,
                     ucontext_t * = 0)
  {
    ACE_DEBUG ((LM_INFO,
                ACE_TEXT ("Resetting interval of timer ")
                ACE_TEXT ("%d to %d\n"),
                this->timerId_,
                ++this->currentInterval_));
    ACE_Time_Value newInterval (this->currentInterval_);
    ACE_Reactor::instance()->
      reset_timer_interval (this->timerId_, newInterval);
    return 0;
  }

private:
  long timerId_;
  int currentInterval_;
};
```

Our `SigintHandler` constructor is given the `timerId` of the timer we wish to reset, as well as the current interval. Each time `handle_signal()` is called, it will increase the interval by 1 second.

We schedule the to-be-reset handler as before, but now we keep the return value of `schedule_timer()`:

```
MyTimerHandler *handler = new MyTimerHandler ();
long timerId =
  ACE_Reactor::instance ()->schedule_timer (handler,
                                            0,
                                            initialDelay,
                                            interval);
```

We can then provide this `timerId` value to our `SigintHandler` instance:

```
SigintHandler *handleSigint =
  new SigintHandler (timerId, 5);
ACE_Reactor::instance ()->register_handler (SIGINT,
                                            handleSigint);
```

Another thing you can do with the timer ID is cancel a timer. To illustrate this, we will modify and rename our `SigintHandler` to cancel the scheduled timer when `SIGTSTP` is received:

```
class SignalHandler : public ACE_Event_Handler
{
public:
  SignalHandler (long timerId, int currentInterval)
    : ACE_Event_Handler(),
      timerId_(timerId),
      currentInterval_(currentInterval)
  { }

  int handle_signal (int sig,
                     siginfo_t * = 0,
                     ucontext_t * = 0)
  {
    if (sig == SIGINT)
      {
        ACE_DEBUG ((LM_INFO,
                    ACE_TEXT ("Resetting interval of timer ")
                    ACE_TEXT ("%d to %d\n"),
                    this->timerId_,
                    ++this->currentInterval_));
```

```
        ACE_Time_Value newInterval (this->currentInterval_);
        ACE_Reactor::instance ()->
          reset_timer_interval (this->timerId_, newInterval);
      }
    else if (sig == SIGTSTP)
      {
        ACE_DEBUG ((LM_INFO,
                    ACE_TEXT ("Canceling timer %d\n"),
                    this->timerId_));
        ACE_Reactor::instance ()->cancel_timer (this->timerId_);
      }

    return 0;
  }

private:
  long timerId_;
  int currentInterval_;
};
```

As before, `SIGINT` will increase the interval of the timer. `SIGTSTP`, typically `^Z`, will cause the timer to be canceled. To use this functionality, we simply register a `SignalHandler` instance with the reactor twice:

```
SignalHandler *mutateTimer =
  new SignalHandler (timerId, 5);
ACE_Reactor::instance ()->register_handler (SIGINT,
                                            mutateTimer);
ACE_Reactor::instance ()->register_handler (SIGTSTP,
                                            mutateTimer);
```

7.6 Using the Acceptor-Connector Framework

In Section 7.2, we hinted that making two classes that know something of each other's internal needs was asking for some trouble down the road. We also said that ACE had already addressed this issue, and we discuss that here. The Acceptor-Connector framework implements the common need of making a connection—not necessarily TCP/IP, but that's obviously a common case—and creating a service handler to run the service on the new connection. The framework's main classes were also designed so that most everything can be changed by

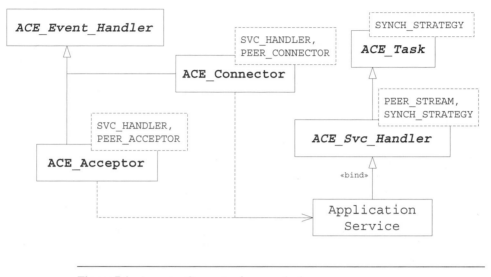

Figure 7.1. Acceptor-Connector framework classes

specifying different template arguments. The classes involved in the framework can seem a bit tangled and difficult to grasp at first. You can refer to Figure 7.1 to see how they relate. In this section, we rework the example from Section 7.2 to use the Acceptor-Connector framework.

7.6.1 Using ACE_Acceptor and ACE_Svc_Handler

The actions we had to take in our previous example are very common. In terms of creating new connections, we had to open the ACE_SOCK_Acceptor, register it with the reactor, and handle new connections by creating service-handling objects and initializing them. As we said in Section 1.1, a framework implements a semi-complete application by codifying the canonical way of performing a number of related tasks. ACE_Acceptor plays a role in the Acceptor-Connector framework by codifying the usual way the preceding tasks are done. However, the framework stays flexible by allowing the particular acceptor-type and service handler-type classes to be specified using template arguments. Let's take a look at how our new acceptor code looks:

```
#include "ace/Log_Msg.h"
#include "ace/INET_Addr.h"
#include "ace/SOCK_Acceptor.h"
#include "ace/Reactor.h"
#include "ace/Acceptor.h"

typedef ACE_Acceptor<ClientService, ACE_SOCK_ACCEPTOR>
  ClientAcceptor;
```

That's it. All the behavior we had to write code for previously is part of the framework, and we need write it no more. That was easy. We simply created a type definition specifying that ACE_SOCK_Acceptor is the class that accepts new service connections and that each new service is handled by a new instance of ClientService. Note that we used the ACE_SOCK_ACCEPTOR macro because ACE_Acceptor also needs to know the addressing trait of the acceptor class; the macro makes it compile correctly with compilers that handle this kind of trait correctly and those that don't.

The main program changed a bit to use the new type:

```
int ACE_TMAIN (int, ACE_TCHAR *[])
{
  ACE_INET_Addr port_to_listen ("HAStatus");
  ClientAcceptor acceptor;
  if (acceptor.open (port_to_listen) == -1)
    return 1;

  ACE_Reactor::instance ()->run_reactor_event_loop ();

  return (0);
}
```

Note that we didn't need to set the acceptor object's ACE_Reactor instance. Well, we did, but it's defaulted in the open() call: one more line of code gone.

Charging right along to the ClientService class, let's look at how it's declared now:

```
#include "ace/Message_Block.h"
#include "ace/SOCK_Stream.h"
#include "ace/Svc_Handler.h"

class ClientService :
  public ACE_Svc_Handler<ACE_SOCK_STREAM, ACE_NULL_SYNCH>
```

```
{
  typedef ACE_Svc_Handler<ACE_SOCK_STREAM, ACE_NULL_SYNCH> super;

public:
  int open (void * = 0);

  // Called when input is available from the client.
  virtual int handle_input (ACE_HANDLE fd = ACE_INVALID_HANDLE);

  // Called when output is possible.
  virtual int handle_output (ACE_HANDLE fd = ACE_INVALID_HANDLE);

  // Called when this handler is removed from the ACE_Reactor.
  virtual int handle_close (ACE_HANDLE handle,
                            ACE_Reactor_Mask close_mask);
};
```

ACE_Svc_Handler is quite flexible, allowing you to specify the stream class type and a locking type. As with ACE_Acceptor, ACE_Svc_Handler needs to use the stream's address trait, so we use the ACE_SOCK_STREAM macro to use this code on systems with and without template traits type support.

The locking type is required because ACE_Svc_Handler is derived from ACE_Task, which includes an ACE_Message_Queue member whose synchronization type must be supplied. We're not going to use the threading capabilities afforded by ACE_Task (we'll see those in Chapter 12), but we are going to use the inherited ACE_Message_Queue member, so we removed the ACE_Message_Queue member from our earlier example. Because we're using only one thread, we don't need any synchronization on the queue, and we specify ACE_NULL_SYNCH as before.

For convenience, we've created the super typedef. This gives us much more readable code when invoking a base class method from our class.

As with the ClientAcceptor, note that our get_handle() method is gone. ACE_Svc_Handler implements it the way we usually need it, so we need not do it. Our peer() method is also gone, subsumed by ACE_Svc_Handler as well.

When it accepts a new connection, an ACE_Acceptor creates a new sevice handler instance—in our case, a ClientService object. After creating it, ACE_Acceptor calls the new service handler's open() hook method; see Figure 7.2 for the complete sequence of steps during connection acceptance. This tells the service that it is now connected and should begin doing whatever is required for the service.

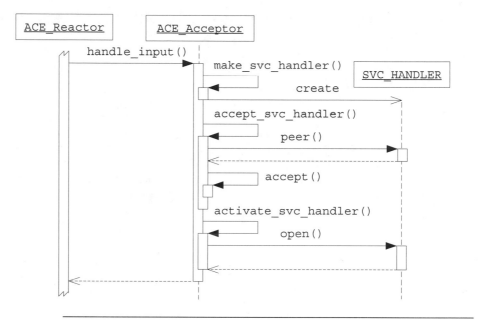

Figure 7.2. Steps in ACE_Acceptor connection acceptance

Let's look at our open() method:

```
int
ClientService::open (void *p)
{
  if (super::open (p) == -1)
    return -1;

  ACE_TCHAR peer_name[MAXHOSTNAMELEN];
  ACE_INET_Addr peer_addr;
  if (this->peer ().get_remote_addr (peer_addr) == 0 &&
      peer_addr.addr_to_string (peer_name, MAXHOSTNAMELEN) == 0)
    ACE_DEBUG ((LM_DEBUG,
                ACE_TEXT ("(%P|%t) Connection from %s\n"),
                peer_name));
  return 0;
}
```

It too is smaller than it used to be. In fact, if we didn't want to log the peer's
address, we could have completely removed this too, as the default action of

`ACE_Svc_Handler::open()` is to register the new handle for READ events. And because `ACE_Acceptor` sets the `reactor()` pointer for each new service handler, that works just like we wanted, too, no matter which `ACE_Reactor` instance we use.

If you ever need to know, the pointer passed into `open()` is a pointer to the `ACE_Acceptor` that created the handler object. The `open()` method is where the handler implements such things as its concurrency policy if it were, for example, to spawn a new thread or fork a new process. The default `open()` implementation does what we want: register the handler with its reactor for READ events. If `open()` returns –1, `ACE_Acceptor` will immediately call the handler's `close()` hook method, a method inherited from `ACE_Task`. The default implementation will cause the handler to be deleted.

Let's now look at our new `handle_input()` method. This is, in fact, very much like the previous version:

```
int
ClientService::handle_input (ACE_HANDLE)
{
  const size_t INPUT_SIZE = 4096;
  char buffer[INPUT_SIZE];
  ssize_t recv_cnt, send_cnt;

  recv_cnt = this->peer ().recv (buffer, sizeof(buffer));
  if (recv_cnt <= 0)
    {
      ACE_DEBUG ((LM_DEBUG,
                  ACE_TEXT ("(%P|%t) Connection closed\n")));
      return -1;
    }

  send_cnt =
    this->peer ().send (buffer,
                        ACE_static_cast (size_t, recv_cnt));
  if (send_cnt == recv_cnt)
    return 0;
  if (send_cnt == -1 && ACE_OS::last_error () != EWOULDBLOCK)
    ACE_ERROR_RETURN ((LM_ERROR,
                       ACE_TEXT ("(%P|%t) %p\n"),
                       ACE_TEXT ("send")),
                      0);
  if (send_cnt == -1)
    send_cnt = 0;
  ACE_Message_Block *mb;
  size_t remaining =
```

```
                ACE_static_cast (size_t, (recv_cnt - send_cnt));
    ACE_NEW_RETURN
      (mb, ACE_Message_Block (&buffer[send_cnt], remaining), -1);
    int output_off = this->msg_queue ()->is_empty ();
    ACE_Time_Value nowait (ACE_OS::gettimeofday ());
    if (this->putq (mb, &nowait) == -1)
      {
        ACE_ERROR ((LM_ERROR,
                    ACE_TEXT ("(%P|%t) %p; discarding data\n"),
                    ACE_TEXT ("enqueue failed")));
        mb->release ();
        return 0;
      }
    if (output_off)
      return this->reactor ()->register_handler
        (this, ACE_Event_Handler::WRITE_MASK);
    return 0;
  }
```

The differences between the two versions follow.

- We access the underlying `ACE_SOCK_Stream` by using the `ACE_Svc_Handler::peer()` method.

- We access the inherited `ACE_Message_Queue` with the inherited `ACE_Task::msg_queue()` method.

- To enqueue items, we can use the inherited `ACE_Task::putq()` method.

Similarly, our new `handle_output()` method is similar but takes advantage of inherited methods:

```
int
ClientService::handle_output (ACE_HANDLE)
{
  ACE_Message_Block *mb;
  ACE_Time_Value nowait (ACE_OS::gettimeofday ());
  while (-1 != this->getq (mb, &nowait))
    {
      ssize_t send_cnt =
        this->peer ().send (mb->rd_ptr (), mb->length ());
      if (send_cnt == -1)
        ACE_ERROR ((LM_ERROR,
                    ACE_TEXT ("(%P|%t) %p\n"),
                    ACE_TEXT ("send")));
      else
        mb->rd_ptr (ACE_static_cast (size_t, send_cnt));
```

```
          if (mb->length () > 0)
            {
              this->ungetq (mb);
              break;
            }
          mb->release ();
        }
    return (this->msg_queue ()->is_empty ()) ? -1 : 0;
}
```

Lest you think that our improvements are done, we've got one more bunch of code to not write any more. Look at the new `handle_close()` method:

```
int
ClientService::handle_close (ACE_HANDLE h, ACE_Reactor_Mask mask)
{
  if (mask == ACE_Event_Handler::WRITE_MASK)
    return 0;
  return super::handle_close (h, mask);
}
```

We left in the check for ignoring the `WRITE_MASK`, but other than that, all the old code is gone too. As depicted in Figure 7.3, the default `handle_close()` method removes all reactor registrations, cancels all timers, and deletes the handler.

As you can see, use of the `ACE_Svc_Handler` greatly simplifies our service handler and allows us to focus completely on the problem we need to solve rather than getting distracted by all the connection management issues.

7.6.2 Template Details

When working with templates, we must do one last chore before our application can be considered complete. We must give the compiler some help in applying the template code to create the real classes:

```
#if defined (ACE_HAS_EXPLICIT_TEMPLATE_INSTANTIATION)
template class ACE_Acceptor<ClientService, ACE_SOCK_ACCEPTOR>;
template class ACE_Svc_Handler<ACE_SOCK_STREAM, ACE_NULL_SYNCH>;
#elif defined (ACE_HAS_TEMPLATE_INSTANTIATION_PRAGMA)
#pragma instantiate ACE_Acceptor<ClientService, ACE_SOCK_ACCEPTOR>
#pragma instantiate \
    ACE_Svc_Handler<ACE_SOCK_STREAM, ACE_NULL_SYNCH>
#endif /* ACE_HAS_EXPLICIT_TEMPLATE_INSTANTIATION */
```

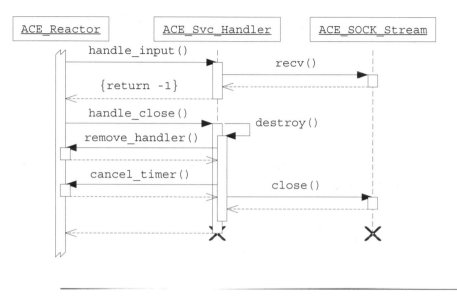

Figure 7.3. Reactive shutdown of an ACE_Svc_Handler

Because different compilers behave differently, we must use different techniques for template instantiation, depending on what the compiler is capable of. This can get tedious quickly but is necessary when creating a truly portable application.

7.6.3 Using ACE_Connector, and Other Features

ACE_Connector is the Acceptor-Connector framework class that actively connects to a peer. Like ACE_Acceptor, it produces an ACE_Svc_Handler-derived object to run the service once connected. It's all very much like we explained when talking about ACE_Acceptor. In this section, we present an example of a client program that talks to the server that's using the ACE_Acceptor. Because it would otherwise be very similar, we threw in some new, interesting tricks. Let's start with the declaration of our Client class:

```
#include "ace/Reactor.h"
#include "ace/INET_Addr.h"
#include "ace/SOCK_Stream.h"
#include "ace/SOCK_Connector.h"
```

```
#include "ace/Connector.h"
#include "ace/Svc_Handler.h"
#include "ace/Reactor_Notification_Strategy.h"

class Client :
    public ACE_Svc_Handler<ACE_SOCK_STREAM, ACE_NULL_SYNCH>
{
  typedef ACE_Svc_Handler<ACE_SOCK_STREAM, ACE_NULL_SYNCH> super;

public:
  Client () : notifier_ (0, this, ACE_Event_Handler::WRITE_MASK)
      {}

  virtual int open (void * = 0);

  // Called when input is available from the client.
  virtual int handle_input (ACE_HANDLE fd = ACE_INVALID_HANDLE);

  // Called when output is possible.
  virtual int handle_output (ACE_HANDLE fd = ACE_INVALID_HANDLE);

  // Called when a timer expires.
  virtual int handle_timeout (const ACE_Time_Value &current_time,
                              const void *act = 0);

private:
  enum { ITERATIONS = 5 };
  int iterations_;
  ACE_Reactor_Notification_Strategy notifier_;
};
```

That code is standard stuff. (ACE is like that, by the way: very consistent. Once you learn how to do something, the knowledge carries well.) However, we encounter our first new feature. `ACE_Reactor_Notification_Strategy` is a class in the *strategies* category and implements the Strategy pattern [3], which allows you to customize another class's behavior without changing the subject class. Let's look a little more closely at what it does; it's used in the `open()` method:

```
int Client::open (void *p)
{
  ACE_Time_Value iter_delay (2);   // Two seconds
  if (super::open (p) == -1)
    return -1;
```

```
    this->notifier_.reactor (this->reactor ());
    this->msg_queue ()->notification_strategy (&this->notifier_);
    return this->reactor ()->schedule_timer
      (this, 0, ACE_Time_Value::zero, iter_delay);
}
```

First, we call the superclass's `open()` method to register this handler with the
reactor for READ events. As with `ACE_Acceptor`, `ACE_Connector` automatically calls the handler's `open()` hook method when the connection is established. As with `ACE_Acceptor`, if `open()` returns −1, `close()` will be called
immediately. If that goes well, we set up the notification strategy on our inherited
`ACE_Message_Queue`, using its `notification_strategy()` method.

Recall from the preceding constructor that we set up the strategy object to
specify `this` handler and the WRITE_MASK. The 0 was a reactor pointer. At the
constructor point, we didn't know which `ACE_Reactor` instance would be used
with this `Client` object, so we left it 0. We now know it, as `ACE_Connector`
assigns it before calling the `open()` method. So we set the correct
`ACE_Reactor` pointer in our `notifier_` object. What is all this for? The
`ACE_Message_Queue` can be strategized with an object, such as
`ACE_Reactor_Notification_Strategy`. When it has one of these
strategy objects, `ACE_Message_Queue` calls the strategy's `notify()` method
whenever an `ACE_Message_Block` is enqueued. As we've set up
`notifier_`, it will do a `notify()` call on the `Client`'s reactor to queue a
notification for `handle_output()` in our `Client` object. This facility is very
useful for incorporating `ACE_Message_Queue` enqueue operations into a
reactor's event loop. The last thing our `open()` method does is set up a recurring
timer for now and every 2 seconds after that.

Recall that our server example will simply echo back whatever it receives
from the client. When the server sends data back, the following method is called:

```
int Client::handle_input (ACE_HANDLE)
{
  char buf[64];
  ssize_t recv_cnt = this->peer ().recv (buf, sizeof (buf) - 1);
  if (recv_cnt > 0)
    {
      ACE_DEBUG ((LM_DEBUG, ACE_TEXT ("%*C"),
                  ACE_static_cast (int, recv_cnt),
                  buf));
      return 0;
    }
```

```
    if (recv_cnt == 0 || ACE_OS::last_error () != EWOULDBLOCK)
      {
        this->reactor ()->end_reactor_event_loop ();
        return -1;
      }
    return 0;
}
```

This is all second nature by now, right? Just to recap: If we receive data, we log it, this time using a counted string, as the received data does not have a 0 terminator byte. If there's an error, we end the event loop and return −1 to remove this handler from the reactor.

Let's look at what happens when a timeout occurs:

```
int Client::handle_timeout(const ACE_Time_Value &, const void *)
{
  if (this->iterations_ >= ITERATIONS)
    {
      this->peer ().close_writer ();
      return 0;
    }

  ACE_Message_Block *mb;
  char msg[128];
  ACE_OS::sprintf (msg, "Iteration %d\n", this->iterations_);
  ACE_NEW_RETURN (mb, ACE_Message_Block (msg), -1);
  this->putq (mb);
  return 0;
}
```

If we've run all the iterations we want—we send a predetermined number of strings to the server—we use the `close_writer()` method to close our end of the TCP/IP socket. This will cause the server to see that we've closed, and it, in turn, will close its end, and we'll end up back in `handle_input()`, doing a 0-byte receive to close everything down.

Note that for each string we want to send to the server, we insert it into a `ACE_Message_Block` and enqueue it. This will cause the message queue to use our `notifier_` object to queue a notification to the reactor; when it's processed, the reactor will call our `handle_output()` method:

```
int Client::handle_output (ACE_HANDLE)
{
  ACE_Message_Block *mb;
  ACE_Time_Value nowait (ACE_OS::gettimeofday ());
  while (-1 != this->getq (mb, &nowait))
    {
      ssize_t send_cnt =
        this->peer ().send (mb->rd_ptr (), mb->length ());
      if (send_cnt == -1)
        ACE_ERROR ((LM_ERROR,
                    ACE_TEXT ("(%P|%t) %p\n"),
                    ACE_TEXT ("send")));
      else
        mb->rd_ptr (ACE_static_cast (size_t, send_cnt));
      if (mb->length () > 0)
        {
          this->ungetq (mb);
          break;
        }
      mb->release ();
    }
  if (this->msg_queue ()->is_empty ())
    this->reactor ()->cancel_wakeup
      (this, ACE_Event_Handler::WRITE_MASK);
  else
    this->reactor ()->schedule_wakeup
      (this, ACE_Event_Handler::WRITE_MASK);
  return 0;
}
```

We continue to dequeue and send data until the queue is empty or the socket becomes flow controlled and we have to wait for more. To manage the callbacks to this method, we use two alternative reactor registration methods: cancel_wakeup() and schedule_wakeup(). Each assumes that the handler being specified is already registered with the reactor for at least one other I/O event type. (Client is registered for READ events from the open() method.) cancel_wakeup() removes the specified mask bit(s) from this handler's reactor registration, and schedule_wakeup() adds the specified mask. The handler is not added or removed in either case, so there's no handle_close() call as a result of removing WRITE_MASK. Therefore, we don't need to implement handle_close() this time to special-case handling of a closed WRITE mask; we reuse the default handle_close() method from ACE_Svc_Handler. Yet more code we don't need to write!

One more feature of `ACE_Svc_Handler` is illustrated via the `main()` function:

```
int ACE_TMAIN (int, ACE_TCHAR *[])
{
  ACE_INET_Addr port_to_connect ("HAStatus", ACE_LOCALHOST);
  ACE_Connector<Client, ACE_SOCK_CONNECTOR> connector;
  Client client;
  Client *pc = &client;
  if (connector.connect (pc, port_to_connect) == -1)
    ACE_ERROR_RETURN ((LM_ERROR, ACE_TEXT ("%p\n"),
                       ACE_TEXT ("connect")), 1);

  ACE_Reactor::instance ()->run_reactor_event_loop ();
  return (0);
}
```

We used `ACE_Connector` without using `typedef`, but that's not the trick. In our `ACE_Acceptor` example, all the service handlers were allocated dynamically. Indeed, that's usually the best model to use with all service handlers. To do that in this case, we could have set `pc` to 0, and `ACE_Connector` would have dynamically allocated a `Client` for the new connection. We previously stated that the default `ACE_Svc_Handler::handle_close()` method unregisters the handler with the reactor, cancels all the timers, and deletes the object. In reality, the method deletes the handler object only if it was dynamically allocated; if it wasn't dynamically allocated, `handle_close()` doesn't try to delete it. How does the method know whether the handler was dynamically allocated? It uses the C++ *Storage Class Tracker* idiom [13]. *C++ Network Programming, Volume 2* [7] has a good description of how `ACE_Svc_Handler` uses this technique internally.

7.7 Reactor Implementations

Most applications will use the default reactor instance provided by `ACE_Reactor::instance()`. In some applications, however, you may find it necessary to specify a preferred implementation. In fact, nine reactor implementations are available at the time of this writing. The API declared by `ACE_Reactor` has proved flexible enough to allow for easy integration with third-party toolkits, such as the Xt framework of the X Window System and the Windows COM/DCOM framework.

You may even create your own extension of one of the existing implementations. ACE's internal design simplifies this extensibility by using the Bridge pattern [3]. The Bridge pattern uses two separate classes: one is the programming interface, and the second is the implementation that the first forwards operations to. When using the defaults in ACE, you need never know how this works. However, if you wish to change the implementation, a new implementation class must be specified for the Bridge. For example, to use the thread-pool reactor implementation, your application would first create the `ACE_TP_Reactor` implementation instance and then a new `ACE_Reactor` object that specifies the implementation:

```
ACE_TP_Reactor *tp_reactor = new ACE_TP_Reactor;

ACE_Reactor *my_reactor = new ACE_Reactor (tp_reactor, 1);
```

The second argument to the `ACE_Reactor` constructor directs `ACE_Reactor` to also delete the `tp_reactor` object when `my_reactor` is destroyed.

To use the specialized reactor object as your program's singleton, use:

```
ACE_Reactor::instance (my_reactor, 1);
```

The second argument directs ACE to delete the `my_reactor` instance at program termination time. This is a good idea to prevent memory leaks and to allow for a clean shutdown.

7.7.1 ACE_Select_Reactor

`ACE_Select_Reactor` is the default reactor implementation used on every platform except Windows. The `select()` system function is ultimately used on these systems to wait for activity. The `ACE_Select_Reactor` is designed to be used by one thread at a time. That thread is referred to as the *owner*. The thread that creates the `ACE_Select_Reactor`—in most cases, the initial program thread—is the initial owner. The owner thread is set by using the `owner()` method. Only the owner thread can run the reactor's event loop. Most times when the call to run the event loop returns –1 immediately, it's because it was called by a thread that doesn't own the reactor.

7.7.2 ACE_WFMO_Reactor and ACE_Msg_WFMO_Reactor

ACE_WFMO_Reactor is the default reactor implementation on Windows. Instead of using the select() demultiplexer, the implementation uses Wait-ForMultipleObjects(). There are some tradeoffs to remember when using ACE_WFMO_Reactor. These tradeoffs favor use of ACE_WFMO_Reactor in the vast majority of use cases; however, it's prudent to be aware of them and evaluate the tradeoffs in the context of your projects:

- *Handle limit.* The ACE_WFMO_Reactor can register only 62 handles. The underlying WaitForMultipleObjects() function imposes a limit of 64, and ACE uses 2 of them internally.

- *I/O types.* ACE_WFMO_Reactor supports the handle_input(), handle_output(), and handle_exception() I/O callbacks only on socket handles. Handles for other IPC types, such as ACE_SPIPE_Stream, are not registerable for the I/O callbacks we've discussed in this chapter. However, it's possible to use overlapped I/O with an associated event and to register the event with the reactor. Overlapped I/O is often easier, however, using the Proactor framework described in Chapter 8.

- *Waitable handles.* ACE_WFMO_Reactor can react to any handle that's legitimate for use with WaitForMultipleObjects(), such as file change notification handles and event handles. To register one of these handles, use this ACE_Reactor method:

```
int register_handler (ACE_Event_Handler *handler,
                ACE_HANDLE event_handle = ACE_INVALID_HANDLE);
```

When the event becomes signaled, the reactor will dispatch to the handler's handle_signal() callback method.

- *Multiple threads.* The ACE_WFMO_Reactor event loop can be executed by multiple threads at once. When using this feature, be aware that callbacks can occur from multiple threads simultaneously, so you need to defend against race conditions and data access serialization issues.

- *Delayed handler removal.* Because multiple threads can all be running the event loop, ACE_WFMO_Reactor doesn't just rip handlers out from event-processing threads. To avoid this very unpolite action, this reactor implementation will defer handler removal until it can let all the event processing threads finish what they're doing. For your purposes, you must remember that when you remove an event handler from ACE_WFMO_Reactor, either by returning −1 from a callback or by calling remove_handler(), some time may elapse before the reactor calls `handle_close()`. Therefore, if you must delete the handler object immediately after unregistering it, you must supply the `DONT_CALL` flag to `remove_handler()`. Following our advice to delete your handler from the `handle_close()` method will avoid this issue completely when you use dynamically allocated handlers; however, you must keep this issue in mind, especially when using statically allocated handlers whose destruction time you don't control.

If your application will be a COM/DCOM server, you should use the `ACE_Msg_WFMO_Reactor` instead. It is much like the `ACE_WFMO_Reactor` but also dispatches Windows messages.

7.7.3   ACE_TP_Reactor

The `ACE_TP_Reactor` extends the `ACE_Select_Reactor` to allow it to operate in multiple threads at the same time: a thread pool. `ACE_TP_Reactor` doesn't create the threads; you are still responsible for that. Once you have your threads running, one or more of them runs the event loop; typically:

```
ACE_Reactor::instance()->run_reactor_event_loop()
```

`ACE_TP_Reactor` implements the Leader/Followers pattern [5]. One of the threads will be the leader and take ownership of the reactor to wait for events while the other threads—the followers—wait their turn. When activity occurs, the leader thread will pass ownership to one of the follower threads while the original leader processes the activity. This pattern continues until the reactor is shut down, at which point the threads—and program—can exit.

7.7.4   ACE_Priority_Reactor

The `ACE_Priority_Reactor` also extends the `ACE_Select_Reactor`. This implementation takes advantage of the `priority()` method on the `ACE_Event_Handler` class. When it is registered with this reactor, an event handler is placed into a priority-specific bucket. When events take place, they are dispatched in their priority order. This allows higher-priority events to be processed first.

7.7.5   GUI Integrated Reactors

Recognizing the need to write reactor-based GUI applications, the ACE community has created several reactor extensions for use with the X Window System.

Each of these extends the `ACE_Select_Reactor` to work with a specific toolkit. By using these reactors, your GUI application can remain single threaded yet still respond to both GUI events, such as button presses, and your own application events.

Qt Reactor

The `ACE_QtReactor` extends both the `ACE_Select_Reactor` and the Trolltech Qt library's `QObject` class. Rather than using `select()`, the `QtWaitForMultipleEvents()` function is used.

FastLight Reactor

The `ACE_FlReactor` integrates with the FastLight toolkit's `Fl::wait()` method.

Tk Reactor

The `ACE_TkReactor` provides reactor functionality around the popular Tcl/Tk library. The underlying Tcl/Tk method used is `Tcl_DoOneEvent()`.

Xt Reactor

Last, but not least, is the `ACE_XtReactor`, which integrates with the X Toolkit library, using `XtWaitForMultipleEvents()`.

7.8 Summary

The Reactor framework is a very powerful and flexible system for handling events from many sources, seemingly simultaneously, without incurring the overhead of multiple threads. At the same time, you can use the reactor in a multithreaded application and have the best of both worlds. A single reactor instance can easily handle activity of timers, signals, and I/O events. In addition to its use with sockets, as shown in this chapter, most reactor implementations can handle I/O from any selectable handle: pipes, UNIX-domain sockets, UDP sockets, serial and parallel I/O devices, and so forth. With a little ingenuity, your reactor-based application can turn on the foyer light when someone pulls into your driveway or mute the television when the phone rings!

Chapter 8
Asynchronous I/O and the ACE Proactor Framework

Applications that must perform I/O on multiple endpoints—whether network sockets, pipes, or files—historically use one of two I/O models:

1. *Reactive*. An application based on the reactive model registers event handler objects that are notified when it's possible to perform one or more desired I/O operations, such as receiving data on a socket, with a high likelihood of immediate, successful completion. The ACE Reactor framework, described in Chapter 7, supports the reactive model.

2. *Multithreaded*. An application spawns multiple threads that each perform synchronous, often blocking, I/O operations. This model doesn't scale very well for applications with large numbers of open endpoints.

Reactive I/O is the most common model, especially for networked applications. It was popularized by wide use of the `select()` function to demultiplex I/O across file descriptors in the BSD Sockets API. Asynchronous I/O, also known as proactive I/O, is often a more scalable way to perform I/O on many endpoints. It is asynchronous because the I/O request and its completion are separate, distinct events that occur at different times. Proactive I/O allows an application to initiate one or more I/O requests on multiple I/O endpoints in parallel without blocking for their completion. As each operation completes, the OS notifies a completion handler that then processes the results.

Asynchronous I/O has been in use for many years on such OS platforms as OpenVMS and on IBM mainframes. It's also been available for a number of years

187

on Windows and more recently on some POSIX platforms. This chapter explains more about asynchronous I/O and the proactive model and then explains how to use the ACE Proactor framework to your best advantage.

8.1 Why Use Asynchronous I/O?

Reactive I/O operations are often performed in a single thread, driven by the reactor's event-dispatching loop. Each thread, however, can execute only one I/O operation at a time. This sequential nature can be a bottleneck, as applications that transfer large amounts of data on multiple endpoints can't use the parallelism available from the OS and/or multiple CPUs or network interfaces.

Multithreaded I/O alleviates the main bottleneck of single-threaded reactive I/O by taking advantage of concurrency strategies, such as the thread-pool model, available using the ACE_TP_Reactor and ACE_WFMO_Reactor reactor implementations, or the thread-per-connection model, which often uses synchronous, blocking I/O. Multithreading can help parallelize an application's I/O operations, which may improve performance. This technique can also be very intuitive, especially when using serial, blocking function calls. However, it is not always the best choice, for the following reasons:

- *Threading policy tightly coupled to concurrency policy*. A separate thread is required for each desired concurrent operation or request. It would be much better to define threading policy by available resources, possibly factoring in the number of available CPUs, using a thread pool.

- *Increased synchronization complexity*. If request processing requires shared access to data, all threads must serialize data access. This involves another level of analysis and design, as well as further complexity.

- *Synchronization performance penalty*. Overhead related to context switching and scheduling, as well as interlocking/competing threads, can degrade performance significantly.

Therefore, using multiple threads is not always a good choice if done solely to increase I/O parallelism.

The proactive I/O model entails two distinct steps.

1. Initiate an I/O operation.

2. Handle the completion of the operation at a later time.

These two steps are essentially the inverse of those in the reactive I/O model.

1. Use an event demultiplexer to determine when an I/O operation is possible and likely to complete immediately.

2. Perform the operation.

Unlike conventional reactive or synchronous I/O models, the proactive model allows a single application thread to initiate multiple operations simultaneously. This design allows a single-threaded application to execute I/O operations concurrently without incurring the overhead or design complexity associated with conventional multithreaded mechanisms.

Choose the proactive I/O model when

• The IPC mechanisms in use, such as Windows Named Pipes, require it

• The application can benefit significantly from parallel I/O operations

• Reactive model limitations—limited handles or performance—prevent its use

8.2 How to Send and Receive Data

The procedure for sending and receiving data asynchronously is a bit different from using synchronous transfers. We'll look at an example, explore what the example does, and point out some similarities and differences between using the Proactor framework and the Reactor framework.

The Proactor framework encompasses a relatively large set of highly related classes, so it's impossible to discuss them in order without forward references. We will get through them all by the end of the chapter. Figure 8.1 shows the Proactor framework's classes in relation to each other; you can use the figure to keep some context as we progress through the chapter.

The following code declares a class that performs the same basic work as the examples in the previous two chapters, introducing the primary classes involved in initiating and completing I/O requests on a connected TCP/IP socket:

```
#include "ace/Asynch_IO.h"

class HA_Proactive_Service : public ACE_Service_Handler
{
public:
  ~HA_Proactive_Service ()
    {
      if (this->handle () != ACE_INVALID_HANDLE)
        ACE_OS::closesocket (this->handle ());
    }
```

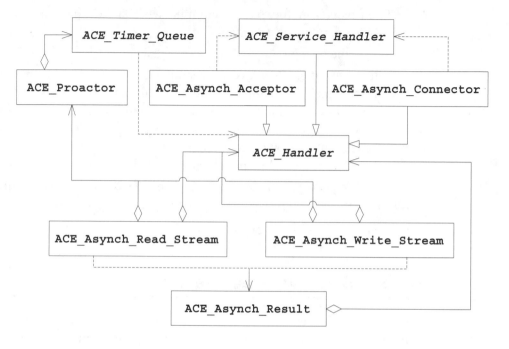

Figure 8.1. Classes in the Proactor framework

```
virtual void open (ACE_HANDLE h, ACE_Message_Block&);

// This method will be called when an asynchronous read
// completes on a stream.
virtual void handle_read_stream
  (const ACE_Asynch_Read_Stream::Result &result);

// This method will be called when an asynchronous write
// completes on a stream.
virtual void handle_write_stream
  (const ACE_Asynch_Write_Stream::Result &result);

private:
  ACE_Asynch_Read_Stream reader_;
  ACE_Asynch_Write_Stream writer_;
};
```

This example begins by including the necessary header files for the Proactor framework classes that this example uses:

- `ACE_Service_Handler`, the target class for creation of new service handlers in the Proactor framework, similar to the role played by `ACE_Svc_Handler` in the Acceptor-Connector framework.

- `ACE_Handler`, the parent class of `ACE_Service_Handler`, which defines the interface for handling asynchronous I/O completions via the Proactor framework. The `ACE_Handler` class is analogous to the `ACE_Event_Handler` in the Reactor framework.

- `ACE_Asynch_Read_Stream`, the I/O factory class for initiating read operations on a connected TCP/IP socket.

- `ACE_Asynch_Write_Stream`, the I/O factory class for initiating write operations on a connected TCP/IP socket.

- `Result`, which each I/O factory class defines as a nested class to contain the result of each operation the factory initiates. All the `Result` classes are derived from `ACE_Asynch_Result` and have added data and methods particular to the type of I/O they're defined for. Because the initiation and completion of each asynchronous I/O operation are separate and distinct events, a mechanism is needed to "remember" the operation parameters and relay them, along with the result, to the completion handler.

So why are there all these classes, many of which seem so close in purpose to classes in the Acceptor-Connector framework we saw in Chapter 7? The asynchronous I/O model splits the I/O initiation and completion actions, as they're not coupled. ACE needs to do this without cluttering the classes that are designed for reactive or synchronous operation.

8.2.1 Setting up the Handler and Initiating I/O

When a TCP connection is opened, the handle of the new socket should be passed to the handler object—in this example's case, `HA_Proactive_Service`. It's helpful to put the handle in the handler for the following reasons.

- It is a convenient point of control for the socket's lifetime, as it's the target of the connection factories.

- It's most often the class from which I/O operations are initiated.

When using the Proactor framework's asynchronous connection establishment classes (we'll look at these in Section 8.3), the ACE_Service_Handler:: open() hook method is called when a new connection is established. Our example's open() hook follows:

```
void
HA_Proactive_Service::open (ACE_HANDLE h, ACE_Message_Block&)
{
  this->handle (h);
  if (this->reader_.open (*this) != 0 ||
      this->writer_.open (*this) != 0   )
    {
      ACE_ERROR ((LM_ERROR, ACE_TEXT ("%p\n"),
                  ACE_TEXT ("HA_Proactive_Service open")));
      delete this;
      return;
    }

  ACE_Message_Block *mb;
  ACE_NEW_NORETURN (mb, ACE_Message_Block (1024));
  if (this->reader_.read (*mb, mb->space ()) != 0)
    {
      ACE_ERROR ((LM_ERROR, ACE_TEXT ("%p\n"),
                  ACE_TEXT ("HA_Proactive_Service begin read")));
      mb->release ();
      delete this;
      return;
    }

  // mb is now controlled by Proactor framework.
  return;
}
```

Right at the beginning, the new socket's handle is saved using the inherited ACE_Handler::handle() method. This method stores the handle in a convenient place for, among other things, access by the HA_Proactive_Service destructor, shown on page 189. This is part of the socket handle's lifetime management implemented in this class.

In order to initiate I/O, you have to initialize the I/O factory objects you need. After storing the socket handle, our open() method initializes the reader_ and writer_ I/O factory objects in preparation for initiating I/O operations. The complete signature of the open() method on both classes is:

```
int open (ACE_Handler &handler,
          ACE_HANDLE handle = ACE_INVALID_HANDLE,
          const void *completion_key = 0,
          ACE_Proactor *proactor = 0);
```

This first argument represents the completion handler for operations initiated by the factory object. The Proactor framework will call back to this object when I/O operations initiated via the factory object complete. That's why the handler object is referred to as a *completion handler.* In our example, the HA_Proactive_Service class is a descendant of ACE_Handler and will be the completion handler for both read and write operations, so *this is the handler argument. All other arguments are defaulted. Because we don't pass a handle, the I/O factories will call HA_Proactive_Service::handle() to obtain the socket handle. This is another reason we stored the handle value immediately on entry to open().

The completion_key argument is used only on Windows; it is seldom used, so we don't discuss it here. The proactor argument is also defaulted. In this case, a processwide singleton ACE_Proactor object will be used. If a specific ACE_Proactor instance is needed, the proactor argument must be supplied.

The last thing our open() hook method does is initiate a read operation on the new socket by calling the ACE_Asynch_Read_Stream::read() method. The signature for ACE_Asynch_Read_Stream::read() is:

```
int read (ACE_Message_Block &message_block,
          size_t num_bytes_to_read,
          const void *act = 0,
          int priority = 0,
          int signal_number = ACE_SIGRTMIN);
```

The most obvious difference between asynchronous read operations and their synchronous counterparts is that an ACE_Message_Block rather than a buffer pointer or iovec array is specified for the transfer. This makes buffer management easier, as you can take advantage of ACE_Message_Block's capabilities and integration with other parts of ACE, such as ACE_Message_Queue. ACE_Message_Block is described in more detail starting on page 261. When a read is initiated, data is read into the block starting at the block's write pointer, as the read data will be written into the block.

8.2.2 Completing I/O Operations

Both the Proactor framework and the Reactor framework (Chapter 7) are event based. However, rather than registering event handler objects to be notified when I/O is possible, the I/O factories establish an association between each operation and the completion handler that should be called back when the operation completes. Each type of I/O operation has its own callback method. In our example using TCP/IP, the Proactor framework calls the `ACE_Handler::handle_read_stream()` hook method when the read completes. Our example's hook method follows:

```
void
HA_Proactive_Service::handle_read_stream
  (const ACE_Asynch_Read_Stream::Result &result)
{
  ACE_Message_Block &mb = result.message_block ();
  if (!result.success () || result.bytes_transferred () == 0)
    {
      mb.release ();
      delete this;
    }
  else
    {
      if (this->writer_.write (mb, mb.length ()) != 0)
        {
          ACE_ERROR ((LM_ERROR,
                      ACE_TEXT ("%p\n"),
                      ACE_TEXT ("starting write")));
          mb.release ();
        }
      else
        {
          ACE_Message_Block *new_mb;
          ACE_NEW_NORETURN (new_mb, ACE_Message_Block (1024));
          this->reader_.read (*new_mb, new_mb->space ());
        }
    }
  return;
}
```

The passed-in `ACE_Asynch_Read_Stream::Result` refers to the object holding the results of the read operation. Each I/O factory class defines its own `Result` class to hold both the parameters each operation is initiated with and the results of the operation. The message block used in the operation is referred to via the `message_block()` method. The Proactor framework automatically advances the block's write pointer to reflect the added data, if any. The `handle_read_stream()` method first checks whether the operation either failed or completed successfully but read 0 bytes. (As in synchronous socket reads, a 0-byte read indicates that the peer has closed its end of the connection.) If either of these cases is true, the message block is released and the handler object deleted. The handler's destructor will close the socket.

If the read operation read any data, we do two things:

1. Initiate a write operation to echo the received data back to the peer. Because the Proactor framework has already updated the message block's write pointer, we can simply use the block as is. The read pointer is still pointing to the start of the data, and a write operation uses the block's read pointer to read data out of the block and write it on the socket.

2. Allocate a new `ACE_Message_Block` and initiate a new read operation to read the next set of data from the peer.

When the write operation completes, the Proactor framework calls the following `handle_write_stream()` method:

```
void
HA_Proactive_Service::handle_write_stream
(const ACE_Asynch_Write_Stream::Result &result)
{
  result.message_block ().release ();
  return;
}
```

Regardless of whether the write completed successfully, the message block that was used in the operation is released. If a socket is broken, the previously initiated read operation will also complete with an error, and `handle_read_stream()` will clean up the object and socket handle. More important, note that the same `ACE_Message_Block` object was used to read data from the peer and echo it back. After it has been used for both operations, it is released.

The sequence of events in this example is illustrated in Figure 8.2. The example presented in this section illustrates the following principles and guidelines for using asynchronous I/O in the ACE Proactor framework.

- *ACE_Message_Block is used for all transfers.* All read and write transfers use `ACE_Message_Block` rather than other types of buffer pointers and counts. This enables ease of data movement around other parts of ACE, such as queueing data to an `ACE_Message_Queue`, or other frameworks that

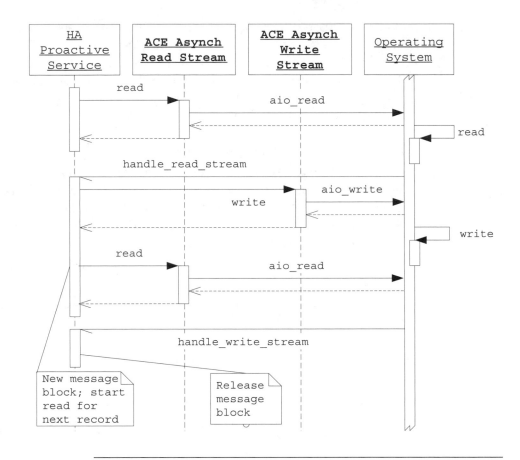

Figure 8.2. Sequence diagram for asynchronous data echo example

reuse ACE_Message_Queue, such as the ACE Task framework (described in Chapter 12) or the ACE Streams framework (described in Chapter 18). Using the common message block class makes it possible for the Proactor framework to automatically update the block's read and write pointers as data is transferred, relieving you of this tedious task. When you design the class(es) involved in initiating and completing I/O operations, you must decide on how the blocks are allocated: statically or dynamically. However, it is generally more flexible to allocate the blocks dynamically.

- *Cleanup has very few restrictions but must be managed carefully.* In the preceding example, the usual response to an error condition is to delete the handler object. After working with the ACE Reactor framework and its rules for event handler registration and cleanup, this "just delete it" simplicity may seem odd. Remember that the Proactor framework has no explicit handler registrations, as there are with the Reactor framework.[1] The only connection between the Proactor and the completion handler object is an outstanding I/O operation. Therein lies an important restriction on completion handler cleanup. If any I/O operations are outstanding, you can't release the `ACE_Message_Block` that an outstanding operation refers to. Even if the Proactor event loop isn't running, an initiated operation may be processed by the OS. If it is a receive, the data will still be put where the original message block used to be. If the operation is a send, something will be sent; if the block has since been released, you don't know what will be sent. If the Proactor event loop is still running, the Proactor framework will, when the I/O operation(s) complete, issue callback(s) to the associated handler, which must be valid, or your program's behavior will be undefined and almost surely wrong.

Each I/O factory class offers a `cancel()` method that can be used to attempt to cancel any outstanding I/O operations. Not all operations can be canceled, however. Different operating systems offer different levels of support for canceling operations, sometimes varying with I/O type on the same system. For example, many disk I/O requests that haven't started to execute can be canceled, but many socket operations cannot. Sometimes, closing the I/O handle on which the I/O is being performed will abort an I/O request and sometimes not. It's often a good idea to keep track of the number of outstanding I/O requests and wait for them all to complete before destroying a handler.

8.3 Establishing Connections

ACE provides two factory classes for proactively establishing TCP/IP connections using the Proactor framework:

1. `ACE_Asynch_Acceptor`, to initiate passive connection establishment
2. `ACE_Asynch_Connector` to initiate active connection establishment

---

1. Use of timers in the Proactor framework does require cleanup, however. The cleanup requirements for timer use in the Proactor framework are similar to those for the Reactor framework.

When a TCP/IP connection is established using either of these classes, the ACE Proactor framework creates a service handler derived from `ACE_Service_Handler`, such as `HA_Proactive_Service`, to handle the new connection. The `ACE_Service_Handler` class, the base class of all asynchronously connected services in the ACE Proactor framework, is derived from `ACE_Handler`, so the service class can also handle I/O completions initiated in the service.

`ACE_Asynch_Acceptor` is a fairly easy class to program with. It is very straightforward in its default case and adds two hooks for extending its capabilities. The following example uses one of the hooks:

```
#include "ace/Asynch_Acceptor.h"
#include "ace/INET_Addr.h"

class HA_Proactive_Acceptor :
    public ACE_Asynch_Acceptor<HA_Proactive_Service>
{
public:
  virtual int validate_connection
    (const ACE_Asynch_Accept::Result& result,
     const ACE_INET_Addr &remote,
     const ACE_INET_Addr &local);
};
```

We declare `HA_Proactive_Acceptor` to be a new class derived from `ACE_Asynch_Acceptor`. As you can see, `ACE_Asynch_Acceptor` is a class template, similar to the way `ACE_Acceptor` is. The template argument is the type of `ACE_Service_Handler`-derived class to use for each new connection.

The `validate_connection()` method is a hook method defined on both `ACE_Asynch_Acceptor` and `ACE_Asynch_Connector`. The framework calls this method after accepting a new connection, before obtaining a new service handler for it. This method gives the application a chance to verify the connection and/or the address of the peer. Our example checks whether the peer is on the same IP network as we are:

```
int
HA_Proactive_Acceptor::validate_connection (
    const ACE_Asynch_Accept::Result&,
    const ACE_INET_Addr& remote,
    const ACE_INET_Addr& local)
{
```

```
struct in_addr *remote_addr =
  ACE_reinterpret_cast (struct in_addr*,
                        remote.get_addr ());
struct in_addr *local_addr =
  ACE_reinterpret_cast (struct in_addr*,
                        local.get_addr ());
if (inet_netof (*local_addr) == inet_netof (*remote_addr))
  return 0;

return -1;
}
```

This check is fairly simple and works only for IPv4 networks but is an example of the hook's use. The handle of the newly accepted socket is available via the `ACE_Asynch_Accept::Result::accept_handle()` method, so it is possible to do more involved checks that require data exchange. For example, an SSL (Secure Sockets Layer) handshake could be added at this point. If `validate_connection()` returns –1, the new connection is immediately aborted.

The other hook method available via `ACE_Asynch_Acceptor` is a protected virtual method: `make_handler()`. The Proactor framework calls this method to obtain an `ACE_Service_Handler` object to service the new connection. The default implementation simply allocates a new handler and is, essentially:

```
template <class HANDLER>
class ACE_Asynch_Acceptor : public ACE_Handler
      . . .
protected:
  virtual HANDLER *make_handler (void)
  {
    return new HANDLER;
  }
```

If your application requires a different way of obtaining a handler, you should override the `make_handler()` hook method. For example, a singleton handler could be used, or you could keep a list of handlers in use.

The following code shows how we use the `HA_Proactive_Acceptor` class just described:

```
ACE_INET_Addr listen_addr;      // Set up with listen port
HA_Proactive_Acceptor aio_acceptor;
if (0 != aio_acceptor.open (listen_addr,
                            0,      // bytes_to_read
                            0,      // pass_addresses
                            ACE_DEFAULT_BACKLOG,
                            1,      // reuse_addr
                            0,      // proactor
                            1))     // validate_new_connection
  ACE_ERROR_RETURN ((LM_ERROR, ACE_TEXT ("%p\n"),
                     ACE_TEXT ("acceptor open")), 1);
```

To initialize the acceptor object and begin accepting connections, call the
`open()` method. The only required argument is the first: the address to listen on.
The `backlog` and `reuse_addr` parameters are the same as for
`ACE_SOCK_Acceptor`, and the default `proactor` argument selects the
process's singleton instance. The nonzero `validate_new_connection`
argument directs the framework to call the `validate_connection()`
method on the new handler when accepting a new connection, as discussed earlier.

The `bytes_to_read` argument can specify a number of bytes to read
immediately on connection acceptance. This is not universally supported by
underlying protocol implementations and is very seldom used. If used, however, it
would be what causes data to be available in the message block passed to
`ACE_Service_Handler::open()`, as we saw in our example on page 192.

The `pass_addresses` argument is of some importance if your handler
requires the local and peer addresses when running the service. The only portable
way to obtain the local and peer addresses for asynchronously established connections is to implement the `ACE_Service_Handler::addresses()` hook
method and pass a nonzero value as the `pass_addresses` argument to
`ACE_Asynch_Acceptor::open()`.

Actively establishing connections is very similar to passively accepting them.
The hook methods are similar. The following could be used to actively establish a
connection and instantiate an `HA_Proactive_Service` object to service the
new connection:

```
ACE_INET_Addr peer_addr;      // Set up peer addr
ACE_Asynch_Connector<HA_Proactive_Service> aio_connect;
aio_connect.connect (peer_addr);
```

8.4 The ACE_Proactor Completion Demultiplexer

The `ACE_Proactor` class drives completion handling in the ACE Proactor framework. This class waits for completion events that indicate that one or more operations started by the I/O factory classes have completed, demultiplexes those events to the associated completion handlers, and dispatches the appropriate hook method on each completion handler. Thus, for any asynchronous I/O completion event processing to take place—whether I/O or connection establishment—your application must run the proactor's event loop. This is usually as simple as inserting the following in your application:

```
ACE_Proactor::instance ()->proactor_run_event_loop ();
```

Asynchronous I/O facilities vary wildly between operating systems. To maintain a uniform interface and programming method across all of them, the `ACE_Proactor` class , like `ACE_Reactor`, uses the Bridge pattern to maintain flexibility and extensibility while allowing the Proactor framework to function with differing asynchronous I/O implementations. We briefly describe the implementation-specific Proactor classes next.

8.4.1 ACE_WIN32_Proactor

`ACE_WIN32_Proactor` is the `ACE_Proactor` implementation on Windows. This class works on Windows NT 4.0 and newer Windows platforms, such as Windows 2000 and Windows XP, but not on Windows 95, 98, ME, or CE, however, as these platforms don't support asynchronous I/O.

`ACE_WIN32_Proactor` uses an I/O completion port for completion event detection. When initializing an asynchronous operation factory, such as `ACE_Asynch_Read_Stream` or `ACE_Asynch_Write_Stream`, the I/O handle is associated with the Proactor's I/O completion port. In this implementation, the Windows `GetQueuedCompletionStatus()` function paces the event loop. Multiple threads can execute the `ACE_WIN32_Proactor` event loop simultaneously.

8.4.2 ACE_POSIX_Proactor

The ACE Proactor implementations on POSIX systems present multiple mechanisms for initiating I/O operations and detecting their completions. Moreover, Sun's Solaris Operating Environment offers its own proprietary version of asynchronous I/O. On Solaris 2.6 and higher, the performance of the Sun-specific asynchronous I/O functions is significantly higher than that of Solaris's POSIX.4 AIO implementation. To take advantage of this performance improvement, ACE also encapsulates this mechanism in a separate set of classes.

The encapsulated POSIX asynchronous I/O mechanisms support `read()` and `write()` operations but not TCP/IP connection related operations. To support the functions of `ACE_Asynch_Acceptor` and `ACE_Asynch_Connector`, a separate thread is used to perform connection-related operations. Therefore, you should be aware that your program will be running multiple threads when using the Proactor framework on POSIX platforms. The internals of ACE keep you from needing to handle events in different threads, so you don't need to add any special locking or synchronization. Just be aware of what's going on if you're in the debugger and see threads that your program didn't spawn.

8.5 Using Timers

In addition to its I/O-related capabilities, the ACE Proactor framework offers settable timers, similar to those offered by the ACE Reactor framework. They're programmed in a manner very similar to programming timers with the Reactor framework, but the APIs are slightly different. Check the reference documentation for complete details.

8.6 Other I/O Factory Classes

As with the Reactor framework, the Proactor framework has facilities to work with many different types of I/O endpoints. Unlike the synchronous IPC wrapper classes in ACE, which have a separate class for each type of IPC, the Proactor framework offers a smaller set of factory classes and relies on you to supply each with a handle. An I/O handle from any ACE IPC wrapper class, such as `ACE_SOCK_Stream` or `ACE_FILE_IO`, may be used with these I/O factory classes as listed:

- `ACE_Asynch_Read_File` and `ACE_Asynch_Write_File` for files and Windows Named Pipes
- `ACE_Asynch_Transmit_File` to transmit files over a connected TCP/IP stream

- `ACE_Asynch_Read_Dgram` and `ACE_Asynch_Write_Dgram` for UDP/IP datagram sockets

8.7 Combining the Reactor and Proactor Frameworks

Sometimes, you have a Reactor-based system and need to add an IPC type that doesn't work with the Reactor model. Or, you may want to use a Reactor feature, such as signals or signalable handles, with a Proactor-based application. These situations occur most often on Windows or in a multiplatform application in which Windows is one of its platforms. Sometimes, your application's I/O needs work better with the Proactor in some situations and better with the Reactor in others and you want to simplify development and maintenance as much as possible. Three different scenarios can usually be used to accommodate mixing of the two frameworks.

8.7.1 Compile Time

It's possible to derive your application's service handler class(es) from either `ACE_Svc_Handler` or `ACE_Service_Handler`, switchable at compile time, based on whether you're building for the Reactor framework or the Proactor framework. Rather than perform any real data processing in the callbacks, arrange your class to follow these guidelines.

- Standardize on handling data in `ACE_Message_Block` objects. Using the Proactor framework, you already need to do this, so this guideline has the most effect when working in the Reactor world. You simply need to get used to working with `ACE_Message_Block` instead of native arrays.

- Centralize the data-processing functionality in a private, or protected, method that's not one of the callbacks. For example, move the processing code to a method named `do_the_work()` or `process_input()`. The work method should accept an `ACE_Message_Block` with the data to work on. If the work requires that data also be sent in the other direction, put it in another `ACE_Message_Block` and return it.

- (Proactor): In the completion handler callback—for example, `handle_read_stream()`, after checking transfer status, pass the message block with the data to the work method.

- (Reactor): When receiving data in `handle_input()`, read it into an `ACE_Message_Block` and then call the work method, just as you do in the Proactor code.

8.7.2   Mix Models

Recall that it's possible to register a signalable handle with the `ACE_WFMO_Reactor` on Windows. Thus, if you want to use overlapped Windows I/O, you could use an event handle with the overlapped I/O and register the event handle with the reactor. This is a way to add a small amount of nonsockets I/O work—if, for example, you need to work with a named pipe—to the reactor on Windows but don't have the inclination or the interest in mixing Reactor and Proactor event loops.

8.7.3   Integrating Proactor and Reactor Events Loops

Both the Proactor and Reactor models require event-handling loops, and it is often useful to be able to use both models in the same program. One possible method for doing this is to run the event loops in separate threads. However, that introduces a need for multithreaded synchronization techniques. If the program is single threaded, however, it would be much better to integrate the event handling for both models into one mechanism. ACE provides this integration mechanism for Windows programs by providing a linkage from the Windows implementation of the `ACE_Proactor` class to the `ACE_WFMO_Reactor` class, which is the default reactor type on Windows.

   The ACE mechanism is based on the `ACE_WFMO_Reactor` class's ability to include a `HANDLE` in the event sources it waits for (see Section 7.7.2). The `ACE_WIN32_Proactor` class uses an I/O completion port internally to manage its event dispatching. However, because an I/O completion port handle is not waitable, it can't be registered with the `ACE_WFMO_Reactor`. Therefore, `ACE_WIN32_Proactor` includes some optional functionality to associate a Windows event handle with each asynchronous I/O operation. The event handle is waitable and is signaled when each I/O operation completes. The event handle is registered with `ACE_WFMO_Reactor`, and `ACE_WIN32_Proactor` is the event handler class. Thus, when the reactor's event loop reacts to the event signaling the I/O completion, the `handle_signal()` callback in `ACE_WIN32_Proactor` simply runs the completion events on the I/O completion port, completing the integration of the two mechanisms.

To make use of this link, follow these steps.

1. Instantiate an `ACE_WIN32_Proactor` object with second argument 1. This directs the `ACE_WIN32_Proactor` object to associate an event handle with I/O operations and make the handle available via the `get_handle()` method.

2. Instantiate an `ACE_Proactor` object with the `ACE_WIN32_Proactor` as its implementation.

3. Register the `ACE_WIN32_Proactor`'s handle with the desired `ACE_Reactor` object.

The following code shows the steps for creating an `ACE_Proactor` as described, making it the singleton, and registering it with the singleton reactor:

```
ACE_WIN32_Proactor proactor_impl (0, 1);
ACE_Proactor proactor (&proactor_impl);
ACE_Proactor::instance (&proactor);
ACE_Reactor::instance ()->register_handler (&proactor_impl,
proactor_impl.get_handle ());
```

After the program has completed its work and before the preceding proactors are destroyed, unregister the event handle to prevent any callbacks to an invalid object:

```
ACE_Reactor::instance ()->remove_handler
(impl->get_handle (), ACE_Event_Handler::DONT_CALL);
```

8.8 Summary

The ACE Proactor framework provides a portable way to implement asynchronous I/O capabilities into your application. Asynchronous I/O can often be an efficient way to handle more I/O endpoints than you can efficiently use with the Reactor framework. Asynchronous I/O can also be a good choice for situations in which you can benefit from highly parallelized I/O operations but don't want to use multiple threads.

This chapter described the Proactor framework's capabilities and showed how to implement the example server from earlier chapters, using the Proactor framework. Because asynchronous I/O is not universally available and not completely interchangeable with the Reactor framework, we also discussed ways to work with both frameworks in the same application.

Chapter 9
Other IPC Types

So far, we have focused on TCP/IP (`ACE_SOCK_Stream` and friends). ACE also offers many other IPC wrapper classes that support both interhost and intrahost communication. Keep in mind that intrahost communications is a very simplified host-to-host communication situation, and interhost IPC mechanisms all work perfectly fine for communication between collocated entities. Like the TCP/IP Sockets wrappers, most of the IPC wrappers offer an interface compatible with using them in the ACE Acceptor-Connector framework (`ACE_Acceptor`, `ACE_Connector`, and `ACE_Svc_Handler` classes).

9.1 Interhost IPC with UDP/IP

UDP is a datagram-oriented protocol that operates over IP. Therefore, as with TCP/IP, UDP uses IP addressing. Also as with TCP, datagrams are demultiplexed within each IP address, using a port number. UDP port numbers have the same range as TCP port numbers but are distinct. Because the addressing information is so similar between UDP and TCP, ACE's UDP classes use the same addressing class as those wrapping TCP do: `ACE_INET_Addr`.

When deciding whether to use UDP communication, consider these three differences between UDP and TCP.

1. UDP is datagram based, whereas TCP is stream based. If a TCP peer sends, for example, three 256-byte buffers of data, the connected peer application will receive 768 bytes of data in the same order they were transmitted but may receive the data in any number of separate chunks, without any guarantee of where the breaks between chunks will be, if any. Conversely, if a UDP peer sends three 256-byte datagrams, the receiving peer will receive anywhere from zero to all three of them. Any datagram that is received will, however, be the complete 256-byte datagram sent; none will be broken up or coalesced. Therefore, UDP transmissions are more record oriented, whereas with TCP, you need a way to extract the streamed data correctly, referred to as *unmarshaling*.

2. UDP makes no guarantees about the arrival or order of data. Whereas TCP guarantees that any data received is precisely what was sent and that it arrives in order, UDP makes only best-effort delivery. As hinted at earlier, three 256 byte datagrams sent may not all be received. Any that are received will be the complete, correct datagram that was sent; however, datagrams may be lost or reordered in transit. Thus, although UDP relieves you of the need to marshal and unmarshal data on a stream of bytes, you are responsible for any needed reliability that your protocol and/or application requires.

3. Whereas TCP is a one-to-one connection between two peers, UDP offers several modes of operation: unicast, broadcast, and multicast. *Unicast* is a one-to-one operation, similar to TCP. In *Broadcast* mode, each datagram sent is broadcast to every listener on the network or subnetwork the datagram is broadcast on. This mode requires a broadcastable network medium, such as Ethernet. Because it must be processed by each station on the attached network, broadcast network traffic can cause network traffic problems and is generally frowned on. The third mode—multicast—solves the traffic issue of broadcast. Interested applications must join *multicast groups* that have unique IP addresses. Any datagram sent to a multicast group is received only by those stations subscribed to the group. Thus, multicast has the one-to-many nature of broadcast without all the attendant traffic issues.

We'll look at brief examples using UDP in the three addressing modes. Note that all the UDP classes we'll look at can be used with the ACE Reactor framework and that the I/O UDP classes can be used as the peer stream template argument with the `ACE_Svc_Handler` class template. The unicast mode `ACE_SOCK_CODgram` class can also produce a handle that's usable with the Proactor framework's `ACE_Asynch_Read_Dgram` and `ACE_Asynch_Write_Dgram` I/O factory classes.

9.1.1 Unicast Mode

Let's see an example of how to send some data on a unicast UDP socket. For this use case, ACE offers the `ACE_SOCK_Dgram` class:

```
#include "ace/OS.h"
#include "ace/Log_Msg.h"
#include "ace/INET_Addr.h"
#include "ace/SOCK_Dgram.h"

int send_unicast (const ACE_INET_Addr &to)
{
  const char *message = "this is the message!\n";
  ACE_INET_Addr my_addr (ACE_static_cast (u_short, 10101));
  ACE_SOCK_Dgram udp (my_addr);
  ssize_t sent = udp.send (message,
                           ACE_OS_String::strlen (message) + 1,
                           to);
  udp.close ();
  if (sent == -1)
    ACE_ERROR_RETURN ((LM_ERROR, ACE_TEXT ("%p\n"),
                       ACE_TEXT ("send")), -1);
  return 0;
}
```

You'll note two differences from our earlier examples using TCP.

1. You simply open and use `ACE_SOCK_Dgram`. No acceptor or connector is needed.

2. You need to explicitly specify the peer's address when sending a datagram.

These differences are a result of UDP's datagram nature. There is no formally established connection between any two peers; you obtain the peer's address and send directly to that address. Although our simple example sends one datagram and closes the socket, the same socket could be used to send and receive many datagrams, from any mixture of different addresses. Thus, even though UDP unicast mode is one to one, there is no one fixed peer. Each datagram is directed from the sending peer to one other.

If the application you are writing specifies a sending port number—for example, your application is designed to receive datagrams at a known port—you must set that information in an `ACE_INET_Addr` object that specifies the local address. If there is no fixed port, you can pass `ACE_Addr::sap_any` as the address argument to `ACE_SOCK_Dgram::open()`.

You have two ways to obtain the destination address to send a datagram to. First, you can use a well-known or configured IP address and port number, similar to the way you obtain the peer address when actively connecting a TCP socket using `ACE_SOCK_Connector`. This is often the way a client application addresses a known service. The second method, however, is often used in UDP server applications. Because each `ACE_SOCK_Dgram` object can send and receive datagrams from any number of peers, there isn't one fixed address to send to. In fact, the destination can vary with every sent datagram. To accommodate this use case, the sender's address is available with every received datagram. The following example shows how to obtain a datagram sender's address and echo the received data back to the sender:

```
void echo_dgram (void)
{
  ACE_INET_Addr my_addr (ACE_static_cast (u_short, 10102));
  ACE_INET_Addr your_addr;
  ACE_SOCK_Dgram udp (my_addr);
  char buff[BUFSIZ];
  size_t buflen = sizeof (buff);
  ssize_t recv_cnt = udp.recv (buff, buflen, your_addr);
  if (recv_cnt > 0)
    udp.send (buff, ACE_static_cast (size_t, buflen), your_addr);
  udp.close ();
  return;
}
```

The third argument in our use of `ACE_SOCK_Dgram::recv()` receives the address of the datagram sender. We use the address to correctly echo the data back to the original sender. Again, for simplicity, the example uses and closes the UDP socket. This is also a reminder that `ACE_SOCK_Dgram` objects do not close the underlying UDP socket when the object is destroyed. The socket must be explicitly closed before destroying the `ACE_SOCK_Dgram` object, or a handle leak will result.

This may seem like a lot of trouble for cases in which an application uses UDP but always exchanges data with a single peer. It is. For cases in which all communication takes place with a single peer, ACE offers the `ACE_SOCK_CODgram` class (connection-oriented datagram). No formal connection is established at the UDP level; however, the addressing information is set when the object is opened—there's also a constructor variant that accepts the send-to address—so it need not be specified on every data transfer operation. There is still no need for an

acceptor or connector class, as with UDP. The following example briefly shows
how to open an `ACE_SOCK_CODgram` object:

```
#include "ace/SOCK_CODgram.h"
// ...
  const ACE_TCHAR *peer = ACE_TEXT ("other_host:8042");
  ACE_INET_Addr peer_addr (peer);
  ACE_SOCK_CODgram udp;
  if (0 != udp.open (peer_addr))
    ACE_ERROR ((LM_ERROR, ACE_TEXT ("%p\n"), peer));

  // ...

  if (-1 == udp.send (buff, buflen))
    ACE_ERROR ((LM_ERROR, ACE_TEXT ("%p\n"), ACE_TEXT ("send")));
```

The example specifies UDP port 8042 at host `other_host` as the peer to
always send data to. If the `open()` succeeds, the `send()` operations need not
specify an address. All sent data will be directed to the prespecified address.

9.1.2 Broadcast Mode

In broadcast mode, the destination address must still be specified for each send
operation. However, the UDP port number part is all that changes between sends,
because the IP address part is always the IP broadcast address, which is a fixed
value. The `ACE_SOCK_Dgram_Bcast` class takes care of supplying the correct
IP broadcast address for you; you need specify only the UDP port number to
broadcast to. The following is an example:

```
#include "ace/OS.h"
#include "ace/Log_Msg.h"
#include "ace/INET_Addr.h"
#include "ace/SOCK_Dgram_Bcast.h"

int send_broadcast (u_short to_port)
{
  const char *message = "this is the message!\n";
  ACE_INET_Addr my_addr (ACE_static_cast (u_short, 10101));
  ACE_SOCK_Dgram_Bcast udp (my_addr);
  ssize_t sent = udp.send (message,
                           ACE_OS_String::strlen (message) + 1,
                           to_port);
  udp.close ();
```

```
  if (sent == -1)
    ACE_ERROR_RETURN ((LM_ERROR, ACE_TEXT ("%p\n"),
                       ACE_TEXT ("send")), -1);
  return 0;
}
```

The `ACE_SOCK_Dgram_Bcast` class is a subclass of `ACE_SOCK_Dgram`, so all datagram receive operations are similar to those in the unicast examples.

9.1.3 Multicast Mode

UDP multicast mode involves a group of network nodes called a multicast group. The underlying OS-supplied protocol software manages multicast groups by using specialized protocols. The OS directs the group operations based on applications' requests to join—subscribe to—or leave—unsubscribe from—a particular multicast group. Once an application has joined a group, all datagrams sent on the joined socket are sent to the multicast group without specifying the destination address for each send operation.

Each multicast group has a separate IP address. Multicast addresses are IP class D addresses, which are separate from the class A, B, and C addresses that individual host interfaces are assigned. Applications define and assign class D addresses specific to the application.

The following example shows how to join a multicast group and transmit a datagram to the group, using the `ACE_SOCK_Dgram_Mcast` class:

```
#include "ace/OS.h"
#include "ace/Log_Msg.h"
#include "ace/INET_Addr.h"
#include "ace/SOCK_Dgram_Mcast.h"

int send_multicast (const ACE_INET_Addr &mcast_addr)
{
  const char *message = "this is the message!\n";
  ACE_SOCK_Dgram_Mcast udp;
  if (-1 == udp.join (mcast_addr))
    ACE_ERROR_RETURN ((LM_ERROR, ACE_TEXT ("%p\n"),
                       ACE_TEXT ("join")), -1);

  ssize_t sent = udp.send (message,
                           ACE_OS_String::strlen (message) + 1);
  udp.close ();
  if (sent == -1)
```

```
             ACE_ERROR_RETURN ((LM_ERROR, ACE_TEXT ("%p\n"),
                                ACE_TEXT ("send")), -1);
        return 0;
   }
```

As with `ACE_SOCK_Dgram_Mcast`, `ACE_SOCK_Dgram_Mcast` is a subclass of `ACE_SOCK_Dgram`; therefore, `recv()` methods are inherited from `ACE_SOCK_Dgram`.

9.2   Intrahost Communication

The classes described in this section can be used for intrahost communication only. They can offer some simplicity over interhost communications, owing to simplified addressing procedures. Intrahost IPC can also be significantly faster than interhost IPC, owing to the absence of heavy protocol layers and network latency, as well as the ability to avoid relatively low bandwidth communications channels. However, some interhost communications facilities, such as TCP/IP sockets, also work quite well for intrahost application because of improved optimization in the protocol implementations. TCP/IP sockets are also the most commonly available IPC mechanism across a wide variety of platforms, so if portability is a high concern, TCP/IP sockets can simplify your code greatly. The bottom line in IPC mechanism selection is to weigh the options, maybe do your own performance benchmarks, and decide what's best in your particular case. Fortunately, ACE's IPC mechanisms offer very similar programming interfaces, so it's relatively easy to exchange them for testing.

9.2.1   Files

The `ACE_FILE_IO` and `ACE_FILE_Connector` classes implement file I/O in a way that allows their use in the Acceptor-Connector framework, albeit only with the Connector side. The associated addressing class is `ACE_FILE_Addr`, which encapsulates the pathname to a file.

9.2.2   Pipes and FIFOs

Pipes and FIFOs are UNIX mechanisms. FIFOs are also sometimes referred to as named pipes but are not the same thing as Windows Named Pipes. Following are the more common classes in this area. Most are platform specific, so check the reference documentation for full details.

- `ACE_FIFO_Recv`, `ACE_FIFO_Send`, `ACE_FIFO_Recv_Msg`, and `ACE_FIFO_Send_Msg` work with UNIX/POSIX FIFOs in both stream and message mode. There is no addressing class; specify the FIFO name to the particular data transfer class you need.

- `ACE_Pipe` provides a simple UNIX/POSIX pipe. Although the pipe is distinctly a UNIX/POSIX capability, `ACE_Pipe` emulates it on Windows, using loopback TCP/IP sockets. It works in a pinch, but be aware of the difference. If you must grab one of the pipe handles and use it for low level I/O, `ACE_OS::read()` and `ACE_OS::write()` will not work on Windows, although it will most everywhere else, because it's a socket handle on Windows; use `ACE_OS::recv()` and `ACE_OS::send()` if you must use one of these handles for low-level I/O on Windows. As with the FIFO classes, there's no addressing class, as pipes don't have names or any other addressing method.

- `ACE_SPIPE_Acceptor`, `ACE_SPIPE_Connector`, `ACE_SPIPE_Stream`, and `ACE_SPIPE_Addr` follow the scheme for easy substitution in the Acceptor-Connector framework. Beware, though; these classes wrap the STREAMS pipe facility on UNIX/POSIX, where it's available, and Named Pipes on Windows. The two aren't really the same, but they program similarly, and if you need to use one on a given platform, you simply need to know to use `ACE_SPIPE`.

9.2.3 Shared Memory Stream

This set of classes comprises `ACE_MEM_Acceptor`, `ACE_MEM_Connector`, `ACE_MEM_Stream`, and `ACE_MEM_Addr`. The classes in the shared memory stream facility fits into the Acceptor-Connector framework but uses shared memory—memory-mapped files, actually—for data transfer. This can result in very good performance because data isn't transferred but rather is placed in memory that's shared between processes.

As you may imagine, synchronizing access to this shared data is where the tricky parts of this facility enter. Also, because there's no way to use `select()` on one of these objects, the `ACE_MEM_Stream` class can adapt its synchronization mechanism to one that allows the facility to be registered with a reactor implementation that's based on TCP/IP sockets.

9.3 Summary

Interprocess Communication (IPC) is an important part of many applications and is absolutely foundational to networked applications. Today's popular operating environments offer a wide range of IPC mechanisms, accessible via varying APIs, for both interhost and intrahost communication.

ACE helps to unify the programming interfaces to many disparate IPC types, as well as avoid the accidental complexity associated with programming at the OS API level. This uniformity of class interfaces across ACE's IPC classes makes it fairly easy to substitute them to meet changing requirements or performance needs.

Part III

Process and Thread Management

Chapter 10
Process Management

Processes are the primary abstraction an operating system uses to represent running programs. Unfortunately, the meaning of the term *process* varies widely. On most general-purpose operating systems, such as UNIX and Windows, a process is seen as a resource container that manages the address space and other resources of a program. This is the abstraction that is supported in ACE. Some operating systems, such as VxWorks, do not have processes at all but instead have one large address space in which *tasks* run. The ACE process classes are not pertinent for these operating systems.

In this chapter, we first explain how to use the simple `ACE_Process` wrapper class to create a process and then manage child process termination. Next, we discuss how you can protect globally shared system resources from concurrent access by one or more processes, using special mutexes for process-level locking. Finally, we look at the high-level process manager class that offers integration with the Reactor framework.

10.1 Spawning a New Process

ACE hides all process creation and control APIs from the user in the `ACE_Process` wrapper class. This wrapper class allows a programmer to spawn new processes and subsequently wait for their termination. You usually use one

ACE_Process object for each new process and are allowed to set several options for the child process:

- Setting standard I/O handles
- Specifying how handle inheritance will work between the two processes
- Setting the child's environment block and command line
- Specifying security attributes on Windows or set uid/gid/euid on UNIX.

For those of you from the UNIX world, the spawn() method does not have semantics similar to the fork() system call but is instead similar to the system() function available on most UNIX systems. You can force ACE_Process to do a simple fork() but in most cases are better off using ACE_OS::fork() to accomplish a simple process fork, if you need it.

Spawning a process using the ACE_Process class is a two-step process.

1. Create a new ACE_Process_Options object specifying the desired properties of the new child process.

2. Spawn a new process using the ACE_Process::spawn() method.

In the next example, we illustrate creating a slave process and then waiting for it to terminate. To do this, we create an object of type Manager, which spawns another process running the same example program, albeit with different options. Once the slave process is created, it creates an object of type Slave, which performs some artificial work and exits. Meanwhile, the master process waits for the slave process to complete before it too exits.

Because the same program is run as both the master and the slave, the command line arguments are used to distinguish which mode it is to run in; if there are arguments, the program knows to run in slave mode and otherwise runs in master mode:

```
int ACE_TMAIN (int argc, ACE_TCHAR *argv[])
{
  if (argc > 1)    // Slave mode
    {
      Slave s;
      return s.doWork ();
    }

  // Else, Master mode
  Manager m (argv[0]);
  return m.doWork ();
}
```

The `Manager` class has a single public method that is responsible for setting the options for the new slave process, spawning it, and then waiting for its termination:

```
class Manager : public ACE_Process
{
public:
  Manager (const ACE_TCHAR* program_name)
  {
    ACE_TRACE (ACE_TEXT ("Manager::Manager"));
    ACE_OS::strcpy (programName_, program_name);
  }

  int doWork (void)
  {
    ACE_TRACE (ACE_TEXT ("Manager::doWork"));

    // Spawn the new process; prepare() hook is called first.
    ACE_Process_Options options;
    pid_t pid = this->spawn (options);
    if (pid == -1)
      ACE_ERROR_RETURN((LM_ERROR, ACE_TEXT ("%p\n"),
                        ACE_TEXT ("spawn")), -1);

    // Wait forever for my child to exit.
    if (this->wait () == -1)
      ACE_ERROR_RETURN ((LM_ERROR, ACE_TEXT ("%p\n"),
                        ACE_TEXT ("wait")), -1);

    // Dump whatever happened.
    this->dumpRun ();
    return 0;
  }
```

An `ACE_Process_Options` object carries the options for the new process. A single options object can be used for multiple `ACE_Process` objects if desired. The `ACE_Process` object on the stack represents the process to be spawned. The process object is used to spawn a new process, based on the process options passed in. The `spawn()` method uses `execvp()` on UNIX and `CreateProcess()` on Windows. Once the child process has been spawned successfully, the parent process uses the `wait()` method to wait for the child to finish and exit. The `wait()` method collects the exit status of the child process and avoids zombie processes on UNIX. On Windows, the `wait()` method causes

the closing of the process and thread HANDLEs that CreateProcess()
created. Once the slave returns, the master prints out the activity performed by the
slave and the master to the standard output stream.

Let's take a closer look at how we set up the options for the child process. The
ACE_Process::spawn() method calls the ACE_Process::prepare()
hook method on the process object before creating the new process. The
prepare() method enables us to inspect and modify the options for the new
process. This method is a very convenient place to set platform-specific options.
Our example's prepare() hook method follows:

```cpp
// prepare() is inherited from ACE_Process.
int prepare (ACE_Process_Options &options)
{
  ACE_TRACE (ACE_TEXT ("Manager::prepare"));

  options.command_line ("%s 1", this->programName_);
  if (this->setStdHandles (options) == -1 ||
      this->setEnvVariable (options) == -1)
    return -1;
#if !defined (ACE_WIN32)
  return this->setUserID (options);
#else
  return 0;
#endif
}


int setStdHandles (ACE_Process_Options &options)
{
  ACE_TRACE(ACE_TEXT ("Manager::setStdHandles"));

  ACE_OS::unlink ("output.dat");
  this->outputfd_ =
    ACE_OS::open ("output.dat", O_RDWR | O_CREAT);
  return options.set_handles
    (ACE_STDIN, ACE_STDOUT, this->outputfd_);
}


int setEnvVariable (ACE_Process_Options &options)
{
  ACE_TRACE (ACE_TEXT ("Manager::setEnvVariables"));
  return options.setenv ("PRIVATE_VAR=/that/seems/to/be/it");
}
```

First, we set the command line to be the same program name as the current program (as the child and parent processes are both represented by the same program) plus a single argument. The extra argument indicates that the program is to run in slave mode. After this, the standard input, output, and error handles for the child process are set up. The input and output handles will be shared between the two processes, whereas the STDERR handle for the child is set to point to a newly created file, output.dat. We also show how to set up an environment variable in the parent process that the child process should be able to see and use.

For non-Windows runs, we also set the effective user ID we want the child process to run as. We discuss this in a little detail later.

If the prepare() hook returns 0, ACE_Process::spawn() continues to spawn the new process. If prepare() returns −1, the spawn() method will not attempt to spawn the new process.

To reiterate, the Manager goes through the following steps:

1. Calls spawn() to spawn the child process
2. ACE_Process::spawn() calls back to the prepare() hook to set up process options, including the command line, environment variables, and I/O streams
3. Waits for the child to exit
4. Displays the results of the child process run.

Now let's look at the how the Slave runs. The Slave class has a single method that exercises the validity of the input, output, and error handles, along with the environment variable that was created, and displays its own and its parent's process ID:

```
class Slave
{
public:
  Slave ()
  {
    ACE_TRACE (ACE_TEXT ("Slave::Slave"));
  }

  int doWork (void)
  {
    ACE_TRACE (ACE_TEXT ("Slave::doWork"));

    ACE_DEBUG ((LM_INFO,
                ACE_TEXT ("(%P) started at %T, parent is %d\n"),
                ACE_OS::getppid ()));
```

```
    this->showWho ();
    ACE_DEBUG ((LM_INFO,
                ACE_TEXT ("(%P) the private environment is %s\n"),
                ACE_OS::getenv ("PRIVATE_VAR")));

    ACE_TCHAR str[128];
    ACE_OS::sprintf (str, ACE_TEXT ("(%d) Enter your command\n"),
                     ACE_OS::getpid ());
    ACE_OS::write (ACE_STDOUT, str, ACE_OS::strlen (str));
    this->readLine (str);
    ACE_DEBUG ((LM_DEBUG, ACE_TEXT ("(%P) Executed: %C\n"),
                str));
    return 0;
}
```

After the slave process is created, the doWork() method is called. This
method

- Checks what the effective user ID of the program is.
- Checks and prints the private environment variable PRIVATE_VAR.
- Asks the user for a string command.
- Reads the string command from standard input.
- Prints the string back out again to the standard error stream. (Remember that
  all ACE_DEBUG() messages are set to go to the standard error stream by
  default.)

After determining that the slave has completed and exited, the master displays
the output that the slave generated in the debug log. Because the standard error
stream was set to the file output.dat, all the Manager object needs to do is
dump this file. Note that when we set the STDERR handle for the child, we kept a
reference to it open in the Master. We can use this open handle to do our dump.
Because the file handle was shared between the slave and the master, we first seek
back to the beginning of the file and then move forward:

```
int dumpRun (void)
{
  ACE_TRACE (ACE_TEXT ("Manager::dumpRun"));

  if (ACE_OS::lseek (this->outputfd_, 0, SEEK_SET) == -1)
    ACE_ERROR_RETURN ((LM_ERROR, ACE_TEXT ("%p\n"),
                       ACE_TEXT ("lseek")), -1);

  char buf[1024];
```

```
    int length = 0;

    // Read the contents of the error stream written
    // by the child and print it out.
    while ((length = ACE_OS::read (this->outputfd_,
                                   buf, sizeof(buf)-1)) > 0)
      {
        buf[length] = 0;
        ACE_DEBUG ((LM_DEBUG, ACE_TEXT ("%C\n"), buf));
      }

    ACE_OS::close (this->outputfd_);
    return 0;
}
```

10.1.1   Security Parameters

As mentioned earlier, `ACE_Process_Options` allows you to specify the
effective, real, and group IDs that you want the child process to run with.
Continuing with the previous example, the following code illustrates setting the
effective user ID of the child process to be the user ID of the user `nobody`. Of
course, for this to run on your system, you must make sure that there is a `nobody`
account and that the user running the program has permission to perform the
effective user ID switch.

```
int setUserID (ACE_Process_Options &options)
{
  ACE_TRACE (ACE_TEXT ("Manager::setUserID"));
  passwd* pw = ACE_OS::getpwnam ("nobody");
  if (pw == 0)
    return -1;
  options.seteuid (pw->pw_uid);
  return 0;
}
```

Note that this code works only for those systems that have a UNIX-like notion of
these IDs. If you are using a Windows system, you can instead use the
`get_process_attributes()` and `set_process_attributes()`
methods to specify the `SECURITY_ATTRIBUTES` for the new process and its
primary thread; however, you cannot use `ACE_Process` to spawn a process for
client impersonation.

10.1.2 Other ACE_Process Hook Methods

In addition to the `prepare()` hook method that prepares process options, the `ACE_Process` class offers two other hook methods that can be overridden to customize processing:

1. `parent(pid_t child)` is called back in the parent process immediately after the `fork()` call on UNIX platforms or the `CreateProcess()` call on Windows.

2. `child(pid_t parent)` is called back in the child process after `fork()` completes but before the subsequent `exec()` call, which occurs if you do not specify `ACE_Process_Options::NO_EXEC` in the creation flags for the process options, the default case. At this point, the new enviroment, including handles and working directory, are not set. This method is not called back on Windows platforms, as there is no concept of a `fork()` and subsequent `exec()` here.

10.2 Using the ACE_Process_Manager

Besides the relatively simple `ACE_Process` wrapper, ACE also provides a sophisticated process manager, `ACE_Process_Manager`, which allows a user, with a single call, to spawn and wait for the termination of multiple processes. You can also register event handlers that are called back when a child process terminates.

10.2.1 Spawning and Terminating Processes

The `spawn()` methods available in the `ACE_Process_Manager` class are similar to those available with `ACE_Process`. Using them entails creating an `ACE_Process_Options` object and passing it to the `spawn()` method to create the process. With `ACE_Process_Manager`, you can additionally spawn multiple processes at once, using the `spawn_n()` method. You can also wait for *all* these processes to exit and correctly remove all the resources held by them. In addition, you can forcibly terminate a process that was previously spawned by `ACE_Process_Manager`.

The following example illustrates some of these new process manager features:

```cpp
#include "ace/Process_Manager.h"

static const int NCHILDREN = 2;

int ACE_TMAIN (int argc, ACE_TCHAR *argv[])
{
  if (argc > 1)       // Running as a child.
    {
      ACE_OS::sleep (10);
    }
  else               // Running as a parent.
    {
      // Get the processwide process manager.
      ACE_Process_Manager* pm = ACE_Process_Manager::instance ();

      // Specify the options for the new processes
      // to be spawned.
      ACE_Process_Options options;
      options.command_line (ACE_TEXT ("%s a"), argv[0]);

      // Spawn two child processes.
      pid_t pids[NCHILDREN];
      pm->spawn_n (NCHILDREN, options, pids);

      // Destroy the first child.
      pm->terminate (pids[0]);

      // Wait for the child we just terminated.
      ACE_exitcode status;
      pm->wait (pids[0], &status);

      // Get the results of the termination.

#if !defined(ACE_WIN32)
      if (WIFSIGNALED (status) != 0)
        ACE_DEBUG ((LM_DEBUG,
                    ACE_TEXT ("%d died because of a signal ")
                    ACE_TEXT ("of type %d\n"),
                    pids[0], WTERMSIG (status)));
#else
      ACE_DEBUG
        ((LM_DEBUG,
          ACE_TEXT ("The process terminated with exit code %d\n"),
          status));
#endif /*ACE_WIN32*/
```

```
            // Wait for all (only one left) of the
            // children to exit.
            pm->wait (0);
        }

    return 0;
}
```

The ACE_Process_Manager is used to spawn NCHILDREN child
processes. (Note that once again, we spawn the same program.) Once the child
processes start, they immediately fall asleep. The parent process then explicitly
terminates the first child, using the terminate() method. This should cause
the child process to abort immediately. The only argument to this call is the
process ID of the process that you wish to terminate. If you pass in the process ID
0, the process manager waits for any of its managed processes to exit. On UNIX
platforms, that does not work as well as one would hope, and you may end up
collecting the status for a process that is not managed by your process manager.
(For more on this, see the ACE reference documentation.) Immediately after
issuing the termination call on the child process, the parent uses the process
manager to do a blocking wait() on the exit of that child. Once the child exits,
the wait() call returns with the termination code of the child process.

Note that on UNIX systems, ACE_Process_Manager issues a signal to
terminate the child once you invoke the terminate() method. You can observe
this by examining the termination status of the process.

After completing the wait on the first process, the parent process waits for all
the rest of its children by using another blocking wait() call on the process
manager. To indicate this, we pass a 0 timeout value to the wait() method. Note
that you can also specify a relative timeout value after which the blocking wait
will return. If the wait is unsuccessful and a timeout does occur, the method
returns 0.

10.2.2   Event Handling

In the previous example, we showed how a parent can block, waiting for all its
children to complete. Most of the time, you will find that your parent process has
other work to do besides waiting for terminating children, especially if you have
implemented a traditional network server that spawns child processes to handle
network requests. In this case, you will want to keep the parent process free to
handle further requests besides reaping your child processes.

To handle this use case, the `ACE_Process_Manager` exit-handling methods have been designed to work in conjunction with the ACE Reactor framework. This next example illustrates how you can set up a termination callback handler that is called back whenever a process is terminated:

```
class DeathHandler: public ACE_Event_Handler
{
public:
  DeathHandler () : count_(0)
  {
    ACE_TRACE (ACE_TEXT ("DeathHandler::DeathHandler"));
  }

  virtual int handle_exit (ACE_Process * process)
  {
    ACE_TRACE (ACE_TEXT ("DeathHandler::handle_exit"));

    ACE_DEBUG
      ((LM_DEBUG,
        ACE_TEXT ("Process %d exited with exit code %d\n"),
        process->getpid (), process->return_value ()));

    if (++count_ == NCHILDREN)
      ACE_Reactor::instance ()->end_reactor_event_loop ();

    return 0;
  }

private:
  int count_;
};
```

In this program, we create an `ACE_Event_Handler` subclass called `DeathHandler` that is used to handle process termination events for all the `NCHILDREN` processes that are spawned by the process manager. When a process exits, the reactor synchronously invokes the `handle_exit()` method on the event handler, passing in a pointer to the `ACE_Process` object representing the process that has just exited. This works under the hood as follows.

- On POSIX platforms, `ACE_Process_Manager` is registered to receive the `SIGCHLD` signal. On receipt of the signal, `ACE_Process_Manager` uses the reactor's notification mechanism to regain control in normal process context.

- On Windows platforms, ACE_Process_Manager is registered to receive event notifications on the process handle via the Reactor framework. Because only the ACE_WFMO_Reactor reactor implementation supports the handle notification capability, child exit notification does not work if you change the reactor implementation on Windows.

When ACE_Process_Manager is notified that the child process has exited, it invokes the handler's handle_exit() method:

```
int ACE_TMAIN (int argc, ACE_TCHAR *argv[])
{
  if (argc > 1)         // Running as a child.
    return 0;

  // Instantiate a process manager with space for
  // 10 processes.
  ACE_Process_Manager pm (10, ACE_Reactor::instance ());

  // Create a process termination handler.
  DeathHandler handler;

  // Specify the options for the new processes to be spawned.
  ACE_Process_Options options;
  options.command_line (ACE_TEXT ("%s a"), argv[0]);

  // Spawn two child processes.
  pid_t pids[NCHILDREN];
  pm.spawn_n (NCHILDREN, options, pids);

  // Register handler to be called when these processes exit.
  for (int i = 0; i < NCHILDREN; i++)
    pm.register_handler (&handler, pids[i]);

  // Run the reactor event loop waiting for events to occur.
  ACE_Reactor::instance ()->run_reactor_event_loop ();

  return 0;
}
```

10.3 Synchronization Using ACE_Process_Mutex

To synchronize threads, you need synchronization primitives, such as mutexes or semaphores. (We discuss these primitives in significant detail in Section 12.2.) When executing in separate processes, the threads are running in different address spaces. Synchronization between such threads becomes a little more difficult. In such cases, you can either

- Create the synchronization primitives that you are using in shared memory and set the appropriate options to ensure that they work between processes
- Use the special process synchronization primitives that are provided as a part of the ACE library

ACE provides a number of process-scope synchronization classes that are analogous to the thread-scope wrappers discussed in Chapter 14. This section explains how you can use the ACE_Process_Mutex class to ensure synchronization between threads running in different processes.

ACE provides, in the form of the ACE_Process_Mutex class, for named mutexes that can be used across address spaces. Because the mutex is named, you can recreate an object representing the same mutex by passing in the same name to the constructor of ACE_Process_Mutex.

In the next example, we create a named mutex: GlobalMutex. We then create two processes that cooperatively share an imaginary global resource, coordinating their access by using the mutex. The two processes both do this by creating an instance of the GResourceUser, an object that intermittently uses the globally shared resource.

We use the same argument-length trick that we used in the previous example to start the same program in different modes. If the program is started to be the parent, it spawns two child processes. If started as a child process, the program gets the named mutex GlobalMutex from the OS by instantiating an ACE_Process_Mutex object, passing it the name GlobalMutex. This either creates the named mutex—if this is the first time we asked for it—or attaches to the existing mutex—if the second process does the construction. The mutex is passed to a resource-acquirer object that uses it to ensure protected access to a global resource.

Again, note that even though we create separate ACE_Process_Mutex objects—each child process creates one—they both refer to the same shared mutex. The mutex itself is managed by the operating system, which recognizes that both mutex instances refer to the same GlobalMutex:

```
int ACE_TMAIN (int argc, ACE_TCHAR *argv[])
{
  if (argc > 1)        // Run as the child.
    {
      // Create or get the global mutex.
      ACE_Process_Mutex mutex ("GlobalMutex");

      GResourceUser acquirer (mutex);
      acquirer.run ();
    }
  else                 // Run as the parent.
    {
      ACE_Process_Options options;
      options.command_line ("%s a", argv[0]);
      ACE_Process processa, processb;

      pid_t pida = processa.spawn (options);
      pid_t pidb = processb.spawn (options);

      ACE_DEBUG ((LM_DEBUG,
                  ACE_TEXT ("Spawned processes; pids %d:%d\n"),
                  pida, pidb));

      if (processa.wait () == -1)
        ACE_ERROR_RETURN ((LM_ERROR, ACE_TEXT ("%p\n"),
                           ACE_TEXT ("processa wait")), -1);

      if (processb.wait () == -1)
        ACE_ERROR_RETURN ((LM_ERROR, ACE_TEXT ("%p\n"),
                           ACE_TEXT ("processb wait")), -1);
    }

  return 0;
}
```

The GResourceUser class represents a user of an unspecified global resource that is protected by a mutex. When this class's run() method is called, it intermittently acquires the global mutex, works with the global resource, and then releases the mutex. Because it releases the resource between runs, the second process a chance to acquire it:

```
class GResourceUser
{
public:
  GResourceUser (ACE_Process_Mutex &mutex) : gmutex_(mutex)
```

```
    {
      ACE_TRACE (ACE_TEXT ("GResourceUser::GResourceUser"));
    }

    void run (void)
    {
      ACE_TRACE (ACE_TEXT ("GResourceUser::run"));

      int count = 0;
      while (count++ < 10)
        {
          int result = this->gmutex_.acquire ();
          ACE_ASSERT (result == 0);

          ACE_DEBUG ((LM_DEBUG,
                      ACE_TEXT ("(%P| %t) has the mutex\n")));

          // Access Global resource
          ACE_OS::sleep (1);

          result = this->gmutex_.release ();
          ACE_ASSERT (result == 0);
          ACE_OS::sleep (1);     // Give other process a chance.
        }
    }

private:
  ACE_Process_Mutex &gmutex_;
};
```

The results from running the program show the two processes competing with each other to acquire the shared resource:

```
(8077| 1024) has the mutex
Spawned processes; pids 8077:8078
(8078| 1024) has the mutex
(8077| 1024) has the mutex
(8078| 1024) has the mutex
(8077| 1024) has the mutex
(8078| 1024) has the mutex
(8077| 1024) has the mutex
(8078| 1024) has the mutex
(8077| 1024) has the mutex
(8078| 1024) has the mutex
(8077| 1024) has the mutex
```

```
(8078|  1024)  has  the  mutex
(8077|  1024)  has  the  mutex
(8078|  1024)  has  the  mutex
(8077|  1024)  has  the  mutex
(8078|  1024)  has  the  mutex
(8077|  1024)  has  the  mutex
(8078|  1024)  has  the  mutex
(8077|  1024)  has  the  mutex
(8078|  1024)  has  the  mutex
```

For UNIX users, the `ACE_Process_Mutex` maps to a System V shared semaphore. Unlike most resources, these semaphores are not automatically released once all references to it are destroyed. Therefore, be careful when using this class, and make sure that the destructor of the `ACE_Process_Mutex` is called, even in the case of abnormal exits. Another option for UNIX users is to use `ACE_SV_Semaphore_Complex`, which will automatically reference count and remove the mutex once all processes referencing it have exited. This automatic reference counting/removal process will work if any process other than the last does an exit, intentional or unintentional, without properly closing the mutex.

10.4 Summary

In this chapter, we introduced the ACE classes that support process creation, life-cycle management, and synchronization. We looked at the simple `ACE_Process` wrapper and the sophisticated `ACE_Process_Manager`. We also looked at synchronization primitives that can be used to synchronize threads that are running in separate processes.

Chapter 11
Signals

Signals act as software interrupts and indicate to the application such asynchronous events as a user pressing the interrupt key on a terminal, a broken pipe between processes, job control functions, and so on. To handle signals, a program can associate a signal handler with a particular signal type. For example, for the interrupt key signal, you can set up a handler that instead of terminating the process, first asks whether the user wishes to terminate. In most cases, your application will want to handle most error signals so that you can either gracefully terminate or retry the current task.

Once the signal is raised, the associated signal handler is invoked in *signal context*, which is separate the interrupted main execution context. After the signal handler returns, execution continues back in the main context from wherever it happened to be right before the signal was received, as if the interruption never occurred.

Windows provides minimal support for signals for ANSI (American National Standards Institute) compatibility. A minimal set of signals is available, but even fewer are raised by the operating system. Therefore, the usefulness of signals is generally somewhat limited for Windows programmers.

In Chapter 7, we explained how you can use the ACE Reactor framework to handle signal events, along with several other event types. Here, we talk about how to use the signal-handling features of ACE, independent of the Reactor framework. This comes in handy in the following situations.

- You do not want to add the extra complexity of the reactor, as it isn't needed.

- The signal-handling actions aren't associated with any of your event handlers.
- You are developing a resource-constrained system in which you cannot afford to waste any memory.

In this chapter, we explain how ACE makes it easy to set up one or more handlers for a signal type. We start by looking at the simple `ACE_Sig_Action` wrapper, which calls a user-specified handler function when a signal occurs. We then look at the higher-level `ACE_Sig_Handler` class, which invokes an `ACE_Event_Handler::handle_signal()` callback when the specified signal occurs. Finally, we talk about the `ACE_Sig_Guard` class, which allows you to guard certain sections of your code from signal interruptions.

11.1 Using Wrappers

The POSIX `sigaction()` call enables a programmer to associate an action, such as the execution of a callback function, with the occurrence of a particular signal. ACE provides a wrapper around the `sigaction()` call. This wrapper provides a type-safe interface for signal registration. ACE also provides a type-safe wrapper to one of its argument types, `sigset_t`. This type represents a collection of signals and is discussed in detail in Section 7.3.2.

The following example illustrates the use of wrappers to register callback functions for a few signals:

```
#include "ace/Signal.h"

// Forward declarations.
static void my_sighandler (int signo);
static void register_actions ();

int ACE_TMAIN (int, ACE_TCHAR *[])
{
  ACE_TRACE (ACE_TEXT ("::main"));

  ::register_actions ();    // Register actions to happen.

  // This will be raised immediately.
  ACE_OS::kill (ACE_OS::getpid (), SIGUSR2);

  // This will pend until the first signal is completely
  // handled and returns, because we masked it out
  // in the registerAction call.
```

```
ACE_OS::kill (ACE_OS::getpid (), SIGUSR1);

while (ACE_OS::sleep (100) == -1)
  {
    if (errno == EINTR)
      continue;
    else
      ACE_OS::exit (1);
  }
return 0;
}
```

When we enter the program, we first register actions, using the ACE-provided `ACE_Sig_Action` class. Then we explicitly raise certain signals, using the `ACE_OS::kill ()` method. In this case, we are asking for `SIGUSR2` to be sent to the current process, followed by `SIGUSR1`; both of these signal types are meant to be user definable.

Our signal handler function follows:

```
static void my_sighandler (int signo)
{
  ACE_TRACE (ACE_TEXT ("::my_sighandler"));

  ACE_OS::kill (ACE_OS::getpid (), SIGUSR1);

  if (signo == SIGUSR1)
    ACE_DEBUG ((LM_DEBUG, ACE_TEXT ("Signal SIGUSR1\n")));
  else
    ACE_DEBUG ((LM_DEBUG, ACE_TEXT ("Signal SIGUSR2\n")));

  ACE_OS::sleep (10);
}
```

Note the signature of the function. It returns `void` and is passed an integer argument representing the signal that occurred. Under the current model for signals, only one signal handler function can be associated for any particular signal number. This means that you can't have multiple functions be called back when a single signal is raised. You can, of course, associate the same signal handler function for multiple signals, as we have done in this example.

In this particular handler, once a signal is received, we sleep for 10 seconds before returning to regular program execution. *Never do something like this in actual programs.* In general, signal handler functions should be very light and should return immediately; otherwise, you will block execution of the rest of your program. Furthermore, the actions allowed in signal context are restricted; check your OS documentation for details. Signal handler functions are generally used to indicate to the application the occurrence of a signal.

The work that must be done owing to the signal occurs after the signal handler has returned. One way to do this is to use the ACE_Reactor notification mechanism (see Section 7.4) to transfer control back to normal execution context.

The following code shows how we register our signal handler:

```
static void register_actions ()
{
  ACE_TRACE (ACE_TEXT ("::register_actions"));

  ACE_Sig_Action sa (my_sighandler);

  // Make sure we specify that SIGUSR1 will be masked out
  // during the signal handler's execution.
  ACE_Sig_Set ss;
  ss.sig_add (SIGUSR1);
  sa.mask (ss);

  // Register the same handler function for these
  // two signals.
  sa.register_action (SIGUSR1);
  sa.register_action (SIGUSR2);
}
```

During registration, we create an ACE_Sig_Action object on the stack, passing in the address of a signal handler function that will be called back. We don't in fact register for the callback in the constructor. Instead, we defer that and do a series of register_action() calls, registering our callback function for SIGUSR1 and SIGUSR2.

Before registration, we also create an ACE_Sig_Set container and add SIGUSR1 to it. We then add this set of signals as a mask to the our sa object. When the sa object registers its action, it passes in this mask to the OS, informing it to automatically disable these signals during the execution of the signal handler function. This is why even though we explicitly raise SIGUSR1 during the execution of the signal handler, we don't see the signal handler being executed for SIGUSR1 until after the handler returns.

Be careful that you specify the mask before you register your action with the OS using the `register_action()` method. Otherwise, the OS will be unaware of this specification.

Note that you do not need to keep the `ACE_Sig_Action` object around after you register the action you want for a particular signal. If you wish to change the disposition of a certain signal you set up previously, you can create another `ACE_Sig_Action` object and do this.

You probably noticed the strange, `errno`-checking loop that we executed around the `ACE_OS::sleep()` in the `main` function of the previous example. The reason we needed to do this is that certain blocking system calls, such as `read()`, `write()`, and `ioctl()`, become unblocked on the occurrence of a signal. Once these calls become unblocked, they return with `errno` set to `EINTR`, or interrupted by a signal.

This can be painful to deal with in programs that make use of signals. Therefore, most implementations that provide the `sigaction()` function allow you to specify a flag, `SA_RESTART`, to cause signal-interrupted calls to automatically continue transparent to the programmer. Be careful though; every version of UNIX and UNIX-like operating systems deals differently with which calls are and are not restarted. Check your OS documentation for details.

In general, however, most SVR4 UNIX platforms provide `sigaction()` and the `SA_RESTART` flag. Using ACE, you can call the `ACE_Sig_Action::flags()` method to set `SA_RESTART`, or you can pass it in as an argument to the constructor of an `ACE_Sig_Action` object.

11.2 Event Handlers

Bundled above the type-safe C++ wrappers for `sigaction` and `sigset_t` is an object-oriented event handler-based signal registration and dispatching scheme. This is available through the `ACE_Sig_Handler` class, which allows a client programmer to register `ACE_Event_Handler`-based objects for callback on the occurrence of signals. The `ACE_Event_Handler` type is central to the ACE Reactor framework, but there is no registration with a reactor when used with `ACE_Sig_Handler`.

As client programmers, we must subclass from `ACE_Event_Handler` and implement the callback method `handle_signal()`:

```
class MySignalHandler : public ACE_Event_Handler
{
public:
  MySignalHandler (int signum) : signum_(signum)
  { }

  virtual ~MySignalHandler()
  { }

  virtual int handle_signal (int signum,
                             siginfo_t * = 0,
                             ucontext_t * = 0)
  {
    ACE_TRACE (ACE_TEXT ("MySignalHandler::handle_signal"));

    // Make sure the right handler was called back.
    ACE_ASSERT (signum == this->signum_);

    ACE_DEBUG ((LM_DEBUG, ACE_TEXT ("%S occured\n"), signum));
    return 0;
  }

private:
  int signum_;
};
```

We start by creating a signal handler class that publicly derives from the
ACE_Event_Handler base class. We need to implement only the
handle_signal() method here, as our event handler can handle only
"signal"-based events. The siginfo_t and ucontext_t are also passed back
to the handle_signal() method, in addition to the signal number, when the
signal event occurs. This is in accordance with the new sigaction() signature;
we will discuss the siginfo_t and ucontext_t types in Section 11.2.1 and
Section 11.2.2, respectively.

```
int ACE_TMAIN (int, ACE_TCHAR *[])
{
  MySignalHandler h1 (SIGUSR1), h2 (SIGUSR2);
  ACE_Sig_Handler handler;
  handler.register_handler (SIGUSR1, &h1);
  handler.register_handler (SIGUSR2, &h2);

  ACE_OS::kill (ACE_OS::getpid (), SIGUSR1);
  ACE_OS::kill (ACE_OS::getpid (), SIGUSR2);
```

```
    int time = 10;
    while ((time = ACE_OS::sleep (time)) == -1)
      {
        if (errno == EINTR)
          continue;
        else
          {
            ACE_ERROR_RETURN ((LM_ERROR,
                               ACE_TEXT ("%p\n"),
                               ACE_TEXT ("sleep")), -1);
          }
      }
    return 0;
}
```

After the program starts, we create two signal event handler objects on the stack and register them to be called back for different signals. Registration occurs using the `ACE_Sig_Handler::register_handler()` method. This method accepts a signal number and a pointer to an `ACE_Event_Handler` object that you want to be called back when the signal occurs. You can also pass in a new `ACE_Sig_Action` that contains the mask and flags you want set up for the action associated with the signal you are currently registering for. This method can also be used to return the old event handler and old `ACE_Sig_Action` struct.

After we register our event handlers to be called back, we raise two signals that are caught in their respective event handlers. After sleeping until the signals have been handled, exit the program.

11.2.1 Introducing siginfo_t

Thus far, we have ignored the `siginfo_t` parameter of the `handle_signal()` method. This parameter contains more information about the causes and attributes of the signal that is being delivered. To illustrate what `siginfo_t` provides, we touch on a few examples here and encourage you to study the `sigaction()` man page for more detail on the data available in the `siginfo_t` structure.

The meaning of the information in the `siginfo_t` structure varies, depending on the signal caught. In our next example, we switch on the value of the signal to determine what information is relevant.

We begin our signal-handling method by using the `%S` format specifier to display a description of the signal received. If the `siginfo_t` structure was not provided, we exit:

```
int handle_signal (int signum,
                    siginfo_t * siginfo = 0,
                    ucontext_t * = 0)
{
  ACE_DEBUG ((LM_INFO, ACE_TEXT ("Received signal [%S]\n"),
             signum));
  if (siginfo == 0)
    {
      ACE_DEBUG ((LM_INFO,
                  ACE_TEXT ("No siginfo_t available for ")
                  ACE_TEXT ("signal [%S]\n"),
                  signum));
      return 0;
    }
```

Now, `si_signo`, `si_errno`, and `si_code` are available for all signals received. We already printed the signal number but now will print the `errno` value. We also print the process ID and user ID that sent the signal. These values are valid only for POSIX.1b signals, but our simple example doesn't make that distinction.

The `si_code` member gives us information about why the signal was sent. Some values are signal specific, and others are relevant to all signals. Here, we look at some of this latter set and print a description of the reason code:

```
ACE_DEBUG ((LM_INFO,
            ACE_TEXT ("errno for this signal is %d [%s]\n"),
            siginfo->si_errno,
            strerror (siginfo->si_errno)));
ACE_DEBUG ((LM_INFO,
            ACE_TEXT ("signal was sent by process %d")
            ACE_TEXT (" / user %d\n"),
            siginfo->si_pid,
            siginfo->si_uid));

switch (siginfo->si_code)
  {
  case SI_TIMER:
    ACE_DEBUG ((LM_INFO, ACE_TEXT ("Timer expiration\n")));
    break;
```

```
      case SI_USER:
        ACE_DEBUG ((LM_INFO,
                    ACE_TEXT ("Sent by kill, sigsend or raise\n")));
        break;

      case SI_KERNEL:
        ACE_DEBUG ((LM_INFO,
                    ACE_TEXT ("Sent by kernel\n")));
        break;
        // ...
      };
```

As our example continues, we now have to inspect the signal value before we can determine which parts of `siginfo_t` are applicable. The `si_address` attribute, for instance, is valid only for SIGILL, SIGFPE, SIGSEGV, and SIGBUS. For SIGFPE (floating-point exception), we will display a description of `si_code` along with `si_address`, indicating both why the signal was raised and the memory location that raised it:

```
switch (signum)
  {
  case SIGFPE:
    switch (siginfo->si_code)
      {
      case FPE_INTDIV:
      case FPE_FLTDIV:
        ACE_DEBUG ((LM_INFO,
                    ACE_TEXT ("Divide by zero at %@\n"),
                    siginfo->si_addr));
        break;

      case FPE_INTOVF:
      case FPE_FLTOVF:
        ACE_DEBUG ((LM_INFO,
                    ACE_TEXT ("Numeric overflow at %@\n"),
                    siginfo->si_addr));
        break;

        // ...
      }
    break;
```

As our outer `switch()` continues, we may also display similar details for
SIGSEGV (segmentation violation):

```
case SIGSEGV:
  switch (siginfo->si_code)
    {
      // ...
    };
  break;
```

Our rather lengthy `handle_signal()` concludes by displaying the appropriate `siginfo_t` attributes when our process receives notification of a child
process's termination:

```
case SIGCHLD:
  ACE_DEBUG ((LM_INFO,
              ACE_TEXT ("A child process has exited\n")));
  ACE_DEBUG ((LM_INFO,
              ACE_TEXT ("The child consumed %1/%1 time\n"),
              siginfo->si_utime,
              siginfo->si_stime));
  ACE_DEBUG ((LM_INFO,
              ACE_TEXT ("and exited with value %d\n"),
              siginfo->si_status));
  break;
  // ...
}
```

In our `main()` function, we create a full signal set so that we can listen for all
signals. We also add a small snippet of code that will create a short-lived child
process, allowing us to test our SIGCHLD-handling code:

```
ACE_Sig_Set signalSet;
signalSet.fill_set ();

MySignalHandler h1;
ACE_Reactor::instance ()->register_handler (signalSet, &h1);
pid_t childPid = ACE_OS::fork ();
if (childPid == 0)        // This is the parent process.
  {
    // ...
  }
ACE_Reactor::instance ()->run_reactor_event_loop ();
```

We have not shown all attributes of `siginfo_t` here. For information about these, as well as which attributes apply to each signal, refer to the `sigaction` documention of your operating system.

11.2.2 Introducing ucontext_t

The final parameter of the `handle_signal()` method is `ucontext_t`. This structure contains the application's execution context, such as CPU state and FPU (floating-point unit) registers, from just before the signal was raised. A thorough discussion of this topic is very much beyond the scope of this chapter. Consult the operating system and vendor documentation for details on the exact content and manner of interpreting the `ucontext_t` structure.

11.2.3 Stacking Signal Handlers

In certain cases, you may want to register more than one signal handler function for a particular signal event. In previous sections, we mentioned that the POSIX model of signals allows only a single handler to be called back when a signal occurs. You can use the `ACE_Sig_Handlers` class to modify this behavior. This class provides for the stacking of signal handler objects for a particular signal event. By making a simple modification to the previous example, we get:

```
int ACE_TMAIN (int, ACE_TCHAR *[])
{
  MySignalHandler h1 (SIGUSR1), h2 (SIGUSR1);
  ACE_Sig_Handlers handler;
  handler.register_handler (SIGUSR1, &h1);
  handler.register_handler (SIGUSR1, &h2);

  ACE_OS::kill (ACE_OS::getpid (), SIGUSR1);

  int time = 10;
  while ((time = ACE_OS::sleep (time)) == -1)
    {
      if (errno == EINTR)
        continue;
      else
        ACE_ERROR_RETURN ((LM_ERROR, ACE_TEXT ("%p\n"),
                           ACE_TEXT ("sleep")), -1);
    }
  return 0;
}
```

The only thing we do differently here is create an `ACE_Sig_Handlers` object instead of an `ACE_Sig_Handler` object. This allows us to register multiple handlers for the same signal number. When the signal occurs, all handlers are automatically called back.

11.3 Guarding Critical Sections

Signals act a lot like asynchronous software interrupts. These interrupts are usually generated external to the application—not the way we have been generating them, using `kill()`, to run our examples. When a signal is raised, the thread of control in a single-thread application—or one of threads in a multithreaded application—jumps off to the signal-handling routine, executes it, and then returns to regular processing. As in all such scenarios, certain small regions of code can be treated as critical sections, during the execution of which you do not want to be interrupted by any signal.

ACE provides a scope-based signal guard class that you can use to disable or mask signal processing during the processing of a critical section of code, although some signals, such as `SIGSTOP` and `SIGKILL`, cannot be masked:

```
class MySignalHandler : public ACE_Event_Handler
{
public:
  virtual int handle_signal (int signo,
                             siginfo_t * = 0,
                             ucontext_t * = 0)
  {
    ACE_DEBUG ((LM_DEBUG, ACE_TEXT ("Signal %d\n"), signo));
    return 0;
  }
};

int ACE_TMAIN (int, ACE_TCHAR *[])
{
  MySignalHandler sighandler;
  ACE_Sig_Handler sh;
  sh.register_handler (SIGUSR1, &sighandler);

  ACE_Sig_Set ss;
  ss.sig_add (SIGUSR1);
  ACE_Sig_Guard guard (&ss);
```

```
{
  ACE_DEBUG ((LM_DEBUG,
             ACE_TEXT ("Entering critical region\n")));
  ACE_OS::sleep (10);
  ACE_DEBUG ((LM_DEBUG,
             ACE_TEXT ("Leaving  critical region\n")));
}

// Do other stuff.

return 0;
}
```

Here, an `ACE_Sig_Guard` is used to protect the critical region of code against all the signals that are in the `ACE_Sig_Set` `ss`. In this case we have added only the signal `SIGUSR1`. This means that the scoped code is "safe" from `SIGUSR1` until the scope closes.

To test this, we ran this program and used the UNIX **kill(1)** utility to send the process `SIGUSR1` (signal number 16):

```
$ SigGuard&
[1]           15191
$ Entering critical region
$kill 16 15191
$ Leaving critical region
$ Signal   16
[1]    +   Done                    SigGuard&
```

Note that even though we sent the signal `SIGUSR1` before the program had left the scope block of the critical region, the signal was received and processed after we had left the critical region. This happens because while in the critical region, we were guarded against `SIGUSR1`, and thus the signal remains pending on the process. Once we leave the critical section scope, the guard is released and the pending signal delivered to our process.

11.4 Signal Management with the Reactor

As we mentioned in the beginnning of this chapter, the reactor is a general-purpose event dispatcher that can handle the dispatching of signal events to event handlers in a fashion similar to `ACE_Sig_Handler`. In fact, in most reactor implementations, `ACE_Sig_Handler` is used behind the scenes to handle the signal dispatching. It is important to remember that signal handlers are invoked in signal context, unlike the other event types that are handled by the Reactor framework. You can, however, transfer control back to a defined point of control in user context using reactor notifications. For more on this topic, see Section 7.4.

11.5 Summary

In this chapter, we looked at how signals, which are asynchronous software interrupts, are handled portably with ACE. We explained how to use the low-level `sigaction` and `sigset_t` wrappers to set up our own signal handler functions. We then discussed how ACE supports object-based callbacks with the `ACE_Event_Handler` abstract base class. Stacking signal handlers for a single signal number was also introduced. Finally, we showed you how to protect regions of code from being interrupted by signals by using the `ACE_Sig_Guard` class.

Chapter 12
Basic Multithreaded Programming

Multithreaded programming has become more and more of a necessity in today's software. Whereas yesterday, most general-purpose operating systems provided programmers with only user-level thread libraries, most of today's operating systems provide real preemptive multitasking. As the prices of multiprocessor machines fall, their use has also become prevalent. The scale of new software also appears to be growing. Whereas formerly, concurrent users numbered in the hundreds or thousands, today that number has jumped tenfold. Development of real time software has always required the use of thread priorities; with the surge of intelligent embedded devices, many more developers are getting involved in this field. All these factors combined make it more and more important for developers to be familiar with threading concepts and their productive use.

This chapter introduces the basics of using threads with the ACE toolkit. Because ACE provides so much in the area of threads, we have divided the discussion on threads into two chapters. This chapter covers the basics: creating new threads of control, safety primitives that ensure consistency when you have more than one thread accessing a global structure, and event and data communication between threads. Chapter 13 discusses more advanced topics, such as thread scheduling and management.

12.1 Getting Started

By default, a process is created with a single thread, which we call the main thread. This thread starts executing in the main() function of your program and ends when main() completes. Any extra threads that your process may need have to be explicitly created. To create your own thread with ACE, all you have to do is create a subclass of the ACE_Task_Base class and override the implementation of the virtual svc() method. The svc() method serves as the entry point for your new thread; that is, your thread starts in the svc() method and ends when the svc() method returns, in a fashion similar to the main thread.

You will often find yourself using extra threads to help process incoming messages for your network servers. This prevents clients that do not require responses from blocking on the network server, waiting for long-running requests to complete. In our first example, we create a home automation command handler class, HA_CommandHandler, that is responsible for applying long-running command sequences to the various devices that are connected on our home network. For now, we simulate the long-running processing with a sleep call. We print out the thread identifier for both the main thread and the command handler thread, using the ACE_DEBUG() macro's %t format specifier, so that we can see the two threads running in our debug log:

```
#include "ace/Task.h"

class HA_CommandHandler : public ACE_Task_Base
{
public:
  virtual int svc (void)
  {
    ACE_DEBUG
      ((LM_DEBUG, ACE_TEXT ("(%t) Handler Thread running\n")));
    ACE_OS::sleep (4);
    return 0;
  }
};

int ACE_TMAIN (int, ACE_TCHAR *[])
{
  ACE_DEBUG
    ((LM_DEBUG, ACE_TEXT ("(%t) Main Thread running\n")));

  HA_CommandHandler handler;
  int result = handler.activate ();
```

```
    ACE_ASSERT (result == 0);

    handler.wait ();
    return 0;
}
```

To start the thread, you must create an instance of HA_CommandHandler and call activate() on it. Before doing this, we print out the main thread's identifier so that we can compare both child and main identifiers in our output debug log.

After activating the child thread, the main thread calls wait() on the handler object, waiting for its threads to complete before continuing and falling out of the main() function. Once the child thread completes the svc() method and exits, the wait() call in the main thread will complete, control will fall out of the main() function, and the process will exit. Why does the main thread have to wait for the child thread to complete? On many platforms, once the main thread returns from the main() function, the C runtime sees this as an indication that the process is ready to exit and destroys the entire running process, including the child thread. If we allowed this to happen, the program might exit before the child thread ever got scheduled and got a chance to execute.

The output shows the two threads—the main thread and the child command handler thread—running:

```
(496) Main Thread running
(3648) Handler Thread running
```

12.2 Basic Thread Safety

One of the most difficult problems you deal with when writing multithreaded programs is maintaining consistency of all globally available data. Because you have multiple threads accessing the same objects and structures, you must make sure that any updates made to these objects are safe. What safety means in this context is that all state information remains in a consistent state.

ACE provides a rich array of primitives to help you to achieve this goal. We cover a few of the most useful and commonly used primitives in the next few sections and continue coverage on the rest of these components in Chapter 14.

12.2.1 Using Mutexes

Mutexes, the simplest protection primitive available, provide a simple
`acquire()`, `release()` interface. If successful in getting the mutex, the
acquiring thread, `acquire()`, continues forward; otherwise, it blocks until the
holder of the mutex releases it by using `release()`.

As shown in Table 14.1, ACE provides several mutex classes. `ACE_Mutex`
can be used as a lightweight synchronization primitive for threads and as a heavy-
weight cross-process synchronization primitive.

In the next example, we add a device repository to our home automation
example. This repository contains references to all the devices connected to our
home network, as well as the interface to apply command sequences to the various
devices connected to our home network. Let us suppose that only one thread can
make updates in the repository at a time, without causing consistency problems.

The repository creates and manages an `ACE_Thread_Mutex` object as a data
member that it uses to ensure the consistency constraint. This is a common idiom
that you will find yourself using on a regular basis. Whenever it calls the
`update_device()` method, a thread first has to acquire the mutex before
continuing forward, as only one thread can have the mutex at a time; at no point
will two threads simultaneously update the state of the repository. It is important
that `release()` be called on the mutex so that other threads can acquire the
repository mutex and update the repository after the first thread is done. When the
repository is destroyed, the destructor of the mutex will ensure that it properly
releases all resources that it holds:

```
class HA_Device_Repository
{
public:
  HA_Device_Repository ()
  { }

  void update_device (int device_id)
  {
    mutex_.acquire ();
    ACE_DEBUG ((LM_DEBUG, ACE_TEXT ("(%t) Updating device %d\n"),
               device_id));
    ACE_OS::sleep (1);
    mutex_.release ();
  }
```

```
private:
  ACE_Thread_Mutex mutex_;
};
```

To illustrate the mutex in action, we modify `HA_CommandHandler` to call `update_device()` on the repository and then create two handler tasks that compete with each other, trying to update devices in the repository at the same time:

```cpp
class HA_CommandHandler : public ACE_Task_Base
{
public:
  enum {NUM_USES = 10};

  HA_CommandHandler (HA_Device_Repository& rep) : rep_(rep)
  { }

  virtual int svc (void)
  {
    ACE_DEBUG
      ((LM_DEBUG, ACE_TEXT ("(%t) Handler Thread running\n")));
    for (int i=0; i < NUM_USES; i++)
      this->rep_.update_device (i);
    return 0;
  }

private:
  HA_Device_Repository & rep_;
};

int ACE_TMAIN (int, ACE_TCHAR *[])
{
  HA_Device_Repository rep;
  HA_CommandHandler handler1 (rep);
  HA_CommandHandler handler2 (rep);
  handler1.activate ();
  handler2.activate ();

  handler1.wait ();
  handler2.wait ();
  return 0;
}
```

The output from this program shows the two handler threads competing to update devices in the repository:

```
(3768) Handler Thread running
(3768) Updating device 0
(1184) Handler Thread running
(1184) Updating device 0
(3768) Updating device 1
(1184) Updating device 1
(3768) Updating device 2
(1184) Updating device 2
(3768) Updating device 3
(1184) Updating device 3
(3768) Updating device 4
```

You may notice that on your platform, one thread may hang onto the repository until it is done before it lets go or that the threads run amok among one another, with no particular order as to which thread uses the repository. You can ensure strict ordering—if that is what you need—by using an `ACE_Token`, which is discussed in Section 14.1.4. But be aware that although tokens support strict ordering and are recursive, they are slower and heavier than mutexes.

12.2.2 Using Guards

In many cases, exceptional conditions cause deadlock in otherwise perfectly working code. This usually happens when we overlook an exceptional path and forget to unlock a mutex. Let's illustrate this with a piece of code:

```
int
HA_Device_Repository::update_device (int device_id)
{
  this->mutex_.acquire ();
  ACE_DEBUG ((LM_DEBUG, ACE_TEXT ("(%t) Updating device %d\n"),
             device_id));

  // Allocate a new object.
  ACE_NEW_RETURN (object, Object, -1);
  // ...
  // Use the object

  this->mutex_.release ();
}
```

You can spot the problem here pretty easily: The ACE_NEW_RETURN() macro returns when an error occurs, thereby preventing the lock from being released, and we have a nasty deadlock. In real code, it becomes more difficult to spot such returns, and having multiple release() calls all over your code can quickly become very ugly.

ACE provides a convenience class that solves this problem. The ACE_Guard set of classes and macros help simplify your code and prevent deadlock situations. The guard is based on the familiar C++ idiom of using the constructor and destructor calls for resource acquisition and release. The guard classes acquire a specified lock when they are constructed, and release the lock when they are destroyed. Using a guard on your stack, you are always assured that the lock will be released, no matter what pathological path your code may wind through.

Using a guard instead of explicit calls to acquire and release the mutex makes the previous snippet of code much easier to read:

```
int
HA_Device_Repository::update_device (int device_id)
{
  // Construct a guard specifying the type of the mutex as
  // a template parameter and passing in the mutex to hold
  // as a parameter.
  ACE_Guard<ACE_Thread_Mutex> guard (this->mutex_);

  // This can throw an exception that is not caught here.
  ACE_NEW_RETURN (object, Object, -1);
  // ..
  // Use the object.
  // ..
  // Guard is destroyed, automatically releasing the lock.
}
```

All we do here is create an ACE_Guard object on the stack. This automatically acquires and releases the mutex on function entry and exit: just what we want. The ACE_Guard template class takes the lock type as its template parameter and also requires you to pass in a lock object that the guard will operate on.

Table 12.1 lists the rich variety of guards that ACE provides. Most of these guards are self-explanatory; we talk about them and use them in several examples in Chapter 14. For further details on each of the guards, consult the ACE reference documentation.

ACE also provides a set of convenient macros that you can use to allocate guards on the stack. These macros expand to use the guard classes listed in

Table 12.1. ACE Guard Classes

Guard	Description
ACE_Guard<T>	Uses the acquire() and release() methods of lock class T during guard creation and destruction. Thus, you get the semantics of acquire() and release() methods for the specified type T.
ACE_Read_Guard<T>	Uses acquire_read() for acquisition instead of the regular acquire().
ACE_Write_Guard<T>	Uses acquire_write() for acquisition instead of the regular acquire().
ACE_TSS_Guard<T>	Allocates the guard on the heap and keeps a reference to it in thread-specific storage. This ensures that the lock is always released even if the thread exits explicitly, using ACE_Thread::exit().
ACE_TSS_Read_Guard<T>	Read version of a thread-specific guard.
ACE_TSS_Write_Guard<T>	Write version of a thread-specific guard.

Table 12.1 and perform error checking on the underlying acquire() and release() calls. They return on an error, optionally with a return value. In the lists of macros below, LockType is used as T in the guard class template, GuardName is the name of the guard object that's created, and LockObject is the lock object referenced by the guard.

The following guard macros do not return values:

- ACE_GUARD (LockType, GuardName, LockObject)
- ACE_WRITE_GUARD (LockType, GuardName, LockObject)
- ACE_READ_GUARD (LockType, GuardName, LockObject)

These guard macros return ReturnValue on an error:

- ACE_GUARD_RETURN (LockType, GuardName, LockObject, ReturnValue)
- ACE_WRITE_GUARD_RETURN (LockType, GuardName, LockObject, ReturnValue)
- ACE_READ_GUARD_RETURN (LockType, GuardName, LockObject, ReturnValue)

In the following code snippet, the guard return macro is used with the device repository:

```
int
HA_Device_Repository::update_device (int device_id)
{
  ACE_GUARD_RETURN (ACE_Thread_Mutex, mon, mutex_, -1);

  ACE_NEW_RETURN (object, Object, -1);
  // Use the object.
  // ...
}
```

If there is an error, the macro returns −1 from the method; otherwise, it creates an `ACE_Guard<ACE_Thread_Mutex>` instance called mon on the stack. If the mutex-protected method does not return a value, the not-return-value guards should be used in conjunction with the `errno` facility.

12.3 Intertask Communication

When writing multithreaded programs, you will often feel the need for your tasks to communicate with one another. This communication may take the form of something simple, such as one thread informing another that it is time to exit, or something more complicated, such as communicating threads passing data back and forth.

In general, intertask communication can be divided into two broad categories:

1. *State change or event notifications*, whereby only the event occurrence needs to be communicated, but no data is passed between the two threads
2. *Message passing*, whereby data is passed between the two threads, possibly forming a work chain, in which the first thread processes the data and then passes it along to the next for further processing

12.3.1 Using Condition Variables

A thread can use condition variables to communicate a state change, an event arrival, or the satisfaction of another condition to other interested threads. A condition variable is always used in conjunction with a mutex. These variables also have a special characteristic in that you can do a *timed block* on the variable.

This makes it easy to use a condition variable to manage a simple event loop. We show an example of this when we talk about timers in Chapter 20.

We can easily change our command handler example to use a condition variable to coordinate access to the device repository instead of using a mutex for protection. We start by modifying the repository so that it can record which task currently owns it:

```cpp
class HA_Device_Repository
{
public:
  HA_Device_Repository() : owner_(0)
  { }

  int is_free (void)
    { return (this->owner_ == 0); }

  int is_owner (ACE_Task_Base* tb)
    { return (this->owner_ == tb); }

  ACE_Task_Base *get_owner (void)
    { return this->owner_; }

  void set_owner (ACE_Task_Base *owner)
    { this->owner_ = owner; }

  int update_device (int device_id);

private:
  ACE_Task_Base * owner_;
};
```

Next, we modify the command handler such that it uses a condition variable (waitCond_) and mutex (mutex_), to coordinate access to the repository. Both the condition variable and the mutex are created on the main() thread stack and are passed to the command handlers during construction.

To use a condition variable, you must first acquire the mutex, check whether the system is in the required state—the required condition is true—and, if so perform the required action and then release the mutex. If the condition is not in the required state, you must call wait() on the condition variable, waiting for the system state to change. Once the system state changes, the thread that is making the change signals the condition variable, waking up one or more of the threads that are waiting for the change. The waiting threads wake up, check the system state again, and, if the state is still amenable, perform the required action; otherwise, they wait again.

In the command handler, the handler thread is waiting for the is_free() condition to become true on the repository. If this happens to be the case, the handler thread successfully acquires the repository and marks itself as the owner, after which it frees the mutex. If any other competing handler tries to acquire the repository for update at this time, the is_free() method will return 0, and the thread will block by calling wait() on the condition variable.

Once the successful thread is done updating, it removes itself as the owner of the repository and calls signal() on the condition variable. This causes the blocked thread to wake up, check whether the repository is free, and, if so, go on its merry way acquiring the repository for update.

You may notice that the blocking thread does not release the mutex before it falls asleep on wait(); nor does it try to acquire it once it wakes up. The reason is that the condition variable ensures the automatic release of the mutex right before falling asleep and acquisition of the mutex just before waking up:

```
int
HA_CommandHandler::svc (void)
{
  ACE_DEBUG ((LM_DEBUG,
              ACE_TEXT ("(%t) Handler Thread running\n")));

  for (int i = 0; i < NUM_USES; i++)
    {
      this->mutex_.acquire ();
      while (!this->rep_.is_free ())
        this->waitCond_.wait ();
      this->rep_.set_owner (this);
      this->mutex_.release ();

      this->rep_.update_device (i);

      ACE_ASSERT (this->rep_.is_owner (this));
      this->rep_.set_owner (0);

      this->waitCond_.signal ();
    }

  return 0;
}
```

As usual, we create two handlers that compete with each other to acquire the repository. Both are passed the condition variable, mutex, and repository by reference when the handler is constructed.

The ACE_Condition class is a template and requires the type of mutex being used as its argument. Because we are coordinating access between threads, we use ACE_Thread_Mutex as the mutex type. The condition variable instance also keeps a reference to the mutex, so that it can automatically acquire and release it on the wait() call, as described earlier. This reference is passed to the condition variable during construction:

```
int ACE_TMAIN (int, ACE_TCHAR *[])
{
  HA_Device_Repository rep;
  ACE_Thread_Mutex rep_mutex;
  ACE_Condition<ACE_Thread_Mutex> wait (rep_mutex);

  HA_CommandHandler handler1 (rep, wait, rep_mutex);
  HA_CommandHandler handler2 (rep, wait, rep_mutex);

  handler1.activate ();
  handler2.activate ();

  handler1.wait ();
  handler2.wait ();

  return 0;
}
```

12.3.2 Message Passing

As mentioned earlier, message passing is often used to communicate data and event occurrences between threads. The sender creates a message that it enqueues on a message queue for the receiver to pick up. The receiver is either blocked or polling the queue, waiting for new data to arrive. Once the data is in the queue, the receiver dequeues the data, uses it, and then goes back to waiting for new data on the queue.

The queue acts as a shared resource between the two threads, and thus the enqueue and dequeue operations must be protected. (See Figure 12.1.) It also would be handy if the queue supports a blocking dequeue call that unblocks when new data arrives. Finally, it would be convenient if each task object that we

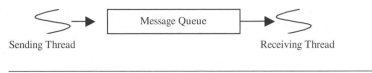

Figure 12.1. Using a queue for communication

created comes out of the box with a message queue attached to it. That way, we wouldn't have to have a global queue. Instead, if a task has a reference to any other task, it can send it messages.

Fortunately, all these features come out of the box with ACE. Up to this point, we have been using `ACE_Task_Base` as the base class for all our example threads. ACE also provides a facility to queue messages between threads that are derived from the `ACE_Task` template. By deriving your class from `ACE_Task`, you automatically inherit a message queue of type `ACE_Message_Queue`, which you can use in your new class. `ACE_Message_Queue` is modeled after the queueing facilities available with System V streams. However, unlike their System V counterparts, the ACE facility allows for efficient intertask communication within a single process and does not provide for interprocess communication.

The message queue provides a type-safe interface, allowing you to enqueue messages that are instances of `ACE_Message_Block`.

Message Blocks

The `ACE_Message_Block` is an efficient data container that can be used to efficiently store and share messages. You can think of the message block as an advanced data buffer that supports such nice features as reference counting and data sharing. Each message block contains two pointers: a `rd_ptr()`, which points to the next byte to be read, and a `wr_ptr()`, which points to the next available empty byte. You can use these pointers to copy data into and get data out of the message block.

You can use the `copy()` method to copy data into the message block:

```
ACE_Message_Block *mb;
ACE_NEW_RETURN (mb, ACE_Message_Block (128), -1);

const char *deviceAddr= "Dev#12";
mb->copy (deviceAddr, ACE_OS::strlen (deviceAddr)+1);
```

Or, you can use the wr_ptr() directly. When doing so, you must move the wr_ptr() forward manually, so that the next write is at the end of the buffer:

```
ACE_Message_Block *mb;
ACE_NEW_RETURN (mb, ACE_Message_Block (128), -1);

const char *commandSeq= "CommandSeq#14";
ACE_OS::sprintf (mb->wr_ptr (), commandSeq);
// Move the wr_ptr() forward in the buffer by the
// amount of data we just put in.
mb->wr_ptr (ACE_OS::strlen (commandSeq) +1);
```

The rd_ptr() is similar to the write pointer. You can use it directly to get the data, but you must be careful to move it forward by the number of bytes you have already read so that you don't read the same data over and over. Once you are done working with the message block, release it using the release() method, causing the reference count to be decremented. When the count reaches 0, ACE will automatically release the memory that was allocated for the block:

```
ACE_DEBUG((LM_DEBUG,
          ACE_TEXT ("Command Sequence --> %s\n"),
          mb->rd_ptr ()));
mb->rd_ptr (ACE_OS::strlen (mb->rd_ptr ())+1);
mb->release ();
```

Message blocks also include a type field, which can be set during construction or through the msg_type() modifier. The message-type field comes in handy when you want to distinguish processing of the message based on its type or to send a simple command notification. An example of the latter is the use of ACE_Messsage_Block::MB_HANGUP message type to inform the message receiver that the source has shut down:

```
// Send a hangup notification to the receiver.
ACE_NEW_RETURN
  (mb, ACE_Message_Block (128, ACE_Message_Block::MB_HANGUP), -1);
// Send an error notification to the receiver.
mb->msg_type (ACE_Message_Block::MB_ERROR);
```

ACE_Message_Block also offers the methods duplicate(), to create a new reference to the block's data, incrementing the reference count, and clone(), to create a deep copy of the message block.

Using the Message Queue

To illustrate the use of ACE_Task and its underlying message queue, we extend our previous automation handler example to include a handler derived from ACE_Svc_Handler<ACE_SOCK_STREAM, ACE_MT_SYNCH>, called Message_Receiver, that receives command messages for the devices on the network from TCP-connected remote clients. (For more on this, see Chapter 6.) On receipt of the commands, Message_Receiver first encapsulates them in message blocks and then enqueues them on the command handler's message queue. The HA_Command_Handler derives from ACE_Task instead of ACE_Task_Base, thus inheriting the required message queue functionality. The command handler thread spends its time waiting for command message blocks to arrive on its message queue; on receiving these messages, the handler proceeds to process the commands.

The remote command messages have a simple header, DeviceCommand-Header, followed by a payload that consists of a null-terminated command string:

```
struct DeviceCommandHeader
{
  int length_;
  int deviceId_;
};
```

The Message_Receiver service handler uses the length_ field of the header to figure out the size of the payload. Once it knows the length of the payload, the service handler can create an ACE_Message_Block of the exact size: the length of the payload plus the length of the header. The handler then copies the header and payload into the message block and enqueues it on the command handler task's message queue, using the ACE_Task::putq() method. (A reference to the HA_Command_Handler is kept by the Message_Receiver, which it receives on construction.) If the device ID read in from the header is negative, we use it as an indication that the system needs to shut down; to do this, we send a hangup message to HA_Command_Handler:

```
int
Message_Receiver::handle_input (ACE_HANDLE)
{
  DeviceCommandHeader dch;
  if (this->read_header (&dch) < 0)
    return -1;
```

```
      if (dch.deviceId_ < 0)
        {
          // Handle shutdown.
          this->handler_->putq (shut_down_message ());
          return -1;
        }

      ACE_Message_Block *mb;
      ACE_NEW_RETURN
        (mb, ACE_Message_Block (dch.length_ + sizeof dch), -1);
      // Copy the header.
      mb->copy ((const char*)&dch, sizeof dch);
      // Copy the payload.
      if (this->copy_payload (mb, dch.length_) < 0)
        ACE_ERROR_RETURN ((LM_ERROR, ACE_TEXT ("%p\n"),
                           ACE_TEXT ("Recieve Failure")), -1);
      // Pass it off to the handler thread.
      this->handler_->putq (mb);
      return 0;
    }
```

It is instructive to look at how the payload is copied into the provided message block. We pass the `wr_ptr()` directly to `ACE_SOCK_Stream::read_n()`, which copies the data directly into the block. After the data is copied into the block, we advance the `wr_ptr()` by the size of the payload. Recall that we had moved the `wr_ptr()` for the message block forward by the size of the header before we made this call; therefore, the message block now contains the header, followed immediately by the payload:

```
int
Message_Receiver::copy_payload (ACE_Message_Block *mb,
                                int payload_length)
{
  int result =
    this->peer ().recv_n (mb->wr_ptr (), payload_length);

    if (result <= 0)
      {
        mb->release ();
        return result;
      }
```

```
    mb->wr_ptr (payload_length);
    return 0;
}
```

When it gets a command to shut down the system, the message receiver creates a new message block that has no data in it but has the MB_HANGUP type set. When it receives a message, the HA_Command_Handler first checks the type; if it is a hang-up message, it shuts down the system:

```
ACE_Message_Block *
Message_Receiver::shut_down_message (void)
{
  ACE_Message_Block *mb;
  ACE_NEW_RETURN
    (mb, ACE_Message_Block (0, ACE_Message_Block::MB_HANGUP), 0);
  return mb;
}
```

On the other side of the fence, the HA_CommandHandler thread blocks, waiting for messages to arrive on its queue by calling getq() on itself. Once a message arrives, getq() will unblock; the handler then reads the messages and applies the received command to the device repository. Finally, it releases the message block, which will deallocate the used memory as the block's reference count drops to 0.

As we said earlier, the system uses a message of type MB_HANGUP to inform the server to shut down. On receiving a message of this type, the handler stops waiting for incoming messages and shuts down the reactor, using the ACE_Reactor::end_reactor_event_loop() method. This causes the command handler process to shut down.

Other Queue Types

ACE provides various ACE_Message_Queue subclasses that provide more than the vanilla FIFO queueing available with ACE_Message_Queue. The ACE_Dynamic_Message_Queue offers priority queues, which include dynamic priority adjustments based on various algorithms. ACE also offers several platform-specific queues that incorporate OS-specific characteristics.

You can specify the queue type used by an ACE_Task during construction or by using the msg_queue() modifier. The queue types are listed in Table 12.2.

Table 12.2. Various Queue Types

Name	Description
`ACE_Dynamic_Message_Queue`	A priority-queue implementation that dynamically readjusts the priority of a message, using variants of the earliest-deadline-first scheme and a laxity (time to deadline minus worst-case execution time) schemes. For details, see the ACE reference documentation.
`ACE_Message_Queue_Vx`	Wrapper around the Wind River VxWorks message queue facility.
`ACE_Message_Queue_Ex`	An even more type-safe version of `ACE_Message_Queue`.
`ACE_Message_Queue_NT`	Implementation that is built on Windows NT's I/O completion port features.[a]

a. `ACE_Message_Queue_NT` does not derive from `ACE_Message_Queue` and therefore cannot be used with `ACE_Task`.

12.4 Summary

The basic high-level ACE threading components provide an easy-to-use object interface to multithreaded programming. In this chapter, we explained how to use the `ACE_Task` objects to create new threads of control, how to use `ACE_Mutex` and `ACE_Guard` to ensure consistency, and how to use `ACE_Condition` and the `ACE_Message_Queue`, `ACE_Message_Block`, and `ACE_Task` message-passing constructs to incorporate communication between threads.

Chapter 13
Thread Management

Previously, we introduced the `ACE_Task` family and thread creation. This chapter goes into the details of how you can create various types of threads in varying states in accordance with your requirements. We also discuss how running threads can be managed: suspending and resuming threads, creating and waiting on threads that are in "thread groups," canceling running threads, and incorporating start-up and exit hooks for the threads that you create.

13.1 Types of Threads

In the previous chapter, we glossed over the fact that you can create threads with special *attributes* by passing various flags to the `ACE_Task_Base::activate()` method. These attributes define, among other things, how the new thread will be created, scheduled, and destroyed. Table 13.1 lists all the possible thread creation flags that control the assignment of various attributes to the new thread.

Because the ACE threads library tries to hide a wide array of operating systems, you may find that some of these flags to do not work exactly as you may expect them to work on your particular operating system. For example, if your particular OS does not support round-robin scheduling, don't expect ACE to do magic to make that work for you. However, on most major OSs, you will find that everything works as expected.

Table 13.1. Thread Creation Flags

Flag	Description
THR_CANCEL_DISABLE	Do not allow this thread to be canceled.
THR_CANCEL_ENABLE	Allow this thread to be canceled.
THR_CANCEL_DEFERRED	Allow for deferred cancellation only.
THR_BOUND	Create a thread that is bound to a kernel-schedulable entity.
THR_NEW_LWP	Create a kernel-level thread.
THR_DETACHED	Create a detached thread.
THR_SUSPENDED	Create the thread but keep the new thread in suspended state.
THR_DAEMON	Create a daemon thread.
THR_JOINABLE	Allow the new thread to be *joined* with.
THR_SCHED_FIFO	Schedule the new thread using the FIFO policy, if available.
THR_SCHED_RR	Schedule the new thread using a round-robin scheme, if available.
THR_SCHED_DEFAULT	Use whatever default scheduling scheme is available on the operating system.

You can OR the flags together and pass them as the first argument to the `activate()` method. For example, the following call would cause the thread to be created as a kernel-schedulable thread, with a default scheduling scheme, and start in the suspended state, and it would be possible to join with this thread:

```
handler.activate (THR_NEW_LWP | THR_SCHED_DEFAULT |
                  THR_SUSPENDED | THR_JOINABLE);
```

13.1.1 Scheduling Contention Scope

Most operating systems make the distinction between kernel-level threads and user-level threads. Kernel-level threads are schedulable entities that the OS is aware of and schedules with a kernel-level scheduler. On the other hand, user-level threads are lighter-weight threads that are scheduled with a library-based

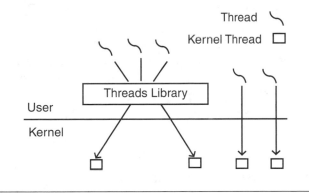

Figure 13.1. Kernel- and User-Level Threads

scheduler within the process's address space. These threads allow for fast context switching but could block on each other. As a programmer, you can deal *only* with user-level threads. Your process is assigned a pool of kernel-level threads that are used to schedule all your user-level threads. You can explicitly bind a user-level thread to a particular kernel-level thread by using the THR_BOUND flag. Doing this would cause the bound user-level thread to be scheduled using the underlying kernel-level thread. Figure 13.1 illustrates these concepts.

If you specify that you want to create a thread with the THR_NEW_LWP flag set, you are assured that a new kernel-level schedulable entity will also be created; that is, the new user-level thread is bound to a new kernel-level thread. This is the default behavior for the ACE_Task_Base::activate() method. However, if you specify your own attribute flags parameter and do not include the THR_NEW_LWP flag, the library will create the thread as a user-level thread.

13.1.2 Detached and Joinable Threads

Threads can be created as detached or joinable by using the THR_DETACHED or THR_JOINABLE flags. If you specify a thread as detached, ACE will automatically clean up all resources the thread held upon thread exit. Unfortunately, the exit status of this thread is not available for any other thread to look at. On the other hand, if a thread is created as joinable, another thread can *join* with it when it terminates. However, be aware that if you do not join with a joinable thread, you will leak resources.

We have been using the THR_JOINABLE feature in all of our previous examples; the main thread waits, or *joins*, with the child thread by calling wait() on the task object. As you may have guessed, all ACE_Task threads are created as joinable by default, thereby making the wait() method possible. If several threads wait for the same thread to complete, only one will join with it. The other waiting threads will unblock and return with a failure status. Once again, if you do specify a thread as being joinable you *must* join with it at some later point in your program. Thus, when using the default task flags, ACE requires you to wait on each task to ensure proper cleanup. If you fail to do this, you may leak system resources.

13.1.3   Initial Thread Scheduling State

Once the ACE_Task_Base::activate() method returns, a new thread has been created by the OS. However, this does not say anything about the current running state of the new thread. The OS will use an internal OS-specific scheduling scheme to decide when to run the new thread. So even after the thread has been created, it may not be running when activate() returns.

You can control the initial running state of a thread to some degree by specifying the THR_SUSPENDED flag. This flag will cause the OS to create the new thread in a suspended state. This flag often comes in handy when you are activating a new thread and do not want it to race for some resource that is currently held by the spawning thread:

```
HA_CommandHandler handler;
int result = handler.activate (THR_NEW_LWP |
                               THR_JOINABLE |
                               THR_SUSPENDED);
ACE_ASSERT (result == 0);

ACE_DEBUG ((LM_DEBUG,
           ACE_TEXT ("(%t) The current thread count is %d\n"),
           handler.thr_count ()));
ACE_DEBUG ((LM_DEBUG,
           ACE_TEXT ("(%t) The group identifier is %d\n"),
           handler.grp_id ()));
handler.resume ();
handler.wait ();
```

Here, we use activate() on the thread; however, because we specify the THR_SUSPENDED flag, the new thread is created in the suspended state and does not run. This allows us to display the current thread count, which is 1, and the automatically assigned group ID of the handler task, without worrying about the child thread completing and altering the handler's state before we are done displaying this information. After we complete, we call `resume()` on the handler, causing the thread to be scheduled and run by the OS for the first time.

13.2 Priorities and Scheduling Classes

One important reason to use threads is to have various parts of your application run at different priorities. Many applications require such characteristics. In our home automation example, we can incorporate priorities to create two `HA_CommandHandler` instances that run at differing priorities. The high-priority command handler receives critical commands that must be executed before any of the noncritical commands are; for example, changing the temperature on the oven could be more critical than recording your favorite TV program. If you were using strict priority-based scheduling, this would mean that the low-priority handler would run only if the application was not busy processing critical commands in the high-priority handler thread.

Each OS defines priorities in a proprietary fashion. For example, Solaris defines priorities to range from 0–127, with 127 being the highest priority. Windows specifies a range of 0–15, with 15 being the highest, and VxWorks has 0–255, with 0 being the highest priority.

Most general-purpose operating systems offer a single time-shared scheduling class. Time-shared schedulers attempt to enforce fairness by allowing the highest priority thread to execute for a finite period of time called a *time slice*. If a higher-priority thread becomes runnable before the end of the executing thread's time slice, the lower-priority thread is preempted and the higher-priority thread begins its time slice.

Some operating systems offer a real-time scheduling class. Threads in the real-time scheduling class are always at a higher priority than any thread in the time-shared class, if the operating system supports a time-shared scheduling class. There are two scheduling policies offered in the real-time scheduling class.

1. *Round-robin*, where a time quantum specifies the maximum time a thread can run before it's preempted by another real-time thread with the same priority.

2. *First-in, first-out (FIFO)*, where the highest-priority thread can run for as long as it chooses, until it voluntarily yields control or is preempted by a real-time thread with an even higher priority.

Table 13.2. Thread Priority Macros

Macro	Meaning
ACE_THR_PRI_OTHER_MIN	Minimum priority for the time-shared scheduling class
ACE_THR_PRI_OTHER_DEF	Default priority for the time-shared scheduling class
ACE_THR_PRI_OTHER_MAX	Maximum priority for the time-shared scheduling class
ACE_THR_PRI_RR_MIN	Minimum priority for the real-time scheduling class with the round-robin policy
ACE_THR_PRI_RR_DEF	Default priority for the real-time scheduling class with the round-robin policy
ACE_THR_PRI_RR_MAX	Maximum priority for the real-time scheduling class with the round-robin policy
ACE_THR_PRI_FIFO_MIN	Minimum priority for the real-time scheduling class with the FIFO policy
ACE_THR_PRI_FIFO_DEF	Default priority for the real-time scheduling class with the FIFO policy
ACE_THR_PRI_FIFO_MAX	Maximum priority for the real-time scheduling class with the FIFO policy

ACE passes your thread scheduling parameters to the OS without trying to mask the differences across platforms. Therefore, it is your responsibility to be sure that the scheduling parameters passed in to calls that set the priority and class work correctly on the particular platform you are dealing with. However, ACE does offer some thread scheduling macros you can use to ease portability in many cases. The scheduling class is requested using either the THR_SCHED_RR or THR_SCHED_FIFO flags described in Table 13.1. If neither is specified, the time-shared scheduling class, also called *other*, is selected.

To create tasks with different priorities, you simply specify the required priority as the fourth parameter to the activate() call. If your use case requires a specific priority for your OS, specify it. However, ACE offers the macros described in Table 13.2 to help specify priorities in a portable manner. For finer control over priority values, please see the ACE_Sched_Params class and the ACE_OS::sched_params() method in the ACE reference documentation.

In this case, we create two instances of our home automation command handler and give them the appropriate names—HighPriority and LowPriority—and use the activate() method to spawn them with low- and high-priority values. We then proceed to pump 100 messages onto each handler's message queue, expecting to see the high-priority handler process these messages before the low-priority handler does:

```
int ACE_TMAIN (int, ACE_TCHAR *[])
{
  HA_CommandHandler hp_handler ("HighPriority");
  hp_handler.activate (THR_NEW_LWP | THR_JOINABLE,
                       1, 1, ACE_THR_PRI_OTHER_MAX);

  HA_CommandHandler lp_handler ("LowPriority");
  lp_handler.activate (THR_NEW_LWP | THR_JOINABLE,
                       1, 1, ACE_THR_PRI_OTHER_DEF);

  ACE_Message_Block mb;
  for (int i = 0; i < 100; i++)
    {
      hp_handler.putq (&mb);
      lp_handler.putq (&mb);
    }

  hp_handler.wait ();
  lp_handler.wait ();

  return 0;
}
```

On receipt of the message, the handler calls process_message(), which displays the task's name and then simulates a compute-bound task:

```
class HA_CommandHandler : public ACE_Task<ACE_MT_SYNCH>
{
public:
  HA_CommandHandler (const char *name) : name_ (name)
  { }

  virtual int svc (void)
  {
    ACE_DEBUG ((LM_DEBUG, ACE_TEXT ("(%t) starting up %C\n"),
               name_));

    ACE_OS::sleep (2);
```

```
    ACE_Message_Block *mb;
    while (this->getq (mb) != -1)
      process_message (mb);
    return 0;
  }

  void process_message (ACE_Message_Block *mb)
  {
    ACE_DEBUG ((LM_DEBUG,
                ACE_TEXT ("(%t) Processing message %C\n"),
                name_));
    // Simulate compute bound task.
    for (int i = 0; i < 100; i++)
      ;
  }

private:
  const char *name_;
};
```

The results are as expected: The high-priority handler always gets to run before the low-priority handler:

```
(2932) starting up HighPriority
(1116) starting up LowPriority
(2932) Processing message HighPriority
(2932) Processing message HighPriority
(2932) Processing message HighPriority
<continues 100 times>
(1116) Processing message LowPriority
(1116) Processing message LowPriority
(1116) Processing message LowPriority
<continues 100 times>
```

Once again: Setting thread priorities that work correctly for your application is a task that *you* must take onto yourself. ACE does not provide much help in this area. Make sure that the values you pass to `activate()` work as you expect them to.

13.3   **Thread Pools**

So far, we have been creating an `ACE_Task` subclass instance and then activating it, causing a single thread of control to be created and start from the `svc()` method. However, the `activate()` method allows multiple threads to be started at the same time, all starting at the same `svc()` entry point. When creating a group of threads in a task, ACE internally assigns to all the threads in a task a group identifier, available through the `grp_id()` accessor, that can be used for subsequent management operations on the group. All the created threads share the same `ACE_Task` object but have their own separate stacks.

This is a handy way to create a simple pool of worker threads that share the same message queue. All the threads wait on the queue for a message to arrive. Once a message arrives, the queue unblocks a single thread that gets the message and continues to process it. Of course, when doing something like this, you must either ensure that the worker threads do not share any data with one another or use property safety constructs in the right places. The advantage is that you can improve message-processing throughput on a multiprocessor or may be able to improve latency on a uniprocessor, especially if the message processing is not compute bound. You must be careful that you don't make things worse by having all your worker threads lock on a single resource; the locking overhead may be high enough to obviate any performance advantage you gain because of the threads.

In the next example, we spawn multiple threads inside a single `ACE_Task` object. These threads display their identifiers by using the `ACE_Log_Msg %t` format specifier and then block, waiting for messages on the underlying message queue:

```
class HA_CommandHandler : public ACE_Task<ACE_MT_SYNCH>
{
public:
  virtual int svc (void)
  {
    ACE_DEBUG ((LM_DEBUG, ACE_TEXT ("(%t) starting up \n")));
    ACE_Message_Block *mb;
    if (this->getq (mb) == -1)
      return -1;
    // ... do something with the message.
    return 0;
  }
};
```

We specify as the second argument to the `activate()` method the number of threads to be created: in this case, 4. This will cause four new threads to start at the `HA_CommandHandler::svc()` entry point:

```
int ACE_TMAIN (int, ACE_TCHAR *[])
{
  HA_CommandHandler handler;

  // Create 4 threads.
  handler.activate (THR_NEW_LWP | THR_JOINABLE, 4);
  handler.wait ();
  return 0;
}
```

The output shows us that four distinct threads start up and then block inside the single `svc()` method of the `HA_CommandHandler` subclass:

```
(2996) starting up
(3224) starting up
(3368) starting up
(876) starting up
```

We discuss thread pools in further detail later, in Chapter 16.

13.4 Thread Management Using ACE_Thread_Manager

So far, we have been using the `ACE_Task` family of classes to help us create and manage tasks. We used the `wait()` management call to wait for handler threads to complete so that the main thread can exit after the handler threads. In addition, we saw the `suspend()` and `resume()` methods, available to suspend and resume threads that are run within tasks. In most cases, you will find the `ACE_Task` interface to be rich enough to provide all the management functionality you need. However, ACE also provides a behind-the-scenes class, `ACE_Thread_Manager`, to help manage all ACE-created tasks, such as providing operations that suspend, resume, and cancel all threads in all tasks. The manager provides a rich interface that includes group management, creation, state retrieval, cancellation, thread start-up and exit hooks, and so on. The thread manager is also tightly integrated with the ACE Streams framework, which we cover in Chapter 18.

ACE allows a programmer to register an unlimited number of exit functions, or exit functors, that will be automatically called when a thread exits. These exit handlers can be used to do last-second cleanup or to inform other threads of the imminent termination of a thread. One of the nice things about the exit handlers is that they are always called, even if the thread exits forcefully with a call to the low-level `ACE_Thread::exit()` method, which causes a thread to exit immediately.

To set up an exit functor, you create a subclass of `ACE_At_Thread_Exit`, implement the `apply()` method, and then register an instance of this class with the `ACE_Thread_Manager`. In this case, we want the `ExitHandler` functor to be called when our home automation command handler thread shuts down. The exit functor then sends out commands to all the devices on the home network, informing them that the network has closed down:

```
#include "ace/Task.h"
#include "ace/Log_Msg.h"

class ExitHandler : public ACE_At_Thread_Exit
{
public:
  virtual void apply (void)
  {
    ACE_DEBUG ((LM_INFO, ACE_TEXT ("(%t) is exiting \n")));

    // Shut down all devices.
  }
};
```

The registration of the exit functor, with the thread manager, must occur within the context of the thread whose exit functor this is. In this case, we want the functor to be applied when the home automation handler thread exits, so we make sure that the exit functor is registered with the thread manager as soon as the command handler thread starts. We get a pointer to the thread manager by calling the task's `thr_mgr()` accessor and then register the exit handler, using the `at_exit()` method:

```
class HA_CommandHandler : public ACE_Task_Base
{
public:
  HA_CommandHandler(ExitHandler& eh) : eh_(eh)
  { }
```

```
  virtual int svc (void)
  {
    ACE_DEBUG ((LM_DEBUG, ACE_TEXT ("(%t) starting up \n")));

    this->thr_mgr ()->at_exit (eh_);

    // Do something.

    // Forcefully exit.
    ACE_Thread::exit ();

    // NOT REACHED
    return 0;
  }

private:
  ExitHandler& eh_;
};
```

The exit handler and command handler objects are created on the stack of the main() function, as usual. An interesting twist here is that instead of using the ACE_Task_Base::wait() method to wait for the handler thread to exit, we use the ACE_Thread_Manager's wait() method. The thread manager waits on all child threads, no matter what task they are associated with. This proves convenient when you have more than one executing task:

```
int ACE_TMAIN (int, ACE_TCHAR *[])
{
  ExitHandler eh;

  HA_CommandHandler handler (eh);
  handler.activate ();

  ACE_Thread_Manager::instance ()->wait ();
  return 0;
}
```

Note that we treat the thread manager as a singleton object; the reason is that the ACE default is to manage all threads with this thread manager singleton. Although in most cases you will find the default behavior to be sufficient, you can create and specify more than one thread manager:

```
int ACE_TMAIN (int, ACE_TCHAR *[])
{
  ExitHandler eh;
  ACE_Thread_Manager tm;

  HA_CommandHandler handler (eh);
  handler.thr_mgr (&tm);
  handler.activate ();

  tm.wait ();
  return 0;
}
```

13.5 Signals

Chapter 11 is devoted to the topic of signals and their use within the ACE toolkit. This section explains how signals are done differently in a multithreaded application and a single-threaded application, respectively.

First, each thread has its own private signal mask, which by default is inherited during creation. This means that all the threads that are created by the main thread inherit its signal mask.

On the other hand, the signal handlers are global to the process. ACE maintains this invariant when you use it to handle a signal; that is, you can have only a single signal handler for a particular signal type.

13.5.1 Signaling Threads

You can explicitly send targeted synchronous signals to threads by using the thread manager. ACE_Thread_Manager allows you to send a signal to all threads, to a thread group or task, or to a particular thread. As ACE_Task inherits from ACE_Event_Handler, the best place to handle the signal is to use the built-in handle_signal() method and use one of the previously discussed signal dispatchers. In the next example, we use the ACE_Sig_Handler dispatcher and the handle_signal() method to illustrate sending signals to all threads in a thread group. We start by creating a routine message-processing task that implements its handle_signal() event-handling method:

```
class SignalableTask : public ACE_Task<ACE_MT_SYNCH>
{
public:
  virtual int handle_signal (int signum,
                               siginfo_t *  = 0,
                               ucontext_t * = 0)
  {
    if (signum == SIGUSR1)
      {
        ACE_DEBUG ((LM_DEBUG,
                    ACE_TEXT ("(%t) received a %S signal\n"),
                    signum));
        handle_alert ();
      }
    return 0;
  }

  virtual int svc (void)
  {
    ACE_DEBUG ((LM_DEBUG, ACE_TEXT ("(%t) Starting thread\n")));

    while (1)
      {
        ACE_Message_Block* mb;
        ACE_Time_Value tv (0, 1000);
        tv += ACE_OS::time (0);
        int result = this->getq (mb, &tv);
        if (result == -1 && errno == EWOULDBLOCK)
          continue;
        else
          process_message (mb);
      }

    return 0;
  }

  void handle_alert ();
  void process_message (ACE_Message_Block *mb);
};
```

We first create the task and activate it with five new threads. We then register the task as the handler for SIGUSR1 with an ACE_Sig_Handler dispatcher object. This will ensure that the handle_signal() method of the task is automatically called back when a signal of type SIGUSR1 is received by a thread.

Finally, we use the thread manager's `kill_grp()` method to send a `SIGUSR1` signal to all the threads within the group. The group ID we use is the group identifier for the threads in the `SignalableTask`; therefore, our `kill_grp()` causes each of the threads in the task to receive a `SIGUSR1` signal that each handles in its own context:

```
int ACE_TMAIN (int, ACE_TCHAR *[])
{
  SignalableTask handler;
  handler.activate (THR_NEW_LWP | THR_JOINABLE , 5);

  ACE_Sig_Handler sh;
  sh.register_handler (SIGUSR1, &handler);

  ACE_OS::sleep (1);

  ACE_Thread_Manager::instance () ->
    kill_grp (handler.grp_id (), SIGUSR1);
  handler.wait ();
  return 0;
}
```

The output shows each thread receiving and then handling the signal in its own context:

```
(1026) Starting thread
(2051) Starting thread
(3076) Starting thread
(4101) Starting thread
(5126) Starting thread
(1026) received a signal 10 signal
(2051) received a signal 10 signal
(5126) received a signal 10 signal
(4101) received a signal 10 signal
(3076) received a signal 10 signal
```

13.5.2 Signaling Processes in Multithreaded Programs

One difficult question is which thread of control is used to handle the signal when a signal is sent to a process. The answer is, of course, that it depends—on many things, in fact. If the signal is synchronous—was raised owing to an error in execution of a thread, such as a `SIGSEGV` or a `SIGFPE`—it's handled by the same thread that caused it be raised. On the other hand, if the signal is asynchronous—for example, `SIGINT`, `SIGTERM`, and so on—it can be handled by any thread running in the application.

These rules are, of course, affected by whatever platform you are running on. In general, Windows programmers do not use signals, whereas UNIX or UNIX-like platforms that support POSIX do support these rules. This includes general-purpose and real-time operating systems.

We modify our previous example to send `SIGUSR1`, a synchronous signal, several times to the process instead of using the thread manager to send signals to particular threads. Because these signals are synchronous and are sent by the main thread, we expect them to be handled by the main thread:

```
int ACE_TMAIN (int, ACE_TCHAR *[])
{
  ACE_DEBUG ((LM_DEBUG, ACE_TEXT ("(%t) Main thread \n")));
  SignalableTask handler;
  handler.activate (THR_NEW_LWP | THR_JOINABLE, 5);

  ACE_Sig_Handler sh;
  sh.register_handler (SIGUSR1, &handler);

  ACE_OS::sleep (1);       // Allow threads to start

  for (int i = 0; i < 5; i++)
    ACE_OS::kill (ACE_OS::getpid (), SIGUSR1);
  handler.wait ();
  return 0;
}
```

The output, generated on Linux, illustrates how the signal is handled by the same thread—in this case, the main thread—every single time:

```
(1024) Main thread
(1026) Starting thread
(2051) Starting thread
(3076) Starting thread
(4101) Starting thread
(5126) Starting thread
(1024) received a 10 signal
(1024) received a 10 signal
(1024) received a 10 signal
(1024) received a 10 signal
(1024) received a 10 signal
```

Signal handling in multithreaded programs varies, based on the platform, and is plagued with inconsistencies. Therefore, we suggest that if you do combine asynchronous signals with multithreaded programs, take some time to understand the exact semantics on your particular platform.

13.6 Thread Start-Up Hooks

ACE provides a global thread start-up hook that can be used to intercept the call to the thread start-up function. This allows a programmer to perform any kind of initialization that is globally applicable to all the threads being used in your application. This is an especially good spot to add thread-specific data to a thread (see Section 14.3).

To set up a start-up hook, you must first subclass ACE_Thread_Hook and implement the virtual start() method. This method is passed a pointer to the thread's entry function, and a void* argument that must be passed to this function. In most cases, you will execute your special start-up code and then call the passed entry point with the supplied argument. In our case, we add a special security context to thread-specific storage. We use this context to record the current client that is using our command handler thread, which helps us to determine whether the client has permission to execute specified commands. After setting up the security context, we execute the specified thread function:

```
class HA_ThreadHook : public ACE_Thread_Hook
{
public:
  virtual ACE_THR_FUNC_RETURN start (ACE_THR_FUNC func, void* arg)
  {
    ACE_DEBUG ((LM_DEBUG, ACE_TEXT("(%t) New Thread Spawned\n")));

    // Create the context on the thread's own stack.
    ACE_TSS<SecurityContext> secCtx;
    // Special initialization.
    add_sec_context_thr (secCtx);

    return (*func) (arg);
  }

  void add_sec_context_thr (ACE_TSS<SecurityContext> &secCtx);
};
```

After creating your new start-up hook, you need to set it as the new start-up hook. To do this, you simply call the `ACE_Thread_Hook::thread_hook()` static method, passing in an instance of the new hook:

```
int ACE_TMAIN (int, ACE_TCHAR *[])
{
  HA_ThreadHook hook;
  ACE_Thread_Hook::thread_hook (&hook);

  HA_CommandHandler handler;
  handler.activate ();
  handler.wait();
  return 0;
}
```

13.7 Cancellation

Except for cooperative cancellation, cancellation is best avoided unless you can justify a real need for it. With that said, let's delve into what cancellation is and why we consider it to be a feature best shunned.

Cancellation is a way by which you can *zap* current running threads into oblivion. No thread exit handlers will be called; nor will thread-specific storage be released. Your thread will simply cease to exist. In certain instances, cancellation may be a necessary evil: to exit a long-running compute-bound thread or to terminate a thread that is blocked on a blocking system call, such as I/O. In most cases, cancellation will make sense when the application is terminating. In other cases, it is difficult to ensure that proper thread termination occurs with cancellation. Cooperative cancellation, which we discuss in Section 13.7.1, is the only cancellation mode that does not suffer from these ungraceful-exit problems.

Cancellation has several *modes*:

- *Deferred cancelability.* When a thread is in this mode, all cancels are deferred until the thread in question reaches the next *cancellation point*. Cancellation points are well-defined points in the code at which either the thread has blocked, as on an I/O call, or an explicit cancellation point is coded by using the `ACE_Thread_Manager::testcancel()` method. This mode is the default for applications built with ACE.

- *Cooperative cancellation.* In this mode, threads are not really canceled but instead have their state marked as canceled within the instance of the `ACE_Thread_Manager` that spawned it. You can call `ACE_Thread_Manager::testcancel()` to determine whether the thread is in the canceled state; if it is, you can choose to exit the thread. This mode also gets around most of the nasty side effects that come with regular cancellation. If you wish to build portable applications, it is best to stick with this cancellation mode.

- *Asynchronous cancelability.* When a thread is in this mode, cancels can be processed at any instant. Threads run in this mode can be difficult to manage. You can change the cancel state of any thread from enabled to disabled to ensure that the threads are not canceled when executing critical sections of code. You can also use cleanup handlers, which are called when a thread is canceled, to ensure that program invariants are maintained during cancellation. ACE does not support POSIX cleanup handler features, as many operating systems that ACE runs on do not support them. If you are running on a POSIX platform, look for these features if you *really* need to use cancellation.

- *Disabled.* Cancellation can be totally disabled for a thread by using the `ACE_Thread::disablecancel()` call.

13.7.1 Cooperative Cancellation

Let's first look at an example of cooperative cancellation. We start by creating a task that first makes sure that is has not been canceled and then does a timed wait of 1 ms for messages to arrive on its queue. If no messages arrive and it times out, the task checks whether it was canceled again; if it has, the thread exits explicitly. Using this scheme, the thread will notice that it has been canceled within 1 ms of cancellation, assuming that message processing is a short process. The `testcancel()` method of the thread manager requires the thread identifier of the thread whose cancel state is being checked. We can easily obtain this by using the `ACE_Thread_Manager::thr_self()` method or the low-level `ACE_Thread::self()` method:

```
class CanceledTask : public ACE_Task<ACE_MT_SYNCH>
{
public:

  virtual int svc (void)
  {
    ACE_DEBUG ((LM_DEBUG, ACE_TEXT ("(%t) starting up \n")));
```

```
        // Cache our ACE_Thread_Manager pointer.
        ACE_Thread_Manager *mgr = this->thr_mgr ();
        while (1)
          {
            if (mgr->testcancel (mgr->thr_self ()))
              return 0;

            ACE_Message_Block *mb;
            ACE_Time_Value tv (0, 1000);
            tv += ACE_OS::time (0);
            int result = this->getq (mb, &tv);
            if (result == -1 && errno == EWOULDBLOCK)
              continue;
            else
              {
                // Do real work.
              }
          }

        return 0;
      }
};
```

The task itself can be canceled from anywhere by using the thread manager's `cancel_task()` method; in this case, the main thread cancels the task after waiting for 1 second:

```
int ACE_TMAIN (int, ACE_TCHAR *[])
{
  CanceledTask task;
  task.activate ();

  ACE_OS::sleep (1);

  ACE_Thread_Manager::instance ()->cancel_task (&task);
  task.wait ();
  return 0;
}
```

13.7.2 Asynchronous Cancellation

This next example illustrates how to use asynchronous cancelability to zap a thread in a tight compute loop. (Note that this example is platform dependent.) Such a thread can't be canceled in deferred cancellation mode, as there are no cancellation points; therefore, we switch the cancel state of this thread to be asynchronous:

```cpp
class CanceledTask : public ACE_Task<ACE_MT_SYNCH>
{
public:
  virtual int svc (void)
  {
    ACE_DEBUG ((LM_DEBUG, ACE_TEXT ("(%t) Starting thread\n")));

    if (this->set_cancel_mode () < 0)
      return -1;

    while (1)
      {
        // Put this thread in a compute loop.. no
        // cancellation points are available.
      }
  }

  int set_cancel_mode (void)
  {
    cancel_state new_state;

    // Set the cancel state to asynchronous and enabled.
    new_state.cancelstate = PTHREAD_CANCEL_ENABLE;
    new_state.canceltype = PTHREAD_CANCEL_ASYNCHRONOUS;
    if (ACE_Thread::setcancelstate (new_state, 0) == -1)
      ACE_ERROR_RETURN ((LM_ERROR,
                         ACE_TEXT ("%p\n"),
                         ACE_TEXT ("cancelstate")), -1);
    return 0;
  }
};
```

We cancel the thread by using the thread manager `cancel_task()` method as we did before. However, in this case, we pass a second argument of 1, indicating that we want the task to be canceled asynchronously; in other words, we want it to be zapped:

```
int ACE_TMAIN (int, ACE_TCHAR *[])
{
  CanceledTask task;
  task.activate ();
  ACE_OS::sleep (1);
  ACE_Thread_Manager::instance ()->cancel_task (&task, 1);
  task.wait ();

  return 0;
}
```

13.8 Summary

In this chapter, we explained how to create various types of threads by using the
ACE_Task::activate() method with varying parameters. We also used the
ACE_Thread_Manager to help us better manage the threads that we create,
going over signal handling, exit handlers, and thread cancellation using the
manager. Finally, we illustrated how you can use ACE_Thread_Hook to better
control thread start-up in your applications.

Chapter 14
Thread Safety and Synchronization

We covered the basics of both thread safety and synchronization in Chapter 12, explaining how you can use mutexes and guards to ensure the safety of your global data and how condition variables can help two threads communicate events between each other synchronizing their actions. This chapter extends that discussion. In the safety arena, you will get to see readers/writer locks, the atomic operation wrapper, using tokens for fine-grain locking on data structures, and an introduction to recursive mutexes. We also introduce semaphores and barriers as new synchronization mechanisms.

14.1 Protection Primitives

To ensure consistency, multithreaded programs must use protection primitives around shared data. Some examples of protection were given in Chapter 12, where we introduced mutexes and guards. Here, we consider the remaining ACE-provided protection primitives.

Table 14.1 lists the primitives that are available in ACE. All these primitives have a common interface but do not share type relationships and therefore cannot be polymorphically substituted at runtime.

Table 14.1. Protection Primitives in ACE

Primitive	Description
`ACE_Mutex`	Wrapper class around the mutual-exclusion mechanism and used to provide a simple, efficient mechanism to serialize access to a shared resource. Similar in functionality to a binary sempahore. Can be used for mutual exclusion among both threads and processes.
`ACE_Thread_Mutex`	Can be used in place of `ACE_Mutex` and is specific for synchronization of threads.
`ACE_Recursive_Thread_Mutex`	Mutex that is *recursive*, that is, can be acquired multiple times by the same thread. Note that to work correctly, it must be released as many times as it was acquired.
`ACE_RW_Mutex`	Wrapper class that encapsulates readers/writer locks. These locks are acquired differently for reading and writing, thus enabling multiple readers to read while no one is writing. These locks are nonrecursive.
`ACE_RW_Thread_Mutex`	Can be used in place of `ACE_RW_Mutex` and is specific for synchronization of threads.
`ACE_Token`	Tokens are the richest and heaviest locking primitive available in ACE. The locks are recursive and allow for read and write locking. Also, strict FIFO ordering of acquisition is enforced; all threads that call `acquire()` enter a FIFO queue and acquire the lock in order.
`ACE_Atomic_Op`	Template wrapper that allows for *safe* arithmetic operations on the specified type.
`ACE_Guard`	Template-based guard class that takes the lock type as a template parameter.
`ACE_Read_Guard`	Guard that uses `acquire_read()` on a read/write guard during construction.
`ACE_Write_Guard`	Guard that uses `acquire_write()` on a read/write guard during construction.

14.1.1 Recursive Mutexes

If a thread acquires the same mutex twice, what do you think will happen: Will the thread block or not? If you think it won't, you are wrong. In most cases, the thread will block, deadlocking on itself! The reason is that in general, mutexes are unaware of the identity of the acquiring thread, thus making it impossible for the mutex to make the smart decision of not blocking.

If you are using a mutex from several intercalling methods, it sometimes becomes difficult to track whether a thread already has acquired a particular mutex. In the following code, the logger will deadlock on itself once it receives a critical log message; the guard has already acquired the mutex in the `log()` method and will then try to reacquire it from within `logCritical()`:

```
typedef ACE_Thread_Mutex MUTEX;
class Logger
{
public:
  void log (LogMessage *msg)
  {
    ACE_GUARD (MUTEX, mon, mutex_);
    if (msg->priority () == LogMessage::CRITICAL)
      logCritical (msg);
  }

  void logCritical (LogMessage *msg)
  {
    // Acquires the same mutex as log()!
    ACE_GUARD(MUTEX, mon, mutex_);
  }

private:
  MUTEX mutex_;
};

static Logger logger;

int ACE_TMAIN (int, ACE_TCHAR *[])
{
  CriticalLogMessage cm;
  logger.log(&cm);  // Will cause deadlock.
  return 0;
}
```

This situation can be avoided by using a recursive mutex. Recursive mutexes, unlike regular mutexes, allow the same thread to acquire the mutex multiple times without blocking on itself. To achieve this, we simply modify the initial typedef:

```
typedef ACE_Recursive_Thread_Mutex MUTEX;
```

The `ACE_Recursive_Thread_Mutex` has the same API as regular mutexes, making them readily substitutable wherever a regular mutex is used.

14.1.2 Readers/Writer Locks

A readers/writer lock allows many threads to hold the lock simultaneously for reading, but only one thread can hold it for writing. This can provide efficiency gains, especially if the data being protected is frequently read by multiple threads but is infrequently written or is written to by only a few threads. In most cases, readers/writer locks are slower than mutexes; therefore, it important for you to apply them only when contention on reads is much higher than on writes.

ACE includes readers/writer locks in the form of the `ACE_RW_Mutex` and `ACE_RW_Thread_Mutex` classes. To acquire these mutexes for reading, you need to call `acquire_read()`; to acquire the mutex for writing, you must call `acquire_write()`.

Let's say that our home network includes a network discovery agent that keeps track of all the devices currently connected on the home network. The agent keeps a list of all devices that are currently on the network, and clients can ask it whether a current device is currently present. Let's also say, for this example's sake, that this list could be very long and that devices are added or removed from the network infrequently. This gives us a good opportunity to apply a readers/writer lock, as the list is traversed, or read, much more than it is modified. We use the guard macros we saw in Chapter 12 to ensure that the `acquire_read()`/ `release()` and `acquire_write()`/`release()` are called in pairs; that is, we don't forget to call `release()` after we are done with the mutex:

```
class HA_DiscoveryAgent
{
public:
  void add_device (Device *device)
  {
    ACE_WRITE_GUARD (ACE_RW_Thread_Mutex, mon, rwmutex_);
    list_add_item_i (device);
  }
```

```
      void remove_device (Device *device)
      {
        ACE_READ_GUARD (ACE_RW_Thread_Mutex, mon, rwmutex_);
        list_remove_item_i(device);
      }

      int contains_device (Device *device)
      {
        ACE_READ_GUARD_RETURN
          (ACE_RW_Thread_Mutex, mon, rwmutex_, -1);
        return list_contains_item_i (device);
      }

  private:
      void list_add_item_i (Device * device);
      int list_contains_item_i (Device * device);
      void list_remove_item_i (Device* device);

  private:
      DeviceList deviceList_;
      ACE_RW_Thread_Mutex rwmutex_;
};
```

14.1.3   Atomic Operation Wrapper

On most machine architectures, changes to basic types are atomic; that is, an increment of an integer variable does not require the use of synchronization primitives. However, on most multiprocessors, this is not true and is dependent on the memory *ordering* properties of the machine. If the machine memory is *strongly ordered*, modifications made to memory on one processor are immediately visible to the other processors and so synchronization is not required around global variables; otherwise, it is.

To help achieve transparent synchronization around basic types, ACE provides the ACE_Atomic_Op template wrapper. This class overloads all basic operations and ensures that a synchronization guard is used before the operation is performed.

To illustrate the use of ACE_Atomic_Op, we will solve the classic producer/ consumer problem using busy waiting. To implement our solution, we create a producer and a consumer task. Both tasks share a common buffer: The items that are produced are put into the buffer by the producer, and the consumer in turn picks up these items. To ensure that the producer doesn't overflow the buffer and that the consumer doesn't underflow, we use in and out counters. Whenever the producer adds an item, it increments the in counter by 1; similarly, when the client consumes an item, it increments the out counter by 1. The producer can produce only if (in – out) is not equal to the buffer size—the buffer isn't full—otherwise, it must wait. The client can consume only if (in – out) is not zero—the buffer isn't empty. Let's also assume that the program is running on a multi-processor on which memory is not *strongly ordered*. This means that if we use regular integers as our in and out counters, the increments will *not* be consistent; the producer may increment the in count, but the client will not see the increment, and vice versa. To ensure consistency, we first need to create a safe unsigned int type that we can use for the counters in our example:

```
typedef ACE_Atomic_Op<ACE_Thread_Mutex, unsigned int> SafeUInt;
```

The data passed between consumer and producer is an integer that, let's imagine for the example's sake, must be safely incremented to be produced correctly. We create a safe int type as:

```
typedef ACE_Atomic_Op<ACE_Thread_Mutex, int> SafeInt;
```

The producer and consumer tasks share the common production buffer and the in and out counter types, which we create on the main stack and pass by reference to each of the tasks. The producer uses a SafeInt, itemNo as the production variable, which it increments on each production and then adds to the buffer. We add a termination condition to each one of the threads such that after producing and consuming a fixed number of items, both threads terminate gracefully. To read the actual value stored in all the ACE_Atomic_Op objects, we use the value() accesor throughout the program:

```cpp
class Producer : public ACE_Task_Base
{
public:
  Producer (int *buf, SafeUInt &in, SafeUInt &out)
    : buf_(buf), in_(in), out_(out)
  { }

  int svc (void)
  {
    SafeInt itemNo = 0;
    while (1)
      {
```

```
                    // Busy wait.
                    do
                      { }
                    while (in_.value () - out_.value () == Q_SIZE);

                    itemNo++;
                    buf_[in_.value () % Q_SIZE] = itemNo.value ();
                    in_++;

                    ACE_DEBUG ((LM_DEBUG, ACE_TEXT ("Produced %d \n"),
                               itemNo.value ()));

                    if (check_termination (itemNo.value ()))
                      break;
                  }

              return 0;
            }

            int check_termination (int item)
            {
              return (item == MAX_PROD);
            }

        private:
            int * buf_;
            SafeUInt& in_;
            SafeUInt& out_;
        };

        class Consumer : public ACE_Task_Base
        {
        public:
            Consumer (int *buf, SafeUInt &in, SafeUInt& out)
              : buf_(buf), in_(in), out_(out)
            { }

            int svc (void)
            {
              while (1)
                  {
                    int item;

                    // Busy wait.
                    do
                      { }
```

```
        while (in_.value () - out_.value () == 0);

        item = buf_[out_.value () % Q_SIZE];
        out_++;

        ACE_DEBUG ((LM_DEBUG, ACE_TEXT ("Consumed %d\n"),
                   item));

        if (check_termination (item))
          break;
      }

    return 0;
  }

  int check_termination (int item)
  {
    return (item == MAX_PROD);
  }

private:
  int * buf_;
  SafeUInt& in_;
  SafeUInt& out_;
};
```

The threads themselves are created as usual on the main stack:

```
int ACE_TMAIN (int, ACE_TCHAR *[])
{
  int shared_buf[Q_SIZE];
  SafeUInt in = 0;
  SafeUInt out = 0;

  Producer producer (shared_buf, in, out);
  Consumer consumer (shared_buf, in, out);

  producer.activate();
  consumer.activate();
  producer.wait();
  consumer.wait();

  return 0;
}
```

14.1.4 Token Management

So far, we have been using synchronization and protection primitives on simplistic resources. In many cases, however, global resources are more complex structures, such as records in a memory-resident table or tree. Multiple threads act on individual records on the table by first obtaining the records, making sure that they have exclusive access to the record, making the desired modification, and then releasing the record. A simplistic solution to this problem is to create a separate lock structure that maintains a lock for each record that is to be managed as a unit. However, many complex issues come into play, such as how the lock structure is managed efficiently or how one avoids or detects deadlock situations, and what happens if the record table also needs to be accessed by remote threads.

ACE provides a framework solution that solves all these problems: the Token framework. Each record has associated with it an `ACE_Token` lock that internally maintains a strict FIFO ordering of threads that are waiting on the token. Before using a record, you acquire the token; after the modification, you release the token to the next waiter in line. Furthermore, a token manager is used to handle the tokens themselves, managing the creation, reference counting, and deletion of tokens.

The following example illustrates the use of tokens to provide record-level locking on a fixed-size table of device records that are maintained for our automated household. The records are kept within an `HA_Device_Repository` that supports update operations. We will assume that a device can be updated only by one client at any particular instant of time. To enforce this invariant, we create a token, an `ACE_Local_Mutex`, for every device that must first be acquired by a thread before it can perform an update. Once the token has been acquired, the thread can go into the device table, obtain the appropriate device, and update it. After completing the modification, the token is released, and the next thread in line can obtain the token:

```
class HA_Device_Repository
{
public:

  enum { N_DEVICES = 100 };

  HA_Device_Repository ()
  {
    for (int i = 0; i < N_DEVICES; i++)
      tokens_[i] = new ACE_Local_Mutex (0, 0, 1);
  }
```

```
  ~HA_Device_Repository ()
  {
    for (int i = 0; i < N_DEVICES; i++)
      delete tokens_[i];
  }

  int update_device (int device_id, char *commands)
  {
    this->tokens_[device_id]->acquire ();

    Device *curr_device = this->devices_[device_id];
    internal_do (curr_device);

    this->tokens_[device_id]->release ();

    return 0;
  }

  void internal_do (Device *device);

private:
  Device *devices_[N_DEVICES];
  ACE_Local_Mutex *tokens_[N_DEVICES];
  unsigned int seed_;
};
```

To illustrate the device repository, we modify our `HA_CommandHandler`
task so that it invokes `update_device()` on the repository, using multiple
threads:

```
class HA_CommandHandler : public ACE_Task_Base
{
public:
  enum { N_THREADS = 5 };

  HA_CommandHandler (HA_Device_Repository &rep) : rep_(rep)
  { }

  int svc (void)
  {
    for (int i = 0; i < HA_Device_Repository::N_DEVICES; i++)
      rep_.update_device (i, "");
    return 0;
  }
```

```
private:
  HA_Device_Repository &rep_;
};

int ACE_TMAIN (int, ACE_TCHAR *[])
{
  HA_Device_Repository rep;
  HA_CommandHandler handler (rep);
  handler.activate (THR_NEW_LWP | THR_JOINABLE,
                    HA_CommandHandler::N_THREADS);
  handler.wait ();
  return 0;
}
```

One of the nice features that the ACE Token framework provides is deadlock detection, which comes in handy to make sure that the algorithms you are designing for your system do not cause deadlock. To illustrate a deadlock situation and the ACE deadlock detection features, we create two tasks, each running a single thread. Both tasks share two resources—`resource1` and `resource2`—that are protected by named tokens of the same name. Unlike the previous example, in which we precreated and shared unnamed tokens, this example uses the framework to manage the tokens for us by name. This allows both threads to create an `ACE_Local_Mutex` named `resource1`, secure in the knowledge that they are indeed sharing a single token. The `mutex1` object acts as a proxy to a shared token for `resource1`. The shared token itself is reference counted; when both `mutex1` objects for threads one and two go out of scope, the token is deleted:

```
class ThreadOne : public ACE_Task_Base
{
public:
  virtual int svc (void)
  {
    ACE_Local_Mutex mutex1 ("resource1",
                            0, // Deadlock detection enabled.
                            1);// Debugging enabled.
    mutex1.acquire ();
    ACE_OS::sleep (2);
    ACE_Local_Mutex mutex2 ("resource2", 0, 1);
    mutex2.acquire ();
    return 0;
  }
};
```

```
class ThreadTwo : public ACE_Task_Base
{
public:
  virtual int svc (void)
  {
    ACE_Local_Mutex mutex2 ("resource2",
                             0, // Deadlock detection enabled.
                             1);// Debugging enabled.
    mutex2.acquire ();
    ACE_OS::sleep (2);
    ACE_Local_Mutex mutex1 ("resource1",
                             0, // Deadlock detection enabled.
                             1);// Debugging enabled.
    mutex1.acquire ();
    return 0;
  }
};

int ACE_TMAIN (int, ACE_TCHAR *[])
{
  ThreadOne t1;
  ThreadTwo t2;

  t1.activate ();
  ACE_OS::sleep (1);
  t2.activate ();
  t1.wait ();
  t2.wait ();

  return 0;
}
```

Resource acquisitions are forced to occur in the following order:

- Thread one acquires a lock on `resource1`
- Thread two acquires a lock on `resource2`
- Thread one blocks trying to acquire `resource2`
- Thread two blocks trying to acquire `resource1`

This order eventually leads to a deadlock situation in which thread one is waiting for `resource2` and can't get it because thread two has it and thread two wants `resource1` but can't get it because thread one has it. Both threads end up waiting for each other forever.

Note that when we created the ACE_Local_Mutex, we specified that we did not want deadlock detection to be ignored and wanted debugging on. This causes ACE to detect the deadlock; when it occurs, the acquire() call on the local mutex fails, setting errno to EDEADLOCK. Enabling debugging causes the following output to be displayed when the program is run:

```
(3224) acquired resource1
(1192) acquired resource2
(3224) waiting for resource2, owner is /USYYID/612/1192, total
waiters == 2
(1192) Deadlock detected.
/USYYID/612/1192 owns resource2 and is waiting for resource1.
/USYYID/612/3224 owns resource1 and is waiting for resource2.
```

Note that although it can detect deadlock, the Token framework cannot prevent it. An appropriate prevention scheme must be devised by the application programmer; this could, for example, include a try and back-off strategy. That is, if deadlock is detected, back off releasing all your own locks and start acquiring them all over again.

14.2 Thread Synchronization

Synchronization is a process by which you can control the order in which threads execute to complete a task. We have already seen several examples of this; we often try to order our code execution such that the main thread doesn't exit before the other threads are done. In fact, the *protection* code in the previous section also has a similar flavor to it; we try to control the order of the threads as they access shared resources. However, we believe that synchronization and protection are sufficiently different to warrant separate sections.

In many instances, you want to make sure that one thread executes before the other or some other specific ordering is needed. For example, you might want a background thread to execute if a certain condition is true, or you may want one thread to *signal* another thread that it is time for it to go. ACE provides a number of primitives that are specifically designed for these purposes. We list them in Table 14.2.

Table 14.2. ACE Synchronization Primitives

Primitive	Description
`ACE_Condition`	A condition variable; allows *signaling* other threads to indicate event occurrence
`ACE_Semaphore`	A counting semaphore; can be used as a signaling mechanism and also for synchronization purposes
`ACE_Barrier`	Blocks all threads of execution until they all reach the *barrier line*, after which all threads continue
`ACE_Event`	A simple synchronization object that is used to signal events to other threads

14.2.1 Using Semaphores

A semaphore is a non-negative integer count that is used to coordinate access among multiple resources. *Acquiring* a semaphore causes the count to decrement, and *releasing* a semaphore causes the count to increment. If the count reaches 0— no resources left—and a thread tries to acquire the semaphore, it will block until the semaphore count is incremented to a value that is greater than 0. This happens when another thread releases on the semaphore. A semaphore count *will never be negative.* When using a semaphore, you initialize the semaphore count to a non-negative value that represents the number of resources you have.

Mutexes assume that the thread that acquires the mutex will also be the one that releases it. Semaphores, on the other hand, are usually acquired by one thread but released by another. It is this unique characteristic that allows one to use semaphores so effectively.

Semaphores are probably the most versatile synchronization primitive provided by ACE. In fact, a *binary* semaphore can be used in place of a mutex, and a regular semaphore can be used in most places where a condition variable is being used.

Once again, we implement a solution to the producer/consumer problem, this time using counting semaphores. We use the built-in `ACE_Message_Queue` held by the consumer as the shared data buffer between the producer and consumer. Using semaphores, we control the maximum number of messages the message queue can have at any particular instant. In other words, we implement a high-water-mark mechanism; the message queue already has this functionality built in; we essentially reproduce it in an inefficient way for the sake of the example. To make things interesting, the consumer task has multiple threads.

The `Producer` produces `ACE_Message_Blocks` that it enqueues on the consumer task's message queue. Each block contains an integer identifier as the only payload. When the producer is done producing, it sends a hang-up message to the consumer, making it shut down.

Before the producer can produce any items, it must acquire the producer semaphore, `psema_`, which represents the maximum capacity of the consumer's message queue, or the high-water mark. The initial count value for `psema_` is set to the high water mark to begin with. Each time `psema_` is acquired, this number is atomically decremented. Finally, when this count becomes 0, the producer cannot enqueue more elements on the consumer's queue:

```cpp
class Producer : public ACE_Task_Base
{
public:
  enum { MAX_PROD = 128 };

  Producer (ACE_Semaphore& psema, ACE_Semaphore& csema,
            Consumer &consumer)
    : psema_(psema), csema_(csema), consumer_(consumer)
  { }

  int svc (void)
  {
    for (int i = 0; i <= MAX_PROD; i++)
      produce_item (i);
    hang_up ();
    return 0;
  }

  void produce_item (int item)
  {
    psema_.acquire ();
    ACE_Message_Block *mb
      = new ACE_Message_Block (sizeof (int),
                               ACE_Message_Block::MB_DATA);
    ACE_OS::memcpy (mb->wr_ptr (), &item, sizeof item);
    mb->wr_ptr (sizeof (int));
    this->consumer_.putq (mb);

    ACE_DEBUG ((LM_DEBUG, ACE_TEXT ("(%t) Produced %d\n"), item));
    csema_.release();
  }
```

```
    void hang_up ()
    {
      psema_.acquire ();
      ACE_Message_Block *mb =
        new ACE_Message_Block (0, ACE_Message_Block::MB_HANGUP);
      this->consumer_.putq (mb);
      csema_.release ();
    }

private:
    ACE_Semaphore& psema_;
    ACE_Semaphore& csema_;
    Consumer& consumer_;
};
```

The csema_ semaphore, on the other hand, is initialized to 0 in the beginning; its value is incremented, by calling csema_.release(), by the producer
every time it produces a new element. If the consumer threads are blocked on an
acquire() of the csema_ variable, one thread will wake up each time the
producer calls release(), causing the woken thread to consume the new
element.

Once a consumer thread unblocks, it consumes the element from the queue
and then calls release() on psema_, the producer semaphore, as the
consumption has freed up a space in the shared message queue. This increments
the psema_ count by 1, allowing the producer to continue and use up the free
space in the queue:

```
class Consumer : public ACE_Task<ACE_MT_SYNCH>
{
public:
  enum { N_THREADS = 5 };

  Consumer (ACE_Semaphore& psema, ACE_Semaphore& csema)
    : psema_(psema), csema_(csema), exit_condition_(0)
  { }

  int svc (void)
  {
    while (!is_closed ())
      consume_item ();
    return 0;
  }
```

```
void consume_item ()
{
  csema_.acquire ();
  if (!is_closed ())
    {
      ACE_Message_Block *mb;
      this->getq (mb);
      if (mb->msg_type () == ACE_Message_Block::MB_HANGUP)
        {
          shutdown ();
          mb->release ();
          return;
        }
      else
        {
          ACE_DEBUG ((LM_DEBUG,
                      ACE_TEXT ("(%t) Consumed %d\n"),
                      *((int*)mb->rd_ptr ())));
          mb->release();
        }
      psema_.release ();
    }
}

void shutdown (void)
{
  exit_condition_ = 1;
  this->msg_queue ()->deactivate ();
  csema_.release (N_THREADS);
}

int is_closed (void)
{
  return exit_condition_;
}

private:
  ACE_Semaphore& psema_;
  ACE_Semaphore& csema_;
  int exit_condition_;
};
```

Shutdown of the consumer task is a little complicated because of the multiple threads that are running in it. Because the producer sends only a single hang-up message to the consumer task, only one thread will receive the hangup; the others are blocked, either waiting for messages on the queue or on the consumer semaphore. Therefore, the consumer thread that receives the hangup must mark the state of the task as closed and then wake up all the other threads so that they notice the closed condition and exit. The consumer's `shutdown()` method does this by first setting the `exit_condition_` to true and then waking up all the threads on the message queue by calling `deactivate()` on it and then decrementing the semaphore count by the number of consumer threads, thereby releasing all the threads waiting on the semaphore:

```
int ACE_TMAIN (int, ACE_TCHAR *[])
{
  ACE_Semaphore psem (5);
  ACE_Semaphore csem (0);

  Consumer consumer (psem, csem);
  Producer producer (psem, csem, consumer);

  producer.activate ();
  consumer.activate (THR_NEW_LWP | THR_JOINABLE,
                     Consumer::N_THREADS);

  producer.wait ();
  consumer.wait ();

  return 0;
}
```

The code here is pretty much boilerplate, except for the initialization of the two semaphores `psem` and `csem`. Once again, note that `psem` is initialized to the maximum number of allowable elements on the queue, five, indicating that the producer can produce until the queue is full. On the other hand, `csem` is initialized to 0, indicating that the consumer can't consume at all until the producer calls release on `csem`.

14.2.2   Using Barriers

Barriers have a role very similar to their name. A group of threads can use a barrier to collectively synchronize with one another. In essence, each thread calls `wait()` on the barrier when it has reached some well-known state and then blocks, waiting for all other participating threads to call `wait()`, indicating that they too have reached the mutual state. Once they have reached the barrier, all the threads unblock and continue together.

The ACE barrier component is `ACE_Barrier`. The constructor of this class takes as its first argument a count of the number of threads that are synchronizing with the barrier. The following example illustrates how barriers can be used to ensure that threads in our home automation command handler task start up and shut down together. To achieve this, we start by creating two barriers: a `startup_barrier` and a `shutdown_barrier`. Each barrier is passed a count of the number of threads running in the handler task. The barriers are then passed to the handler by reference:

```
int ACE_TMAIN (int, ACE_TCHAR *[])
{
  ACE_Barrier startup_barrier (HA_CommandHandler::N_THREADS);
  ACE_Barrier shutdown_barrier (HA_CommandHandler::N_THREADS);

  HA_CommandHandler handler (startup_barrier, shutdown_barrier);
  handler.activate (THR_NEW_LWP | THR_JOINABLE,
                    HA_CommandHandler::N_THREADS);
  handler.wait ();
  return 0;
}
```

When a new handler thread is created, it enters the `svc()` method and initializes itself by calling `initialize_handler()`, after which it calls `wait()` on the start-up barrier. This blocks the thread on the barrier until all the other handler threads initialize themselves and also call `wait()` on the start-up barrier. After completing start-up, the handler begins handling command requests by calling `handle_command_requests()`. When the handler receives the command to shut down, `handle_command_requests()` returns −1, and the threads block on the shutdown barrier. Once all threads reach this barrier, they all exit together:

```
class HA_CommandHandler : public ACE_Task<ACE_MT_SYNCH>
{
public:
  enum { N_THREADS = 5 };

  HA_CommandHandler (ACE_Barrier& startup_barrier,
                     ACE_Barrier &shutdown_barrier)
    : startup_barrier_(startup_barrier),
      shutdown_barrier_(shutdown_barrier)
    { }
```

```
    void initialize_handler (void);
    int handle_command_requests (void);

    int svc (void)
    {
      initialize_handler ();
      startup_barrier_.wait ();
      ACE_DEBUG ((LM_DEBUG, ACE_TEXT ("(%t: %D) Started\n")));

      while (handle_command_requests () > 0)
        ;

      shutdown_barrier_.wait ();
      ACE_DEBUG ((LM_DEBUG, ACE_TEXT ("(%t: %D) Ended\n")));

      return 0;
    }

private:
  ACE_Barrier& startup_barrier_;
  ACE_Barrier& shutdown_barrier_;
};
```

For illustrative purposes, we set up the `initialize_handler()` method and `handle_command_requests()` method to sleep for random time periods, thus ensuring that each handler thread takes a different time period to initialize and to shut down. The barriers will ensure that they all start up and exit at the same time; we display the start-up and shut-down times for each thread by using the `%D` current timestamp format specifier for the `ACE_DEBUG` macro. The resultant output shows that start-up and shut-down times are indeed in synch for all threads:

```
(764: 08/12/2001 23.40.11.214000) Started
(720: 08/12/2001 23.40.11.214000) Started
(1108: 08/12/2001 23.40.11.214000) Started
(1168: 08/12/2001 23.40.11.214000) Started
(1080: 08/12/2001 23.40.11.214000) Started
(1168: 08/12/2001 23.40.11.334000) Ended
(720: 08/12/2001 23.40.11.334000) Ended
(764: 08/12/2001 23.40.11.334000) Ended
(1108: 08/12/2001 23.40.11.334000) Ended
(1080: 08/12/2001 23.40.11.334000) Ended
```

14.3 Thread-Specific Storage

When you create a thread, all you create is a thread stack, a signal mask, and a task control block for the new thread. The thread carries no other state information on creation. Nonetheless, it is convenient to be able to store state information that is specific to a thread: *thread-specific storage (TSS),* or *thread local storage.*

One classic example of the use of TSS is with the application global `errno`. The global `errno` is used to indicate the most recent error that has occurred within an application. When multithreaded programs first appeared on UNIX platforms, `errno` posed a problem. Different errors can occur within different threads of the application, so if `errno` is global, which error would it hold? Putting `errno` in thread-specific storage solves this problem. Logically, the variable is global but is kept in TSS.

Thread-specific storage should be used for all objects that you consider to be part and parcel of a thread. ACE uses TSS internally to store a thread-specific output stream for the purposes of logging. By doing this, no locks are required on any of the logging streams, as only the owning thread can access the TSS stream. This helps keeps the code efficient and lightweight.

The `ACE_Thread` class provides access to the low-level OS TSS methods, but in most cases, you can avoid these tedious APIs by using the `ACE_TSS` class template. This class is very simple to use. You simply pass it the data you want to be stored in TSS as its template parameter and then use the `operator->()` method to access the data when you need it. The `operator->()` creates and stores the data in TSS when called the first time. The destructor for `ACE_TSS` ensures that the TSS data is properly removed and destroyed.

One useful application of TSS is the addition of a context object that can hold information specific to the current client that is using the thread. For example, if you were to use a thread-per-connection model, you could keep connection-specific information within TSS, where you can get to it easily and efficiently. At least one database server we know keeps transactional context within TSS for each connection it hands out.

We can use the same idea to improve our home automation command handler. The handler keeps a generic-client context object in TSS. The context can then hold any arbitrary, named tidbit of information, using an internal attribute map:

```
// Client-specific context information.
class ClientContext
{
public:
  void *get_attribute (const char *name);
```

```
     void set_attribute (const char *name, void *value);

private:
  Map attributeMap_;
};
```

To store this object in TSS, all you need to do is wrap the object within the
ACE_TSS template. The first access causes an instance of the type ClassCon-
text to be created on the heap and stored within thread-specific storage. For
illustrative purposes, we store the current thread ID in the context, only to obtain it
at a later point and display it:

```
class HA_CommandHandler : public ACE_Task<ACE_MT_SYNCH>
{
public:
  virtual int svc (void)
  {
    ACE_thread_t tid = this->thr_mgr ()->thr_self ();
    // Set our identifier in TSS
    this->tss_ctx_->set_attribute ("thread_id", &tid);

    while (handle_requests () > 0)
      ;

    return 0;
  }

  int handle_requests (void)
  {
    ACE_thread_t *tid =
      (ACE_thread_t*)this->tss_ctx_->get_attribute ("thread_id");
    ACE_DEBUG ((LM_DEBUG, ACE_TEXT ("(%t) TSS TID: %d \n"),
                *tid));

    // do work.
    return -1;
  }

private:
  ACE_TSS<ClientContext> tss_ctx_;
};
```

14.4 Summary

In this chapter, we covered some of the more advanced synchronization and protection primitives that are available from the ACE toolkit. We discussed recursive mutex locks, using the `ACE_Recursive_Mutex` and `ACE_Recursive_Thread_Mutex` classes, readers/writer locks with `ACE_RW_Mutex` and `ACE_RW_Thread_Mutex`, introduced the Token framework with `ACE_Local_Mutex`, and talked about enforcing atomic arithmetic operations on multiprocessors with the `ACE_Atomic_Op` wrapper as new protection primitives. We also introduced several new synchronization primitives, including counting semaphores with `ACE_Semaphore` and barriers with `ACE_Barrier`. Finally, we introduced thread-specific storage as an efficient means to get around protection with thread-specific data and the `ACE_TSS` wrapper.

Chapter 15
Active Objects

Threads need to cooperate with one another. Various illustrations of thread cooperation were given in previous chapters, including cooperation using condition variables, semaphores, and message queues.

The Active Object pattern has been specifically designed to provide an object-based solution to cooperative processing between threads. The pattern is based on the requirement that two Active Objects should communicate through what look like regular method calls, but these methods will be executed in the context of the receiver, not that of the invoker; hence the name Active Object. In other words, every object that is active has a private thread of control that is used to execute any methods that a client invokes on the object.

This comes in handy when you have an object whose method calls take a long time to complete: for example, a proxy to a remote service. You can make this proxy an Active Object and free up the main thread of control to do other things, such as interact with the user or run a GUI event loop.

This chapter examines the Active Object pattern and illustrates how you can make this pattern work in your applications. We also introduce several new components used to implement the pattern; these components will also be useful when we talk about thread pools (Chapter 16).

Main Thread   Logger Thread

```
//the main thread                   //the logger thread..
int main()                          Logger::log(const char* data)
{                                   {
ActiveLogger logger;                  ..
logger.activate();
//create an active                   //logs the data in a separate
//logger object                      //thread of control. Context
                                     //switch occurs here.
logger.log(data);
//this occurs in the
//context of the
//logger thread, that                 ..
//returns immediately in            }
//main i.e., this is
 //an asynchronous call. ..
}
```

Figure 15.1. Asynchronous `log()` method

15.1 The Pattern

Figure 15.1 illustrates the behavior of an active Logger object. The main thread starts by creating a object and then activating it. The `activate()` call causes the `Logger` object to spawn its own private thread of control. Next, the main thread invokes the `log()` method. Here is where the Active Object magic steps in. The `log()` method is executed in the context of the `Logger`-spawned thread, *not* in the context of the main thread. Therefore, when it returns in the main thread, there is no guarantee that the `log()` method has completed execution or, for that matter, even started execution. In Active Object parlance, the `Logger` object is *active*.

15.1.1 Pattern Participants

The Active Object pattern is a combination of the Command pattern and the Proxy pattern. The participants in the pattern, illustrated in Figure 15.2, are as follows:

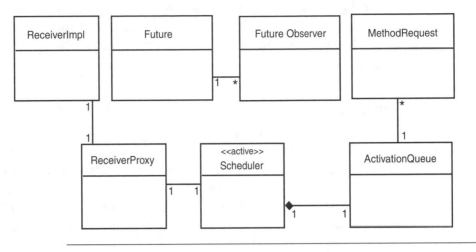

Figure 15.2. Active Object pattern participants

- *Receiver Implementation*. The Receiver Implementation is independent of threading details.
- *Scheduler*. The `Scheduler` class has a reference to an Activation Queue on which the private thread of control used by the Active Object remains blocked until a new method request arrives. When a request arrives, the private thread wakes up, dequeues the request, and executes it.
- *Proxy*. Proxy to the Receiver object that will be used by the client to invoke requests. This class converts method invocations to method requests and inserts them on the activation queue. The Proxy object keeps a reference to the real Receiver Implementation object (Proxy pattern).
- *Method Request*. An object that encapsulates a method call in the form of an object (Command pattern). Each method on the Receiver interface will have one method request class associated with it. To invoke the method on the `ReceiverImpl`, the method request will need to have a reference to the `ReceiverImpl`.
- *Activation Queue*. A priority queue that is held by the Scheduler. All method requests are placed on this queue by the Proxy object and are picked up by the private thread of the Active Object.
- *Future*. Returned to the client, a token that can be redeemed at a later time to obtain the result of the asynchronous operation.

- *Future Observer.* A callback object (Command pattern) that is associated with a Future and is automatically called when the return value of the asynchronous call is set in the Future object, that is, is called when the asynchronous operation has completed.

15.1.2 Collaborations

The collaborations between the various participants are illustrated by a sequence diagram in Figure 15.3. When it wishes to execute a method on the `Receiver-Impl` object, a client thread first obtains a reference to the receiver's `RemoteProxy` object. Once it has a reference, the client thread can invoke any of the active methods on the receiver. In the diagram, the client invokes `active_operation()` on the `RemoteProxy`.

The `RemoteProxy` object then creates the corresponding concrete Method Request object, named `ActiveOp`, and enqueues it on the `Activation-Queue`. Note that the `Scheduler`, which encapsulates the private thread of the Active Object, has already issued a blocking `dequeue()` call on the `Activa-tionQueue` and is waiting for method requests to arrive on the queue. When the `RemoteProxy` object enqueues the Method Request, the scheduler thread wakes up, dequeues the Method Request object, and invokes the `call()` method on it, which in turns invokes `active_operation()` on the `ReceiverImpl` object.

Note that to keep things simple, the sequence diagram did not show Futures. If `active_operation()` does not have a return value, you may not need to use Futures. When it invokes `active_operation()` on `RemoteProxy`, the client immediately returns a Future object to the client. The client can either block or poll on the Future, waiting for a result. Alternatively, you can attach a Future Observer to the Future object. In the latter case, the Future Observer is automatically called back—by the private thread of control owned by the Active Object—when the asynchronous operation completes and the result is available.

15.2 Using the Pattern

In this example, we have a home automation controller on our home network. This controller is capable of providing status information about itself to any clients on the network. The client devices on the network use an agent object to talk to the controller. The agent object encapsulates the remoting protocol and other network

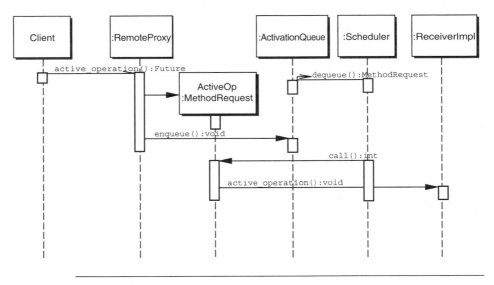

Figure 15.3. Active Object collaborations

details, providing clients with an easy-to-use representation of the controller: once again, the Proxy pattern:

```
class HA_ControllerAgent
{
  // Proxy to the HA_Controller that is on the network.
public:
  HA_ControllerAgent ()
  {
    ACE_TRACE
      (ACE_TEXT ("HA_ControllerAgent::HA_ControllerAgent"));
    status_result_ = 1;
  }

  int status_update (void)
  {
    ACE_TRACE (ACE_TEXT ("HA_ControllerAgent::status_update"));
    ACE_DEBUG ((LM_DEBUG,
                ACE_TEXT ("Obtaining a status_update in %t ")
                ACE_TEXT ("thread of control\n")));
    // Simulate time to send message and get status.
    ACE_OS::sleep (2);
    return next_result_id ();
  }
```

```
private:
  int next_result_id (void)
  {
    ACE_TRACE (ACE_TEXT ("HA_ControllerAgent::next_cmd_id"));
    return status_result_++;
  }

  int status_result_;
};
```

Let's assume that it takes a while for the agent to talk to the controller, obtain the status, and get back. This seems like an ideal object to turn into an Active Object (Figure 15.4). Note that we will not change any code within the agent object, and it will therefore contain no details about how threads are going to be used to dispatch its methods:

```
class StatusUpdate : public ACE_Method_Request
{
public:
  StatusUpdate (HA_ControllerAgent& controller,
                ACE_Future<int>& returnVal)
    : controller_(controller), returnVal_(returnVal)
  {
    ACE_TRACE (ACE_TEXT ("StatusUpdate::StatusUpdate"));
  }

  virtual int call (void)
  {
    ACE_TRACE (ACE_TEXT ("StatusUpdate::call"));

    // status_update with the controller.
    this->returnVal_.set (this->controller_.status_update ());
    return 0;
  }

private:
  HA_ControllerAgent& controller_;
  ACE_Future<int> returnVal_;
};
```

The StatusUpdate class is a method request Command object that encapsulates the activation record needed to perform a deferred call to the agent. The

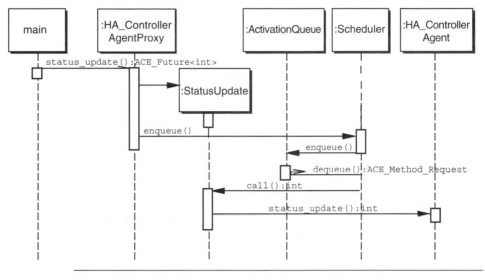

Figure 15.4. Active Object pattern applied to example

method request object is created when the client of the Active Object makes a request on the Proxy. At a later point, the Active Object obtains the method request and issues `call()` on it. This in turn causes the method request object to invoke the right method on the implementation object of the Active Object (`HA_ControllerAgent`).

In this case, when a client uses an `HA_ControllerAgentProxy` to obtain a status update, a `StatusUpdate` object that keeps a reference to the real `HA_ControllerAgent` implementation object and a reference to the Future object is created. Later, the `Scheduler` object will pick up the `StatusUpdate` object from its queue in the thread of control of the Active Object and will issue `call()` on it. This invokes `status_update()` on the real implementation object.

You will need to create one method request object for each method of your Active Object. To keep things simple for the sake of our example, we show the `HA_ControllerAgent` as having only two methods, which is not very realistic. The first method is `status_update()`, and the second is `exit()`. The `ExitMethod` class is the method request object used when the client programmer calls `exit()` on the `HA_ControllerAgentProxy`. Note that in this case, the call method returns –1. We will see how we use this to cause the active object to shut down:

```
class ExitMethod : public ACE_Method_Request
{
public:
  virtual int call (void)
  {
    // Cause exit.
    return -1;
  }
};
```

The Scheduler class is the heart of the Active Object. This class "holds" the thread of control. This Scheduler derives from ACE_Task_Base (see Chapter 12), which will start a new thread of control in the svc() method once the activate() method is called. Note that Scheduler constructor calls activate() with no arguments, causing a single thread to start up once a Scheduler object is constructed:

```
class Scheduler : public ACE_Task_Base
{
public:
  Scheduler ()
  {
    ACE_TRACE (ACE_TEXT ("Scheduler::Scheduler"));
    this->activate ();
  }

  virtual int svc (void)
  {
    ACE_TRACE (ACE_TEXT ("Scheduler::svc"));

    while (1)
      {
        // Dequeue the next method object
        auto_ptr<ACE_Method_Request>
          request (this->activation_queue_.dequeue ());

        // Invoke the method request.
        if (request->call () == -1)
          break;
      }

    return 0;
  }
```

```
      int enqueue (ACE_Method_Request *request)
      {
        ACE_TRACE (ACE_TEXT ("Scheduler::enqueue"));
        return this->activation_queue_.enqueue (request);
      }

  private:
    ACE_Activation_Queue activation_queue_;
  };
```

The `Scheduler` keeps an underlying activation queue on which method request objects are enqueued when the client requests service. The `Scheduler` uses its thread to dequeue method objects from its activation queue and then invoke the `call()` method on these objects. Thus, whatever happens in `call()` happens in the context of the `Scheduler`'s thread, not in that of the client thread.

Also, note that our `Scheduler` has been built such that if the `call()` method returns –1, the Active Object thread gracefully exits. This is exactly what happens if an `ExitMethod` object is placed on the activation queue by the client. Now you probably understand why we returned –1 from the call method in the `ExitMethod` class.

Finally, we get to the `HA_ControllerAgentProxy` class, which is used by the client. `HA_ControllerAgentProxy` aggregates both the `Scheduler` class and the agent implementation:

```
class HA_ControllerAgentProxy
{
  // This acts as a Proxy to the controller impl object.
public:
  ACE_Future<int> status_update (void)
  {
    ACE_TRACE
      (ACE_TEXT ("HA_ControllerAgentProxy::status_update"));
    ACE_Future<int> result;

    // Create and enqueue a method request on the scheduler.
    this->scheduler_.enqueue
      (new StatusUpdate (this->controller_, result));

    // Return Future to the client.
    return result;
  }
```

```
  void exit (void)
  {
    ACE_TRACE (ACE_TEXT ("HA_ControllerAgentProxy::exit"));
    this->scheduler_.enqueue (new ExitMethod);
  }

private:
  Scheduler scheduler_;
  HA_ControllerAgent controller_;
};
```

When it issues a request on the Proxy, all a client does is create the corresponding method request object and pass it along to the `Scheduler`. It is the `Scheduler`'s responsibility to use the method object and then destroy it—done by using the C++ `auto_ptr` template class in this example.

In the case of the `status_update()` method, the client is returned a Future object, which holds a reference to the result that will be returned to the client. Next, let's look at how the client can redeem the Future for its actual value:

```
int ACE_TMAIN (int, ACE_TCHAR *[])
{
  HA_ControllerAgentProxy controller;
  ACE_Future<int> results[10];

  for (int i = 0 ; i < 10; i++)
    results[i] = controller.status_update ();

  ACE_OS::sleep (5);  // Do other work.

  // Get results...
  for (int j = 0; j < 10; j++)
    {
      int result;
      results[j].get (result);
      ACE_DEBUG ((LM_DEBUG,
                  ACE_TEXT ("New status_update %d\n"), result));
    }

  // Cause the status_updater threads to exit.
  controller.exit ();
  ACE_Thread_Manager::instance ()->wait ();
  return 0;
}
```

Here, the client of the active agent object uses its `status_update()` method to issue requests to get the current status of the controller. The agent returns Futures to the client, which the client redeems by using the `get()` method of the Future object. If the agent has not finished obtaining the status, which is a distinct possibility in our example, the client will block on the `get()` method of the Future until the results are obtained from the remote controller.

The `ACE_Future` class also allows you to do a timed wait for results that are returned using Futures. To do this, simply pass in an `ACE_Time_Value` with the absolute time until which you are willing to block. If the value is not available and a timeout occurs, the `get()` method returns –1 and sets the errno to `ETIME`.

Instead of blocking on the future and waiting for results, the client can attach a concrete `ACE_Future_Observer` to the `ACE_Future` returned by the Proxy. To create a concrete observer, simply subclass `ACE_Future_Observer` and implement the `update()` method, which takes a single argument: an `ACE_Future` class. Because our `status_update()` method returns an `int`, the template is instantiated as `ACE_Future<int>` and the observer as `ACE_Future_Observer<int>`:

```
class CompletionCallBack : public ACE_Future_Observer<int>
{
public:
  CompletionCallBack (HA_ControllerAgentProxy& proxy)
    : proxy_(proxy)
  { }

  virtual void update (const ACE_Future<int>& future)
  {
    int result;
    ((ACE_Future<int>)future) get (result);
    ACE_DEBUG ((LM_INFO,
                ACE_TEXT ("(%t) New Status %d\n"), result));
    if (result == 10)
      this->proxy_.exit ();
  }

private:
  HA_ControllerAgentProxy& proxy_;
};
```

To attach the observer to a Future, you simply call `attach()` on the Future object when it is returned by the Proxy object:

```
int ACE_TMAIN (int, ACE_TCHAR *[])
{
  HA_ControllerAgentProxy controller;
  ACE_Future<int> results[10];
  CompletionCallBack cb (controller);

  for (int i = 0 ; i < 10; i++)
    {
      results[i] = controller.status_update ();
      results[i].attach (&cb);
    }

  ACE_Thread_Manager::instance ()->wait ();
  return 0;
}
```

This makes the code a bit more simple. Now when a `status_update ()` method completes, we are assured that the Observer's `update ()` method is automatically called. This frees up the client thread of control to do other things instead of simply waiting for the call to complete.

15.3 Summary

In this chapter, we described the Active Object pattern and all its component participants. This pattern allows you to build an object whose methods are run asynchronously. This comes in handy when you have long-running I/O calls that you wish to run in a separate thread of control. We also illustrated how you can obtain the result of asynchronous operations; that is, you can either block on an `ACE_Future` object, or you can attach an Observer to the Future and receive a callback on method completion. In the next chapter, we reuse the Active Object pattern and the ACE Task framework to build thread pools.

Chapter 16
Thread Pools

Most network servers are designed to handle multiple client requests simultaneously. As we have seen, there are multiple ways to achieve this, including using reactive event handling, multiple processes, or multiple threads in our servers. When building a multithreaded server, many design options are available, including

- Spawning a new thread for each request
- Spawning a new thread for each connection/session
- Prespawning a managed pool of threads, or creating a thread pool

In this chapter, we explore thread pools in some detail. We start by defining what we mean by a thread pool and what advantages it provides over some of the other approaches to building multithreaded servers. We then go into some detail about various types of thread pools and their performance characteristics, illustrating a few types with example pools that are built using the ACE components. Finally, we look at two ACE_Reactor implementations that can use thread pools for concurrent event handling.

16.1 Understanding Thread Pools

In the thread pool model, we do not create a new thread for each session or request and then destroy it; rather, we prespawn all the threads we are going to use and keep them around in a pool. This bounds the cost of the resources that the server is going to use, so you as a developer always know how many threads are running in the server.

Contrast this with the thread-per-request model, in which a new thread is created for each request. If it receives a large spurt of requests in a short period of time, the server will spawn a large number of threads to handle the load. This will cause degradation in service for all requests and may cause resource allocation failures as the load increases. In the thread pool model, when a request arrives, a thread is chosen from the queue to handle the request; if there are no threads in the pool when the request arrives, it is enqueued until one of the worker threads returns to the pool.

The thread pool model has several variants, each with different performance characteristics:

- *Half-sync/half-async model.* In this model, a single listener thread asynchronously receives requests and buffers them in a queue. A separate set of worker threads synchronously processes the requests.

- *Leader/followers model.* In this model, a single thread is the leader and the rest are followers in the thread pool. When a request arrives, the leader picks it up, selects one of the followers as the new leader, and then continues to process the request. Thus in this case, the thread that receives the request is also the one that handles it.

16.2 Half-Sync/Half-Async Model

This model breaks the thread pool into three separate layers:

1. The asynchronous layer, which receives the asynchronous requests
2. The queueing layer, which buffers the requests
3. The synchronous layer, which contains several threads of control blocked on the queueing layer

When the queueing layer indicates that there is new data, the synchronous layer handles the request synchronously in a separate thread of control. This model has the following advantages.

- The queuing layer can help handle bursty clients; if there are no threads to handle a request, they are simply buffered in the queueing layer.

- The synchronous layer is simple and independent of any asynchronous processing details. Each synchronous thread blocks on the queueing layer, waiting for a request.

This model also has disadvantages.

- Because a thread switch occurs at the queueing layer, we must incur synchronization and context switch overhead. Furthermore, on a multiprocessor machine, we may experience data copying and cache coherency overhead.

- We cannot keep any request information on the stack or in thread-specific storage, as the request is processed in a different worker thread.

Let's go through a simple example implementation of this model. In this example, the asynchronous layer is implemented as an `ACE_Task` subclass, `Manager`, which receives requests on its underlying message queue. Each worker thread is implemented by the `Worker` class, which is also an `ACE_Task` derivative. When it receives a request, the `Manager` picks a `Worker` object from the worker thread pool and enqueues the request on the `Worker` object's underlying `ACE_Message_Queue`. This queue acts as the queueing layer between the asynchronous `Manager` and the synchronous `Worker` class.

First, let's look at the `Manager` task:

```
class Manager: public ACE_Task<ACE_MT_SYNCH>, IManager
{
public:
  enum {POOL_SIZE = 5, MAX_TIMEOUT = 5};

  Manager ()
    : shutdown_(0), workers_lock_(), workers_cond_(workers_lock_)
  {
    ACE_TRACE (ACE_TEXT ("Manager::Manager"));
  }

  int svc (void)
  {
    ACE_TRACE (ACE_TEXT ("Manager::svc"));

    ACE_DEBUG ((LM_INFO, ACE_TEXT ("(%t) Manager started\n")));

    // Create pool.
    create_worker_pool ();

    while (!done ())
      {
        ACE_Message_Block *mb = NULL;
```

```
      ACE_Time_Value tv ((long)MAX_TIMEOUT);
      tv += ACE_OS::time (0);

      // Get a message request.
      if (this->getq (mb, &tv) < 0)
        {
          shut_down ();
          break;
        }

      // Choose a worker.
      Worker *worker;
      {
        ACE_GUARD_RETURN (ACE_Thread_Mutex,
                          worker_mon, this->workers_lock_, -1);

        while (this->workers_.is_empty ())
          workers_cond_.wait ();

        this->workers_.dequeue_head (worker);
      }

      // Ask the worker to do the job.
      worker->putq (mb);
    }

  return 0;
}

int shut_down (void);

int thread_id (Worker *worker);

virtual int return_to_work (Worker *worker)
{
  ACE_GUARD_RETURN (ACE_Thread_Mutex,
                    worker_mon, this->workers_lock_, -1);
  ACE_DEBUG ((LM_DEBUG,
             ACE_TEXT ("(%t) Worker %d returning to work.\n"),
             worker->thr_mgr ()->thr_self ()));
  this->workers_.enqueue_tail (worker);
  this->workers_cond_.signal ();

  return 0;
}
```

```
private:
  int create_worker_pool (void)
  {
    ACE_GUARD_RETURN (ACE_Thread_Mutex,
                      worker_mon,
                      this->workers_lock_,
                      -1);
    for (int i = 0; i < POOL_SIZE; i++)
      {
        Worker *worker;
        ACE_NEW_RETURN (worker, Worker (this), -1);
        this->workers_.enqueue_tail (worker);
        worker->activate ();
      }

    return 0;
  }

  int done (void);

private:
  int shutdown_;
  ACE_Thread_Mutex workers_lock_;
  ACE_Condition<ACE_Thread_Mutex> workers_cond_;
  ACE_Unbounded_Queue<Worker* > workers_;
};
```

First, note that the `Manager` has an `ACE_Unbounded_Queue` of `Worker` objects. This represents the worker thread pool, which is protected by the `workers_lock_` mutex. When it starts in its `svc()` method, the `Manager` thread first creates the underlying worker thread pool and then blocks on its underlying message queue waiting for requests.

When a request does arrive, the `Manager` dequeues the request and then dequeues the first worker off the worker pool and enqueues the request onto its message queue. Note that if no workers are available, perhaps because they are all busy processing messages, we block on the `workers_cond_` condition variable, waiting for a thread to return to work. When a thread does return to work, it enqueues itself back on the worker queue and notifies the `Manager` by signaling the condition variable. The `Manager` thread then wakes up and hands the new request off to the worker thread that has just returned to the pool:

```
class Worker : public ACE_Task<ACE_MT_SYNCH>
{
public:
  Worker (IManager *manager) : manager_(manager)
  { }

  virtual int svc (void)
  {
    thread_id_ = ACE_Thread::self ();
    while (1)
      {
        ACE_Message_Block *mb = NULL;
        ACE_ASSERT (this->getq (mb) != -1);
        if (mb->msg_type () == ACE_Message_Block::MB_HANGUP)
          {
            ACE_DEBUG ((LM_INFO,
                        ACE_TEXT ("(%t) Shutting down\n")));
            break;
          }

        // Process the message.
        process_message (mb);

        // Return to work.
        this->manager_->return_to_work (this);
      }

    return 0;
  }
```

The worker thread sits in an infinite loop waiting for a request to arrive on its queue. When a request does arrive, the worker thread picks it up and then processes it. Once the processing completes, the worker thread notifies its Manager, where it is once again enqueued in the worker thread pool.

16.2.1   Taking Advantage of ACE_Task

The previous example illustrated how to build a half-sync/half-async thread pool from available ACE components. Often, however, you can take advantage of the multithreaded queueing capability of ACE_Task to considerably simplify the implementation of such a thread pool. Making use of this capability yields the following revised Manager class:

```
class Manager : public ACE_Task<ACE_MT_SYNCH>
{
public:
  enum {POOL_SIZE = 5, MAX_TIMEOUT = 5};

  Manager () : shutdown_(0)
  {
    ACE_TRACE (ACE_TEXT ("Manager::Manager"));
  }

  int svc (void)
  {
    ACE_TRACE (ACE_TEXT ("Manager::svc"));

    ACE_DEBUG ((LM_INFO, ACE_TEXT ("(%t) Manager started\n")));

    // Create pool.
    Workers pool;
    pool.activate (THR_NEW_LWP | THR_JOINABLE, POOL_SIZE);

    while (!done ())
      {
        ACE_Message_Block *mb = NULL;
        ACE_Time_Value tv ((long)MAX_TIMEOUT);
        tv += ACE_OS::time (0);

        // Get a message request.
        if (this->getq (mb, &tv) < 0)
          {
            pool.msg_queue ()->deactivate ();
            pool.wait ();
          }

        // Ask the worker pool to do the job.
        pool.putq (mb);
      }

    return 0;
  }

private:
  int done (void);

  int shutdown_;
};
```

That's it. All of the locking and condition variable logic is contained in the ACE_Message_Queue class. We also illustrated another way to notify the threads in the worker pool that it's time to shut down: we used the `deactivate()` method to shut the ACE_Message_Queue down.

The revised `Workers` class shows how to respond to the queue shutting down, as well as the simpler logic resulting from fuller use of the ACE_Message_Queue class's capabilities:

```
class Workers : public ACE_Task<ACE_MT_SYNCH>
{
public:
  Workers ()
  { }

  virtual int svc (void)
  {
    while (1)
      {
        ACE_Message_Block *mb = NULL;
        if (this->getq (mb) == -1)
          {
            ACE_DEBUG ((LM_INFO,
                        ACE_TEXT ("(%t) Shutting down\n")));
            break;
          }

        // Process the message.
        process_message (mb);
      }

    return 0;
  }
}
```

Remember that all the threads in the pool are executing in the same `Workers` object. The ACE_Message_Queue class contains all the logic necessary to safely and fairly dequeue message blocks for processing.

16.2.2   Using an Activation Queue and Futures

In the previous example, we kept things simple by using simple message blocks as the unit of work. We also assumed that the client thread that enqueues the work on the `Manager`'s queue did not require any results. Although both of these conditions are often true, sometimes a more object-oriented solution is more appropriate: using method requests as the unit of work and futures as results.

In this next example, we add these features to our previous example. Let's begin with a new Method Request object that expects to return a string as the result of the operation:

```
class LongWork : public ACE_Method_Request
{
public:
  virtual int call (void)
  {
    ACE_TRACE (ACE_TEXT ("LongWork::call"));
    ACE_DEBUG
      ((LM_INFO, ACE_TEXT ("(%t) Attempting long work task\n")));
    ACE_OS::sleep (1);

    char buf[1024];
    ACE_OS::strcpy (buf, ACE_TEXT ("Completed assigned task\n"));
    ACE_CString *msg;
    ACE_NEW_RETURN
      (msg, ACE_CString (buf, ACE_OS::strlen (buf) + 1), -1);
    result_.set (msg);
    return 0;
  }

  ACE_Future<ACE_CString*> &future (void)
  {
    ACE_TRACE (ACE_TEXT ("LongWork::future"));
    return result_;
  }

  void attach (CompletionCallBack *cb)
  {
    result_.attach (cb);
  }

private:
  ACE_Future<ACE_CString*> result_;
};
```

Next, let's add a Future Observer that will automatically get called back when the result from the `LongWork` operation is available:

```
class CompletionCallBack: public ACE_Future_Observer<ACE_CString*>
{
public:
  virtual void update (const ACE_Future<ACE_CString*> & future)
  {
    ACE_CString *result;

    // Block for the result.
    ((ACE_Future<ACE_CString*>)future).get (result);
    ACE_DEBUG ((LM_INFO, ACE_TEXT("%C\n"), result->c_str ()));
    delete result;
  }
};
```

The Manager and Worker both need to be modified so that they use an
ACE_Activation_Queue instead of an ACE_Message_Queue. Also, as it
will not be using the underlying message queue in ACE_Task, Manager will
inherit from the lighter ACE_Task_Base class, which does not include the
message queue. Worker, however, illustrates how to use the ACE_Task
message queue in an ACE_Activation_Queue:

```
class Worker: public ACE_Task<ACE_MT_SYNCH>
{
public:
  Worker (IManager *manager)
    : manager_(manager), queue_ (msg_queue ())
  { }

  int perform (ACE_Method_Request *req)
  {
    ACE_TRACE (ACE_TEXT ("Worker::perform"));
    return this->queue_.enqueue (req);
  }

  virtual int svc (void)
  {
    thread_id_ = ACE_Thread::self ();
    while (1)
      {
        ACE_Method_Request *request = this->queue_.dequeue();
        if (request == 0)
          return -1;

        // Invoke the request
```

```
        int result = request->call ();
        if (result == -1)
          break;

        // Return to work.
        this->manager_->return_to_work (this);
      }

    return 0;
  }

  ACE_thread_t thread_id (void);

private:
  IManager *manager_;
  ACE_thread_t thread_id_;
  ACE_Activation_Queue queue_;
};
```

The Worker class has not changed much, except that now, instead of dequeueing an ACE_Message_Block, the svc () method dequeues and then immediately invokes the Method Request object. Once the method request has returned, the worker thread returns to the worker thread pool that is held by the Manager:

```
class Manager : public ACE_Task_Base, IManager
{
public:
  enum {POOL_SIZE = 5, MAX_TIMEOUT = 5};

  Manager ()
    : shutdown_ (0), workers_lock_ (), workers_cond_ (workers_lock_)
  {
    ACE_TRACE (ACE_TEXT ("Manager::TP"));
  }

  int perform (ACE_Method_Request *req)
  {
    ACE_TRACE (ACE_TEXT ("Manager::perform"));
    return this->queue_.enqueue (req);
  }

  int svc (void)
  {
    ACE_TRACE (ACE_TEXT ("Manager::svc"));
```

```
      ACE_DEBUG ((LM_INFO, ACE_TEXT ("(%t) Manager started\n")));

      // Create pool when you get in the first time.
      create_worker_pool ();

      while (!done ())
        {
          ACE_Time_Value tv ((long)MAX_TIMEOUT);
          tv += ACE_OS::time (0);

          // Get the next message
          ACE_Method_Request *request = this->queue_.dequeue (&tv);
          if (request == 0)
            {
              shut_down ();
              break;
            }

          // Choose a worker.
          Worker *worker = choose_worker ();

          // Ask the worker to do the job.
          worker->perform (request);
        }

      return 0;
    }

  int shut_down (void);

  virtual int return_to_work (Worker *worker)
    {
      ACE_GUARD_RETURN
        (ACE_Thread_Mutex, worker_mon, this->workers_lock_, -1);
      ACE_DEBUG
        ((LM_DEBUG, ACE_TEXT ("(%t) Worker returning to work.\n")));
      this->workers_.enqueue_tail (worker);
      this->workers_cond_.signal ();

      return 0;
    }

private:
  Worker *choose_worker (void)
    {
```

```
        ACE_GUARD_RETURN
          (ACE_Thread_Mutex, worker_mon, this->workers_lock_, 0)

          while (this->workers_.is_empty ())
            workers_cond_.wait ();

        Worker *worker;
        this->workers_.dequeue_head (worker);
        return worker;
      }

      int create_worker_pool (void)
      {
        ACE_GUARD_RETURN
          (ACE_Thread_Mutex, worker_mon, this->workers_lock_, -1);
        for (int i = 0; i < POOL_SIZE; i++)
          {
            Worker *worker;
            ACE_NEW_RETURN (worker, Worker (this), -1);
            this->workers_.enqueue_tail (worker);
            worker->activate ();
          }

        return 0;
      }

      int done (void)
      {
        return (shutdown_ == 1);
      }

      int thread_id (Worker *worker)
      {
        return worker->thread_id ();
      }

  private:
    int shutdown_;
    ACE_Thread_Mutex workers_lock_;
    ACE_Condition<ACE_Thread_Mutex> workers_cond_;
    ACE_Unbounded_Queue<Worker* > workers_;
    ACE_Activation_Queue queue_;
  };
```

The Manager class is also almost the same, the only difference being the use of the ACE_Activation_Queue instead of the underlying message queue. The Manager also has a new public method, perform(), that clients can use to enqueue Method Requests onto the Manager's activation queue:

```
int ACE_TMAIN (int, ACE_TCHAR *[])
{
  Manager tp;
  tp.activate ();

  ACE_Time_Value tv;
  tv.msec (100);

  // Wait for a few seconds every time you send a message.
  CompletionCallBack cb;
  LongWork workArray[OUTSTANDING_REQUESTS];
  for (int i = 0; i < OUTSTANDING_REQUESTS; i++)
    {
      workArray[i].attach (&cb);
      ACE_OS::sleep (tv);
      tp.perform (&workArray[i]);
    }

  ACE_Thread_Manager::instance ()->wait ();
  return 0;
}
```

16.3 Leader/Followers Model

In this model, a single group of threads is used to wait for new requests and to handle the request. One thread is chosen as the leader and blocks on the incoming request source. When a request arrives, the leader thread first obtains the request, promotes one of the followers to leader status, and goes on to process the request it had received. The new leader waits on the request source for any new requests while the old leader processes the request that was just received. Once the old leader is finished, it returns to the end of thread pool as a follower thread.

The leader/followers model has the advantage that performance improves, as there is no context switch between threads. This also allows for keeping request data on the stack or in thread-specific storage.

This model also has some disadvantages.

- It is not easy to handle bursty clients, as there might not be an explicit queueing layer.

- This model is more complex to implement.

The following simple example implements the leader/followers thread pool model. In this case, a single `ACE_Task` (the `LF_ThreadPool` class) encapsulates all the threads in the thread pool. Remember, there can be only one leader at any given time; the thread ID of the current leader of the pool is maintained in `current_leader_`. As in our first example, the `LF_ThreadPool` is given new work as an `ACE_Message_Block` on its message queue; that is, a unit of work is a message:

```cpp
class LF_ThreadPool : public ACE_Task<ACE_MT_SYNCH>
{
public:
  LF_ThreadPool () : shutdown_(0), current_leader_(0)
  {
    ACE_TRACE (ACE_TEXT ("LF_ThreadPool::TP"));
  }

  virtual int svc (void);

  void shut_down (void)
  {
    shutdown_ = 1;
  }

private:
  int become_leader (void);

  Follower *make_follower (void);

  int elect_new_leader (void);

  int leader_active (void)
  {
    ACE_TRACE (ACE_TEXT ("LF_ThreadPool::leader_active"));
    return this->current_leader_ != 0;
  }

  void leader_active (ACE_thread_t leader)
  {
    ACE_TRACE (ACE_TEXT ("LF_ThreadPool::leader_active"));
    this->current_leader_ = leader;
  }
```

```
      void process_message (ACE_Message_Block *mb);

      int done (void)
      {
        return (shutdown_ == 1);
      }

  private:
    int shutdown_;
    ACE_thread_t current_leader_;
    ACE_Thread_Mutex leader_lock_;
    ACE_Unbounded_Queue<Follower*> followers_;
    ACE_Thread_Mutex followers_lock_;
    static long LONG_TIME;
  };
```

The `svc()` method for the `LF_ThreadPool` follows:

```
int
LF_ThreadPool::svc (void)
{
  ACE_TRACE (ACE_TEXT ("LF_ThreadPool::svc"));
  while (!done ())
    {
      become_leader ();  // Block until this thread is the leader.

      ACE_Message_Block *mb = NULL;
      ACE_Time_Value tv (LONG_TIME);
      tv += ACE_OS::gettimeofday ();

      // Get a message, elect new leader, then process message.
      if (this->getq (mb, &tv) < 0)
        {
          if (elect_new_leader () == 0)
            break;
          continue;
        }

      elect_new_leader ();
      process_message (mb);
    }

  return 0;
}
```

As each thread starts, it first tries to become a leader by calling
`become_leader()`. If it can't become a leader, the thread blocks in the
`become_leader()` method and will return only once it has indeed become
leader. Once a thread becomes leader, it blocks on the message queue until a
message arrives. When it receives a new message, the leader first selects a new
leader by calling `elect_new_leader()` and then processes the incoming
message. The new leader will wake up from its previous `become_leader()`
call and then block on the message queue, waiting for the next request:

```
int
LF_ThreadPool::become_leader (void)
{
  ACE_TRACE (ACE_TEXT ("LF_ThreadPool::become_leader"));

  ACE_GUARD_RETURN
    (ACE_Thread_Mutex, leader_mon, this->leader_lock_, -1);
  if (leader_active ())
    {
      Follower *fw = make_follower ();
      {
        // Wait until told to do so.
        while (leader_active ())
          fw->wait ();
      }

      delete fw;
    }

  ACE_DEBUG ((LM_DEBUG, ACE_TEXT ("(%t) Becoming the leader\n")));

  // Mark yourself as the active leader.
  leader_active (ACE_Thread::self ());
  return 0;
}

Follower*
LF_ThreadPool::make_follower (void)
{
  ACE_TRACE (ACE_TEXT ("LF_ThreadPool::make_follower"));

  ACE_GUARD_RETURN
    (ACE_Thread_Mutex, follower_mon, this->followers_lock_, 0);
  Follower *fw;
```

```
ACE_NEW_RETURN (fw, Follower (this->leader_lock_), 0);
this->followers_.enqueue_tail (fw);
return fw;
}
```

When it calls become_leader(), a thread first checks whether there is
already a current active leader. If there is, the thread creates a new Follower
object, which is enqueued on the followers_ queue. The thread then calls
wait() on the new follower object. The Follower is a thin wrapper around a
condition variable. Once a follower thread wakes up, it is the new leader and
returns in the svc() method as described previously:

```
int
LF_ThreadPool::elect_new_leader (void)
{
  ACE_TRACE (ACE_TEXT ("LF_ThreadPool::elect_new_leader"));

  ACE_GUARD_RETURN
    (ACE_Thread_Mutex, leader_mon, this->leader_lock_, -1);
  leader_active(0);

  // Wake up a follower
  if (!followers_.is_empty ())
    {
      ACE_GUARD_RETURN (ACE_Thread_Mutex,
                        follower_mon,
                        this->followers_lock_,
                        -1);
      // Get the old follower.
      Follower *fw;
      ACE_ASSERT (this->followers_.dequeue_head (fw) ==0);
      ACE_DEBUG ((LM_ERROR,
                 ACE_TEXT ("(%t) Resigning and Electing %d\n"),
                 fw->owner ()));
      ACE_ASSERT (fw->signal () == 0);
      return 0;
    }
  else
    {
      ACE_DEBUG
        ((LM_ERROR, ACE_TEXT ("(%t) Oops no followers left\n")));
      return -1;
    }
}
```

To designate a new leader, the previous leader first changes the `current_leader_` value to 0, indicating that no active leader is in the pool. The old leader then obtains a follower from the `followers_` queue and wakes the `Follower` up by calling `signal()` on it. The blocked follower thread then wakes up, notices that there is no current leader, and marks itself as the current leader.

When it finishes processing a message, the leader thread once again calls the `become_leader()` method and tries to become the leader again. If it can't, it will become a follower and be enqueued in the `followers_` queue.

16.4 Thread Pools and the Reactor

The `ACE_Reactor` has several implementations that you have seen previously in this book. Some of these implementations allow only a single owner thread to run the event loop and dispatch event handlers; others, however, allow you to have multiple threads run the event loop at once. The underlying reactor implementation builds a thread pool using these client-supplied threads and uses them to wait for and then dispatch events.

The two implementations that provide for this functionality are

- `ACE_TP_Reactor`
- `ACE_WFMO_Reactor`

16.4.1 ACE_TP_Reactor

The `ACE_TP_Reactor` uses the leader/followers model for its underlying thread pool. Thus, when several threads enter the event loop method, all but one become followers and wait in a queue. The leader thread waits for events. When an event occurs, the leader selects a new leader and dispatches the event handlers that had been signaled. Before selecting a new leader or dispatching events, the leader first suspends the handlers that it is about to call back. By suspending the handlers, it makes sure that they can never be invoked by two threads at the same time, thereby making our lives easier, as we don't have to deal with protection issues arising from multiple calls into our event handlers. Once it finishes the dispatch, the leader resumes the handler in the reactor, making it available for dispatch once again.

The following example is a rehash from an ACE test that illustrates the `ACE_TP_Reactor`:

```
int ACE_TMAIN (int, ACE_TCHAR *[])
{
  ACE_TP_Reactor sr;
  ACE_Reactor new_reactor (&sr);
  ACE_Reactor::instance (&new_reactor);

  ACCEPTOR acceptor;
  ACE_INET_Addr accept_addr (rendezvous);

  if (acceptor.open (accept_addr) == -1)
    ACE_ERROR_RETURN ((LM_ERROR,
                       ACE_TEXT ("%p\n"),
                       ACE_TEXT ("open")),
                      1);

  ACE_DEBUG ((LM_DEBUG,
              ACE_TEXT ("(%t) Spawning %d server threads...\n"),
              svr_thrno));

  ServerTP serverTP;
  serverTP.activate (THR_NEW_LWP | THR_JOINABLE, svr_thrno);

  Client client;
  client.activate ();

  ACE_Thread_Manager::instance ()->wait ();

  return 0;
}
```

Let's first look at how the ACE_TP_Reactor is set up. We create an
ACE_TP_Reactor instance and set it up as the implementation class for the
reactor by passing it to the constructor of the ACE_Reactor. We also set the
global singleton instance of the ACE_Reactor to be the instance we create here.
This makes it easy for us to obtain the reactor through the global singleton. After
we do this, we open an acceptor and activate two tasks: one to represent the server
thread pool that will run the reactive event loop (ServerTP) and the other to
represent clients that connect to the server (Client):

```
static int
reactor_event_hook (ACE_Reactor *)
{
  ACE_DEBUG ((LM_DEBUG,
              ACE_TEXT ("(%t) handling events ....\n")));
```

```
      return 0;
    }

class ServerTP : public ACE_Task_Base
{
public:
  virtual int svc (void)
  {
    ACE_DEBUG ((LM_DEBUG,
                ACE_TEXT ("(%t) Running the event loop\n")));

    int result =
      ACE_Reactor::instance ()->run_reactor_event_loop
        (&reactor_event_hook);

    if (result == -1)
      ACE_ERROR_RETURN ((LM_ERROR,
                         ACE_TEXT ("(%t) %p\n"),
                         ACE_TEXT ("Error handling events")),
                         0);

    ACE_DEBUG ((LM_DEBUG,
                ACE_TEXT ("(%t) Done handling events.\n")));

    return 0;
  }
};
```

Once the `ServerTP` is activated, multiple threads start up in its `svc()` method. Each thread immediately starts the reactor's event loop. Note that you can use any of the reactor's event-handling methods here. As we described earlier, the reactor then takes charge, creating the thread pool, selecting the leader, and then dispatching events in multiple threads of control.

[7] contains a thorough explanation of how `ACE_TP_Reactor` works.

16.4.2 ACE_WFMO_Reactor

The `ACE_WFMO_Reactor` is available on the Windows platform and uses the `WaitForMultipleObjects()` function to wait for events. Its use is similar to the `ACE_TP_Reactor`, although there are a few noteworthy differences.

- The `ACE_WFMO_Reactor` does *not* suspend and resume handlers the way the `ACE_TP_Reactor` does. This means that you have to ensure that state information is protected in your event handlers.

- The `ACE_WFMO_Reactor` uses the concept of ownership to choose one thread that will handle timeouts. If none of the threads that are running the event loop are designated as the owner, using the `owner()` method, timeouts may not be handled properly.

- State changes to the `ACE_WFMO_Reactor` are not immediate but are delayed until the reactor reaches a "stable state." (Under the covers, when you make a change, the leader thread is informed and this thread makes the state changes.)

  [7] contains a thorough explanation of how `ACE_WFMO_Reactor` works.

16.5 Summary

In this chapter, we looked at thread pools. We first talked about a few design models for thread pools, including the leader/followers and half-sync/half-async models. We then implemented each of these, using the `ACE_Task` and synchronization components. We also saw how to use `ACE_Activation_Queue`, `ACE_Future`, and `ACE_Future_Observer` to implement pools that can execute arbitrary `ACE_Method_Requests` and then allow for clients to obtain results, using Futures. Finally, we talked about the two reactor implementations that support thread pools: the `ACE_TP_Reactor` and the `ACE_WFMO_Reactor`.

Part IV

Advanced ACE

Chapter 17
Shared Memory

Modern operating systems enforce address space protection between processes. This means that the OS will not allow two distinct processes to write to each other's address space. Although this is what is needed in most cases, sometimes you may want your processes to share certain parts of their address space. Shared memory primitives allow you to do just this. In fact, when used correctly, shared memory can prove to be the fastest interprocess communication mechanism between collocated processes, especially if large amounts of data need to be shared.

Shared memory is not used only as an IPC mechanism. Shared memory primitives also allow you to work with files by mapping them into memory. This allows you to perform direct memory-based operations on files instead of using file I/O operations. This comes in handy when you want to provide for a simple way to persist a data structure. (In fact, `ACE_Configuration` can use this technique to provide persistence for your configuration.)

ACE provides several tools to assist in your shared memory adventures. For sharing memory between applications, ACE provides a set of allocators that allow you to allocate memory that is shared. In fact, you can use a shared memory allocator with the containers discussed in Chapter 5 to create containers in shared memory. For example, you could create a hash map in shared memory and share it across processes.

ACE also provides low-level wrappers around the OS shared memory primitives. These wrappers can be used to perform memory-mapped file operations.

17.1   ACE_Malloc and ACE_Allocator

When we talked about containers in Chapter 5, we saw how we could supply
special-purpose allocators to the containers. These allocators were of type
ACE_Allocator and were usually passed in during container construction. The
container then used the allocator to manage any memory it needed to allocate and
deallocate.

ACE also includes another family of allocators, based on the ACE_Malloc
class template. Unlike the ACE_Allocator family, which is based on polymor-
phism, the ACE_Malloc family of classes are template based. The
ACE_Malloc template takes two major parameters: a lock type and a memory
pool type. The lock is used to ensure consistency of the allocator when used by
multiple threads or processes. The memory pool is where the allocator obtains and
releases memory from/to. To vary the memory allocation mechanism you want
ACE_Malloc to use, you need to instantiate it with the right pool type.

ACE comes with several memory pools, including those that allocate shared
memory and those that allocate regular heap memory. The various pools are
detailed in Table 17.1.

As you can see, several pools are OS specific; make sure that you use a pool
that is available on your OS. For example, to create an allocator that uses a pool
that is based on a memory-mapped file, you would do something like this:

```
typedef ACE_Malloc <ACE_MMAP_Memory_Pool, ACE_SYNCH_MUTEX> MALLOC;
```

If your compiler does not support nested typedefs for template classes, you
need to use an ACE-provided macro for the pool type to instantiate the template.
The macro names are provided in Table 17.2. Using a macro, the sample example
would be:

```
typedef ACE_Malloc<ACE_MMAP_MEMORY_POOL, ACE_SYNCH_MUTEX> MALLOC;
```

17.1.1   Map Interface

Besides a memory allocation interface that supports such operations as
malloc(), calloc(), and free(), ACE_Malloc also supports a maplike
interface. This interface is very similar to the interface supported by
ACE_Map_Manager and ACE_Hash_Map_Manager, which we talked about
in Chapter 5. This interface allows you to insert values in the underlying memory
pool and associate them with a character string key. You can then retrieve the
values you stored, using your key. The map also offers LIFO and FIFO iterators

Table 17.1. Memory Pool Types

Memory Pool Name	Description
`ACE_MMAP_Memory_Pool`	A memory pool based on a memory mapped file
`ACE_Lite_MMAP_Memory_Pool`	A lightweight version of a pool that is based on a memory-mapped file
`ACE_Shared_Memory_Pool`	A memory pool that is based on System V shared memory
`ACE_Local_Memory_Pool`	A memory pool that is based on the C++ new operator
`ACE_Pagefile_Memory_Pool`	A memory pool that is based on "anonymous" memory regions allocated from the Windows page file
`ACE_Sbrk_Memory_Pool`	A memory pool that is based on `sbrk(2)`

that iterate through the map in LIFO and FIFO order of insertion. In the next few sections, we will see several examples that use this interface.

17.1.2 Memory Protection Interface

In certain cases, the underlying shared memory pool allows you to change the memory protection level of individual pages in the memory pool. You could, for example, make certain pages read-only and others read/write or executable. To specify protection, `ACE_Malloc` offers several `protect()` methods that allow you to specify the protection attributes for various regions of its underlying memory pool. Note that protection is available only with certain pools, such as `ACE_MMAP_Memory_Pool`.

17.1.3 Sync Interface

If your memory pool is backed to a file, such as when using `ACE_MMAP_Memory_Pool`, you need a way to flush out the mapping file to disk at the appropriate times in your program. To allow this, `ACE_Malloc` includes a `sync()` method.

Table 17.2. Memory Pool Macro Names

Class	Macro
ACE_MMAP_Memory_Pool	ACE_MMAP_MEMORY_POOL
ACE_Lite_MMAP_Memory_Pool	ACE_LITE_MMAP_MEMORY_POOL
ACE_Shared_Memory_Pool	ACE_SHARED_MEMORY_POOL
ACE_Local_Memory_Pool	ACE_LOCAL_MEMORY_POOL
ACE_Pagefile_Memory_Pool	ACE_PAGEFILE_MEMORY_POOL
ACE_Sbrk_Memory_Pool	ACE_SBRK_MEMORY_POOL

17.2 Persistence with ACE_Malloc

Let's look at a simple example of using a shared memory allocator based on the
ACE_MMAP_Memory_Pool class. One of the nice properties of the
ACE_MMAP_Memory_Pool allocator is that it can be backed up by a file. That
is, whatever you allocate using this allocator is saved to a backing file. As we
mentioned earlier, you can use this mechanism to provide a simple persistence
mechanism for your data. We will use this and the map interface to insert several
records into a shared memory allocator with an ACE_MMAP_Memory_Pool.

Let's start by creating a few easy-to-use types that define the allocator type
and iterator on that type. We also declare a global pointer to the allocator we are
going to create:

```
#include "ace/Malloc_T.h"

typedef ACE_Malloc<ACE_MMAP_MEMORY_POOL, ACE_Null_Mutex>
  ALLOCATOR;
typedef ACE_Malloc_LIFO_Iterator <ACE_MMAP_MEMORY_POOL,
                                  ACE_Null_Mutex>
  MALLOC_LIFO_ITERATOR;

ALLOCATOR  *g_allocator;
```

Next, we instantiate the shared memory allocator. The only option we pass to
the constructor is the name of the backing file where we wish to persist the records
we will be adding to the allocator:

```
// Backing file where the data is kept.
#define BACKING_STORE "backing.store"

int ACE_TMAIN (int argc, ACE_TCHAR *[])
{
  ACE_NEW_RETURN (g_allocator,
                  ALLOCATOR (BACKING_STORE),
                  -1);
  if (argc > 1)
    {
      showRecords ();
    }
  else
    {
      addRecords ();
    }

  g_allocator->sync ();
  delete g_allocator;
  return 0;
}
```

The example needs to be run twice. The first time, you need to run it with no command line arguments; in that case, it will add new records to the memory pool. The second time, you need to run with at least one argument—anything will do, as we are looking only at the number of arguments in the command line—in which case, it will iterate through the inserted records and display them on the screen.

Next, let's look at the record type that we are inserting into memory:

```
class Record
{
public:
  Record (int id1, int id2, char *name)
    : id1_(id1), id2_(id2), name_(0)
  {
    size_t len = ACE_OS::strlen (name) + 1;
    this->name_ =
      ACE_reinterpret_cast (char *,
                            g_allocator->malloc (len));
    ACE_OS::strcpy (this->name_, name);
  }

  ~Record () { g_allocator->free (name_); }
```

```
char* name(void) { return name_; }
int id1 (void) { return id1_; }
int id2 (void) { return id2_; }

private:
  int id1_;
  int id2_;
  char *name_;
};
```

The `Record` class has three data members: two simple integers and a char pointer, `name_`, that represents a string. This is where the tricky part comes in; if we allocate the record in shared memory, we would allocate just enough space for the two integers and the pointer. The pointer itself would be pointing somewhere out into heap space. This is definitely not what we want, as the next time the application is run, the pointer will have a value that points to heap space that does not exist anymore—a recipe for looming disaster.

To ensure that the value `name_` is pointing to is in the shared memory pool, we explicitly allocate it by using the shared memory allocator in the constructor:

```
int addRecords ()
{
  char buf[32];

  for (int i = 0; i < 10; i++)
    {
      ACE_OS::sprintf (buf, "%s:%d", "Record", i);
      void *memory = g_allocator->malloc (sizeof (Record));
      if (memory == 0)
        ACE_ERROR_RETURN ((LM_ERROR, ACE_TEXT ("%p\n"),
                           ACE_TEXT ("Unable to malloc")),
                          -1);

      // Allocate and place record
      Record* newRecord = new (memory) Record (i, i+1, buf);
      if (g_allocator->bind (buf, newRecord) == -1)
        ACE_ERROR_RETURN ((LM_ERROR, ACE_TEXT ("%p\n"),
                           ACE_TEXT ("bind failed")),
                          -1);
    }

  return 0;
}
```

To add a record, we allocate enough memory for the record, using the shared memory allocator, and then use the placement new operator to "place" a new Record object into this memory. Next, we bind the record into the allocator, using its map interface. The key is the name of the record, and the value is the record itself:

```
void showRecords ()
{
  ACE_DEBUG ((LM_DEBUG,
             ACE_TEXT ("The following records were found:\n")));
  {
    MALLOC_LIFO_ITERATOR iter (*g_allocator);

    for (void *temp = 0; iter.next (temp) != 0; iter.advance ())
      {
        Record *record =
          ACE_reinterpret_cast (Record *, temp);
        ACE_DEBUG ((LM_DEBUG,
                   ACE_TEXT ("Record name: %C|id1:%d|id2:%d\n"),
                   record->name (),
                   record->id1 (),
                   record->id2 ()));
      }
  }
}
```

Finally, we illustrate LIFO iteration and the fact that the records were indeed persisted by iterating through them and displaying them on the screen. When we run the example again, we get the following results:

```
The following records were found.
Record name: Record:9|id1:9|id2:10
Record name: Record:8|id1:8|id2:9
Record name: Record:7|id1:7|id2:8
Record name: Record:6|id1:6|id2:7
Record name: Record:5|id1:5|id2:6
Record name: Record:4|id1:4|id2:5
Record name: Record:3|id1:3|id2:4
Record name: Record:2|id1:2|id2:3
Record name: Record:1|id1:1|id2:2
Record name: Record:0|id1:0|id2:1
```

17.3 Position-Independent Allocation

In the previous example, we glossed over several important issues that arise when you are using shared memory. The first issue is that it may not be possible for the underlying shared memory pool of an allocator to be assigned the same base address in all processes that wish to share it or even every time you start the same process. What does all this mean? Here is an example.

Let's say that process A creates a shared memory pool that has a base address of 0x40000000. Process B opens up the same shared memory pool but maps it to address 0x7e000000. Process A then inserts a record into the pool at 0x400001a0. If process B attempts to obtain this record at this address, the record will not be there; instead, it is mapped at 0x7e0001a0 in its address space! This issue continues to get worse, as the record itself may have pointers to other records that are all in shared memory space, but none are accessible to process B, as the base address of the pool is different for each process.

In most cases, the operating system will return the same base address for a ACE_MMAP_Memory_Pool by default. This is why the previous example worked. If the OS did not assign the same base address to the allocator, the previous example would not work. Further, if the underlying memory pool needs to grow as you allocate more memory, the system may need to remap the pool to a different base address. This means that if you keep direct pointers into the shared region, they may be invalidated during operation. (This will occur only if you use the special ACE_MMAP_Memory_Pool::NEVER_FIXED option; we talk more about this and other options later.)

As usual, however, ACE comes to the rescue. ACE includes several classes that, when used together, allow you to perform position-independent memory allocation. These classes calculate offsets from the current base address and store them in shared memory. So the allocator knows that the record is located at an offset of 0x01a0 from the base address instead of knowing only that the record is at 0x400001a0. Of course, this comes with some overhead in terms of memory use and processing, but it allows you to write applications that you know will work with shared memory.

Let's modify our previous example to use position-independent allocation:

```
#include "ace/Malloc_T.h"
#include "ace/PI_Malloc.h"

typedef ACE_Malloc_T <ACE_MMAP_MEMORY_POOL,
                      ACE_Null_Mutex,
                      ACE_PI_Control_Block>
```

```
   ALLOCATOR;
typedef ACE_Malloc_LIFO_Iterator_T<ACE_MMAP_MEMORY_POOL,
                                   ACE_Null_Mutex,
                                   ACE_PI_Control_Block>
   MALLOC_LIFO_ITERATOR;

ALLOCATOR  *g_allocator;
```

We start by changing the typedef for our allocator. Instead of using ACE_Malloc, we use its base class, ACE_Malloc_T. This template includes one additional parameter, a control block type. A control block is allocated in the shared memory pool to provide bookkeeping information. Here, we specify that we want to use the position-independent control block, ACE_PI_Control_Block. This ensures that the find() and bind() operations will continue to work even if the underlying pool is mapped to different addresses in different runs or in different processes:

```
class Record
{
public:
  Record (int id1, int id2, char *name)
    : id1_(id1), id2_(id2)
  {
    size_t len = ACE_OS::strlen (name) + 1;
    char *buf =
      ACE_reinterpret_cast (char *,
                            g_allocator->malloc (len));
    ACE_OS::strcpy (buf, name);
    name_ = buf;
  }

  ~Record() { g_allocator->free (name_.addr ()); }

  char *name (void) { return name_; }
  int id1 (void) { return id1_; }
  int id2 (void) { return id2_; }

private:
  int id1_;
  int id2_;
  ACE_Based_Pointer_Basic<char> name_;
};
```

We also need to change our `Record` class a little. Instead of using a raw pointer for the name, we use a position-independent pointer embodied in the `ACE_Based_Pointer_Basic` class. This utility class calculates and keeps the offset of the name string instead of keeping the raw pointer to the string. If the underlying memory region is mapped to a different address, we will still get the right pointer for `name_` because `ACE_Based_Pointer` will recalculate the pointer for different base addresses. This class also overloads several useful operators, including `()`, which for the most part allow you to treat `name_` as a regular pointer.

To illustrate that this works, we explicitly map the allocator to a different base address when we are adding rather than merely showing records. To achieve this, we use the `ACE_MMAP_Memory_Pool_Options` class:

```
// Backing file where the data is kept.
#define BACKING_STORE "backing2.store"

int ACE_TMAIN (int argc, ACE_TCHAR *[])
{
  if (argc > 1)
    {
      ACE_MMAP_Memory_Pool_Options options
        (ACE_DEFAULT_BASE_ADDR,
         ACE_MMAP_Memory_Pool_Options::ALWAYS_FIXED);
      ACE_NEW_RETURN (g_allocator,
                      ALLOCATOR (BACKING_STORE,
                                 BACKING_STORE,
                                 &options),
                      -1);
      ACE_DEBUG ((LM_DEBUG,
                  ACE_TEXT ("Mapped to base address %@\n"),
                  g_allocator->base_addr ()));

      showRecords ();
    }
  else
    {
      ACE_MMAP_Memory_Pool_Options options
        (0, ACE_MMAP_Memory_Pool_Options::NEVER_FIXED);
      ACE_NEW_RETURN (g_allocator,
                      ALLOCATOR (BACKING_STORE,
                                 BACKING_STORE,
                                 &options),
                      -1);
```

```
            ACE_DEBUG ((LM_DEBUG,
                       ACE_TEXT ("Mapped to base address %@\n"),
                       g_allocator->base_addr ()));

            addRecords();
        }

    g_allocator->sync ();
    delete g_allocator;
    return 0;
}
```

`ACE_MMAP_Memory_Pool_Options` allows us to specify various options, including the base address and whether we want the OS to map to a fixed address. Other options are described in Table 17.3.

When we are adding records, we ask the OS to map the address to any address it pleases; however, when we are showing records, we map to a fixed base address. When you run the example, you can see that the allocator is mapped to a different address each time it is run; even though this occurs, the program works flawlessly.

17.4 ACE_Malloc for Containers

As you know, you can specify special-purpose allocators for containers. The container then uses the allocator to satisfy its memory needs. Wouldn't it be nice if we could use an `ACE_Malloc` shared memory allocator with the container and allocate containers in shared memory? This would mean that the container would allocate memory for itself in shared memory. The problem, of course, is that the allocator needs to implement the `ACE_Allocator` interface, but `ACE_Malloc` doesn't.

No need to fret, though, because ACE includes a special adapter class for this purpose. `ACE_Allocator_Adapter` adapts an `ACE_Malloc`-based class to the `ACE_Allocator` interface. This class template is very easy to use. To create the adapter, simply pass in the appropriate `ACE_Malloc` type. For example:

```
typedef ACE_Malloc<ACE_MMAP_MEMORY_POOL, ACE_Null_Mutex> MALLOC;

typedef ACE_Allocator_Adapter<MALLOC> ALLOCATOR;
```

Besides the issue of interface compatibility, another issue crops up. Most of the container classes keep a reference to the allocator they use and use this reference for all memory operations. This reference will point to heap memory, where

Table 17.3. `ACE_MMAP_Memory_Pool_Options` Attributes

Option Name	Description
`base_address`	Specifies a starting address for where the file is mapped into the process's memory space.
`use_fixed_addr`	Specifies when the base address can be fixed; must be one of three constants: • `FIRSTCALL_FIXED`: Use the specified base address on the initial acquire • `ALWAYS_FIXED`: Always use the specified base address • `NEVER_FIXED`: Always allow the OS to specify the base address
`write_each_page`	Write each page to disk when growing the map.
`minimum_bytes`	Initial allocation size.
`flags`	Any special flags that need to be used for `mmap()`.
`guess_on_fault`	When a fault occurs try to guess the faulting address and remap/extend the mapped file to cover it.
`sa`	`LPSECURITY_ATTRIBUTES` on Windows.
`file_mode`	File access mode to use when creating the backing file.

the shared memory allocator itself is allocated. Of course, this pointer is valid only in the original process that created the allocator and not any other processes that wish to share the container. To overcome this problem, you must provide the container with a valid memory allocator reference for all its operations. As an example, ACE overloads the `ACE_Hash_Map` container—the new class is `ACE_Hash_Map_With_Allocator`—to provide this, and you can easily extend the idea to any other containers you wish to use.

Finally, as most, if not all, ACE containers contain raw pointers, you cannot expect to use them between processes that map them to different base addresses. ACE does not include any container class that uses the position-independent pointers we showed you earlier, although you could easily create one on your own. Therefore, if you are going to use a container in shared memory, you must make sure that you can map the entire container into all sharing processes at the same base address.

17.4.1 Hash Map

Now let's get down to an example. We are going to put a hash map into shared memory. We will have a parent process add records into the hash table and have two other worker processes consume these records and remove them from the map. To ensure the map consistency, we create an ACE_Process_Mutex and use it to serialize access to the map:

```
#include "ace/Hash_Map_With_Allocator_T.h"
#include "ace/Malloc_T.h"
#include "ace/PI_Malloc.h"
#include "ace/Process_Mutex.h"
#include "ace/Process.h"

#define BACKING_STORE "map.store"
#define MAP_NAME "records.db"

class Record;

typedef ACE_Allocator_Adapter<ACE_Malloc_T <ACE_MMAP_MEMORY_POOL,
                                            ACE_Process_Mutex,
                                            ACE_Control_Block>
                     > ALLOCATOR;
typedef ACE_Hash_Map_With_Allocator<int, Record> MAP;

ACE_Process_Mutex coordMutex("Coord-Mutex");
```

We start by creating a few convenient type definitions and creating the coordination mutex globally. We create a position-independent allocator and use ACE_Allocator_Adapter to adapt the interface to ACE_Allocator. We define a hash map with simple integer keys and Record values.

Now let's take a quick look at a minor change to the Record class:

```
class Record
{
public:
  Record () { }
  ~Record () { }

  Record (const Record& rec)
    : id1_(rec.id1_), id2_(rec.id2_)
  {
    ACE_OS::strcpy (recName_, rec.name_);
    this->name_ = recName_;
  }
```

```
  Record (int id1, int id2, char *name)
    : id1_(id1), id2_(id2)
  {
    ACE_OS::strcpy (recName_, name);
    this->name_ = recName_;
  }
  char *name (void) { return recName_; }
  int id1 (void) { return id1_; }
  int id2 (void) { return id2_; }

private:
  int id1_;
  int id2_;
  char recName_[128];
  ACE_Based_Pointer_Basic<char> name_;
};
```

We have written a copy constructor for the Record class, as the map requires this. During a copy, we make a deep copy of the record name. This allows the container to safely delete the memory it allocates for a Record object during an unbind. To simplify managing the name, we've also changed from allocating it separately to storing it in a member array, recName_.

Next, let's look at how we create and place the map into our allocator:

```
MAP* smap (ALLOCATOR *shmem_allocator)
{
  void *db = 0;
  if (shmem_allocator->find (MAP_NAME, db) == 0)
    return (MAP *) db;
  size_t hash_table_size = sizeof (MAP);
  void *hash_map = shmem_allocator->malloc (hash_table_size);
  if (hash_map == 0)
    return 0;
  new (hash_map) MAP (hash_table_size, shmem_allocator);
  if (shmem_allocator->bind (MAP_NAME, hash_map) == -1)
    {
      ACE_ERROR ((LM_ERROR, ACE_TEXT ("%p\n"),
                  ACE_TEXT ("allocate_map")));
      shmem_allocator->remove ();
      return 0;
    }
  return (MAP*)hash_map;
}
```

Because the map will be shared among processes, we have written a small routine that helps us find the map if it already exists or creates a new one if it has not been created yet. This helper function assumes that the caller already has control of the coordinating mutex; otherwise, you might leak a map.

First, we look for the map in the allocator, using the convenient find() method. If the map is not found, we allocate memory for a new map and use the placement new operator to place a map in this memory. We then associate it with the key MAP_NAME so that in the future, it will be found there by other processes:

```
int handle_parent (char *cmdLine)
{
  ACE_TRACE (ACE_TEXT ("::handle_parent"));

  ALLOCATOR * shmem_allocator = 0;
  ACE_MMAP_Memory_Pool_Options options
    (ACE_DEFAULT_BASE_ADDR,
     ACE_MMAP_Memory_Pool_Options::ALWAYS_FIXED);

  ACE_NEW_RETURN
    (shmem_allocator,
     ALLOCATOR (BACKING_STORE, BACKING_STORE, &options),
     -1);

  MAP *map = smap (shmem_allocator);

  ACE_Process processa, processb;
  ACE_Process_Options poptions;
  poptions.command_line("%s a", cmdLine);
  {
    ACE_GUARD_RETURN (ACE_Process_Mutex, ace_mon,
                      coordMutex, -1);
    ACE_DEBUG ((LM_DEBUG,
                ACE_TEXT ("(%P|%t) Map has %d entries\n"),
                map->current_size ()));
    ACE_DEBUG ((LM_DEBUG,
                ACE_TEXT ("In parent, map is located at %@\n"),
                map));

    // Then have the child show and eat them up.
    processa.spawn (poptions);

    // First append a few records.
    addRecords (map, shmem_allocator);
  }
```

```
  {
    ACE_GUARD_RETURN (ACE_Process_Mutex, ace_mon,
                      coordMutex, -1);

    // Add a few more records..
    addRecords (map, shmem_allocator);

    // Let's see what's left.
    ACE_DEBUG ((LM_DEBUG,
                ACE_TEXT ("(%P|%t) Parent finished adding, ")
                ACE_TEXT ("map has %d entries\n"),
                map->current_size ()));

    // Have another child try to eat them up.
    processb.spawn (poptions);
  }

  processa.wait ();
  processb.wait ();

  // No processes are left and we don't want to keep the data
  // around anymore; it's now safe to remove it.
  // !!This will remove the backing store.!!
  shmem_allocator->remove ();
  delete shmem_allocator;
  return 0;
}

int ACE_TMAIN (int argc, ACE_TCHAR *argv[])
{
  if (argc == 1) // parent
    ACE_ASSERT (handle_parent (argv[0]) == 0);
  else
    ACE_ASSERT (handle_child () == 0);

  return 0;
}
```

When the program is started, it will call the handle_parent() function.
First, we create the shared memory allocator on the heap. Next, we acquire the
coordinating mutex and add a few records into the map and then start a child
process to process these records. Because we still hold the coordinating mutex, the
child process will not be able to process the records until the guard goes out of

scope. After we release the mutex, we once again try to acquire it and add further records; we also spawn a second child to finish processing these records:

```
int addRecords(MAP *map, ALLOCATOR *shmem_allocator)
{
  ACE_TRACE (ACE_TEXT ("::addRecords"));

  char buf[32];
  int mapLength = ACE_static_cast (int, map->current_size ());
  ACE_DEBUG ((LM_DEBUG,
              ACE_TEXT ("Map has %d entries; adding 20 more\n"),
              mapLength));

  for (int i = mapLength ; i < mapLength + 20; i++)
    {
      ACE_OS::sprintf (buf, "%s:%d", "Record", i);

      // Allocate new record on stack;
      Record newRecord (i, i+1, buf);
      ACE_DEBUG ((LM_DEBUG,
                  ACE_TEXT ("Adding a record for %d\n"), i));

      int result = map->bind (i, newRecord, shmem_allocator);
      if (result == -1)
        ACE_ERROR_RETURN ((LM_ERROR, ACE_TEXT ("%p\n"),
                           ACE_TEXT ("bind failed")), -1);
    }

  return 0;
}
```

The `addRecords()` routine is simple enough. All we do is create a new record on the stack and then bind it into the underlying map. We use a special `bind()` method here that takes a pointer to the allocator in addition to the key/ value pair. As we explained earlier, we must specify the allocator whenever we use the hash map. The internal reference the hash map keeps is valid only in the process that creates the hash map; in this case, the parent process is that process, and this is not strictly necessary, but to avoid errors, you should always follow this rule.

When we bind the record into the hash map, the map will use the allocator to create a copy of the record in shared memory. Now let's look at how the child process will process and then remove the record from the map:

```
int handle_child (void)
{
  ACE_TRACE (ACE_TEXT ("::handle_child"));

  ACE_GUARD_RETURN (ACE_Process_Mutex, ace_mon, coordMutex, -1);

  ALLOCATOR * shmem_allocator = 0;
  ACE_MMAP_Memory_Pool_Options options
    (ACE_DEFAULT_BASE_ADDR,
     ACE_MMAP_Memory_Pool_Options::ALWAYS_FIXED);

  ACE_NEW_RETURN (shmem_allocator,
                  ALLOCATOR (BACKING_STORE,
                             BACKING_STORE,
                             &options),
                  -1);

  MAP *map = smap (shmem_allocator);

  ACE_DEBUG ((LM_DEBUG,
              ACE_TEXT ("(%P|%t) Map has %d entries\n"),
              map->current_size ()));
  ACE_DEBUG ((LM_DEBUG,
              ACE_TEXT ("In child, map is located at %@\n"),
              map));

  processRecords (map, shmem_allocator);
  shmem_allocator->sync ();
  delete shmem_allocator;

  return 0;
}
```

Unlike the parent, the child first acquires the coordinating mutex and then creates the shared memory allocator. As it is going to dereference records that are created by the parent, the child must be sure that the underlying pool does not grow after it has created an allocator and mapped the pool into its address space. If not, the following scenario could occur.

1. The child creates the allocator whose underlying map is, for example, 16K.

2. The parent continues to add records, causing the map to grow to 20K.

3. The child gets the coordinating mutex and starts accessing all the records in the map.

4. The child reaches a record that lies outside its mapping, that is, between the 16K and 20K region. The child dereferences it and receives an address exception.

5. The parent process did not have to worry about this, as it knows that the child never causes the map to grow.

We have solved this problem by locking everyone else out of the entire map. ACE offers another solution, which we talk about in Section 17.4.2. First, let's see how the child processes the records:

```
int processRecords (MAP *map, ALLOCATOR *shmem_allocator)
{
  ACE_TRACE (ACE_TEXT ("::processRecords"));

  size_t mapLength = map->current_size ();
  ACE_DEBUG ((LM_DEBUG,
              ACE_TEXT ("(%P|%t) Found %d records\n\n"),
              mapLength));

  int *todelete = new int[mapLength];
  int i = 0;

  for (MAP::iterator iter = map->begin ();
       iter != map->end ();
       iter++)
    {
      int key = (*iter).ext_id_;
      ACE_DEBUG ((LM_DEBUG,
                  ACE_TEXT ("(%P|%t) [%d] Preprocessing %d:%@\n"),
                  i+1, key, &(*iter).ext_id_));

      todelete[i++] = key;     // Mark message for deletion.

      // Illustrate the find feature of the map.
      Record record;
      int result = map->find (key, record, shmem_allocator);
      if (result == -1)
        ACE_DEBUG ((LM_ERROR,
                    ACE_TEXT ("Could not find record for %d\n"),
                    key));
      else
        ACE_DEBUG ((LM_DEBUG,
                    ACE_TEXT ("Record name: %C|id1:%d|id2:%d\n"),
                    record.name (), record.id1(), record.id2()));
    }
```

```
// Delete everything we processed.
for (int j = 0; j < i ; j++)
  {
    int result = map->unbind (todelete[j],
                             shmem_allocator);
    if (result == -1)
      ACE_ERROR_RETURN ((LM_ERROR,
                         ACE_TEXT ("Failed on key %d: %p\n"),
                         ACE_TEXT ("unbind"),
                         todelete[j]),
                        -1);
    else
      ACE_DEBUG ((LM_INFO,
                  ACE_TEXT ("Fully processed and removed %d\n"),
                  j));
  }

delete [] todelete;

return 0;
}
```

Processing the records involves iterating through the map, collecting all the record IDs that need to removed, and then unbinding them. Note that the `find()` and `unbind()` methods both take an additional allocator argument, just like the `bind()` method did earlier.

Although this example was a little more involved, it illustrates two issues that you need to be aware of when you are using shared memory.

1. You must first realize that this example depends on the fact that all processes—parent and child—manage to map the shared memory pool to the same base address. If you cannot achieve this, the pointers in the hash map will be invalid.

2. If one process causes the underlying memory pool to grow—in this case, the parent does this by calling `addRecords()`—this does not grow the pool in the other processes—in this case, the children calling `processRecords()`. When the child accesses a record that is not in range, dereferencing it will cause a fault.

17.4.2 Handling Pool Growth

You can handle the memory pool growth in three ways.

1. You can make sure that it does not happen, by allocating enough memory to start with, thus preventing the problem from occurring. If this is possible, it is perhaps the easiest, most portable, and most efficient thing to do. However, this approach can limit scalability.

2. You can make sure that the child process maps the pool in and uses it only when sure that the pool will not grow after it has been mapped, similar to the previous example. The problem here is that you lose all opportunities for concurrent read/write access to the entire pool.

3. You can use your OS exception-handling mechanism in conjunction with the ACE-provided `remap()` functionality to remap the pool so that the faulting address is now mapped into the process. OS exception handling comes in two flavors: UNIX-based signal handling and Windows structured exception handling (SEH).

For those of you lucky enough to be using a platform with UNIX signals, ACE will automatically install a signal handler for `SIGSEGV` for you. This will cause the remapping to occur transparently. If you are using Windows, you will have to handle the exception yourself, using structured exception handling.

In this next example, we show you how to handle pool growth using Windows structured exception handling. In this example, we also extend the same idiom ACE uses to create `ACE_Hash_Map_With_Allocator` to build our own `Unbounded_Queue` class that will work with shared memory. The program will start and spawn two child processes. The parent will then add messages into a queue, and the child processes will continuously dequeue them from the queue until they get a special termination message, at which point the child processes will exit.

First, let's look at the `Unbounded_Queue` type that we have created:

```
template <class T>
class Unbounded_Queue : public ACE_Unbounded_Queue<T>
{
public:
  typedef ACE_Unbounded_Queue<T> BASE;

  Unbounded_Queue(ACE_Allocator* allocator)
    : ACE_Unbounded_Queue<T> (allocator)
  { }
```

```
int enqueue_tail (const T &new_item, ACE_Allocator* allocator)
{
  this->allocator_ = allocator;
  return BASE::enqueue_tail (new_item);
}

int dequeue_head (T &item, ACE_Allocator* allocator)
{
  this->allocator_ = allocator;
  return BASE::dequeue_head (item);
}

void delete_nodes (ACE_Allocator* allocator)
{
  this->allocator_ = allocator;
  delete_nodes ();
}
};
```

This simple data type overloads the enqueue and dequeue methods to allow us to specify the shared memory allocator in each method. All we do is reassign the allocator pointer to be sure that the queue uses a valid memory allocator instead of using the invalid allocator pointer it has in shared memory.

Let's look at the parent's actions first:

```
int handle_parent (char *cmdLine)
{
  ALLOCATOR *shmem_allocator = 0;
  ACE_MMAP_Memory_Pool_Options options
    (ACE_DEFAULT_BASE_ADDR,
     ACE_MMAP_Memory_Pool_Options::ALWAYS_FIXED);

  // Create the allocator.
  ACE_NEW_RETURN (shmem_allocator,
                  ALLOCATOR (BACKING_STORE,
                             BACKING_STORE,
                             &options),
                  -1);

  ACE_Process processa, processb;
  ACE_Process_Options poptions;
  poptions.command_line ("%s a", ACE_TEXT_ALWAYS_CHAR (cmdLine));
  processa.spawn (poptions);
  processb.spawn (poptions);
```

```
   // Make sure the child does map a partial pool in memory.
   ACE_OS::sleep (2);

   for (int i = 0; i < 100; i++)
     sendRecord (i, shmem_allocator);
   sendRecord (-1, shmem_allocator);

   processa.wait ();
   processb.wait ();
   shmem_allocator->remove ();
   return 0;
}
```

When the parent starts, it first allocates the shared memory pool and spawns two child processes. At this point, it waits for a bit, just to make sure that each one of the children has mapped in the pool at this point, where it has no queue or messages on the queue. This ensures that after the parent adds messages to the queue, the memory pool will need to grow. The parent then quickly places 100 records on the queue, sends a termination message, and waits for the children to exit.

Now, let's look at the child's actions:

```
int handle_child (void)
{
  ALLOCATOR *shmem_allocator = 0;
  ACE_MMAP_Memory_Pool_Options options
    (ACE_DEFAULT_BASE_ADDR,
     ACE_MMAP_Memory_Pool_Options::ALWAYS_FIXED);
  ACE_NEW_RETURN (shmem_allocator,
                  ALLOCATOR (BACKING_STORE,
                             BACKING_STORE,
                             &options),
                  -1);
  g_shmem_allocator = shmem_allocator;

#if defined (WIN32)
  while (processWin32Record (shmem_allocator) != -1)
    ;
#else
  while (processRecord (shmem_allocator) != -1)
    ;
#endif
  return 0;
}
```

On start-up, the child goes into the `handle_child()` method, which creates the shared memory allocator, and then loops through processing records. Note that we have elected to use polling here; in a realistic application, you would probably want to place a condition variable in shared memory and use that to notify the child when it is appropriate to read.

When running on Windows, we call a special `processWin32Record()` function, which uses structured exception handling to handle the remapping case. Let's first take a quick look at `processRecord()`:

```
int processRecord (ALLOCATOR *shmem_allocator)
{
  ACE_GUARD_RETURN (ACE_Process_Mutex, ace_mon, coordMutex, -1);

  QUEUE* queue = squeue (shmem_allocator);
  if (queue == 0)
    {
      delete shmem_allocator;
      ACE_ERROR_RETURN ((LM_ERROR, ACE_TEXT ("%p\n"),
                         ACE_TEXT ("Could not obtain queue")),
                        -1);
    }

  if (queue->is_empty ())  // Check for anything to process.
    return 0;

  Record record;
  if (queue->dequeue_head (record, shmem_allocator) == -1)
    {
      ACE_ERROR_RETURN ((LM_ERROR, ACE_TEXT ("%p\n"),
                         ACE_TEXT ("dequeue_head\n")),
                        -1);
    }

  ACE_DEBUG ((LM_DEBUG,
              ACE_TEXT ("(%P|%t) Processing record|name: %C")
              ACE_TEXT ("|Record id1:%d|Record id2:%d\n"),
              record.name (), record.id1 (), record.id2 ()));
  if (record.id1 () == -1)
    queue->enqueue_tail (record, shmem_allocator);
  return record.id1 ();
}
```

All we do here is get the queue, check whether any messages are on it, and dequeue the message. If the message was a termination message, we put it back on the queue so that any other children can pick it up and process it.

Finally, we get to `processWin32Record()`:

```
#if defined(WIN32)

int handle_remap (EXCEPTION_POINTERS *ep)
{
  ACE_DEBUG ((LM_INFO, ACE_TEXT ("Handle a remap\n")));

  DWORD ecode = ep->ExceptionRecord->ExceptionCode;
  if (ecode != EXCEPTION_ACCESS_VIOLATION)
    return EXCEPTION_CONTINUE_SEARCH;

  void *addr =
    (void *) ep->ExceptionRecord->ExceptionInformation[1];
  if (g_shmem_allocator->alloc().memory_pool().remap (addr) == -1)
    return EXCEPTION_CONTINUE_SEARCH;
#if __X86__
  // This is 80x86-specific.
  ep->ContextRecord->Edi = (DWORD) addr;
#elif __MIPS__
  ep->ContextRecord->IntA0 =
    ep->ContextRecord->IntV0 = (DWORD) addr;
  ep->ContextRecord->IntT5 =
    ep->ContextRecord->IntA0 + 3;
#endif /* __X86__ */

  return EXCEPTION_CONTINUE_EXECUTION;
}

int processWin32Record (ALLOCATOR *shmem_allocator)
{
  ACE_SEH_TRY
  {
    return processRecord (shmem_allocator);
  }

  ACE_SEH_EXCEPT (handle_remap (GetExceptionInformation ()))
  { }

  return 0;
}
#endif /*WIN32*/
```

Here, we place `processRecord()` in an SEH `_try/_except` clause, wrapped by `ACE_SEH_TRY` and `ACE_SEH_EXCEPT`. If a fault occurs, the `handle_remap()` SEH selector is called. This checks whether an `EXCEPTION_ACCESS_VIOLATION` occurred and, if so, finds the faulting address and uses the allocator's `remap()` feature to map the faulting address into its pool. Once the `remap()` returns, we return `EXCEPTION_CONTINUE_EXECUTION`, causing the program to continue normally.

17.5 Wrappers

Besides the more advanced features provided by `ACE_Malloc` and friends, you may want to do something much simpler. For example, mapping files into memory is a common technique many web servers use to reduce the time it takes to send high hit-rate files back to client browsers.

ACE provides several wrapper classes that wrap lower-level shared memory primitives, such as `mmap()`, `MapViewOfFileEx()`, System V shared memory segments, and so on. We take a brief look at `ACE_Mem_Map`, which is a wrapper around the memory-mapping primitives of the OS.

In this next example, we rewrite the classic Richard Stevens example of copying files [8], using memory mapping. We map both source and destination files into memory and then use a simple `memcpy()` call to copy source to destination:

```
int ACE_TMAIN (int argc, ACE_TCHAR *argv[])
{
  ACE_HANDLE srcHandle = ACE_OS::open (argv[1], O_RDONLY);
  ACE_ASSERT(srcHandle != ACE_INVALID_HANDLE);

  ACE_Mem_Map srcMap (srcHandle, -1, PROT_READ, ACE_MAP_PRIVATE);
  ACE_ASSERT(srcMap.addr () != 0);

  ACE_Mem_Map destMap (argv[2],
                       srcMap.size (),
                       O_RDWR | O_CREAT,
                       ACE_DEFAULT_FILE_PERMS,
                       PROT_RDWR,
                       ACE_MAP_SHARED);
  ACE_ASSERT(destMap.addr () != 0);
```

```
ACE_OS::memcpy (destMap.addr (),
                srcMap.addr (),
                srcMap.size ());
destMap.sync ();

srcMap.close ();
destMap.close ();
return 0;
}
```

We create two ACE_Mem_Map instances that represent the memory mappings of both the source and destination files. To keep things interesting, we map the source by explicitly opening the file ourselves in read-only mode and then supplying the handle to srcMap. However, we let ACE_Mem_Map open the destination file for us in read/write/create mode for us. The PROT_READ and PROT_RDWR specify the protection mode for the pages that are mapped into memory. Here, the source file memory-mapped pages can only be read from, whereas the destination pages can be both read and written to. Finally, we specify the sharing mode as ACE_MAP_PRIVATE for the source file and ACE_MAP_SHARED for the destination. ACE_MAP_PRIVATE indicates that if any changes are made to the in-memory pages, the changes will not be propagated back to the backing store or to any other processes that have the same file mapped into memory. ACE_MAP_SHARED implies that changes are shared and will be seen in the backing store and in other processes.

In many cases, it is not feasible to map an entire file into memory at once. Instead, you can use ACE_Mem_Map to map chunks of the file into memory. You can then operate on the chunk, release it when you are done with it, and map the next chunk. To do this, you must specify the size of the chunk you want to map and the offset into the file where the chunk will begin.[1]

---

1. It is important that the offset you specify into the file be properly aligned. This alignment is platform specific and can be obtained by calling ACE::getpagesize() on UNIX/POSIX platforms and by calling ACE_OS::allocation_granularity() on Windows.

17.6 Summary

In this chapter, we reviewed the `ACE_Malloc` family of allocators. In particular, we talked about the shared memory pools you can use with `ACE_Malloc`. First, we showed how you can use an `ACE_Malloc` allocator to build a simple persistence mechanism. We then showed how you can use position-independent pointers to build portable applications that will work no matter where an allocator pool is mapped to in virtual memory. Next, we showed how to adapt the `ACE_Malloc` class to the `ACE_Allocator` interface and use it with the containers that are supplied with ACE. We also identified the problems that come with dynamic shared memory pool growth and explained how you can tackle them. Finally, we mentioned a few of the wrapper classes that ACE provides to deal with shared memory.

Chapter 18
ACE Streams Framework

The ACE Streams framework implements the Pipes and Filters pattern described in [1]. The framework is an excellent way to model processes consisting of a set of ordered steps. Each step, or *filter* in Pipes and Filters terminology, in the process is implemented as an `ACE_Task` derivative. As each step is completed, the data is handed off to the next step for continuation, using the `ACE_Task` objects' message queues, or *pipes* in Pipes and Filters terminology. Steps can be multithreaded in order to increase throughput if the data lends itself to parallel processing. In this chapter, we explore the following classes: `ACE_Stream`, `ACE_Module`, `ACE_Task`, and `ACE_Message_Block`.

18.1 Overview

Another commonly known implementation of the Pipes and Filters pattern is the UNIX System V STREAMS framework. If you're familiar with System V STREAMS, you will recognize the concepts. The ACE Streams framework allows the flexible, dynamically configurable assembly of a set of modules into a stream through which information travels. Each module has an opportunity to manipulate the data in the stream and can modify it, remove it, or add to it before passing it to the next module in the stream. Data moves bidirectionally in the stream, and each module in the stream has a reader and a writer task—one for each data direction.

The first thing to do when using ACE Streams is to identify the sequence of events you wish to process. The steps should be as discrete as possible, with well-defined outputs and inputs. Where possible, identify and document opportunities for parallel processing within each step.

Once your steps are identified, you can begin implementing each as a derivative of ACE_Task. The svc() method of each will use getq() to get a unit of work and put_next() to pass the completed work to the next step. At this time, identify which tasks are "downstream" and which are "upstream" in nature. Downstream tasks can be thought of as moving "out of" your primary application as they move down the stream. For instance, a stream implementing a protocol stack would use each task to perform a different stage of protocol conversion. The final task would send the converted data, perhaps via TCP/IP, to a remote peer. Similarly, upstream tasks can be thought of as moving data "into" your primary application.

Module instances, or paired downstream and upstream tasks, can be created once the tasks are implemented. In our protocol conversion example, the downstream tasks would encode our data and the upstream tasks would decode it.

The final step is to create the ACE_Stream instance and push the ordered list of modules onto it. You can then use put() to move data onto the stream for processing and obtain the results with get(). See Figure 18.1.

18.2 Using a One-Way Stream

In this section, we look at an answering machine implementation that uses a one-way stream to record and process messages. Each module of the stream performs one function in the set of functions required to implement the system. The functions are

1. Answer incoming call
2. Collect Caller Identification data
3. Play outgoing message
4. Collect incoming message
5. Return recording device to the pool
6. Encode collected message into a normalized form
7. Save message and metadata into message repository
8. Send notification of received message

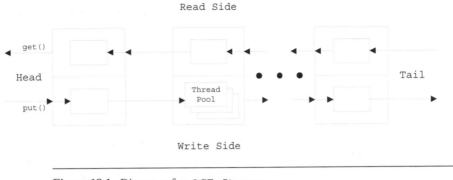

Figure 18.1. Diagram of an ACE_Stream

As defined, each step of the process is very specific in what it must do. This may seem a bit like overkill, but in a more complex application, it is an excellent way to divide the work among team members. Each person can focus on the implementation of his or her own step, as long as the interfaces between each step are well defined.

18.2.1 Main Program

We're going to work through this example from the top down; that is, we start with main() and then dig down into successively lower levels:

```
int ACE_TMAIN (int argc, ACE_TCHAR *argv[])
{
  RecordingDevice *recorder =
    RecordingDeviceFactory::instantiate (argc, argv);
```

Here, main() begins by using the RecordingDeviceFactory to instantiate a RecordingDevice instance based on command line parameters.[1] Our system may have many kinds of recording devices: voice modems, video phones, e-mail receivers, and so on. The command line parameters tell us which kind of device this instance of the application is communicating with.

---

1. Obviously, a more realistic application would be structured to read a list of devices from a configuration file and listen to several at one time.

```
RecordingStream *recording_stream;
ACE_NEW_RETURN (recording_stream, RecordingStream, -1);

if (recording_stream->open () < 0)
  ACE_ERROR_RETURN ((LM_ERROR,
                     ACE_TEXT ("%p\n"),
                     ACE_TEXT ("RecordingStream->open()")),
                    0);
```

Next, our example creates and opens an instance of `RecordingStream`. As we will see, this is a simple derivative of `ACE_Stream`. If the `open()` fails, we will print a brief message and exit with an error code.

The final task of `main()` is to enter an infinite loop, waiting for messages to arrive and recording them when they do:

```
for (;;)
  {
    ACE_DEBUG ((LM_INFO,
                ACE_TEXT ("Waiting for incoming message\n")));
    RecordingDevice *activeRecorder =
      recorder->wait_for_activity ();

    ACE_DEBUG ((LM_INFO,
                ACE_TEXT ("Initiating recording process\n")));

    recording_stream->record (activeRecorder);
  }
```

The `RecordingDevice::wait_for_activity()` method will block until there is some activity, such as a ring, on the physical device. The `RecordingDevice` instance is then given to the `RecordingStream` to process our list of directives.

18.2.2 RecordingStream

As mentioned, the `RecordingStream` object is a simple derivative of `ACE_Stream`. We begin with the constructor, which takes care of the details of initializing the base class:

```
class RecordingStream : public ACE_Stream<ACE_MT_SYNCH>
{
public:
  typedef ACE_Stream<ACE_MT_SYNCH> inherited;
```

```
typedef ACE_Module<ACE_MT_SYNCH> Module;

RecordingStream () : inherited()
{ }
```

A stream will always have at least two modules installed: head and tail. The default downstream task of the head module simply passes any data down the stream. The default tail module, however, will treat any received data as an error. Our example can prevent this from happening in two ways.

1. We can code our last task in the stream to not send data any farther.

2. We can install a replacement for the task in the tail module.

In order to prevent special conditions, which are generally a sign of a bad design, we will use the second option. Therefore, our stream's `open()` method will create a `Module` with an instance of our `EndTask` object and install that at the tail of the stream:

```
int open (void)
{
  Module *endModule;
  ACE_NEW_RETURN (endModule,
                  Module ("End Module", new EndTask ()),
                  -1);
  this->inherited::open ((void *)0, (Module *)0, endModule);
```

The head and tail module instances are the second and third parameters to the `open()` method. By providing a null value for the head, we are asking the stream to use its default head module.

Our design described eight steps in the process, and we've created eight `ACE_Task` derivatives to implement those steps. In the next part of `open()`, we create an instance of each of these eight objects and a `Module` to contain them:

```
Module *answerIncomingCallModule;
ACE_NEW_RETURN (answerIncomingCallModule,
                Module ("Answer Incoming Call",
                        new AnswerIncomingCall ()),
                -1);

Module *getCallerIdModule;
ACE_NEW_RETURN (getCallerIdModule,
                Module ("Get Caller ID", new GetCallerId ()),
                -1);
```

```
Module *playOGMModule;
ACE_NEW_RETURN (playOGMModule,
               Module ("Play Outgoing Message",
                       new PlayOutgoingMessage ()),
               -1);

Module *recordModule;
ACE_NEW_RETURN (recordModule,
               Module ("Record Incoming Message",
                       new RecordIncomingMessage ()),
               -1);

Module *releaseModule;
ACE_NEW_RETURN (releaseModule,
               Module ("Release Device",
                       new ReleaseDevice ()),
               -1);

Module *conversionModule;
ACE_NEW_RETURN (conversionModule,
               Module ("Encode Message",
                       new EncodeMessage ()),
               -1);

Module *saveMetaDataModule;
ACE_NEW_RETURN (saveMetaDataModule,
               Module ("Save Meta-Data",
                       new SaveMetaData ()),
               -1);

Module *notificationModule;
ACE_NEW_RETURN (notificationModule,
               Module ("Notify Someone",
                       new NotifySomeone ()),
               -1);
```

The general design of the Stream framework is that an `ACE_Stream`
contains a list of `ACE_Module` instances and that each `ACE_Module` contains
one or two `ACE_Task` instances. The tasks can be designated either downstream—invoked as data moves away from the stream's head—or upstream—
invoked as data moves toward the stream's head. Our instantiation of `getCall-
erIdModule` follows:

```
Module *getCallerIdModule;
ACE_NEW_RETURN (getCallerIdModule,
                Module ("Get Caller ID", new GetCallerId ()),
                -1);
```

This creates a Module (ACE_Module<ACE_MT_SYNC>) with the name "Get Caller ID" and an instance of the GetCallerId object, which is a derivative of ACE_Task, as required by the ACE_Module constructor signature. The GetCallerId instance is installed as the module's downstream task. We don't provide an upstream task, because our stream will store the recorded messages to disk and not expect anything to return back upstream to main ().

The final part of our RecordingStream's open () method now pushes the modules onto the stream in the correct order:

```
if (this->push (notificationModule) == -1)
  ACE_ERROR_RETURN ((LM_ERROR,
                     ACE_TEXT ("Failed to push %p\n"),
                     ACE_TEXT ("notificationModule")),
                    -1);
if (this->push (saveMetaDataModule) == -1)
  ACE_ERROR_RETURN ((LM_ERROR,
                     ACE_TEXT ("Failed to push %p\n"),
                     ACE_TEXT ("saveMetaDataModule")),
                    -1);
if (this->push (conversionModule) == -1)
  ACE_ERROR_RETURN ((LM_ERROR,
                     ACE_TEXT ("Failed to push %p\n"),
                     ACE_TEXT ("conversionModule")),
                    -1);
if (this->push (releaseModule) == -1)
  ACE_ERROR_RETURN ((LM_ERROR,
                     ACE_TEXT ("Failed to push %p\n"),
                     ACE_TEXT ("releaseModule")),
                    -1);
if (this->push (recordModule) == -1)
  ACE_ERROR_RETURN ((LM_ERROR,
                     ACE_TEXT ("Failed to push %p\n"),
                     ACE_TEXT ("recordModule")),
                    -1);
if (this->push (playOGMModule) == -1)
  ACE_ERROR_RETURN ((LM_ERROR,
                     ACE_TEXT ("Failed to push %p\n"),
                     ACE_TEXT ("playOGMModule")),
                    -1);
```

```
if (this->push (getCallerIdModule) == -1)
  ACE_ERROR_RETURN ((LM_ERROR,
                       ACE_TEXT ("Failed to push %p\n"),
                       ACE_TEXT ("getCallerIdModule")),
                      -1);
if (this->push (answerIncomingCallModule) == -1)
  ACE_ERROR_RETURN ((LM_ERROR,
                       ACE_TEXT ("Failed to push %p\n")
                       ACE_TEXT ("answerIncomingCallModule")),
                      -1);
```

Pushing the modules onto the stream in the correct order is very important. If your process is order dependent and you push the first-used module first, you'll be in for an unpleasant surprise! The push/pop stream terminology is the same as a stack. So be sure that you remember: first pushed, last used.

The remainder of our `RecordingStream` is the `record()` method. Whereas the constructor protected `main()` from the details of stream creation, `record()` protects it from direct interaction with the stream API:

```
int record (RecordingDevice *recorder)
{
  ACE_Message_Block * mb;
  ACE_NEW_RETURN (mb, ACE_Message_Block (sizeof(Message)), -1);

  Message *message = (Message *)mb->wr_ptr ();
  mb->wr_ptr (sizeof(Message));

  ACE_DEBUG ((LM_DEBUG,
              ACE_TEXT ("RecordingStream::record() - ")
              ACE_TEXT ("message->recorder(recorder)\n")));
  message->recorder (recorder);

  int rval = this->put (mb);
  ACE_DEBUG ((LM_DEBUG,
              ACE_TEXT ("RecordingStream::record() - ")
              ACE_TEXT ("this->put() returns %d\n"),
              rval));
  return rval;
}
```

An `ACE_Stream` is, ultimately, a fancy implementation of a linked list of `ACE_Task` objects. Each `ACE_Task` comes from the manufacturer with a built-in ACE_MessageQueue at no extra charge. That's primarily because the message queue is such an easy way to request work from a task.[2]

To give our stream some work to do, we create an ACE_Message_Block that will go into the first downstream task's message queue with put(). As our stream will be dealing with recording messages, we create the message block with enough space to contain our Message[3] object. We will basically be using the message block's data area to contain a Message object's contents.

Once our message is created, we provide it with the RecordingDevice pointer so that it will be able to ask the physical device to do things during the message processing. There may be many RecordingDevice implementations, each able to talk to a different kind of device. The tasks of the recording stream, however, don't need to know any of these details and need only the base class (RecordingDevice) pointer to get the job done.

Finally, the stream's put() method is used to start the message down the stream by putting it on the first module's downstream task's message queue. Recall that when we opened the stream, we allowed it to use the default head module, which simply passes its input on down the stream.

18.2.3 Tasks

Many of the tasks in our simple example need only delegate their action to the RecordingDevice instance, primarily because our design has required the RecordingDevice implementations to do all the "dirty work" required to talk with the physical device. Our tasks serve only as the "glue" to ensure that things happen in the right order.

AnswerIncomingCall

Before we look at our base class, let's look at the first task in our stream:

---

2. Although this example doesn't take advantage of it, don't forget that an ACE_Task can be made to use many threads. Such tasks are allowed and, in fact, encouraged in a stream because they can greatly improve the stream's throughput.

3. Message is a simple data object designed to hold a recorded message and information about that message. It's not a derivative of ACE_Message_Block. Note also that we're doing a very dangerous thing here by treating the data area as a Message instance. We never actually *created* the Message object; therefore, its constructor was never invoked. This is OK because it is a simple data object with no virtual functions. If it were more complex, we would want to use the placement new operator to instantiate the Message into the message block's data area.

```
class AnswerIncomingCall : public BasicTask
{
protected:
  virtual int process (Message *message)
  {
    ACE_TRACE (ACE_TEXT ("AnswerIncomingCall::process()"));

    if (message->recorder ()->answer_call () < 0)
      ACE_ERROR_RETURN ((LM_ERROR,
                         ACE_TEXT ("%p\n"),
                         ACE_TEXT ("AnswerIncomingCall")),
                        -1);
    return 0;
  }
};
```

The job of AnswerIncomingCall is to simply tell the recording device to "pick up the phone." Recall that in main(), we were notified that "the phone is ringing" only by the fact that the recording device's wait_for_activity() unblocked. It is up to our stream's first task to request that the recording device answer the incoming call. In a more robust application, our stream may be in use by many recording devices at one time. Therefore, we have chosen to put the recording device instance pointer into the message, in the recording stream's record() method, which is passed to each task of the stream. AnswerIncomingCall uses the recorder() method to retrieve this pointer and then invokes answer_call() on it to tell the physical device to respond to the incoming call.

BasicTask

AnswerIncomingCall and the tasks that follow all possess a process() method in which they implement their required functionality. They also don't bother to move the Message they're given on to the next task in the stream. These things, and others, are handled by the common base class: BasicTask.

Given that our tasks are all derivatives of ACE_Task and that they expect to get their input from a message queue, it is easy to create a base class for all of them. This base class takes care of reading data from the queue, requesting a derivative to process it, and passing it on to the next task in the stream. The base class also takes care of shutting down the tasks cleanly when the containing stream is shut down, either explicitly or implicitly by destruction:

```
class BasicTask : public ACE_Task<ACE_MT_SYNCH>
{
public:
  typedef ACE_Task<ACE_MT_SYNCH> inherited;

  BasicTask () : inherited()
  { }

  virtual int open (void * = 0)
  {
    ACE_DEBUG ((LM_DEBUG,
                ACE_TEXT ("BasicTask::open() starting ")
                ACE_TEXT ("%d threads\n"),
                this->desired_threads ()));

    return this->activate (THR_NEW_LWP | THR_JOINABLE,
                           this->desired_threads ());
  }
```

BasicTask extends ACE_Task and takes care of the housework our
stream's tasks would have otherwise been bothered with. The virtual open()
method activates the object into one or more threads as required by the virtual
desired_threads() method. For our simple example, none of the tasks
require more than one thread, but we've provided two methods—overriding of
open() or desired_threads()—of customizing this if a task needs to do
so.

We next provide a simple put() method that will put a message block onto
the task's message queue. The put() method is used by the Streams framework
to move messages along the stream. The putq() method could have been used
instead, but then the stream would be tied more closely to the task implementation. That is, the stream would be assuming that all tasks wish to use their message
queue for communication. A put() method could just as well send the message
to a file for the svc() method to pick up at a predefined interval:

```
int put (ACE_Message_Block *message,
         ACE_Time_Value *timeout)
{
  return this->putq (message, timeout);
}
```

Before we investigate `svc()`, we need to take a look at the `close()`[4] method. When shut down via its `close()` method, a stream will cause the `close()` method of each task to be invoked with a `flags` value of 1:

```
virtual int close (u_long flags)
{
  int rval = 0;

  if (flags == 1)
    {
      ACE_Message_Block *hangup = new ACE_Message_Block ();
      hangup->msg_type (ACE_Message_Block::MB_HANGUP);
      if (this->putq (hangup->duplicate ()) == -1)
        {
          ACE_ERROR_RETURN ((LM_ERROR,
                             ACE_TEXT ("%p\n"),
                             ACE_TEXT ("Task::close() putq")),
                            -1);
        }

      hangup->release ();
      rval = this->wait ();
    }

  return rval;
}
```

When closed by the stream, the task needs to take steps to ensure that all its threads are shut down cleanly. We do this by creating a message block of type MB_HANGUP. Our `svc()` method will look for this and close down cleanly when it arrives. After enqueuing the hang-up request, `close()` waits for all threads of the task to exit before returning. The combination of the hang-up message and `wait()` ensures that the stream will not shut down before all its tasks have had a chance to do so.

As with any other task, `svc()` is the workhorse of `BasicTask`. Here, we get the message, ask for our derivatives to do whatever work is necessary, and then send the message on to the next task in the stream:

---

4. The `module_close()` method is better suited to shutting down a task when a stream is closed. Old-time users of ACE will most likely be familiar with the `close()` approach, however, which is why we've presented it here.

```
virtual int svc (void)
{
  for (ACE_Message_Block *message = 0; ; )
    {
      ACE_DEBUG ((LM_DEBUG,
                  ACE_TEXT ("BasicTask::svc() - ")
                  ACE_TEXT ("waiting for work\n" )));

      if (this->getq (message) == -1)
        ACE_ERROR_RETURN ((LM_ERROR, ACE_TEXT ("%p\n"),
                             ACE_TEXT ("getq")),
                            -1);
```

The `svc()` method consists of an infinite loop of the actions described
earlier. The first action is to get a message from the queue. We use the simple form
of `getq()`, which will block until data becomes available.

```
if (message->msg_type () == ACE_Message_Block::MB_HANGUP)
  {
    if (this->putq (message->duplicate ()) == -1)
      {
        ACE_ERROR_RETURN ((LM_ERROR,
                            ACE_TEXT ("%p\n"),
                            ACE_TEXT ("Task::svc() putq")),
                           -1);
      }
    message->release ();
    break;
  }
```

With the message in hand, we check whether it is the special hang-up
message. If so, we put it back into the queue[5] so that peer threads of the task can
also shut down cleanly. We then exit the `for(;;)` loop and allow the task to end.

If the message is not the special hang-up message, we continue to process it:

---

5. Astute readers may think there is a memory leak here. What happens when the last of the task's
   threads puts the message back into the queue? As it turns out, when the message queue is
   destructed, which it will be when its containing task is destructed, it will iterate through any
   remaining message blocks it contains and call `release()` on each of them.

```
Message *recordedMessage =
  (Message *)message->rd_ptr ();

if (this->process (recordedMessage) == -1)
  {
    message->release ();
    ACE_ERROR_RETURN ((LM_ERROR,
                       ACE_TEXT ("%p\n"),
                       ACE_TEXT ("process")),
                      -1);
  }
```

With the message block in hand and a determination that the stream isn't being closed, we extract the read pointer from the message block and cast it into a `Message` pointer. Thus, we get back to the data that was originally put into the stream by the `RecordingStream`'s `record()` method. The virtual `process()` method is now invoked to allow derivatives to do work on the message as required by the design specification:

```
ACE_DEBUG ((LM_DEBUG,
            ACE_TEXT ("BasicTask::svc() - ")
            ACE_TEXT ("Continue to next stage\n") ));

if (this->next_step (message->duplicate ()) < 0)
  ACE_ERROR_RETURN ((LM_ERROR,
                     ACE_TEXT ("%p\n"),
                     ACE_TEXT ("put_next failed")),
                    -1);

message->release ();
```

If all went well with `process()`, we attempt to send the message to the next module of the stream. Remember that in our discussion of `RecordingStream`, we mentioned the issue of the default downstream tail task and the need to create a replacement that would not treat input data as an error. The behavior of `next_step()` in `BasicTask` is to simply invoke `put_next()`:

```
protected:
  virtual int next_step (ACE_Message_Block *message_block)
  {
    return this->put_next (message_block->duplicate ());
  }
```

This will put the message block onto the next task's message queue for processing. Our custom `EndTask` will override this method to do nothing:

```
class EndTask : public BasicTask
{
protected:
  virtual int process (Message *)
  {
    ACE_TRACE (ACE_TEXT ("EndTask::process()"));
    return 0;
  }

  virtual int next_step (ACE_Message_Block *)
  {
    ACE_DEBUG ((LM_DEBUG,
                ACE_TEXT ("EndTask::next_step() - ")
                ACE_TEXT ("end of the line.\n")));
    return 0;
  }
};
```

The nice thing about creating the custom `EndTask` is that we don't have to add any special code to any other task—or even the `BasicTask` base class—to handle the end-of-stream condition. This approach to special conditions is much more powerful and flexible than a host of `if` statements!

Now that we've seen how `AnswerIncomingCall` uses the `BasicTask` and how `BasicTask` itself is implemented, we can move quickly through the rest of the tasks in the stream.

GetCallerId

Like `AnswerIncomingCall`, `GetCallerId` delegates its work to the `RecordingDevice` on which we expect to record the `Message`:

```
class GetCallerId : public BasicTask
{
protected:
  virtual int process (Message *message)
  {
    ACE_TRACE (ACE_TEXT ("GetCallerId::process()"));

    CallerId *id;
    id = message->recorder ()->retrieve_callerId ();
```

```
  if (!id)
    ACE_ERROR_RETURN ((LM_ERROR,
                       ACE_TEXT ("%p\n"),
                       ACE_TEXT ("GetCallerId")),
                       -1);

  message->caller_id (id);
  return 0;
  }
};
```

The `retrieve_callerId()` method returns an opaque `CallerId` object. The `CallerId` object contains a reference to the message's originator. This reference could be a phone number, e-mail address, or even IP address, depending on the physical device that is taking the message for us. We store the `CallerId` in the `Message` for use later when we write the message's metadata.

PlayOutgoingMessage

In this task object, we retrieve an `ACE_FILE_Addr` pointing to an outgoing message appropriate to the recording device: an MP3 to be played through a voice modem, a text file to be sent over a socket, and so on. The recorder's `play_message()` is then given the file for playing. If the recording device is smart enough, it could even convert a text message to audio data:

```
class PlayOutgoingMessage : public BasicTask
{
protected:
  virtual int process (Message *message)
  {
    ACE_TRACE (ACE_TEXT ("PlayOutgoingMessage::process()"));

    ACE_FILE_Addr outgoing_message =
      this->get_outgoing_message (message);

    int pmrv =
      message->recorder ()->play_message (outgoing_message);
    if (pmrv < 0)
      ACE_ERROR_RETURN ((LM_ERROR,
                         ACE_TEXT ("%p\n"),
                         ACE_TEXT ("PlayOutgoingMessage")),
                         -1);
    return 0;
  }
```

```
    ACE_FILE_Addr get_outgoing_message (Message *message)
    {
      // ...
    }
};
```

RecordIncomingMessage

Our survey of trivial objects continues with `RecordIncomingMessage`. The recorder is now asked to capture the incoming message and record it to a queue/spool location where it can be processed later in the stream. The location of the message and its type are remembered by the `Message` so that later modules will be able to quickly locate the recorded data:

```
class RecordIncomingMessage : public BasicTask
{
protected:
  virtual int process (Message *message)
  {
    ACE_TRACE (ACE_TEXT ("RecordIncomingMessage::process()"));

    ACE_FILE_Addr incoming message =
      this->get_incoming_message_queue ();

    MessageType *type =
      message->recorder ()->record_message (incoming_message);
    if (!type)
      ACE_ERROR_RETURN ((LM_ERROR,
                         ACE_TEXT ("%p\n"),
                         ACE_TEXT ("RecordIncomingMessage")),
                        -1);
    message->incoming_message (incoming_message, type);
    return 0;
  }

  ACE_FILE_Addr get_incoming_message_queue (void)
  {
    // ...
  }
};
```

ReleaseDevice

After a message has been collected, we release the physical device. Remember that `main()` is operating in a different thread from the stream tasks. Thus, a new message can come into our application while we're finalizing the processing of the current one. In fact, the recording device could represent many physical channels, and we could implement a system that has many simultaneous "current" calls. In such a system, our `BasicTask` might instantiate each task into many threads instead of only one:

```
class ReleaseDevice : public BasicTask
{
protected:
  virtual int process (Message *message)
  {
    ACE_TRACE (ACE_TEXT ("ReleaseDevice::process()"));
    message->recorder ()->release ();
    return 0;
  }
};
```

EncodeMessage

To keep life easy for other applications using recorded data, it is preferable to encode the three message types—text, audio, video—into a standard format. We might, for instance, require that all audio be encoded into "radio-quality" MP3:

```
class EncodeMessage : public BasicTask
{
protected:
  virtual int process (Message *message)
  {
    ACE_TRACE (ACE_TEXT ("ReleaseDevice::process()"));

    ACE_FILE_Addr &incoming = message->addr ();
    ACE_FILE_Addr addr = this->get_message_destination (message);

    if (message->is_text ())
      Util::convert_to_unicode (incoming, addr);
    else if (message->is_audio ())
      Util::convert_to_mp3 (incoming, addr);
    else if (message->is_video ())
      Util::convert_to_mpeg (incoming, addr);
```

```
    message->addr (addr);
    return 0;
  }

  ACE_FILE_Addr get_message_destination (Message *message)
  {
    // ...
  }
};
```

The `get_message_destination()` method determines the final location of the encoded message. The `Util` object methods take care of encoding the message appropriately and placing the result into the final path. This final path is then added to the `Message` in case remaining tasks need to know what it is.

SaveMetaData

`SaveMetaData` is our most complex task yet consists of only a handful of lines. By now, you should have an appreciation of how the Streams framework, along with a little housekeeping, can eliminate all the tedious coding and allow you to focus on your application logic!

The message's metadata will describe the message for other applications. This information includes the path to the message, the type of message—text, audio, or video—and other interesting bits. We've chosen to create a simple XML (Extensible Markup Language) file to contain the metadata:

```
class SaveMetaData : public BasicTask
{
protected:
  virtual int process (Message *message)
  {
    ACE_TRACE (ACE_TEXT ("SaveMetaData::process()"));

    ACE_CString path (message->addr ().get_path_name ());
    path += ".xml";

    ACE_FILE_Connector connector;
    ACE_FILE_IO file;
    ACE_FILE_Addr addr (path.c_str ());
    if (connector.connect (file, addr) == -1)
      ACE_ERROR_RETURN ((LM_ERROR,
                         ACE_TEXT ("%p\n"),
                         ACE_TEXT ("create meta-data file")),
                        0);
```

```
      file.truncate (0);
      this->write (file, "<Message>\n");
      // ...
      this->write (file, "</Message>\n");
      file.close ();
      return 0;
  }

private:
  int write (ACE_FILE_IO &file, const char *str)
  {
    return file.send (str, ACE_OS::strlen (str));
  }
};
```

NotifySomeone

Our final task is to notify someone that a new message has arrived. This task may
be as simple as log file entry or something more complex, such as sending the
message as an attachment in an e-mail to an interested party:

```
class NotifySomeone : public BasicTask
{
protected:
  virtual int process (Message *message)
  {
    ACE_TRACE (ACE_TEXT ("NotifySomeone::process()"));

    // Format an email to tell someone about the
    // newly received message.
    // ...

    // Display message information in the logfile
    ACE_DEBUG ((LM_INFO,
                ACE_TEXT ("New message from %s ")
                ACE_TEXT ("received and stored at %s\n"),
                message->caller_id ()->string (),
                message->addr ().get_path_name ()));
    return 0;
  }
};
```

18.2.4 Remainder

We have seen that creating and using the ACE_Stream framework is very easy to do. The bulk of our sample code, in fact, had little or nothing to do with the framework itself. If we had included the answering system objects, we would find that the stream interaction code was less than 10 percent of the total. This is as it should be. A good framework should do as much as possible and allow you to focus on your application.

18.3 A Bidirectional Stream

In this section, we use a bidirectional stream to implement a *command stream*. The general idea is that each module on the stream will implement one command supported by a RecordingDevice. The RecordingDevice will configure a Command object and place it on the stream; the first module capable of processing the Command will do so and return the results up the stream for the RecordingDevice to consume. Figure 18.2 shows the logical structure of the Command Stream.

We will work this example from the inside out so that we can focus on the details of the CommandStream itself. The following subsections describe the stream, its tasks, and how the RecordingDevice derivative uses the stream.

18.3.1 CommandStream

For purposes of this example, we have created a RecordingDevice that will record a message delivered on a socket. Each task pair of our command stream will implement a RecordingDevice command by interacting with the socket in an appropriate manner.

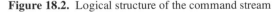

Figure 18.2. Logical structure of the command stream

We begin with the definition of our `CommandStream` class:

```
class CommandStream : public ACE_Stream<ACE_MT_SYNCH>
{
public:
  typedef ACE_Stream<ACE_MT_SYNCH> inherited;

  CommandStream () : inherited()  { }
  int open (ACE_SOCK_Stream *peer);
  Command *execute (Command *command);
};
```

We expect clients of `CommandStream` to do three things:

1. Instantiate the object.

2. Open the object and provide a socket.

3. Request execution of one or more commands.

The `open()` method is where the stream's modules are created and pushed onto the stream. The method begins by invoking the superclass's `open()` method so that we don't have to duplicate that functionality:

```
int CommandStream::open (ACE_SOCK_Stream *peer)
{
  ACE_TRACE (ACE_TEXT ("CommandStream::open(peer)"));

  if (this->inherited::open (0) == -1)
    ACE_ERROR_RETURN ((LM_ERROR, ACE_TEXT ("%p\n"),
                       ACE_TEXT ("Failed to open superclass")),
                      -1);
```

In this example, we are not providing custom head/tail modules. If no task is registered to handle a command, the task will reach the default tail module and cause an error. A more robust implementation would replace the default tail module with one that would return an error back upstream, in much the same way that results will be returned upstream.

We now create a task pair for each `RecordingDevice` command we intend to support:

```
CommandModule *answerCallModule;
ACE_NEW_RETURN (answerCallModule,
                AnswerCallModule (peer),
                -1);
```

```
CommandModule *retrieveCallerIdModule;
ACE_NEW_RETURN (retrieveCallerIdModule,
                RetrieveCallerIdModule (peer),
                -1);

CommandModule *playMessageModule;
ACE_NEW_RETURN (playMessageModule,
                PlayMessageModule (peer),
                -1);

CommandModule *recordMessageModule;
ACE_NEW_RETURN (recordMessageModule,
                RecordMessageModule (peer),
                -1);
```

At this point, we don't care about the specific tasks. Each `CommandModule` is a derivative of `ACE_Module<>` and knows what tasks need to be created to process the command it represents. This approach helps to decouple the module and the stream. As each module is constructed, we provide it with a copy of the pointer to the socket. We'll see later that the module's tasks are then able to fetch this pointer when they need to interact with the socket.

With the stream ready and the modules created, we can now push each one onto the stream. Because this stream doesn't represent an ordered set of steps, we can push them in any order. Because a `Command` must flow down the stream until it is encountered by a task pair to process, it would probably be wise to have the module responsible for the most-used command to be at the beginning of the stream. Our example is pretty much a one-shot sequence of commands, though, so the order doesn't matter:

```
if (this->push (answerCallModule) == -1)
  ACE_ERROR_RETURN ((LM_ERROR,
                     ACE_TEXT ("Failed to push %p\n"),
                     ACE_TEXT (answerCallModule->name())),
                    -1);

if (this->push (retrieveCallerIdModule) == -1)
  ACE_ERROR_RETURN ((LM_ERROR,
                     ACE_TEXT ("Failed to push %p\n"),
                     ACE_TEXT (retrieveCallerIdModule->name())),
                    -1);

if (this->push (playMessageModule) == -1)
  ACE_ERROR_RETURN ((LM_ERROR,
```

```
                              ACE_TEXT ("Failed to push %p\n"),
                              ACE_TEXT (playMessageModule->name())),
                              -1);

if (this->push (recordMessageModule) == -1)
  ACE_ERROR_RETURN ((LM_ERROR,
                     ACE_TEXT ("Failed to push %p\n"),
                     ACE_TEXT (recordMessageModule->name())),
                     -1);
```

The final `CommandStream` method is `execute()`. A client of the stream will construct a `Command` instance and provide it to `execute()` for processing. The `execute()` method will send the command downstream and wait for a result to be returned:

```
Command *CommandStream::execute (Command *command)
{
  ACE_Message_Block *mb;
  ACE_NEW_RETURN (mb, ACE_Message_Block (command), 0);
  if (this->put (mb) == -1)
    ACE_ERROR_RETURN ((LM_ERROR,
                       ACE_TEXT ("Fail on put command %d: %p\n"),
                       command->command_,
                       ACE_TEXT ("")),
                       0);

  this->get (mb);
  command = (Command *)mb->data_block ();
  ACE_DEBUG ((LM_DEBUG,
              ACE_TEXT ("Command (%d) returns (%d)\n"),
              command->command_,
              command->numeric_result_));

  return command;
}
```

The `Command` object is a derivative of `ACE_Data_Block`. This allows us to provide it directly to the `ACE_Message_Block` constructor. It also allows us to take advantage of the fact that the ACE Streams framework—`ACE_Message_Block`, in particular—will free the data block's memory at the appropriate time so that we don't have any memory leaks.

Once the message block is configured, we start it down the stream with the `put()` method. We immediately invoke `get()` to wait for the return data to be given to us. The return data is then cast back to a `Command` instance and returned to the caller. The `TextListener` implementation of `RecordingDevice` uses `execute()` to implement each `RecordingDevice` command. But we first need to look at the objects that do the work.

18.3.2 Supporting Objects and Base Classes

Command

In order for all this to work cleanly, we need a bit of support structure. First and foremost is our `Command` object, the interface between the clients of the `CommandStream`, such as `TextListener`, and the tasks that provide the implementation:

```
class Command : public ACE_Data_Block
{
public:
  // Result Values
  enum {
    PASS    = 1,
    SUCCESS = 0,
    FAILURE = -1
  };

  // Commands
  enum {
    UNKNOWN             = -1,
    ANSWER_CALL         = 10,
    RETRIEVE_CALLER_ID,
    PLAY_MESSAGE,
    RECORD_MESSAGE
  } commands;

  int flags_;
  int command_;

  void *extra_data_;

  int numeric_result_;
  ACE_CString result_;
};
```

The Command class extends ACE_Data_Block so that we can take advantage of the autodestruction provided by ACE_Message_Block. Recall that CommandStream::execute() simply instantiates an ACE_Message_Block with the provided Command. The fact that Command is an ACE_Data_Block makes this trivial. In a more robust application, we would create further derivatives of Command instead of using the generic public member variables.

CommandModule

CommandModule is the base class for all the modules our CommandStream will be using. We got a hint of this in CommandStream::open(). The CommandModule is nothing more than an adapter around its ACE_Module base class so that we can easily provide the socket to the module and easily retrieve the socket. All necessary casting is handled internally by Command-Module so that its clients—the command implementation tasks—can remain cast free:

```
class CommandModule : public ACE_Module<ACE_MT_SYNCH>
{
public:
  typedef ACE_Module<ACE_MT_SYNCH> inherited;
  typedef ACE_Task<ACE_MT_SYNCH> Task;

  CommandModule (const ACE_TCHAR *module_name,
                 CommandTask *writer,
                 CommandTask *reader,
                 ACE_SOCK_Stream *peer);

  ACE_SOCK_Stream &peer (void);
};
```

The constructor has essentially the same signature as that of ACE_Module but with the more specific data types appropriate to our application:

```
CommandModule::CommandModule (const ACE_TCHAR *module_name,
                              CommandTask *writer,
                              CommandTask *reader,
                              ACE_SOCK_Stream *peer)
  : inherited(module_name, writer, reader, peer)
{ }
```

The peer() method makes use of the arg() method of ACE_Module to retrieve its optional data. The arg() result is then cast into an ACE_SOCK_Stream as expected by the clients of CommandModule:

```
ACE_SOCK_Stream &CommandModule::peer (void)
{
  ACE_SOCK_Stream *peer = (ACE_SOCK_Stream *)this->arg ();
  return *peer;
}
```

CommandTask

The workhorse of our CommandStream framework is the CommandTask object, which extends ACE_Task and is the base class for all the tasks that implement each command. CommandTask provides a svc() method that will

- Retrieve Command requests from its message queue
- Determine whether the task can process the Command
- Decide where to pass the Command next

```
class CommandTask : public ACE_Task<ACE_MT_SYNCH>
{
public:
  typedef ACE_Task<ACE_MT_SYNCH> inherited;

  virtual ~CommandTask () { }

  virtual int open (void * = 0 );

  int put (ACE_Message_Block *message,
           ACE_Time_Value *timeout);

  virtual int svc (void);

  virtual int close (u_long flags);

protected:
  CommandTask (int command);

  virtual int process (Command *message);

  int command_;
};
```

Before we look at `svc ()` in detail, let's see what the other methods are doing for us. The constructor simply initializes the `ACE_Task` base class and sets the `command_` attribute. This will be provided by a derivative and should be one of the enumerated values from `Command`. The `svc ()` method will compare the `command_` attribute of an incoming `Command` to this value to determine whether a `CommandTask` derivative instance can process the requested command:

```
CommandTask::CommandTask (int command)
  : inherited (), command_(command)
{ }
```

The `open ()` method is as we've seen before. It simply creates a new thread in which the task will execute. For this example, we need only one thread per command:

```
int CommandTask::open (void *)
{
  return this->activate ();
}
```

The `put ()` method is similarly familiar:

```
int CommandTask::put (ACE_Message_Block *message,
                      ACE_Time_Value *timeout)
{
  return this->putq (message, timeout);
}
```

The `close ()` method is yet another boilerplate from our previous example:

```
int CommandTask::close (u_long flags)
{
  int rval = 0;
  if (flags == 1)
    {
      ACE_Message_Block *hangup = new ACE_Message_Block;
      hangup->msg_type (ACE_Message_Block::MB_HANGUP);
      if (this->putq (hangup->duplicate ()) == -1)
        {
          ACE_ERROR_RETURN ((LM_ERROR,
                             ACE_TEXT ("%p\n"),
                             ACE_TEXT ("Task::close() putq")),
                            -1);
```

```
    }

    hangup->release ();
    rval = this->wait ();
  }

  return rval;
}
```

Next comes our virtual `process ()` method. This base class implementation returns a failure code. The `CommandTask` derivatives are expected to override this method to implement the command they represent. Thus, `process ()` will return `Command::FAILURE` if processing fails, `Command::SUCCESS` if it succeeds, or `Command::PASS` if it chooses not to process the command. On failure or success, the `Command` will be returned upstream to where the command stream's `execute ()` method is blocking on `getq ()`. On `Command::PASS`, the `Command` instance will continue downstream. Any return from an upstream task will allow the `Command` to continue the upstream journey:

```
int CommandTask::process (Command *)
{
  ACE_TRACE (ACE_TEXT ("CommandTask::process()"));
  return Command::FAILURE;
}
```

With the trivia behind us, we can now take a look at `svc ()`. We begin with the usual business of taking a message block off the task's queue and checking for shutdown:

```
int CommandTask::svc (void)
{
  ACE_Message_Block *message;

  for (;;)
    {
      ACE_DEBUG ((LM_DEBUG,
                  ACE_TEXT ("CommandTask::svc() - ")
                  ACE_TEXT ("%s waiting for work\n"),
                  this->module ()->name ()));

      if (this->getq (message) == -1)
        ACE_ERROR_RETURN ((LM_ERROR,
                           ACE_TEXT ("%p\n"),
```

```
                              ACE_TEXT ("getq")),
                          -1);

     if (message->msg_type () == ACE_Message_Block::MB_HANGUP)
       {
         if (this->putq (message->duplicate ()) == -1)
           {
             ACE_ERROR_RETURN ((LM_ERROR,
                                ACE_TEXT ("%p\n"),
                                ACE_TEXT ("Task::svc() putq")),
                               -1);
           }

         message->release ();
         break;
       }
```

Now that we have a valid message block, we extract its data block. We know the data block is a Command instance, so we cast that back. If the command we're being asked to execute is not "ours," the message block is sent on to the next module in the stream. As this is a bidirectional stream, the put_next() could be moving data up- or downstream, but we don't care at this stage:

```
Command *command = (Command *)message->data_block ();

ACE_DEBUG ((LM_DEBUG,
            ACE_TEXT ("CommandTask::svc() - ")
            ACE_TEXT ("%s got work request %d\n"),
            ACE_TEXT (this->module ()->name ()),
            command->command_));

if (command->command_ != this->command_)
  {
    this->put_next (message->duplicate ());
  }
```

If the Command is our responsibility, we need to invoke process() on it. Or, more specifically, our derivative needs to process it. We help by setting the numeric_result_ attribute to –1 if process() failed. This allows our derivative's process() to simply return Command::FAILURE, yet the command stream's client can inspect numeric_result_:

```
else
  {
    int result = this->process (command);
    ACE_DEBUG ((LM_DEBUG,
                  ACE_TEXT ("CommandTask::svc() - ")
                  ACE_TEXT ("%s work request %d result is %d\n"),
                  ACE_TEXT (this->module ()->name ()),
                  command->command_,
                  result));

    if (result == Command::FAILURE)
      {
        command->numeric_result_ = -1;
      }
```

If the Command is intended for this task, the task's process() method can
still decide to let someone else handle the processing. Perhaps a scenario will
require two or more tasks to process the same Command. In any case, a
Command::PASS return value will let the message continue along the stream:

```
else if (result == Command::PASS)
  {
    this->put_next (message->duplicate ());
  }
```

Any other return value must be success, and we need to decide what should be
done with the Command. If the current task is on the downstream side of the
CommandStream (is_writer ()), we want to turn around the Command and
send it back to the stream head. This is simply done by putting the message block
on our sibling task's message queue:

```
else // result == Command::SUCCESS
  {
    if (this->is_writer ())
      {
        this->sibling ()->putq
          (message->duplicate ());
      }
```

On the other hand, if the task is on the upstream side, we want the Command
to keep flowing upstream:

```
else // this->is_reader ()
  {
    this->put_next (message->duplicate ());
  }
```

That completes the section where this task is processing a command. All that is left now is to release the message block taken off the message queue and wrap up the method:

```
message->release ();
    }    // for (;;)

  return 0;
}
```

18.3.3 Implementations

Answer Call

Now that we've seen the CommandModule and CommandTask base classes, we can look at the specific implementations instantiated by Command-Stream::open(). In the life cycle of recording a call, the first thing we must do is answer the call.

To implement the Answer Call function, we've created three objects. AnswerCallModule is a CommandModule (ACE_Module) responsible for creating the upstream and downstream tasks. The only method of Answer-CallModule is the constructor, which simply provides the necessary information to the base class instance. The peer parameter is provided as "extra data" to the base class so that the peer() method can use the arg() method to return the socket to either of the tasks:

```
AnswerCallModule::AnswerCallModule (ACE_SOCK_Stream *peer)
  : CommandModule ("AnswerCall Module",
                   new AnswerCallDownstreamTask (),
                   new AnswerCallUpstreamTask (),
                   peer)
{ }
```

The two tasks are responsible for handling the ANSWER_CALL command; therefore, they must provide this value to the CommandTask constructor:

```
AnswerCallDownstreamTask::AnswerCallDownstreamTask (void)
  : CommandTask(Command::ANSWER_CALL)
{ }


AnswerCallUpstreamTask::AnswerCallUpstreamTask (void)
  : CommandTask(Command::ANSWER_CALL)
{ }
```

All that is left now is to implement the `process()` method that will answer the incoming connection request. The decision to put this on the downstream or upstream side is rather arbitrary and in the end doesn't matter. We've taken the approach that any "active" action will go on the downstream side and any "passive," or "receiving," action on the upstream side. Thus, we implement the connection acceptance on the downstream task:

```
int AnswerCallDownstreamTask::process (Command *command)
{
  ACE_DEBUG ((LM_DEBUG, ACE_TEXT ("Answer Call (downstream)\n")));

  TextListenerAcceptor *acceptor =
    (TextListenerAcceptor *)command->extra_data_;

  CommandModule *module =
    (CommandModule*)this->module ();

  command->numeric_result_ =
    acceptor->accept (module->peer ());

  acceptor->release ();
  return Command::SUCCESS;
}
```

A few things are worth noting here. First, the `Command` instance's extra data is expected to be a `TextListenerAcceptor` instance. This sort of implied API could be avoided by creating derivatives of `Command` for each command verb.

Next of interest is the `module()` method. Any `ACE_Task` has access to this method for retrieving the `ACE_Module` in which the task is contained, if any. Because our module is a `CommandModule`, we cast the `module()` return. On our `CommandModule`, we can then invoke the `peer()` method to get a reference to the socket.

Finally, we return `Command::SUCCESS` to tell `CommandTask::svc()` that we've processed the command and that the data is ready to be sent upstream to the client.

`CommandTask::svc()` will then invoke `putq()` on the upstream task whose `process()` method has nothing important to do:

```
int AnswerCallUpstreamTask::process (Command *)
{
  ACE_DEBUG ((LM_DEBUG, ACE_TEXT ("Answer Call (upstream)\n")));

  return Command::SUCCESS;
}
```

Retrieve Caller ID

The action of retrieving caller ID from a socket consists of gathering up the IP of the remote peer. Like the `AnswerCallModule`, the `RetrieveCallerId-Module` consists of nothing more than a constructor:

```
RetrieveCallerIdModule::RetrieveCallerIdModule
  (ACE_SOCK_Stream *peer)
    : CommandModule ("RetrieveCallerId Module",
                     new RetrieveCallerIdDownstreamTask (),
                     new RetrieveCallerIdUpstreamTask (),
                     peer)
{ }
```

We consider this to be a read operation, so we've implemented it on the upstream side of the stream:

```
RetrieveCallerIdUpstreamTask::RetrieveCallerIdUpstreamTask
  (void)
    : CommandTask(Command::RETRIEVE_CALLER_ID)
{ }

int RetrieveCallerIdUpstreamTask::process (Command *command)
{
  ACE_DEBUG ((LM_DEBUG,
              ACE_TEXT ("Returning Caller ID data\n")));

  ACE_INET_Addr remote_addr;

  CommandModule *module =
    (CommandModule*)this->module ();
```

```
module->peer ().get_remote_addr (remote_addr);
ACE_TCHAR remote_addr_str[256];
remote_addr.addr_to_string (remote_addr_str, 256);
command->result_ = ACE_CString (remote_addr_str);

return Command::SUCCESS;
}
```

There should be nothing surprising here. We again use the `module ()` method to get access to our `CommandModule` and its `peer ()`. The peer's address is returned in the `result_` attribute of the `Command` for our client's consumption.

Our downstream object is expectedly simple:

```
RetrieveCallerIdDownstreamTask::RetrieveCallerIdDownstreamTask
  (void)
    : CommandTask(Command::RETRIEVE_CALLER_ID)
{ }

int RetrieveCallerIdDownstreamTask::process (Command *)
{
  ACE_DEBUG ((LM_DEBUG,
              ACE_TEXT ("Retrieving Caller ID data\n")));

  return Command::SUCCESS;
}
```

Play Message and Record Message

As you can see, our `CommandModule` and `CommandTask` derivatives are well insulated from the mechanics of the `ACE_Stream` framework. As with our unidirectional stream example, we have gone to some effort to ensure that the application programmer can focus on the task at hand—no pun intended—rather than worry about the details of the underlying framework.

Play Message and Record Message each require an appropriate module constructor. Play Message is then implemented on the downstream side:

```cpp
int PlayMessageDownstreamTask::process (Command *command)
{
  ACE_DEBUG ((LM_DEBUG,
              ACE_TEXT ("Play Outgoing Message\n")));

  ACE_FILE_Connector connector;
  ACE_FILE_IO file;

  ACE_FILE_Addr *addr =
    (ACE_FILE_Addr *)command->extra_data_;

  if (connector.connect (file, *addr) == -1)
    {
      command->numeric_result_ = -1;
    }
  else
    {
      command->numeric_result_ = 0;

      CommandModule *module =
        (CommandModule*)this->module ();

      char rwbuf[512];
      int rwbytes;
      while ((rwbytes = file.recv (rwbuf, 512)) > 0)
        {
          module->peer ().send_n (rwbuf, rwbytes);
        }
    }

  return Command::SUCCESS;
}
```

RecordMessage is implemented on the upstream side:

```cpp
int RecordMessageUpstreamTask::process (Command *command)
{
  // Collect whatever the peer sends and write into the
  // specified file.
  ACE_FILE_Connector connector;
  ACE_FILE_IO file;

  ACE_FILE_Addr *addr =
    (ACE_FILE_Addr *)command->extra_data_;
```

```
  if (connector.connect (file, *addr) == -1)
    ACE_ERROR_RETURN ((LM_ERROR,
                       ACE_TEXT ("%p\n"),
                       ACE_TEXT ("create file")),
                      Command::FAILURE);
  file.truncate (0);

  CommandModule *module =
    (CommandModule*)this->module ();

  int total_bytes = 0;
  char rwbuf[512];
  int rwbytes;
  while ((rwbytes = module->peer ().recv (rwbuf, 512)) > 0)
    {
      total_bytes += file.send_n (rwbuf, rwbytes);
    }

  file.close ();

  ACE_DEBUG ((LM_INFO,
              ACE_TEXT ("RecordMessageUpstreamTask ")
              ACE_TEXT ("- recorded %d byte message\n"),
              total_bytes));

  return Command::SUCCESS;
}
```

18.3.4 Using the Command Stream

All our component parts are now in place. We have an opaque CommandStream into which one can place a Command instance and retrieve a response. The CommandStream is built from a list of CommandModule derivatives, each of which contains a pair of CommandTask derivatives. The program logic is implemented in the CommandTask derivatives and, for the most part, is immune to the details of the ACE_Stream framework.

Let's now look at how the TextListener implementation of RecordingDevice uses the CommandStream. Because we can concurrently accept connections on a socket and process established connections, we have two RecordingDevice derivatives to implement our socket recorder. The first, TextListenerAcceptor, implements only the wait_for_activity()

method of `RecordingDevice`. That has nothing to do with the stream interaction, so we won't go into the details. In short, `TextListenerAcceptor::wait_for_activity()` will wait for a connection request on the socket and return a new `TextListener` instance when that happens.

`TextListener` implements the other `RecordingDevice` interface, using the `CommandStream`. We begin with the constructor as invoked by the acceptor:

```
TextListener::TextListener (TextListenerAcceptor *acceptor)
  : acceptor_(acceptor)
{
  ACE_TRACE (ACE_TEXT ("TextListener ctor"));

  ACE_NEW (this->command_stream_, CommandStream ());
  this->command_stream_->open (&(this->peer_));
}
```

The `TextListenerAcceptor` doesn't even accept the incoming socket connection. It shouldn't; that's a job for the Answer Call task, as shown earlier. Therefore, the acceptor's `wait_for_activity()` method provides a pointer to the acceptor object when the `TextListener` is created. This is held in a member attribute until ready to be used in the `answer_call()` method.

We've chosen not to implement an `open()` method for the `TextListenerAcceptor` to invoke. Thus, we create and initialize the `CommandStream` directly in the constructor. The `peer_` attribute is not yet connected, but because it is instantiated, we can safely provide a pointer to it in the command stream at this stage. In fact, we must provide it, API aside, so that the `answer_call` task can perform the connection:

```
int TextListener::answer_call (void)
{
  ACE_DEBUG ((LM_DEBUG,
              ACE_TEXT ("TextListener::answer_call()\n")));

  Command *c = new Command ();
  c->command_ = Command::ANSWER_CALL;
  c->extra_data_ = this->acceptor_;

  c = this->command_stream_->execute (c);

  ACE_DEBUG ((LM_DEBUG,
              ACE_TEXT ("TextListener::answer_call() ")
              ACE_TEXT ("result is %d\n"),
```

```
            c->numeric_result_ ));

  return c->numeric_result_;
}
```

To implement the `answer_call()` method, the `TextListener` first creates a `Command` instance with the `command_` attribute set to `Command::ANSWER_CALL`. This tells the command stream what needs to be done. We also save the `TextListenerAcceptor` instance (`acceptor_`) as extra data on the `Command`. This satisfies the implied API of the `AnswerCall-DownstreamTask` so that it can establish the connection.

The newly created `Command` is then given to the stream for execution. As written, the `execute()` method will block until the command has been completed. For simplicity, `execute()` will return a `Command` instance identical to the one it was given,[6] plus the return values.

The remainder of the `TextListener` methods follow this general pattern. They are presented in life-cycle order.

retrieve_callerId

```
CallerId *TextListener::retrieve_callerId (void)
{
  ACE_DEBUG ((LM_DEBUG,
              ACE_TEXT ("TextListener::retrieve_callerId()\n")));

  Command *c = new Command ();
  c->command_  = Command::RETRIEVE_CALLER_ID;

  c = this->command_stream_->execute (c);

  CallerId *caller_id = new CallerId (c->result_);
  return caller_id;
}
```

---

6. In fact, it will return the same instance in this particular implementation.

play_message

```
int TextListener::play_message (ACE_FILE_Addr &addr)
{
  MessageType *type = Util::identify_message (addr);
  if (type->is_text ())
    {
      Command *c = new Command ();
      c->command_ = Command::PLAY_MESSAGE;
      c->extra_data_ = &addr;

      c = this->command_stream_->execute (c);
      return c->numeric_result_;
    }

  ACE_FILE_Addr temp ("/tmp/outgoing_message.text");
  ACE_FILE_IO *file;

  if (type->is_audio ())
    file = Util::audio_to_text (addr, temp);
  else if (type->is_video ())
    file = Util::video_to_text (addr, temp);

  int rval = this->play_message (temp);
  file->remove ();
  return rval;
}
```

record_message

```
MessageType *TextListener::record_message (ACE_FILE_Addr &addr)
{
  Command *c = new Command ();
  c->command_ = Command::RECORD_MESSAGE;
  c->extra_data_ = &addr;

  c = this->command_stream_->execute (c);

  if (c->numeric_result_ == -1)
    {
      return 0;
    }

  return new MessageType (MessageType::RAWTEXT, addr);
}
```

release

The `release()` method is invoked by our `RecordingStream` framework when the recording process is complete. Because a new `TextListener` is instantiated for each recording, we take this opportunity to free that memory:

```
void TextListener::release (void)
{
  delete this;
}
```

18.4 Summary

In this chapter, we have investigated the ACE Streams framework. An `ACE_Stream` is nothing more than a doubly linked list of `ACE_Module` instances, each of which contains a pair of `ACE_Task` derivatives. Streams are useful for many things, only two of which we've investigated here. The following list enumerates how one would use a stream.

1. Create one or more `ACE_Task` derivatives that implement your application logic.
2. If applicable, pair these tasks into downstream and upstream components.
3. For each pair, construct a module to contain them.
4. Push the modules onto the stream in a last-used/first-pushed manner.

Keep in mind the following when architecting your stream.

- Each task in the stream can exist in one or more threads. Use multiple threads when your application can take advantage of parallel processing.
- The default tail tasks will return an error if any data reaches them. If your tasks don't entirely consume the data, you should at least provide a replacement downstream tail task.
- You can provide your task's `open()` method with arbitrary data by passing it as the fourth parameter (`args`) of module's constructor or `open()` method.
- A task's `open()` method is invoked as a result of pushing its module onto the stream, not as a result of invoking `open()` on the module.

- `ACE_Message_Block` instances are reference counted and will not leak memory if you correctly use their `duplicate()` and `release()` methods.

One last thing: If you're wondering what happened to the protocol stack we mentioned, rest assured that we haven't forgotten it. The ACE source is distributed with online tutorials. Please check out tutorial 15 in the `ACE_wrappers/docs/tutorials` directory for a protocol stream implementation example.

Chapter 19
ACE Service Configurator Framework

As we've shown so far, ACE permits tremendous flexibility when you are designing your applications. You can exchange classes, change behavior by using different strategies and template arguments, and easily change services to use multiple threads, multiple processes, use the Reactor framework, and/or use the Proactor framework.

However, you often need the flexibility to configure your application differently at runtime to use different services. You might need to do this for the following reasons.

- Your customers or users need to be able to move certain services to other machines or processes to make better use of their network or other available resources.

- You may offer optional pieces of a system and don't want them to always take up space in your program or use up memory when they're not used.

- You may have services that you always use but that you want the users to be able to configure differently, with site-specific options, for example.

You may want to allow your users to make all these changes at will, dynamically, while your application is running. This allows you to write services that you don't decide how or if they'll be used until runtime. In this chapter, we look at the ACE Service Configurator framework, which gives you all this flexibility.

19.1 Overview

The ACE Service Configurator framework is an implementation of the Component Configurator pattern [5]. You can dynamically configure services and streams at runtime, whether they are statically linked into your program or the objects are dynamically loaded from shared libraries. You can configure both services—one object representing a service—and streams—assembling modules based on a configuration file rather than at compile time. Both the arrangement of the services/streams and configuration arguments similar to command line arguments can be specified. Further, you can add and remove services to a running program, suspend services, and resume them. All this can be done by using a configuration file or by making method calls on ACE_Service_Config with text lines that would otherwise be read from a configuration file. Runtime configuration is beneficial for the following reasons.

- Multiple types of services are linked into the program or are available in shared libraries, and the set of services to activate is deferred until runtime, enabling site- or configuration-specific sets of services to be activated.

- Different arguments can be passed into the service initialization. For example, the TCP port number for a service to listen on can be specified in the configuration file rather than compiled into the program.

19.2 Configuring Static Services

A static service is one whose code is already linked into the executable program. Configuring a static service is done for the same reasons as for a dynamic service. Additionally, statically linked programs are sometimes favored for simplicity or for security concerns. Following is an example of a statically configured service; note the code involved in initializing the service, stopping the service, and how those are controlled:

```
#include "ace/OS.h"
#include "ace/Acceptor.h"
#include "ace/INET_Addr.h"
#include "ace/SOCK_Stream.h"
#include "ace/SOCK_Acceptor.h"
#include "ace/Service_Object.h"
#include "ace/Svc_Handler.h"
```

```
class ClientHandler :
    public ACE_Svc_Handler<ACE_SOCK_STREAM, ACE_NULL_SYNCH>
{
  // ... Same as previous examples.
};

class HA_Status : public ACE_Service_Object
{
  public:
    virtual int init (int argc, ACE_TCHAR *argv[]);
    virtual int fini (void);
    virtual int info (ACE_TCHAR **str, size_t len) const;

  private:
    ACE_Acceptor<ClientHandler, ACE_SOCK_ACCEPTOR> acceptor_;
    ACE_INET_Addr listen_addr_;
};
```

We're building the HA_Status service as a statically linked, configurable service. Using this technique, the service is not instantiated or activated until the ACE Service Configurator framework explicitly activates it, although all the code will already be linked into the executable program.

The preceding class declaration shows two important items that are central to developing configurable services.

1. Your service class must be a subclass of ACE_Service_Object. Remember that ACE_Task is derived from ACE_Service_Object and that ACE_Svc_Handler is a subclass of ACE_Task; therefore, ACE_Task and ACE_Svc_Handler are often used to implement configurable services.

2. Each service needs to implement the following hook methods:

   - virtual int init (int argc, ACE_TCHAR *argv[]), which is called by the framework when an instance of this service is initialized. If arguments were specified to the service initialization, they are passed via the method's arguments.

   - virtual int fini (void), which is called by the framework when an instance of the service is being shut down.

   - virtual int info (ACE_TCHAR **str, size_t len), which is optional. It is used for the service to report information about itself when asked.

The following are the implementations of the `init()` and `fini()` hook methods for our example service:

```
int
HA_Status::init (int argc, ACE_TCHAR *argv[])
{
  static const ACE_TCHAR options[] = ACE_TEXT (":f:");
  ACE_Get_Opt cmd_opts (argc, argv, options, 0);
  if (cmd_opts.long_option
       (ACE_TEXT ("config"), 'f', ACE_Get_Opt::ARG_REQUIRED) == -1)
    return -1;
  int option;
  ACE_TCHAR config_file[MAXPATHLEN];
  ACE_OS_String::strcpy (config_file, ACE_TEXT ("HAStatus.conf"));
  while ((option = cmd_opts ()) != EOF)
    switch (option)
      {
      case 'f':
        ACE_OS_String::strncpy (config_file,
                                cmd_opts.opt_arg (),
                                MAXPATHLEN);
        break;
      case ':':
        ACE_ERROR_RETURN
          ((LM_ERROR, ACE_TEXT ("-%c requires an argument\n"),
            cmd_opts.opt_opt ()),
           -1);
      default:
        ACE_ERROR_RETURN
          ((LM_ERROR, ACE_TEXT ("Parse error.\n")), -1);
      }

  ACE_Configuration_Heap config;
  config.open ();
  ACE_Registry_ImpExp config_importer (config);
  if (config_importer.import_config (config_file) == -1)
    ACE_ERROR_RETURN ((LM_ERROR,
                       ACE_TEXT ("%p\n"),
                       config_file),
                      -1);

  ACE_Configuration_Section_Key status_section;
  if (config.open_section (config.root_section (),
                           ACE_TEXT ("HAStatus"),
                           0,
                           status_section) == -1)
```

```
        ACE_ERROR_RETURN ((LM_ERROR,
                           ACE_TEXT ("%p\n"),
                           ACE_TEXT ("Can't open HAStatus section")),
                          -1);

    u_int status_port;
    if (config.get_integer_value (status_section,
                                  ACE_TEXT ("ListenPort"),
                                  status_port) == -1)
      ACE_ERROR_RETURN ((LM_ERROR,
                         ACE_TEXT ("HAStatus ListenPort does ")
                         ACE_TEXT ("not exist\n")),
                        -1);
    this->listen_addr_.set (ACE_static_cast (u_short, status_port));

    if (this->acceptor_.open (this->listen_addr_) != 0)
      ACE_ERROR_RETURN ((LM_ERROR,
                         ACE_TEXT ("HAStatus %p\n"),
                         ACE_TEXT ("accept")),
                        -1);

    return 0;
}
```

The `init()` method is called when an instance of the service is initialized. The main purpose of this method is to initialize an `ACE_Acceptor` to listen for service connection requests. It accepts a -f option to specify a configuration file to import to learn what TCP port to listen on for service requests. Note that the constructor for `ACE_Get_Opt` uses the `skip_args` parameter (fourth) with a value of 0 to force option scanning to begin at the first `argv` token. When an `argc`/`argv` pair is passed during service initialization, the arguments begin in `argv[0]` instead of `argv[1]` as in a `main()` program.

If the service initialization completes successfully, the `init()` hook should return 0. Otherwise it should return −1 to indicate an error. In an error situation, ACE will remove the service instance.

When a successfully loaded service is to be shut down, the framework calls the `fini()` hook method:

```
int
HA_Status::fini (void)
{
  this->acceptor_.close ();
  return 0;
}
```

The main responsibility of the `fini()` hook is to perform any cleanup actions
necessary for removing the service instance. On return from the method, the
service object itself will most often be deleted, so `fini()` must ensure that all
cleanup actions are complete before returning. In our example's case, the acceptor
is closed to prevent further service connections from being accepted. Any existing
service requests will be allowed to continue, as they have no coupling to the
`HA_Status` object that's being destroyed.

Now let's see how this service gets loaded and initialized. ACE keeps an
internal repository of known static services that can be configured. Each static
service must insert some bookkeeping information into this repository, using some
macros that ACE supplies for this purpose. The bookkeeping information for our
example service follows. It is located in the .cpp file for the service:

```
ACE_FACTORY_DEFINE (ACE_Local_Service, HA_Status)

ACE_STATIC_SVC_DEFINE (HA_Status_Descriptor,
                       ACE_TEXT ("HA_Status_Static_Service"),
                       ACE_SVC_OBJ_T,
                       &ACE_SVC_NAME (HA_Status),
                       ACE_Service_Type::DELETE_THIS |
                       ACE_Service_Type::DELETE_OBJ,
                       0)  // Service not initially active

ACE_STATIC_SVC_REQUIRE (HA_Status_Descriptor)
```

`ACE_FACTORY_DEFINE(CLS,SERVICE_CLASS)` defines service
factory and tear-down functions that ACE will use to assist in creating and
destroying the service object. `CLS` is the identifier your program/library is using
for import/export declarations (see Section 2.5.1). This can be the special symbol
`ACE_Local_Service` if the service factory function does not need to be
exported outside a DLL, as is the case with a static service that's linked into the
main program. `SERVICE_CLASS` is the name of the `ACE_Service_Object`-
derived class that's instantiated when the service is initialized.

ACE_STATIC_SVC_DEFINE(SERVICE_VAR,NAME,TYPE,FACTORY, FLAGS,ACTIVE) creates a static object that contains all the information needed to register the service with the ACE Service Configurator repository. The arguments are

- SERVICE_VAR. A name for the static object that this macro creates.
- NAME. A text string containing the name the service will be identified as in the service configuration file. This name should not contain whitespace.
- TYPE. The type of object being registered. We'll look at streams later, but whenever you're building a service, use ACE_SVC_OBJ_T.
- FACTORY. A pointer to the factory function used to create the service object's instance. This pointer is usually formed by using the macro ACE_SVC_NAME (SERVICE_CLASS), which creates a reference to the factory function defined with ACE_FACTORY_DEFINE.
- FLAGS. The disposition of the service-related objects when the service is shut down. Unless you are hand creating special objects, use DELETE_THIS and DELETE_OBJ.
- ACTIVE. If this value is 1, the service is activated when the program starts but can't be passed any arguments. If 0, the service is initialized by directive from the service configuration file.

ACE_STATIC_SVC_REQUIRE(SERVICE_VAR) ensures that an instance of your service object is created and registered with the ACE Service Configurator when your program starts. SERVICE_VAR is the same name used with the ACE_STATIC_SVC_DEFINE macro.

Using these three macros will ensure that your service object is prepared and registered with the Service Configurator framework. However, it will not be activated or initialized. That step occurs at runtime, usually by adding an entry for it to the service configuration file. The format of a line to configure a static service is simply:

```
static service-name [arguments]
```

where *service-name* is the name of your service assigned in the ACE_ STATIC_SVC_DEFINE macro. When the service configuration file is processed, your service's init(int argc, ACE_TCHAR *argv[]) method will be called. The *arguments* string will have been separated into tokens before calling the method. The following directive can be used to initialize our example service:

```
static HA_Status_Static_Service "-f status.ini"
```

The following program is typical of one that loads service(s) and executes a reactor event loop to drive all other program actions:

```
#include "ace/OS.h"
#include "ace/Service_Config.h"
#include "ace/Reactor.h"

int ACE_TMAIN (int argc, ACE_TCHAR *argv[])
{
  ACE_STATIC_SVC_REGISTER (HA_Status_Descriptor);
  ACE_Service_Config::open (argc,
                            argv,
                            ACE_DEFAULT_LOGGER_KEY,
                            0);
  ACE_Reactor::instance ()->run_reactor_event_loop ();
  return 0;
}
```

Note the ACE_STATIC_SVC_REGISTER macro use. Owing to differences in platform handling for static objects, this is sometimes not required; the ACE_STATIC_SVC_REQUIRE in the service implementation file is enough. However, for best portability, you should use ACE_STATIC_SVC_REGISTER as well. If it's not needed, it's a no-op.

The ACE_Service_Config::open() call is the mechanism that configures any requested services. The command line options for the main program should be passed to ACE_Service_Config::open() to effect the service processing. By default, open() attempts to process a file in the current directory named svc.conf. If the static service directive shown earlier for the example service were in such a file, the service would be initialized at this point.

The fourth parameter to the open() method is ignore_static_svcs. The default value is 1, so the ACE Service Configurator framework will ignore static services completely. Therefore, if your program will load any static services, you need to either pass 0 as the argument for ignore_static_svcs or pass -y on the command line, which has the same effect. The decision is simply to enable static services at compile time or defer the decision to program start time. The -y option is but one of those available for altering the behavior of the ACE Service Configurator at runtime. Table 19.1 lists all the available options. Note that these options are not passed to individual services' init() hooks; they direct the processing of the Service Configurator itself.

Table 19.1. Service Configurator Command Line Options

Option	Meaning
`-b`	Directs that the program become a daemon. When this option is used, the process will be daemonized before the service configuration file(s) are read. During daemonization on POSIX systems, the current directory will be changed to /, so the caller should either fully specify the file names or execute a `chroot()` to the appropriate directory.
`-d`	Turns on debugging mode. When debugging mode is on, the ACE Service Configurator will log messages describing its actions as they occur.
`-f`	Specifies a service configuration file to replace the default `svc.conf` file. Can be specified multiple times to use multiple files.
`-k`	Specifies the rendezvous point for the ACE distributed logging system (see Section 3.6).
`-y`	Enables the use of static services, overriding the `ignore_static_svcs` parameter.
`-n`	Disables the use of static services, overriding the `ignore_static_svcs` parameter.
`-s`	Specifies the signal number used to trigger a reprocessing of the configuration file(s). This is ignored on platforms that don't have POSIX signals, such as Windows.
`-S`	Specifies a service directive string to process. Enclose the string in quotes and escape any embedded quotes with a backslash. This option specifies service directives, without the need for a configuration file.

19.3 Setting Up Dynamic Services

Dynamic services can be dynamically loaded from a shared library (DLL) when directed at runtime. They need not be linked into the program at all. This dynamic-loading capability allows for great flexibility of substitution at runtime, as the code for the service need not even be written when the program is. Existing services can be removed and new services added dynamically by directives in a service configuration file or programatically.

The procedure for writing a dynamic service is very similar to that for writing a static service. The primary differences are as follows.

- The service class(es) will reside in a shared library (DLL) instead of being linked into the main program. Therefore, when declaring the service class—derived from `ACE_Service_Object`, just as for static services—the proper DLL export declaration must be used. Section 2.5.1 describes these declarations.

- The only service-related macro needed for a dynamic service is `ACE_FACTORY_DEFINE`. The record-keeping macros used for static services are not needed. The record-keeping information for dynamic services is created dynamically at runtime as the services are configured.

The following example shows the same service used in our static-service example but adjusted to work as a dynamic service. First, the class declaration:

```cpp
#include "ace/OS.h"
#include "ace/Acceptor.h"
#include "ace/INET_Addr.h"
#include "ace/SOCK_Stream.h"
#include "ace/SOCK_Acceptor.h"
#include "ace/Service_Object.h"
#include "ace/Svc_Handler.h"

#include "HASTATUS_export.h"

class ClientHandler :
    public ACE_Svc_Handler<ACE_SOCK_STREAM, ACE_NULL_SYNCH>
{
    // ... Same as previous examples.
};

class HASTATUS_Export HA_Status : public ACE_Service_Object
{
  public:
    virtual int init (int argc, ACE_TCHAR *argv[]);

    virtual int fini (void);

    virtual int info (ACE_TCHAR **str, size_t len) const;

  private:
    ACE_Acceptor<ClientHandler, ACE_SOCK_ACCEPTOR> acceptor_;
    ACE_INET_Addr listen_addr_;
};
```

As you can see, the only difference between this version of the service and the static version is the addition of the HASTATUS_Export specification on the HA_Status class declaration and the inclusion of the HASTATUS_export.h header file, which defines the needed import/export specifications.

The code for the service is exactly the same as that used in the static service example in this chapter. The record-keeping macros in the dynamic service have been reduced to simply:

```
ACE_FACTORY_DEFINE (HASTATUS, HA_Status)
```

Note that we use HASTATUS in the first argument this time. The macro will expand this to HASTATUS_Export, matching the service class's import/export specification. The ACE_FACTORY_DEFINE macro generates a short factory function, called _make_HA_Status. The macro also generated a function of this name in the static-service example, but we didn't need to know it then. We'll need the name in this example, as we'll see shortly.

The main program for this example is also shorter than that used in the static-service example:

```
#include "ace/OS.h"
#include "ace/Service_Config.h"
#include "ace/Reactor.h"

int ACE_TMAIN (int argc, ACE_TCHAR *argv[])
{
  ACE_Service_Config::open (argc, argv);
  ACE_Reactor::instance ()->run_reactor_event_loop ();
  return 0;
}
```

There are no service record-keeping macros here. In fact, there is no trace of any specific service information at all. The set of services to load and use is determined completely outside the program's code. There's certainly nothing to prevent you from using both static and dynamic services in the same program, but as this example isn't using static services, the arguments to ACE_Service_Config::open() that allow them have been left out.

Once again, the Service Configurator framework will attempt to load services as directed in the service configuration file: svc.conf, by default. The following configuration file directive will load our example dynamic service:

```
dynamic HA_Status_Dynamic_Service Service_Object *
HA_Status:_make_HA_Status() "-f status.ini"
```

Because the record-keeping information is not compiled into the program, as with static services, the configuration directives contain the information needed to direct ACE to create the proper record-keeping information. `Service_Object` indicates a service. `HA_Status:_make_HA_Status()` indicates that a shared library named `HA_Status` should be dynamically loaded and the `_make_HA_Status()` factory function called to instantiate the service object. This is the factory function generated via the `ACE_FACTORY_DEFINE` macro. The complete syntax definition for configuring a dynamic service is:

```
dynamic ident Service_Object * lib-pathname : object-class
[active|inactive] [parameters]
```

```
dynamic ident Service_Object * lib-pathname : factory-func()
[active|inactive] [parameters]
```

Our example used the second variant.

The `lib-pathname` token illustrates a useful feature of ACE with respect to portability. As you may know, different platforms use different conventions for shared library naming. For example, UNIX and Linux platforms prefix the name with `lib` and use a `.so` suffix; for example, `libHA_Status.so`. Windows doesn't add a prefix but may decorate the name with a trailing `d`, if it's a debug version, and use a `.DLL` suffix; for example, `HA_Statusd.DLL`. ACE knows how to properly deal with all these naming variants, as well as how to use various library searching mechanisms appropriate to the runtime platform, such as the `LD_LIBRARY_PATH` environment variable used on many platforms.

Keep in mind that the proper `(PROG)_BUILD_DLL` preprocessor macro needs to be specified at compile time when building a service DLL on Windows. This procedure, explained in Section 2.5.1, is very important for successfully building a service-containing DLL and bears repeating here.

19.4 Setting Up Streams

Configuring streams by using the configuration file involves a number of lines to specify the modules to be included in the stream and their relationships:

```
stream static|dynamic [modules]
```

```
stream ident [modules]
```

```
modules:
```

```
{ [[service-specification] [service-specification...]] }
```

A set of service specifications is given, listed one per line. Each successive service is created, has its `init()` method called with the arguments from the service specification, then is pushed onto the stream:

```
dynamic ident Module *

dynamic ident STREAM * lib-pathname : object-class [active|inactive]
[parameters]
```

19.5 Reconfiguring Services During Execution

So far, we've looked primarily at how to write code for configurable services and initialize those services at runtime. The other side of configurable services is being able to remove them. This capability makes it possible to add, replace, and remove services without interrupting the program as a whole, including other services executing in the same process. It is also possible to suspend and resume individual services without removing or replacing them.

The directive to remove a service that was previously initialized, such as the two services we previously showed in this chapter, is:

```
remove service
```

where `service` is the service name used in either the static or dynamic directive used to initialize the service. For example, the following directive initiates the removal of the `HA_Status_Dynamic_Service`:

```
remove HA_Status_Dynamic_Service
```

When this directive is processed, the service's `fini()` method is called; then the service object created by the factory function is deleted:

```
int
HA_Status::fini (void)
{
  this->acceptor_.close ();
  return 0;
}
```

We have learned how service configuration directives are processed at program start-up via the `ACE_Service_Config::open()` method. So how do these configuration directives get processed after that point? As we saw in the example programs in this chapter, after the Service Configurator framework is initialized, control often resides in the Reactor framework's event loop. There are two ways to make ACE reprocess the same service configuration file—or set of files—used when `ACE_Service_Config::open()` was called.

1. On systems that have POSIX signal capability, send the process a `SIGHUP` signal. For this to work, the program must be executing the Reactor event loop. As this is often the case, the requirement is not usually a problem. Note that the signal number to use for this can be changed when the program starts, by specifying the **-s** command line option (see Table 19.1).

2. The program itself can call `ACE_Service_Config::reconfigure()` directly. This is the favored option on Windows, as POSIX signals are not available, and can also be used for programs that are not running the Reactor event loop. To make this more automatic on Windows, it's possible to create a file/directory change event, register the event handle with the `ACE_WFMO_Reactor`, and use the event callback to do the reconfiguration.

Both of these options will reprocess the service configuration file(s) previously processed via `ACE_Service_Config::open()`. Therefore, the usual practice is to comment out the `static` and/or `dynamic` service initialization directives and add—or uncomment, if previously added—the desired `remove` directives, save the file(s), and trigger the reconfiguration.

The two other directives that can be used to affect a service while it is active are:

```
suspend service
```

```
resume service
```

These directives suspend and resume a service, respectively. Exactly what suspending and resuming a service entail, however, are completely up to the service implementation, and it is free to ignore the requests completely.

The service implements the suspend and resume operations via two hook methods inherited from `ACE_Service_Object`:

```
virtual int suspend (void);
```

```
virtual int resume (void);
```

Appropriate actions to take in these hook methods are service dependent but may include removing a handler from a reactor or suspending a thread. It's customary to make the `resume()` hook method undo the actions of the `suspend()` hook, resuming normal operations for the service.

19.6   **Using XML to Configure Services and Streams**

ACE version 5.3 added a new, optional way to configure services and streams. It's based on XML service configuration files rather than the syntax we've seen so far. At some future ACE version, the XML form will become the standard configuration file syntax, and the syntax we've seen to this point will become optional but won't be removed. The document type definition (DTD) for the new language follows:

```
<!ELEMENT ACE_Svc_Conf (dynamic|static|suspend|resume
                             |remove|stream|streamdef)*>
<!ELEMENT streamdef ((dynamic|static),module)>
<!ATTLIST streamdef id IDREF #REQUIRED>
<!ELEMENT module (dynamic|static|suspend|resume|remove)+>
<!ELEMENT stream (module)>
<!ATTLIST stream id IDREF #REQUIRED>
<!ELEMENT dynamic (initializer)>
<!ATTLIST dynamic id ID #REQUIRED
                  status (active|inactive) "active"
                  type (module|service_object|stream)
                  #REQUIRED>
<!ELEMENT initializer EMPTY>
<!ATTLIST initializer init CDATA #REQUIRED
                      path CDATA #IMPLIED
                      params CDATA #IMPLIED>
<!ELEMENT static EMPTY>
<!ATTLIST static id ID #REQUIRED
                 params CDATA #IMPLIED>
<!ELEMENT suspend EMPTY>
<!ATTLIST suspend id IDREF #REQUIRED>
<!ELEMENT resume EMPTY>
<!ATTLIST resume id IDREF #REQUIRED>
<!ELEMENT remove EMPTY>
<!ATTLIST remove id IDREF #REQUIRED>
```

The syntax of this XML-based configuration language is different from the current service configuration language in ACE, but its semantics are the same. Although it's more verbose to compose, the ACE XML-based configuration file format is more flexible. For example, users can plug in customized XML event handlers to extend the behavior of the ACE Service Configurator framework without modifying the underlying ACE implementation. You can try this format out by adding the following to your `ace/config.h` file and rebuilding ACE:

```
#define ACE_HAS_XML_SVC_CONF
```

Do not worry about converting all your current configuration files. ACE provides the `svcconf-convert.pl` perl script to translate original-format files into the new XML format. The script is located in the `ACE_wrappers/ bin` directory.

19.7 Configuring Services without svc.conf

In some situations, it may be too restrictive to direct service (re)configuration operations completely by using service configuration files. For example, a program may wish to instantiate or alter a service in direct response to a service request instead of waiting for an external event. To enable this direct action on the Service Configurator framework, the `ACE_Service_Config` class offers the following method:

```
static int process_directive (const ACE_TCHAR directive[]);
```

The argument to this method is a string with the same syntax as a directive you could place in a service configuration file. If you want to process a configuration file's contents, whether or not the Service Configurator framework has seen the file, you can pass the file specification to this method:

```
static int process_file (const ACE_TCHAR file[]);
```

`ACE_Service_Config` also offers methods to finalize, suspend, and resume individual named services:

```
static int remove (const ACE_TCHAR svc_name[]);

static int suspend (const ACE_TCHAR svc_name[]);

static int resume (const ACE_TCHAR svc_name[]);
```

19.8 Singletons and Services

Recall from Section 1.6.3 that the `ACE_Object_Manager` provides a useful facility for ensuring that objects can be cleaned up properly when your program runs down. The `ACE_Singleton` class is integrated with the Object Manager facility, and many application services use this feature to manage singleton lifetimes correctly. However, when using this facility, you must remember when the singleton objects are destroyed: at program rundown, when the `ACE_Object_ Manager` does its cleanup work. Now consider what happens when a dynamically loaded service that makes use of `ACE_Singleton` is unloaded before the Object Manager cleans up singletons. Usually, very bad things happen. The code that was to run the destruction of the service's singleton is probably not mapped into your process when the `ACE_Object_Manager` cleanup happens, and you'll likely get an access violation.

To make the instantiate-when-needed, double-checked locking safety of `ACE_Singleton` available to dynamically loaded services without the danger of having the cleanup performed after the service is unloaded, ACE offers the `ACE_Unmanaged_Singleton` class, which is used exactly like `ACE_Singleton`, except that an unmanaged singleton is not registered with `ACE_Object_Manager` and is not automatically cleaned up at program termination. To delete an unmanaged singleton, you must call its `close()` method. You should do this from your service's `fini()` method, as that's the dynamic service equivalent of program termination.

19.9 Summary

The Service Configurator framework allows you to divide your system into individual services and then include them or not and configure them at runtime instead of when you build your application. Users can customize the behavior of your applications to suit their site's requirements and resources and can reconfigure dynamically, adding to the availability and flexibility of your applications.

In this chapter, we gave some background of the ACE Service Configurator framework, said why it is useful, and explained how to use it. We showed how to write code that can be dynamically loaded, including those pesky Windows-required import/export directives, and how to configure your services via a configuration file and also directly in code that can be executed on demand.

We also gave a glimpse into a new feature of ACE that will become the standard way of configuring services: the XML-based service configuration file. You can use this facility today by building it into ACE, and ACE also provides a conversion script to convert your existing ACE service configuration files to the new XML format.

Finally, we explained why you need to be careful with singletons and their interaction with the ACE Object Manager facility. With the `ACE_Unmanaged_Singleton`, you are completely free of the need to always build services into your applications at link time. Your job will be easier and your customers impressed.

Chapter 20
Timers

Timers are used in almost all types of software but are especially useful for writing systems or network software. Most timers are implemented with the assistance of an underlying hardware timer, accessed through your operating system interface, which indicates timer expiration in an OS-dependent fashion. Once the hardware timer expires, it notifies the operating system, which in turn will notify the calling application. Achieving all this varies greatly, depending on the machine/OS.

In this chapter, we introduce timers and how they are built with timer queues. We then discuss the timer queue facilities provided by ACE and incorporate them into a crude timer dispatcher. Next, we show you some of the prebuilt timer dispatchers that are a part of ACE and that you can use directly in your applications. Finally, we change the event handler hierarchy to build our own private callback classes independent of `ACE_Event_Handler`.

20.1 Timer Concepts

Most operating systems provide for only a few unique timers. However, in most network software, a large number of extremely efficient timers are needed. For example, it is plausible to have one timer associated with each packet that is sent and held within a network queue. In turn, it is also necessary that the process of timer setup and cancellation be extremely efficient.

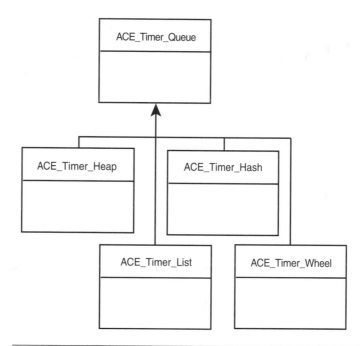

Figure 20.1. Timer queue class hierarchy

Much research has taken place in this arena, resulting in the design of highly efficient data structures called timer queues. These ordered timer queues hold nodes that individually specify the next timeout that the user is interested in. The head of the queue always contains the next timeout value. This value is obtained and then fed back to the underlying hardware timer through an OS interface. Once the timer goes off, a new timeout value is obtained from the timer queue and set as the next timeout.

ACE has implementations for many of these types of timer queues. In addition, these queues directly support interval timers, which expire repeatedly after a specified interval has elapsed. ACE timer queues also offer facilities that can be used to dispatch specified handlers once timeout does occur. ACE is flexible in that to handle timeouts, you can either use the default event handler hierarchy, based on `ACE_Event_Handler`, or you can roll your own.

Table 20.1. Timer Storage Structures and Relative Performance

Timer	Description of Structure	Performance
ACE_Timer_Heap	The timers are stored in a heap implementation of a priority queue.	schedule: O(lg n) cancel: O(lg n) find: O(1)
ACE_Timer_List	The timers are stored in a doubly linked list.	schedule: O(n) cancel: O(1) find: O(1)
ACE_Timer_Hash	A variation on the timer wheel algorithm. The performance is highly dependent on the hashing function used.	schedule (worst case): O(n) schedule (best case): O(1) cancel: O(1) find: O(1)
ACE_Timer_Wheel	The timers are stored in an array of "pointers to arrays," whereby each array being pointed to is sorted.	schedule (worst case): O(n) schedule (best case): O(1) cancel: O(1) find: O(1)

20.2 Timer Queues

All ACE timer queues derive from the abstract base class ACE_Timer_Queue. This means that they are runtime substitutable with one another, as illustrated in Figure 20.1.

Each concrete timer queue uses a different algorithm for maintaining timing nodes in order, each with different time-complexity characteristics (see Table 20.1). These characteristics should drive your decision in moving from one timer queue mechanism to another one. Further, if none of ACE prebuilt timers satisfy your requirements, you can subclass and create your own timer queue.

Each timer data structure also differs in the way it manages memory. ACE_Timer_Heap avoids expensive memory allocation by preallocating memory for internal timer nodes. When using a timer heap, you can specify how many entries are to be created in the underlying heap array. Similarly, ACE_Timer_Wheel can be set up to allocate memory from a free list of timer nodes, the free list can be provided by the programmer. For specific details, refer to the ACE reference documentation.

In the following example, we create a TimerDispatcher, which we use to register event handlers (CB) that are called when scheduled timers expire. The timer dispatcher contains two parts: an ACE timer queue and a timer driver. We use the term *timer driver* to mean the mechanism that instigates, or causes, the indication of a timeout event. You can use various schemes for timer indication, including your private OS timer API, timed condition variables, timed semaphores, timed event loop mechanisms, and so on. In our example, we use an ACE_Event object to drive the timer, as illustrated in Figure 20.2.

ACE provides several prebuilt timer dispatchers that are directly tied to OS timer APIs. These out-of-the-box dispatchers can be used to schedule and cancel timers. We have already seen one such general-purpose timer dispatcher: the ACE_Reactor. We will discuss prebuilt dispatchers in greater detail later in this chapter.

```
class Timer_Dispatcher
{
public:
  void wait_for_event (void);

  long schedule (ACE_Event_Handler *cb,
                 void *arg,
                 const ACE_Time_Value &abs_time,
                 const ACE_Time_Value &interval);

  int cancel (ACE_Event_Handler *cb,
              int dont_call_handle_close = 1);

  int reset_interval (long timer_id,
                      const ACE_Time_Value &interval);

  void set (ACE_Timer_Queue *timer_queue);

private:
  ACE_Timer_Queue *timer_queue_;
  ACE_Event timer_;
};

typedef ACE_Singleton<Timer_Dispatcher, ACE_Null_Mutex> Timer;
```

The dispatcher allows the user to register a timer/event listener object that will be called back when a timer expires. This is done through the schedule() API. This method returns to the newly scheduled timer an identifier that can be used to change or cancel the timer. The event listener class must conform to the ACE

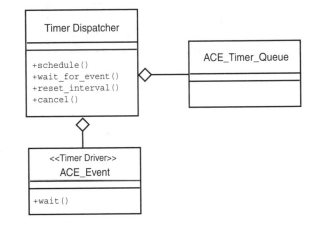

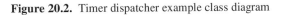

Figure 20.2. Timer dispatcher example class diagram

event-handling scheme: It must be a subtype of the `ACE_Event_Handler` abstract class and implement the `handle_timeout()` method.

A user can cancel a previously scheduled timer event through the `cancel()` method of the timer event dispatcher and reset the interval of an interval timer by using the `reset_interval()` method. Both of these methods use the timer ID returned by the `schedule()` method.

Note that we also create a singleton called `Timer` that makes our dispatcher globally visible within the application.

After scheduling the appropriate timers, the dispatcher's `wait_for_event()` method must be called. This method causes the dispatcher to wait for the underlying `ACE_Event` class to generate a timer event. Once this event occurs, the dispatcher proceeds to call back all registered event handlers (see Figure 20.3):

```
void Timer_Dispatcher::wait_for_event (void)
{
  ACE_TRACE (ACE_TEXT ("Timer_Dispatcher::wait_for_event"));

  while (1)
    {
      ACE_Time_Value max_tv = timer_queue_->gettimeofday ();

      ACE_Time_Value *this_timeout =
        this->timer_queue_->calculate_timeout (&max_tv);
```

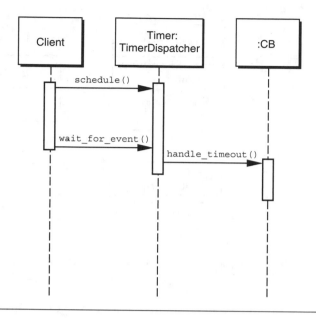

Figure 20.3. Timer dispatcher example sequence diagram

```
if (*this_timeout == ACE_Time_Value::zero)
  this->timer_queue_->expire ();
else
  {
    // Convert to absolute time.
    ACE_Time_Value next_timeout =
      timer_queue_->gettimeofday ();
    next_timeout += *this_timeout;
    if (this->timer_.wait (&next_timeout) == -1 )
      this->timer_queue_->expire ();
  }
  }
}
```

    The `wait_for_event()` method uses the `calculate_timeout()` method on the timer queue to determine the next timer that is set to expire. The time value `max_tv` that is passed in to `calculate_timeout()` is compared to the next timeout on the queue, and the greater of the two is returned. We pass this greater timeout to the underlying timer, as the time for the next expiration.

This behavior can be used to allow for a maximum blocking time for the
`wait_for_event()` method, similar to the timeout specified on the
`ACE_Reactor::handle_events()` method.

The blocking call is made on the `ACE_Event` class that is acting as our timer.
If a timeout does occur, the `wait()` call on `ACE_Event` returns –1. When this
happens, we call `expire()` on the timer queue, which consequently calls
`handle_timeout()` on all event handlers scheduled to expire before the
current time. The `expire()` call returns the number of handlers that were
dispatched.

Let's see how timers are scheduled:

```
long
Timer_Dispatcher::schedule (ACE_Event_Handler *cb,
                            void *arg,
                            const ACE_Time_Value &abs_time,
                            const ACE_Time_Value &interval)
{
  ACE_TRACE (ACE_TEXT ("Timer_Dispatcher::schedule_timer"));

  return this->timer_queue_->schedule
    (cb, arg, abs_time, interval);
}
```

The dispatcher's `schedule()` method forwards the call to `schedule()`
on the underlying timer queue. When a scheduled timer expires, the `handle_`
`timeout()` method of cb is called with the argument `arg`. The timeout occurs
at `abstime`, expressed as an absolute time and not relative time. (ACE users
commonly make the mistake of assuming relative time instead of absolute time.)
If the value of `interval` is anything but `ACE_Time_Value::zero`, the
timer will, after the initial timer expiry, continue to expire at this interval over and
over again. As we mentioned earlier, this method returns a long timer ID that is
used in subsequent timer management calls, such as `cancel()` or `reset_`
`interval()`:

```
int
Timer_Dispatcher::cancel (ACE_Event_Handler *cb,
                          int dont_call_handle_close)
{
  ACE_TRACE (ACE_TEXT ("Timer_Dispatcher::cancel"));
  return timer_queue_->cancel (cb, dont_call_handle_close);
}
```

The `cancel()` method causes all timers that are being handled by the `cb` callback object to be canceled. If the value of `dont_call_handle_close` is 1, the `handle_close()` method of `cb` is not automatically called back.

Finally, we get to the callback handler:

```
class CB : public ACE_Event_Handler
{
public:
  CB ();

  // Set the timer id that is being handled by this instance.
  void setID (long timerID);

  // Get the timer id.
  long getID (void);

  // Handle the timeout.
  virtual int handle_timeout(const ACE_Time_Value &tv,
                             const void *arg = 0);

  virtual int handle_close (ACE_HANDLE handle,
                            ACE_Reactor_Mask close_mask);

private:
  long timerID_;
  int count_;
};
```

The `handle_timeout()` method is called back when a timer expires. The callback method is passed two arguments: the absolute time at which the timer expired and a void pointer that was passed in through the dispatcher's `schedule()` API:

```
int CB::handle_timeout (const ACE_Time_Value &,
                        const void *arg)
{
  ACE_TRACE (ACE_TEXT ("CB::handle_timeout"));

  const int *val = ACE_static_cast (const int*, arg);
  ACE_ASSERT ((*val) == timerID_);
  if (count_ == 5)
    {
      ACE_DEBUG ((LM_DEBUG,
                  ACE_TEXT ("Reseting interval for timer %d\n"),
                  timerID_));
```

```
        // New interval is 10 ms.
        ACE_Time_Value interval (0L, 1000L);
        ACE_ASSERT (Timer::instance ()->reset_interval
                        (timerID_, interval) != -1);
    }

  if (count_++ == 10)
    {
      ACE_DEBUG ((LM_DEBUG, ACE_TEXT ("Canceling %d\n"),
                  timerID_));
      ACE_ASSERT ((Timer::instance ()->cancel (this)) != 0);
    }

  return 0;
}
```

In the `handle_timeout()` method, we first assert that the argument
passed in matches the identifier stored by the callback object. If this particular
callback has been called more then five times, we use the dispatcher singleton,
`Timer`, to reset the time interval for the interval timer. Similarly, if the handler
has been called more than ten times, we cancel all timers that are handled by this
event handler.

Here is the program that uses these classes:

```
#include "ace/Timer_Queue.h"
#include "ace/Timer_Heap.h"
#include "ace/Timer_Wheel.h"
#include "ace/Timer_Hash.h"
#include "ace/Timer_List.h"

#include "CB.h"
#include "TimerDispatcher.h"

int ACE_TMAIN (int argc, ACE_TCHAR *argv[])
{
  ACE_Timer_Queue *timer_queue;

#if defined(HEAP)

  ACE_NEW_RETURN (timer_queue, ACE_Timer_Heap, -1);
#elsif defined(HASH)

  ACE_NEW_RETURN (timer_queue, ACE_Timer_Hash, -1);
```

```
#elsif defined(WHEEL)

  ACE_NEW_RETURN (timer_queue, ACE_Timer_Wheel, -1);
#else

  ACE_NEW_RETURN (timer_queue, ACE_Timer_List, -1);
#endif

  // setup the timer queue
  Timer::instance ()->set (timer_queue);

  CB cb[10];
  long args[10];
  for (int i = 0; i < 10 ; i++)
    {
      long timerID =
        Timer::instance ()->schedule
          (&cb[i],
           &args[i],
           timer_queue->gettimeofday () + (ACE_Time_Value)5,
           i);

      // Set the timerID state variable of the handler.
      cb[i].setID (timerID);

      // Implicitly send the handler it's timer id.
      args[i] = timerID;
    }

  // "run" the timer.
  Timer::instance ()->wait_for_event ();

  return 0;
}
```

Because ACE provides many types of concrete timer queues, we decided to take them all out for a spin in this example. By defining the appropriate preprocessor symbol, you can set up the timer dispatcher with an appropriate timer queue.

Once the timer dispatcher is set up, we create ten callback objects that we schedule to handle ten different timers. We then perform a blocking call on the `wait_for_event()` method of the timer dispatcher.

20.3 Prebuilt Dispatchers

Having described at some length how you can create your own timer dispatcher, we now give you an overview of some of the prebuilt ACE timer dispatchers.

20.3.1 Active Timers

ACE provides an active-timer queue class that not only encapsulates the OS-based timer mechanism but also runs the timer event loop within its own private thread of control; hence the name active-timer queue. In this next example, we use an `ACE_Event_Handler`-based callback, very similar to the one we used in the previous example:

```
#include "ace/Timer_Queue_Adapters.h"
#include "ace/Timer_Heap.h"

typedef ACE_Thread_Timer_Queue_Adapter<ACE_Timer_Heap> ActiveTimer
;
```

The `ActiveTimer` adapter allows you to specify any one of the concrete timer queues as the underlying timer queue for the active timer. In this case, we chose to use the `ACE_Timer_Heap` queue:

```
class CB : public ACE_Event_Handler
{
public:
  CB (int id) : id_(id) { }

  virtual int handle_timeout (const ACE_Time_Value &tv,
                              const void *arg)
  {
    ACE_TRACE (ACE_TEXT ("CB::handle_timeout"));

    const int *val = ACE_static_cast (const int*, arg);
    ACE_ASSERT((*val) == id_);
    ACE_DEBUG ((LM_DEBUG,
                ACE_TEXT ("Expiry handled by thread %t\n")));
    return 0;
  }
```

```
private:
  int id_;
};
```

We start by creating a useful timer callback handler. As the timer dispatcher is active, the `handle_timeout()` method of the event handler will be dispatched, using the active timer's private thread of control. We display this, using the `ACE_DEBUG()` macro's `%t` format specifier:

```
int ACE_TMAIN (int argc, ACE_TCHAR *argv[])
{
  ACE_DEBUG ((LM_DEBUG,
              ACE_TEXT ("the main thread %t has started \n")));

  // Create an "active" timer and start its thread.
  ActiveTimer atimer;
  atimer.activate ();

  CB cb1 (1);
  CB cb2 (2);
  int arg1 = 1;
  int arg2 = 2;

  // Schedule timers to go off 3 & 4 seconds from now
  // and then with an interval of 1.1 seconds.
  const ACE_Time_Value curr_tv = ACE_OS::gettimeofday ();
  ACE_Time_Value interval = ACE_Time_Value (1, 1000);

  long tid1 = atimer.schedule (&cb1,
                               &arg1,
                               curr_tv + ACE_Time_Value (3L),
                               interval);
  long tid2 = atimer.schedule (&cb2,
                               &arg2,
                               curr_tv + ACE_Time_Value (4L),
                               interval);

  ACE_Thread_Manager::instance ()->wait ();  // Wait forever.

  return 0;
}
```

We start the program by creating and then activating the active timer. The `activate()` method of the timer queue gets the timer dispatcher's private thread running.

After starting the dispatcher, we schedule a couple of timers and block the main thread on the `ACE_Thread_Manager::wait()` method. Note that in the case of the active-timer dispatcher, we did not have to run any event loop, and the main thread was free to perform other functions.

20.3.2 Signal Timers

Another ACE-provided dispatcher, `ACE_Async_Timer_Queue_Adapter`, uses UNIX signals to indicate timer expirations. This timer queue works only on platforms that support the interval timer signals. These signals are not supported on Windows.

As we discussed earlier in the book, signals are asynchronous software interrupts that are handled by using any of the application threads to handle the interrupt. This allows for asynchronous behavior in single-threaded applications:

```
#include "ace/Timer_Queue_Adapters.h"
#include "ace/Timer_Heap.h"

typedef ACE_Async_Timer_Queue_Adapter<ACE_Timer_Heap> Timer;
```

We start by creating an asynchronous timer dispatcher, specifying the underlying timer queue as `ACE_Timer_Heap`:

```
int ACE_TMAIN (int, ACE_TCHAR *[])
{
  // Create the timer such that it blocks all signals
  // when it goes off.
  Timer timer;

  // Schedule a timer to go off 2 seconds later and then
  // after every 4 seconds.
  CB cb (1);
  int arg = 1;
  ACE_Time_Value initial (2);
  ACE_Time_Value repeat (4);
  initial += ACE_OS::gettimeofday ();
  timer.schedule (&cb, &arg, initial, repeat);
```

```
while (1)        // Don't let the main thread exit.
  ACE_OS::sleep (2);
return 0;        // Not reached.
}
```

We run the example by creating the timer dispatcher and scheduling a timer. We then block the main thread of control on `ACE_OS::sleep()`. When a timer goes off, a signal is raised, and the `handle_timeout()` method is called back in signal context. Once the signal handler returns, we once again block on the `ACE_OS::sleep()` call.

20.4 Managing Event Handlers

You will probably use the `ACE_Event_Handler` hierarchy almost exclusively for your timer needs unless you need to integrate with a preexisting event-handling hierarchy. In these cases, you can create or integrate with your own event-handling mechanisms. However, before we can go into how you can do this, it is necessary to understand the template types behind the `ACE_Timer_Queue` hierarchy of timer queues.

Underneath the covers of the ACE timer queues used in all our previous examples lie a couple of template-based timer queue classes (Figure 20.4). These template classes allow the template instantiator to specify

- The type of callback handler that will be called back when a timer expires
- The upcall manager, which calls methods on the callback handler when timer expiration or cancellation occurs
- A lock to ensure thread safety of the underlying timer queue

In fact, the `ACE_Timer_Queue` class is created by instantiating the `ACE_Timer_Queue_T` class template with the `ACE_Event_Handler` class as the callback handler type and an ACE internal upcall handler class as the upcall manager.

When an action is performed on any of the ACE timer queue classes, a method of the upcall manager is automatically called. This provides you, the application programmer, with a hook to decide what should happen when the action occurs. This allows you to set up your own upcall manager to call back your specific event handler class methods.

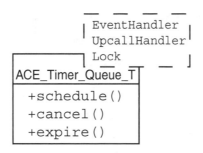

Figure 20.4. Timer queue template classes

Figure 20.5 illustrates how the timer queue, upcall manager, and a private call-back class (PCB) would interoperate. When the timer queue's `expire()` method is called, the `timeout()` method of the supplied upcall handler is invoked. In this case, we call `handleEvent()` on our new callback class, whereas the ACE-provided upcall handler would have invoked `handle_timeout()`. Similarly, when `cancel()` is invoked by the timer queue client, `cancellation()` is called on the upcall handler; when the timer queue is deleted, `deletion()` is called on the upcall handler.

Let's step through an example of creating our own upcall handler. We start by defining our event handler class:

```
class PCB
{
public:
  PCB ();

  // Set/get the timer id that is being handled by this instance.
  void setID (long timerID);
  long getID (void);

  // Handle a timeout event, cancel, and close.
  virtual int handleEvent (const void *arg);
  virtual int handleCancel (void);
  virtual int handleClose (void);

private:
  long timerID_;
  int count_;
};
```

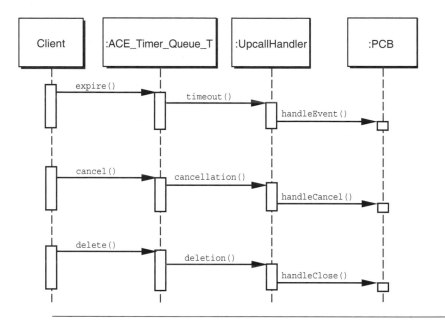

Figure 20.5. Upcall handler sequence diagram

This event handler has one `handleEvent()` method that we want to be called when a timer expires. Similarly, we want `handleCancel()` to be called on timer expiration and `handleClose()` to be called when the timer queue is deleted but the handler is still alive. Each PCB is associated with a single timer, the ID of which is stored within the PCB as `timerID_`.

After defining our callback class, we move on to the upcall handler:

```
class UpcallHandler;

typedef ACE_Timer_Queue_T<PCB*, UpcallHandler, ACE_Null_Mutex>
  PTimerQueue;

// Create a special heap-based timer queue that allows you to
// control exactly how timer evetns are handled.
typedef ACE_Timer_Heap_T<PCB*, UpcallHandler, ACE_Null_Mutex>
  PTimerHeap;
```

First, we need to instantiate the provided ACE timer queue templates with the appropriate parameters. We create the abstract base class PTimerQueue and then create a single heap-based concrete class, `PTimerHeap`. By instantiating these templates, we automatically create the base, derived relationship between these classes.

When it is called on the new timer queue type that we have created (`PTimer-Queue`), `expire()` knows that it needs to call our `UpcallHandler` handler's `timeout()`:

```
int
UpcallHandler::timeout (PTimerQueue &timer_queue,
                        PCB *handler,
                        const void *arg,
                        const ACE_Time_Value &cur_time)
{
  ACE_TRACE (ACE_TEXT ("UpcallHandler::timeout"));

  return (*handler).handleEvent (arg);
}

int
UpcallHandler::cancellation (PTimerQueue &timer_queue,
                             PCB *handler)
{
  ACE_TRACE (ACE_TEXT ("UpcallHandler::cancellation"));

  ACE_DEBUG ((LM_DEBUG,
              ACE_TEXT ("Handler %d has been cancelled\n"),
              handler->getID ()));

  return handler->handleCancel ();
}

// This method is called when the timer is canceled
int
UpcallHandler::deletion (PTimerQueue &timer_queue,
                         PCB *handler,
                         const void *arg)
{
  ACE_TRACE (ACE_TEXT ("UpcallHandler::deletion"));

  ACE_DEBUG ((LM_DEBUG,
              ACE_TEXT ("Handler %d has been deleted\n"),
              handler->getID ()));

  return handler->handleClose ();
}
```

We have set our upcall handler so that it delegates to our own PCB class, specifically invoking the handleEvent() method each time the timer queue informs us of a timeout. We also pass back the args—asynchronous completion token—that were passed to the timer queue when this timer was scheduled. Note that we ignore the cur_time value.

The cancellation() and deletion() methods are also called back at the appropriate times, and we again delegate the call to handleCancel() and handleClose(), as appropriate.

Finally, we get to the main program, which creates two callback objects and schedules timers to go off with a timer dispatcher, PTimer:

```
int ACE_TMAIN (int, ACE_TCHAR *[])
{
  PCB cb1, cb2;
  cb1.setID (1);
  cb2.setID (2);
  int arg1 = 1, arg2 = 2;

  PTimerQueue *timerQueue;

  ACE_NEW_RETURN (timerQueue, PTimerHeap (), -1);

  PTimer::instance ()->set (timerQueue);

  ACE_Time_Value tv = ACE_OS::gettimeofday ();
  tv += 20L;

  // Schedule two different timers to go off.
  PTimer::instance ()->schedule (&cb1, &arg1, tv, 1);
  PTimer::instance ()->schedule (&cb2, &arg2, tv, 2);

  // Run the timer event loop forever.
  PTimer::instance ()->wait_for_event ();

  return 0;
}
```

The PTimer dispatcher is similar to the one we used in previous sections but has been created to use an underlying PTimerQueue instead of the ACE_Timer_Queue. To set up the underlying queue for the dispatcher, we have to pass in a concrete subclass of PTimerQueue, in this case PTimerHeap.

20.5 Summary

In this chapter, we began by talking about timers and how timer queues and timer drivers are combined to create timer dispatchers. We then created our own timer dispatcher that used ACE_Event as the underlying timer driver. Next, we took a look at the timer dispatchers that are provided as a part of the ACE framework. Finally, we decided to go deep down and replace the upcall handler and event handler classes that are used by the timer queues with our own home-grown event handler class.

Chapter 21
ACE Naming Service

The ACE Naming Service provides your application with a persistent key/value mapping mechanism, which can, for instance, create a server-to-address mapping much like DNS but tailored to your application's needs. The name space can cover a single process, all processes on a single node, or many processes on a network.

21.1 The ACE_Naming_Context

The `ACE_Naming_Context` class is the center of the Naming Service universe. Once you have an instance of a naming context, you can begin to provide it with key/value pairs and fetch data from it. In addition to the key/value pair, you can also provide a *type* value. The type does not augment the key in any way. That is, keys are unique within the entire naming context, not just within a type. However, you can use the type to group a set of related keys for later resolution.

A naming context instance is typically used to:

- Bind or rebind a key to a value in the naming context
- Unbind, or remove, an entry from the context
- Resolve, or find, an entry based on a key
- Fetch a list of names, values, or types from the context
- Fetch a list of name/value/type bindings from the context.

Table 21.1. Name Options Attributes

Attribute	Meaning
TCP port	The TCP port at which a client of a network mode naming service will connect.
Host name	The host name at which a client will find a network mode naming service.
Context type	Instructs the naming context to use a process, node, or network local database.
Namespace directory	A location in the file system where the persistent namespace data is kept.
Process name	The name of the current process; in process-local mode, the default database name.
Database	The name of the database to use if the default is not appropriate.
Base address	Allows you to get/set the address of the underlying allocator used for creating entries in the database.
Registry use	Applications in the Windows environment can choose to use the Windows registry.

In addition, you can fetch and set the `ACE_Name_Options` instance used to configure the naming context instance. Using the name options, you can set the behavior and attributes listed in Table 21.1.

The Naming Service supports three contexts from which your application can choose: process-only access, system- or node-only access, and networkwide access. The first two options are essentially the same, differing only in your convention for accessing the persistent database of key/value pairs. When using the `PROC_LOCAL` context, only applications of the same name, such as their `argv[0]` value, should access a particular database. When using the `NODE_LOCAL` context, any application on the local system is permitted access to the database.

The `NET_LOCAL` context requires you to execute a server somewhere on your network. Clients can then query this server to set or get key/value pairs. This would be the most appropriate architecture for our hypothetical DNS look-alike.

Note that access to the persistent data may be implemented using a memory-mapped file. Attempting to access a network-mounted database in a local context could have unpleasant results. If you need multiple hosts accessing the same database, use the NET_LOCAL context (Section 21.4).

One of the best features of the Naming Service is that it presents exactly the same API to your application, regardless of which context you choose. This means that as your application expands, you can switch from process to node to network mode simply by changing one line of code.

21.2 A Single-Process Naming Context: PROC_LOCAL

We will use the PROC_LOCAL context to show a single application accessing the database. By "single application," we mean a named application, that is, having the same argv[0], not necessarily a single instance of an application.

The sample application will poll a thermometer device to request the current temperature. The current and previous temperatures will be stored in the naming context. In addition, a reset mechanism will be implemented such that the thermometer can be reset if there are too many successive failures. The naming context is used to record the first failure time, most recent failure time, number of resets, and so forth, so that the application can reset the thermometer intelligently and notify someone if necessary. By storing the values in the naming context, the data will be preserved even if the application is restarted.

First, our application creates a helper object to manage the command line options. This isn't strictly necessary but is a handy way to delegate that work to another object and keep main() clear of clutter:

```
int ACE_TMAIN (int argc, ACE_TCHAR *argv[])
{
  Temperature_Monitor_Options opt (argc, argv);
```

With that out of the way, we can create a Naming_Context instance and fetch the ACE_Naming_Options from it:

```
Naming_Context naming_context;

ACE_Name_Options *name_options = naming_context.name_options();
```

The Naming_Context is a simple derivative of ACE_Naming_Context and provides a few handy methods. We'll come to those details shortly.

Ordinarily, you would provide `argc`/`argv` directly to the `parse_args()`[1] method of the name context instance. Our sample application has opted to consume those values with its own options manager, however, so we must manually initialize the name options attributes:

```
char *naming_options_argv[] = { argv[0] };
name_options->parse_args
  (sizeof(naming_options_argv) / sizeof(char*),
   naming_options_argv);
name_options->context (ACE_Naming_Context::PROC_LOCAL);
naming_context.open (name_options->context ());
```

After setting the name options attributes, we give it to the context's `open()` method. Once the context has been opened, we're free to instantiate our temperature monitor object and turn control over to it:

```
Temperature_Monitor temperature_monitor (opt, naming_context);
temperature_monitor.monitor ();
```

Although the `monitor()` method is designed to execute forever, we still provide cleanup code for the naming context instance. A future version of the application may provide some sort of clean shutdown mechanism that would cause `monitor()` to exit and, if so, we won't have to worry about the context's cleanup:

```
naming_context.close ();
return 0;
```

21.2.1 Naming_Context and Name_Binding

Because the naming context is your primary interface to the ACE Naming Service, it makes sense to extend the `ACE_Naming_Context` object to the specific needs of your application. In the example, we will be storing temperatures and

---

1. Because the Naming Service is generally considered an advanced topic, it will frequently be used alongside other advanced features of ACE. In particular, it is frequently used in applications that rely on the Service Configurator. In these situations, the context's `parse_args()` is fed from the `svc.conf` file's data. In order to keep the example focused and a little simpler, we've chosen not to use the Service Configurator.

times of failures and resets. To simplify our application code, therefore, our
`ACE_Naming_Context` extension provides methods for storing, or binding,
these datatypes in the Naming Service database:

```
class Naming_Context : public ACE_Naming_Context
{
public:
  typedef ACE_Naming_Context inherited;

  int rebind (const char *name_in,
              const char *value_in,
              const char *type_in = "")
  {
    return this->inherited::rebind (name_in, value_in, type_in);
  }

  int rebind (const char *name_in,
              float value_in,
              const char *type_in = "")
  {
    char buf[BUFSIZ];
    ACE_OS::sprintf (buf, "%2f", value_in);
    return this->inherited::rebind (name_in,
                                    (const char *)buf,
                                    type_in);
  }

  int rebind (const char *name_in,
              int value_in,
              const char *type_in = "")
  {
    char buf[BUFSIZ];
    ACE_OS::sprintf (buf, "%d", value_in );
    return this->inherited::rebind (name_in,
                                    (const char *)buf,
                                    type_in);
  }
```

The Naming Service database ultimately stores its keys and values as wide-
character strings.[2] If we have any other kind of information to store, we must be

---

2. The optional *type* is always stored as a narrow-, or one-byte, character string.

able to represent it this way. Our helper functions simply use the `sprintf()` function to convert `float` (temperature) and `int` (time) values into a string before invoking the base class `rebind()` method.

Before continuing, we need to discuss the difference between `bind()` and `rebind()`. The `bind()` method will put a value into the database only if no value exists at the current key location. On success, `bind()` will return 0; on failure, such as "key already exists," `bind()` will return a nonzero value.

The `rebind()` method, on the other hand, will add a value if the key doesn't exist or will replace an existing value if the key does exist. Like `bind()`, `rebind()` will return 0 on success and nonzero on failure, but an attempt to add a value to an existing key will not be considered a failure.

Whether you use `bind()` or `rebind()` in your application is entirely up to you and the needs of your application. In our temperature-monitoring scenario, it is appropriate to replace any existing values, so we use `rebind()` in all cases.

Returning to our `Naming_Service` object, we have one more value-added feature:

```
Name_Binding *fetch (const char *name)
{
  ACE_NS_WString value;
  char *type;

  if (this->resolve (name, value, type) != 0 ||
      value.length () < 1)
    {
      return 0;
    }

  Name_Binding *rval =
    new Name_Binding (ACE_NS_WString (name),
                      value,
                      type);
  return rval;
}
```

When you know the key, known as the *name* in Naming Service parlance, of an item stored in the naming context, you will use the `resolve()` method to fetch the value and type, if any. You do this by passing a reference to an `ACE_WString` and a reference to a character pointer. If the requested key (name) exists, the `ACE_Naming_Context` will allocate space at the references you provide to contain the value and type. It is up to you to remember to deallocate this space so as not to cause a memory leak.[3]

To avoid the need to remember to delete these instances and to generally make the example code easier to write, read, and maintain, we've created a Name_Binding object to contain the results of a successful resolve() invocation. When the Name_Binding instance is destroyed, it will take care of freeing the memory allocated by the resolve() call.

The name was chosen carefully because an ACE_Name_Binding is used by the Naming Service to contain key/value/type tuples. As our Name_Binding object mirrors this, the name Name_Binding made sense:

```
class Name_Binding
{
public:
  Name_Binding (ACE_Name_Binding *entry)
  {
    this->name_  = entry->name_.char_rep ();
    this->value_ = entry->value_.char_rep ();
    this->type_  = ACE_OS::strdup (entry->type_);
  }

  Name_Binding (const ACE_NS_WString &n,
                const ACE_NS_WString &v,
                const char *t)
  {
    this->name_  = n.char_rep ();
    this->value_ = v.char_rep ();
    this->type_  = ACE_OS::strdup (t);
  }

  ~Name_Binding ()
  {
    delete this->name_;
    delete this->value_;
    delete this->type_;
  }

  char *name (void)
  { return this->name_; }
```

---

3. You can also provide resolve() with a character pointer for the value parameter if you know that's what was stored in the Naming Service in the first place.

```
    char *value (void)
    { return this->value_; }

    const char *type (void)
    { return this->type_; }

    int int_value (void)
    { return ACE_OS::atoi (this->value ()); }
private:
  char *name_;
  char *value_;
  const char *type_;
};

typedef auto_ptr<Name_Binding> Name_Binding_Ptr;
```

To convert an ACE_WString to a character pointer, which is what our application will ultimately want, you must use the char_rep() method, which allocates memory. To keep things as straightforward as possible, we let that happen in the constructor and at the same time use strdup() to create a copy of the type. Our destructor can then delete all the member variables safely, with no special cases.

As our example grows in later sections, we will find a need to do the same memory management for an ACE_Name_Binding instance. A constructor accepting an ACE_Name_Binding that copies that binding's values is just the thing to handle this situation.

The int_value() method is a simple wrapper around the standard atoi() function. This isn't strictly necessary, but it makes certain bits of our application code a little easier to read.

Finally, remember that Naming_Service::fetch() creates a new instance of Name_Binding. Somebody has to remember to free that instance so that the Name_Binding's destructor will free up the key/value/type tuple. The auto_ptr template makes it easy for us to create smart pointers that will do these things for us.

21.2.2 The Temperature Monitor

Now that we have our Naming_Context and Name_Binding objects defined, we can get into the core of the application and investigate the

Temperature_Monitor class. This class will use both of these custom objects to interact with the underlying ACE_Naming_Context for managing the temperature and thermometer status.

The constructor accepts instances of Temperature_Monitor_Options and Naming_Context. The former provides us with runtime behavior configuration, whereas the latter is the access to our persistent name/value pairs:

```
Temperature_Monitor::Temperature_Monitor
  (Temperature_Monitor_Options &opt,
  Naming_Context &naming_context)
    : opt_(opt), naming_context_(naming_context)
{ }
```

We saw this in main() just before invocation of the monitor() method:

```
void Temperature_Monitor::monitor (void)
{
  this->thermometer_ =
    new Thermometer (this->opt_.thermometer_address ());

  for(;;)
    {
      float temp = this->thermometer_->temperature ();
      ACE_DEBUG ((LM_INFO, ACE_TEXT ("Read temperature %.2f\n"),
                  temp));

      if (temp >= 0)
        {
          this->record_temperature (temp);
        }
      else
        {
          this->record_failure ();
        }

      ACE_OS::sleep (this->opt_.poll_interval ());
    }

  delete this->thermometer_;
}
```

The monitor() method is responsible for polling the physical thermometer at periodic intervals. If the physical device returns success, we log the value. If the temperature query fails, we log that also and possibly reset it.

In the `record_temperature()` method, we finally begin interacting with the Naming Service itself. Our first task is to fetch any previous record of the current temperature:

```
void Temperature_Monitor::record_temperature (float temp)
{
  Name_Binding_Ptr current
    (this->naming_context_.fetch ("current"));
  if (current.get ())
    {
      this->naming_context_.rebind ("previous",
                                    current->value ());
    }
```

Recall that `fetch()` is one of our value-added methods in the `Naming_Context` extension of `ACE_Naming_Context`. Internally, `fetch()` invokes the base class method `resolve()`. If it locates the named value—"current," in this case—`resolve()` will return a pointer to a new `Name_Binding` instance. By "wrapping" this pointer with a stack instance of `Name_Binding_Ptr`, a type definition based on `auto_ptr`, we can use the `auto_ptr`'s behavior to ensure that the `Name_Binding` pointer is deleted when the `record_temperature()` method exits.

An `auto_ptr`'s `get()` method will return the pointer it has ownership of. If that value is nonzero, we know that `fetch()` was successful and can rebind the current temperature under the new name "previous." The name binding's `value()` method will return a character pointer to the data associated with the name we queried for. That can then be given directly to the `rebind()` method of the naming context. If a value already exists there, it will be replaced; if not, the new value will be added.

Our next action is to save the new current value. We do that with another call to `rebind()`, this time overwriting the previous "current" value:

```
this->naming_context_.rebind ("current", temp);
```

Finally, we clear out the various reset variables. After all, we're recording a successful temperature fetch, so it doesn't make sense to have failure-state information at this time:

```
this->naming_context_.unbind ("lastReset");
this->naming_context_.unbind ("resetCount");
```

To clear out these values, we use the `unbind()` method. This works much like a database's `delete` keyword. Any subsequent attempt to use `resolve()` on the now unbound name will result in a failure.

Now we take a moment to look at the `record_failure()` method, which is invoked when `monitor()` fails to fetch a temperature from the thermometer device. The first thing here is to fetch the current failure status, if any:

```
void Temperature_Monitor::record_failure (void)
{
  Name_Binding_Ptr lastReset
    (this->naming_context_.fetch ("lastReset"));
  Name_Binding_Ptr resetCount
    (this->naming_context_.fetch ("resetCount"));
```

As with `record_temperature()`, we use the `fetch()` method to locate each named value we're interested in and wrap those results in on-the-stack `Name_Binding_Ptr` instances.

If a previous reset time was recorded, we use the `int_value()` method of our extended name-binding instance to find out when that reset took place. If there was no previous reset, we dummy up the value as "right now":

```
int now = ACE_OS::time ();
int lastResetTime;
if (lastReset.get ())
  {
    lastResetTime = lastReset->int_value ();
  }
else
  {
    this->naming_context_.rebind ("lastReset", now);
    lastResetTime = now;
  }
```

We then compare the `lastResetTime` to the current time. Once this delta reaches a reasonable limit, we reset the physical device:

```
if (now - lastResetTime > this->opt_.reset_interval ())
  {
    this->reset_device (resetCount);
  }
```

Thus, we're done with the `record_failure()` method, and we move on to the `reset_device()` method:

```
void
Temperature_Monitor::reset_device (Name_Binding_Ptr &resetCount)
{
  int number_of_resets = 1;
  if (resetCount.get ())
    {
      number_of_resets = resetCount->int_value () + 1;
      if (number_of_resets > this->opt_.excessive_resets ())
        {
          // ...
        }
    }
  this->thermometer_->reset ();
  this->naming_context_.rebind ("lastReset",
                                (int) ACE_OS::time ());
  this->naming_context_.rebind ("resetCount",
                                number_of_resets);
}
```

The purpose of `reset_device()` is, unsurprisingly, to reset the physical device. If too many consecutive resets have been done, we may want to notify someone of the situation. After the reset action, we record the reset time and current "consecutive resets" count, using another pair of `rebind()` methods.

As the workhorse of our little application, the `Temperature_Monitor` class's job is to monitor a physical device and record its current "state" in the form of the current temperature or failure status. We've used the Naming Service to persist this information between executions of the application. This is particularly important with the failure data.

21.3 Sharing a Naming Context on One Node: NODE_LOCAL

`NODE_LOCAL` mode is what you want to use when you have multiple applications on the same system needing to use a single naming context. In this section's example, we modify the previous application to write the ten most recent successful results to a `NODE_LOCAL` naming service. A second application then polls this naming context periodically to create a graph of the temperature history.

21.3.1 **Saving Shared Data**

We begin with a new version of `main()` to create a second naming context instance in which we'll store the shared information:

```
int ACE_TMAIN (int argc, ACE_TCHAR *argv[])
{
  Temperature_Monitor_Options opt (argc, argv);
  Naming_Context process_context;
  {
    ACE_Name_Options *name_options =
      process_context.name_options ();
    name_options->context (ACE_Naming_Context::PROC_LOCAL);
    ACE_TCHAR *nargv[] = { argv[0] };
    name_options->parse_args (sizeof(nargv) / sizeof(ACE_TCHAR*) ,
                              nargv);
    process_context.open (name_options->context ());
  }

  Naming_Context shared_context;
  {
    ACE_Name_Options *name_options =
      shared_context.name_options ();
    name_options->process_name (argv[0]);
    name_options->context (ACE_Naming_Context::NODE_LOCAL);
    shared_context.open (name_options->context ());
  }

  Temperature_Monitor2 temperature_monitor (opt,
                                            process_context,
                                            shared_context);

  temperature_monitor.monitor ();

  process_context.close ();
  shared_context.close ();

  return 0;
}
```

This is very much like the previous example's `main()`, even though we're creating two `Naming_Context` instances. We've taken the opportunity to initialize the instances in slightly different ways. Both are effective; choose the version that best fits your application's needs.

Next, we look at the modified `Temperature_Monitor` object. The `monitor()` loop is no different: Instantiate a `Thermometer`, fetch the temperature, and record success or failure. The `record_temperature()` method includes a new hook to record the temperature history:

```
void Temperature_Monitor2::record_temperature (float temp)
{
  Name_Binding_Ptr current
    (this->naming_context_.fetch ("current"));
  if (current.get ())
    {
      this->naming_context_.rebind ("previous",
                                    current->value ());
    }

  this->record_history (temp);

  this->naming_context_.unbind ("lastFailure");
  this->naming_context_.unbind ("lastReset");
  this->naming_context_.unbind ("resetCount");
}
```

As before, we save the previous value and store the current one, as well as clear the failure flags. Hiding in between is a call to `record_history()`, where we'll use the shared context:

```
void Temperature_Monitor2::record_history (float temp)
{
  int now = (int)ACE_OS::time ();
  this->shared_context_.rebind ("lastUpdate", now);

  Name_Binding_Ptr counter
    (this->shared_context_.fetch ("counter"));
  int counterValue = counter.get () ? counter->int_value () : 0;

  char name[BUFSIZ];
  ACE_OS::sprintf (name, "history[%d]", counterValue);

  char value[BUFSIZ];
  ACE_OS::sprintf (value, "%d|%.2f", now, temp);

  this->shared_context_.rebind (name, value);
```

```
  counterValue = ++counterValue % this->opt_.history_size ();
  this->shared_context_.rebind ("counter", counterValue);
}
```

As you can see, storing data to the shared context is no different from storing it to the local context. The naming-context keys are simple text strings, so we build a clever string of the format history[n] to store our ten or so most recent temperatures. Likewise, the values we store must also be strings, so we use the format date/temperature to store not just the temperature but also the date and time, in epoch seconds, at which the temperature was stored. Our cooperating application will be aware of these two clever ideas and use them to extract the data we've stored.

The remainder of the second example is identical to the first. In particular, the failure and reset logic work just as before. We now move on to look at our peer application, which will read and process the temperature history.

21.3.2 Reading Shared Data

As you might expect by now, the main() function of the temperature-graphing application is quite similar to the main() of the temperature collector:

```
int ACE_TMAIN (int argc, ACE_TCHAR *argv[])
{
  Temperature_Grapher_Options opt (argc, argv);

  Naming_Context naming_context;
  ACE_Name_Options *name_options = naming_context.name_options ();
  name_options->process_name (argv[0]);
  name_options->context (ACE_Naming_Context::NODE_LOCAL);
  naming_context.open (name_options->context ());

  Temperature_Grapher grapher (opt, naming_context);
  grapher.monitor ();
  naming_context.close ();
  return 0;
}
```

The grapher uses a simple monitor() method to poll the shared naming context from time to time:

```
void Temperature_Grapher::monitor (void)
{
  for (;;)
    {
      this->update_graph ();
      ACE_OS::sleep (this->opt_.poll_interval ());
    }
}
```

First, `update_graph()` checks whether the shared naming context has a `lastUpdate` entry. If there is no such entry, the temperature monitor has not yet successfully queried the thermometer:

```
void Temperature_Grapher::update_graph (void)
{
  Name_Binding_Ptr lastUpdate
    (this->naming_context_.fetch ("lastUpdate"));

  if (!lastUpdate.get ())
    {
      ACE_DEBUG ((LM_DEBUG, ACE_TEXT ("No data to graph\n")));
      return;
    }
```

Once we know that data is available for graphing, we need to decide whether to graph something:

```
Name_Binding_Ptr lastGraphed
  (this->naming_context_.fetch ("lastGraphed"));

if (lastGraphed.get () &&
    lastGraphed->int_value () == lastUpdate->int_value ())
  {
    ACE_DEBUG ((LM_DEBUG, ACE_TEXT ("Data already graphed\n")));
    return;
  }
```

The last thing `update_graph()` will do is record the current time. If the time between the last graphing and the current time is less than desired, we won't do anything.

Recall that in the monitor application that records temperatures, we use the format `history[n]` for the name of each value we store. The grapher doesn't know all possible values of n, so it doesn't know the exact name values to ask for via `fetch()` or `resolve()`. The naming context comes to our rescue here with the `list_name_entries()` method. This `ACE_Naming_Context` method will provide us with a set of `ACE_Name_Binding` instances in which each one's name matches the pattern provided to `list_name_entries()`.[4]

```
ACE_BINDING_SET set;
if (this->naming_context_.list_name_entries
       (set, "history[") != 0)
  {
    ACE_DEBUG ((LM_INFO,
                ACE_TEXT ("There's nothing to graph\n")));
    return;
  }
```

An `ACE_BINDING_SET` is an STL-like container of `ACE_Name_Binding` instances. In a moment, we'll iterate over that list to extract the times and temperatures to graph. Each of those pairs will be put into a list of `Graphable_Element` objects. A `Graphable_Element` is a simple application specific extension of `Name_Binding`, which is itself a derivative of `ACE_Name_Binding`. We'll get into the details of `Graphable_Element` shortly, but first let's see how to iterate over the binding set to create each graphable element:

```
Graphable_Element_List graphable;
ACE_BINDING_ITERATOR set_iterator (set);
for (ACE_Name_Binding *entry = 0;
     set_iterator.next (entry) != 0;
     set_iterator.advance ())
  {
    Name_Binding binding (entry);
    ACE_DEBUG ((LM_DEBUG, ACE_TEXT ("%s\t%s\t%s\n"),
                binding.type (),
                binding.name (),
                binding.value ()));

    Graphable_Element *ge = new Graphable_Element (entry);
    graphable.push_back (*ge);
  }
```

---

4. Several other useful methods allow you to query the context for values or types. In each case, you can receive a set of things—names, values, or types—that match your pattern or a set of `ACE_Name_Binding` instances, as we've done with `list_name_entries()`.

The `Graphable_Element_List` is a simple STL `list` of
`Graphable_Element` instances. As we iterate through the set of
`ACE_Name_Binding` instances, we create a `Name_Binding` wrapper for
each[5] and display a line of debug information describing the data we retrieved. We
then create a `Graphable_Element` instance from the `ACE_Name_Binding`
instance and add it to our growing list of graphable elements.

Our final action is to create a `Graph` instance and use it to draw a graph of the
temperatures we've fetched:

```
Graph g;
g.graph (lastUpdate->value (), graphable);
this->naming_context_.rebind ("lastGraphed",
                              lastUpdate->int_value ());
```

As promised, we also store the `lastGraphed` value so that we don't graph too
often.

Our `Graphable_Element` derives from our previous `Name_Binding`
and provides three important functions. First, it knows how to extract the time and
temperature components from the `value` attribute of the underlying `ACE_
Name_Binding` instance:

```
class Graphable_Element : public Name_Binding
{
public:
  Graphable_Element (ACE_Name_Binding *entry)
    : Name_Binding(entry)
  {
    sscanf (this->value (), "%d|%f", &this->when_, &this->temp_);
  }
```

Second, it provides convenient access to these values for other parts of the
application:

```
inline int when (void)
{
  return this->when_;
}
```

---

5. Remember the memory allocation issues that the `Name_Binding` wrapper solves for us.

```
inline float temp (void)
{
  return this->temp_;
}
```

This adaptation of one interface to another is very useful when you have an opaque data storage mechanism, such as the Naming Service. By taking this approach, we can store any arbitrarily complex information in the Naming Service.

Third, the `Graphable_Element` provides a less-than operator to compare the time components of two graphable element instances. Considering that our graph widget might want to sort the graphable elements by time, this could be quite handy:

```
inline bool operator< (Graphable_Element &other)
{
  return this->when () < other.when ();
}
```

The `Graphable_Element` concludes with its private member data and an STL `list`:

```
private:
  int when_;
  float temp_;
};

typedef std::list<Graphable_Element> Graphable_Element_List;
```

At this point, we need to mention a brief note about `std::list`. Recall that the temperature grabber's `update_graph ()` method dynamically creates instances of `Graphable_Element` and adds them to the element list, yet it never explicitly deletes these instances. Memory leak? Not so. When it goes out of scope at the end of `update_graph ()`, the `std::list` instance is freed from the stack. The list's destructor then iterates through the list and deletes each of the elements. As our `Graphable_Element` is a derivative of our memory-conservative `Name_Binding` object, the space allocated by the conversion of the name and value attributes from `WString` to `char*` is also cleaned up. Thus, there are no memory leaks.

In this section, we've extended our rather simple example to use a naming context that can be shared between processes on the same system. We saw that sharing a naming context in this way is very simple and, in fact, no different from using the process-local naming context. We move on now to consider the network local naming context, and we'll see again that doing so has little effect on our application.

21.4 Sharing a Naming Context across the Network: NET_LOCAL

At the end of Section 21.1, we made a comment about the API presented by the Naming Service. Specifically, the API used by clients of the Naming Service remains constant, regardless of the context—process, node, or network—chosen. In this section, we leverage that consistency to convert the two NODE_LOCAL programs from Section 21.3 to the NET_LOCAL context.

21.4.1 Starting the Naming Service Server

For NET_LOCAL mode, we must have a Naming Service instance executing somewhere in our network. The Naming Service is a part of ACE's network services (netsvcs) functionality. (The client and server logging servers we discussed in Chapter 3 are also part of netsvcs.) The service is dynamically loadable and can be loaded into any process. Possibly the easiest way to do so is to leverage the generic networking services application distributed with the ACE framework. In the netsvcs/servers directory is main.cpp, which can execute one or more of the ACE networking services specified in a svc.conf file. For our purposes, we need only the Naming Service, so we'll create a simple svc.conf:[6]

```
dynamic Name_Server Service_Object *
netsvcs:_make_ACE_Name_Acceptor() "-p 20012"
```

When executed, main will create a Naming Service instance listening on TCP/IP port 20012. Our modified temperature monitor and graphing applications will then look there for their naming service needs.

---

6. Please refer to Section 19.3 for details on configuring dynamic services.

21.4.2 Modifying the Applications

Modifying the two applications from NODE_LOCAL to NET_LOCAL mode is easy. First, we'll modify the temperature monitor process:

```
int ACE_TMAIN (int argc, ACE_TCHAR *argv[])
{
  Temperature_Monitor_Options opt (argc, argv);

  Naming_Context process_context;
  {
    ACE_Name_Options *name_options =
      process_context.name_options ();
    name_options->context (ACE_Naming_Context::PROC_LOCAL);
    ACE_TCHAR *nargv[] = { argv[0] };
    name_options->parse_args (sizeof(nargv) / sizeof(ACE_TCHAR*),
                              nargv);
    process_context.open (name_options->context ());
  }

  Naming_Context shared_context;
  {
    ACE_Name_Options *name_options =
      shared_context.name_options ();
    name_options->process_name (argv[0]);
    name_options->context (ACE_Naming_Context::NET_LOCAL);
    shared_context.open (name_options->context ());
  }

  Temperature_Monitor2 temperature_monitor (opt,
                                            process_context,
                                            shared_context);
  temperature_monitor.monitor ();
  process_context.close ();
  shared_context.close ();
  return 0;
}
```

The only difference between this monitor and the one in the previous section is in the invocation of name_options->context (...)!

Modifying the graph daemon is equally simple:

```
int ACE_TMAIN (int argc, ACE_TCHAR *argv[])
{
  Temperature_Grapher_Options opt (argc, argv);

  Naming_Context naming_context;
  ACE_Name_Options *name_options = naming_context.name_options ();
  name_options->process_name (argv[0]);
  name_options->context (ACE_Naming_Context::NET_LOCAL);
  naming_context.open (name_options->context ());

  Temperature_Grapher grapher (opt, naming_context);
  grapher.monitor ();
  naming_context.close ();
  return 0;
}
```

21.5 Summary

The ACE Naming Service is an easy mechanism for storing and sharing name/
value pairs. The architecture is such that it can easily keep up with the growth of
your application as it grows from a single, stand-alone process to a distributed
application running on several networked nodes.

Bibliography

1. F. Buschmann et al. 1996. *Pattern-Oriented Software Architecture—A System of Patterns.* Wiley.

2. T. Cormen et al. 2001. *Introduction to Algorithms, Second Edition.* MIT Press.

3. E. Gamma et al. 1995. *Design Patterns: Elements of Reusable Object-Oriented Software.* Addison-Wesley.

4. R. Johnson and B. Foote. 1988. "Designing Reusable Classes," *Journal of Object-Oriented Programming*, SIGS, June/July 1988, 1(5): 22–35.

5. D. Schmidt et al. 2000. *Pattern-Oriented Software Architecture: Patterns for Concurrent and Networked Objects, Volume 2.* Wiley.

6. Schmidt, D. C., and S. D. Huston. 2002. *C++ Network Programming, Volume 1: Mastering Complexity with ACE and Patterns.* Addison-Wesley.

7. Schmidt, D. C. and S. D. Huston. 2003. *C++ Network Programming, Volume 2: Systematic Reuse with ACE and Frameworks.* Addison-Wesley.

8. Stevens, W. R. 1992. *Advanced Programming in the UNIX Environment.* Addison-Wesley.

9. Stevens, W. R. 1994. *TCP/IP Illustrated, Volume 1.* Addison-Wesley.

10. Stevens, W. R. 1998. *UNIX Network Programming, Volume 1: Networking APIs: Sockets and XTI, 2d ed.* Prentice-Hall.

11. Stroustrup, B. 1997. *The C++ Programming Language, 3rd Edition.* Addison-Wesley.

12. Tanenbaum, A. 1996. *Computer Networks* 3d ed. Prentice-Hall.

13. van Rooyen, M. "Alternative C++: A New Look at Reference Counting and Virtual Destruction in C++". In *C++ Report* 8(4), April 1996.

14. Vandevoorde, D., and N. M. Josuttis. 2003. *C++ Templates: The Complete Guide*. Addison-Wesley.

Index

Note: Page numbers followed by *f* and *t* indicate figures and tables, respectively.

A

abstract design, reuse of, 7
accept(), for ACE_SOCK_Acceptor
  acceptor and, 135
  for connection requests, 136
  interruption of, by signals, 136–137
accept_handle(), for
    ACE_Asynch_Acceptor, 199
acceptor. *See also* ACE_SOCK_Acceptor
  in Acceptor-Connector framework (*See*
    ACE_Acceptor)
  definition of, 123
  error handling and, 135
  instantiating, 145
  open() method of, 144–145, 146
  port listening with, 135, 145
  register_handler() for, 145
  unicast mode and, 209
Acceptor-Connector framework, 169–182
  ACE_Acceptor in, 169–171
  ACE_Svc_Handler in, 171–172
  classes of, 169, 169*f*
  file I/O in, 213
  SPIPE in, 214
ACE

benefits of, 5–6
building, 27–30
character types in, 19, 20*t*
developer forums for, 22
distribution of, 26–27
history of, 3–5
including, in applications, 30–31
memory allocation macros in, 19, 20*t*
organization of, 6–7
reference documentation for, 21
technical support services for, 22
versions of, 25–26
ACE_Acceptor
  connection accepted by, 172–173, 172*f*
  initialization of, 423
  role of, 169–170
ACE_Activation_Queue. *See also* Activation
    Queue
  in half-sync/half-async thread pool, 334
ACE_Addr, about, 125–126
ACE_Addr::sap_any, 131
ACE_Allocator interface
  ACE_Malloc and, 350–351, 369
  for containers, 115, 116–119
ACE_Allocator_Adapter, 359, 361

ACE_ARGV, 85–86

ACE_Array. *See* array

ACE_ASSERT macro, 43*t*

ACE_Asynch_Acceptor
  about, 198–200
  for passive connection establishment, 198
  on POSIX systems, 202

ACE_Asynch_Connector
  about, 199–200
  for active connection establishment, 198
  on POSIX systems, 202

ACE_Async_Timer_Queue_Adapter, 449–
      450

ACE_Atomic_Op, 293

ACE_At_Thread_Exit, 277

ACE_Barrier, 307

ACE_Based_Pointer_Basic, 358–359

ACE_BINDING_SET, values in, 473

ACE_Bounded_Stack. *See* bounded stack

ACE_Cleanup, 15

ACE_Condition, 259

ACE_Configuration, 77

ACE_Configuration_Heap, 83, 84

ACE_Configuration_Win32Registry,
      83, 84–85

ACE_Connector, 177. *See also*
      ACE_SOCK_Connector

ACE_Data_Block, 401, 402

ACE_DEBUG macro
  about, 38–39, 43*t*
  wrapping, 48–51

ace directory, 27

ACE_DLList container. *See* doubly linked list

ACE_Dynamic_Message_Queue, 266, 266*t*

ACE_Equal_To, specialization in, 89

ACE_ERROR_BREAK macro, 43*t*

ACE_ERROR_INIT macro, 43*t*

ACE_ERROR macro, 38–39, 43*t*

ACE_ERROR_RETURN macro, 43*t*

ACE_Event_Handler. *See also* ClientSer-
      vice handler; event handler
  ACE_Reactor pointer in, 146
  I/O event handles in, 144
  for process termination, 230
  Reactor event handlers and, 142
  for signal callbacks, 239
  in timer event listener, 441

ACE_FACTORY_DEFINE macro, 424, 427, 429

ACE_FIFO classes, 214

ACE_FILE_Addr, 125–126, 213, 392

ACE_FILE_Connector, 214

ACE_FILE_IO, 214

ACE_Fixed_Stack, 95, 96–97, 98

ACE_FlReactor extension, 186

ACE_Future, 323

ACE_Future_Observer, 323–324

ACE_Get_Opt
  altering behavior of, 80–81
  command line arguments and, 78–82
  getopt() *vs.*, 78–82
  parsing with
      at arbitrary index, 80–81
      error reporting during, 81
  purpose of, 77
  for string parsing, 85

ACE_Guard, 255, 256, 256*t*. *See also* guards

ACE_GUARD macro, 256

ACE_GUARD_RETURN macro, 256

ACE_Handler, 191, 192. *See also* completion
      handler

ACE_Hash, 89

ACE_Hash_Map_Manager, 108–111. *See also*
      hash map(s)

ACE_HAS_LAZY_MAP_MANAGER, 104, 108

ACE header files, including, 30–31

ACE_HEX_DUMP macro, 43*t*

ACE_INET_Addr. *See also* address
  address extracted with, 137
  for client, 125–126
  as connect() parameter, 131
  constructor of, 129
  for server, 135
      Reactor-based, 145
  set() methods of, 129–130
  for UDP/IP, 207, 209

ACE_Ini_ImpExp, configuration information
      saved with, 85

ACE kits, availability of, 21–22

ACE_Less_Than, 111, 114–115

ACE_Less_Than functor, 111, 114–115

ACE library, 31, 36*t*

ACE_Local_Mutex, as token, 297

ACE_Log_Msg
  flag values for, 57*t*

log message format in, 45
methods of, 47, 48*t*
ACE_Log_Msg_Callback, 61–64
ACE_Log_Record, 64, 65*t*
ACE_Malloc
    about, 350–351
    ACE_Allocator and, 359
    for containers, 119
    map interface for, 351–352
    memory protection interface for, 352
    parameters for, 350
    persistence with, 352–356
    sync interface for, 352
ACE_Malloc_T, 357
ACE_Map_Manager. *See* map(s)
ACE_MEM classes, for intrahost communication, 214
ACE_Mem_Map, 375–376
ACE_Message_Block
    allocation of, in asynchronous I/O, 197
    in asynchronous read operations, 193–194, 195, 196
    in asynchronous write operations, 195, 196
    data handled with, standardization on, 203–204
    dequeueing, 154
    dequeuing, 154
    in leader/follower thread pool, 338
    in message passing, 260
    in one-way stream, 385
    outstanding operations and, 197
    queueing, 152–153, 180
    queuing, 152–153, 180
    releasing, 155, 195
    with semaphore, 303
ACE_Message_Queue
    access to, with msg_queue(), 175
    in event loop, 179
    flushing, 155
    in half-sync/half-async thread pool, 330–332
    in input processing, 152–153
    notification strategy on, 179
    as shared data buffer, 303
    in threads, 260
ACE_MMAP_Memory_Pool, backing up, 352
ACE_MMAP_Memory_Pool_Options, 358–359, 360*t*
ACE_Module
    command module from, 402–403
    tasks in, 383

ACE_Msg_WFMO_Reactor implementation, 183–185
ACE_Mutex, 252. *See also* mutex
ACE_Name_Binding. *See also* Name_Binding
    memory management for, 464
ACE_Name_Options, 458, 458*t*, 460
ACE_Naming_Context. *See also* naming context
    about, 457–459
    binding in, 474–479
ACE_Null_Mutex, 111
ACE_Object_Manager. *See* Object Manager
ACE_OSTREAM_TYPE, 59
ACE_PI_Control_Block, 357
ACE_Pipe, 214
ACE_POSIX_Proactor implementation, 202
ACE_Priority_Reactor implementation, 185
ACE_Proactor. *See also* Proactor framework
    in completion handling, 201
    implementations of, 201–202
ACE_Process. *See also* process
    about, 219–220
    spawning from, 220–221
ACE_Process_Manager, 226–231
ACE_Process_Mutex
    for hash maps, 361
    synchronization with, 231–234
ACE_Process_Options, for slave process, 220–221
ACE_QtReactor extension, 186
ACE_RB_Tree. *See* self-adjusting binary trees
ACE_Reactor. *See also* reactor
    implementations of, 182–186
    instance of, 146
    pointer to
        in event handler, 146
        passing to event handler, 147
    as timer dispatcher, 440
ACE_Reactor_Notification_Strategy, 178–179
ACE_READ_GUARD macro, 256
ACE_READ_GUARD_RETURN macro, 257
ACE_Recursive_Thread_Mutex, 16, 108, 298. *See also* recursive mutex
ACE_Registry_ImpExp, 85
ACE_RETURN macro, 43*t*

`ACE_RW_Mutex`, 292
`ACE_RW_Thread_Mutex`, 292
`ACE_Select_Reactor` implementation, 183
`ACE_Service_Handler`, 191
`ACE_Service_Object`
    dynamic services from, 427
    static services from, 421
`ACE_Sig_Action`
  for action registration, 237
  creation of, 238
`ACE_Sig_Guard`, 246–247
`ACE_Sig_Handler`
  for event handler registration, 239
  in reactor implementation, 247
  in thread signaling, 279
`ACE_Sig_Handlers`, for multiple handlers,
    245
`ACE_Sig_Set`, 158, 238
`ACE_SOCK_Acceptor`. *See also* acceptor
  in `ACE_Acceptor`, 170
  for connection acceptance, 136–138
  for multiple connections, 143–144
  port listening with, 135, 145
`ACE_SOCK_CODgram`, for UDP unicast, 210–
    211
`ACE_SOCK_Connector`. *See also* connector
  `connect()` method in, 130
  constructors for, 130–132
  nonblocking connection operation with, 132
  quality-of-service parameters with, 132
  for socket connection, 126
`ACE_SOCK_Dgram`, 209, 210
`ACE_SOCK_Dgram_Bcast`, 212
`ACE_SOCK_Dgram_Mcast`, 212–213
`ACE_SOCK_Stream`. *See also* stream
  access, with `peer()`, 175
  in `ACE_Svc_Handler`, 172
  `arg()` result in, 403
  closing, 155
  send and receive methods in, 127
  server connection of, 126
  timeout with, 132
  wrapping, in `ClientService`, 147
`ACE_SPIPE`, 214
`ACE_SPIPE_Addr`, 125–126
`ACE_STATIC_SVC_DEFINE` macro, 424
`ACE_STATIC_SVC_REGISTER` macro, 426
`ACE_STATIC_SVC_REQUIRE` macro, 425, 426

`ACE_Stream`, 379*f. See also* stream
  creation of, 378
  as linked list, 385
  modules in, 383
  in one-way stream, 380, 381–386
`ACE_Svc_Handler`. *See also* `Client` handler
  about, 171–172
  from `ACE_Connector`, 177
  UDP classes with, 208
`ACE_SV_Semaphore_Complex`, *vs.*
    `ACE_Process_Mutex`, 234
`ACE_Synch_Read_Stream`, 191
`ACE_Synch_Result`, 191
`ACE_Synch_Write_Stream`, 191
`ACE_Task`
  message queueing in, 334
  message queuing in, 334
  multithreaded queueing in, 330
  multithreaded queuing in, 330
  stream tasks from, 382
  thread creation from, 260
`ACE_Task_Base`
  in half-sync/half-async thread pool, 334
  Scheduler from, 320
  thread creation from, 250
`ACE_Thread_Manager`, 277
`ACE_Thread_Mutex`
  in `ACE_Condition`, 259
  as consistency constraint, 252–254
  for maps, 108
`ACE_Timer_Heap`
  for active timer, 447–448
  memory allocation in, 439
  for signal timer, 449–450
`ACE_Timer_Queue`, 439
`ACE_Timer_Wheel`, 439
`ACE_Time_Value`, 132, 323
`ACE_TkReactor` extension, 186
`ACE_Token`
  locking with, 297
  strict ordering with, 254
`ACE_TP_Reactor` implementation, 185, 343–
    345
`ACE_TRACE` macro
  about, 39–42, 44*t*
  customizing, 51–55
  features enabled in, 42
`ACE_TSS`, 310

`ACE_Unbounded_Queue`, 98–100, 329. *See also* queue(s)

`ACE_Unbounded_Stack`, 94, 95–96, 97. *See also* unbounded stack

`ACE_UNIX_Addr`, 125–126

`ACE_Unmanaged_Singleton`, 435

`ACE_WFMO_Reactor` implementation
  about, 183–185
  event loop integration with, 205
  proactor integration with, 204
  thread pool support in, 345

`ACE_Win32_Proactor`, 201–202, 204–205

`ACE_wrappers` directory, 26

`ACE_WRITE_GUARD` macro, 256

`ACE_WRITE_GUARD_RETURN` macro, 257

`ACE_WString`, 462, 464

`ACE_XtReactor` extension, 186

`acquire()` function
  in deadlock detection, 301
  for mutex, 252, 258
  semaphores and, 304
  vs. guard, 255

`acquire_read()`, for readers/writer lock, 292

`acquire_write()`, for readers/writer lock, 292

`activate()`
  for active object, 314
  for active-timer dispatcher, 449
  priority specified in, 274
  for thread of control, 320
  thread started with, 251

Activation Queue
  in Active Object pattern, 316
  in half-sync/half-async thread pool, 333–338
  in Scheduler, 321

Active Object pattern
  about, 314, 314*f*
  collaboration in, 316, 317*f*
  for cooperative processing, 313
  participants in, 315–316, 315*f*
  using, 317–324, 319*f*

Active Object thread, exit of, 321

active timer dispatcher, 447–449

active-timer queue, 447

Adapter pattern, 16

ADAPTIVE Communication Environment. *See* ACE

address. *See also* `ACE_INET_Addr`
  from `ACE_INET_Addr`, 137
  `addresses()` for, 200
  for client, 125–126
  definition of, 123
  for shared memory pool, 356–357, 369
  in UDP broadcast, 211
  in UDP multicast, 212
  in UDP unicast, 209–210

address space, protection of, 349

`addr_to_string()`, 137

agent implementation, aggregation of, 321

algorithms
  in C++ library, 90, 95
  reuse of, 7

allocators. *See also* `ACE_Allocator`; `ACE_Malloc`; shared memory allocator
  about, 115–119, 116*t*
  cached, 116–119
  type awareness and, 116

`answer_call()`
  for AnswerIncomingCall, 386–387
  implementation of, 416
  implantation of, 416

AnswerCallModule, 409–411

AnswerIncomingCall, 386–387

answering machine application, one-way stream for, 378–397

API
  in C, *vs.* C++, 5
  finalize from, 18
  initialize from, 18
  of Naming Serice, 459
  vs. OS methods, 9–10

applications
  building, 31–35
  networked, difficulty in writing, 5

`apply()`, for exit handler, 277

apps directory, 27

arbitrary index, parsing at, 80–81

architecture, layered, of ACE toolkit, 6–7

`arg()`, for command module, 403, 409

argument vector. *See* command line argument vector

array, 97, 100–101

associative containers, 104–115

asynchronous cancelability, 285, 287–288

asynchronous I/O model. *See also* Proactor frame-

work
about, 187
benefits of, 188–189
steps in, 188
asynchronous layer, of half-sync/half-async thread
pool, 326–327
code for, 327–329
asynchronous signals, in multithreaded programs,
282
asynchronous timer dispatcher, 449–450
at_exit(), for exit handler registration, 277–
278
atoi(), for PROC_LOCAL context, 464
atomic operation wrapper, 293–297
attributes
of name options, 460
of threads, 267–268

B

backlog argument, of open(), 200
barriers, for thread synchronization, 301–303
basic task, in one-way stream, 387–392
become_leader(), 340, 343
begin(), for maps, 106
Berkeley Software Distribution (BSD) Sockets programming. See Sockets programming
beta versions, 25
BFO (bug fix only) versions, 26
bidirectional stream, 397–418. See also command
stream
binary ordering functor, 111
binary semaphore, vs. mutex, 303
bind()
acceptor and, 135
allocator pointer in, 366
vs. rebind(), 462
binding set
iteration over, 473–474
name values in, 474
bin directory, 27
block
with getq(), 265
timed, on condition variable, 257
block size, for cached allocators, 117
bounded set, 101–103
bounded stack, 94–96
Bridge pattern, 182–183, 201

broadcast connection, in UDP, 208, 211–212
BSD (Berkeley Software Distribution) Sockets programming. See Sockets programming
bucket size, in hash map, 109
buffer
ACE_Message_Queue as, 303
for addr_to_string(), 137
allocation of, with recvv(), 134–135
counter for, 294
noncontiguous, 133
recv_n() method and, 127
send_n() method and, 127
bug fix only (BFO) versions, 26
build
of ACE, 27–30
of applications, 31–35
in Microsoft C++, 34–35
from multiple source files, 32
bytes_to_read argument, 200

C

C programming language
for APIs, 5
memory allocation in, 18–19
typeless pointers in, 88
C++ programming language. See also Microsoft
Visual C++
for APIs, 5–6
compilers for, differences among, 11–19
data types in, 14, 15t
in heap memory allocation, 18–19
templates in, 11–14
containers in, 87, 93
memory allocation in, 18–19
wide characters in, 19
cached allocators, 116–119
calculate_timeout(), on timer queue,
441–443
callbacks. See also specific methods
deleting, 61
event handler (See also handle_close();
handle_input())
in Reactor implementation, 141
return values of, 148, 149t
inheritance in, 61
for I/O operations, 194
for logging, 61–64
for logging server, direct communication with,
68–69

for process termination, 229

queueing, with notifications, 159

queuing, with notifications, 159

for signals, 236–237, 238, 245

`cancel()`

for outstanding I/O operations, 197

for timer dispatcher, 441, 444

for timer queue, 451

`cancellation()`, for upcall handler, 451, 453

cancellation, of threads, 284–288

`cancel_task()`, for thread cancellation, 286, 288

`cancel_wakeup()`, 181

`cancel_wakup()`, 181

`ChangeLog` file, 26–27

character sets, narrow *vs.* wide, 19–21

`char_rep()`, memory allocation with, 464

`child(pid_t parent)`, 226

child process. *See* slave process

class(es)

in Acceptor-Connector framework, 169, 169*f*

reuse of, by layers, 7

template argument, types defined in, 13–14

vs. namespace, 10

class libraries

extension of, 7–8

reuse by, 7

class templates, in compilers, differences among, 11–14

`cleanup()`, 16

cleanup handlers, during cancellation, 285

client. *See also* I/O sources

addressing in, 125–126

constructing, 124–129

querying with, 125, 129

with `iovec` structures, 133–134

send and receive in, 127, 137–138

`ClientAcceptor` handler. *See also* connection-accepting handler

declaration of, 143

`handle_input` method of, 146–147

instantiation of, in Reactor-based server, 145

`Client` handler. *See also* `ACE_Svc_Handler`

declaration of, 177–178

methods in, 178–181

`ClientService` handler. *See also* service handler

in Acceptor-Connector framework, 170

creation of, 172

declaration of, 171

`handle_output()` method for, 175

`open()` method for, 172–173

in Reactor framework

creation of, 147

declaration of, 149–150

`peer()` method for, 147

queueing in, 152–153

queuing in, 152–153

`clone()`, for message blocks, 263

`close()`

for command task, 405–406

for stream tasks, 388

for unmanaged singleton, 435

`close_writer()`, for `Client` handler, 180

code

conditionally compiled, 10

porting, to multiple operating systems, 8–10

private method for, 203–204

reuse of, templates for, 11–12

`collectCallerIdModule`, 383

`CollectCallerId` task, 392

command line

processing, 79

static service configuration at, 425

command line argument

`ACE_Get_Opt` and, 78–82

in one-way stream, 379–380

ordering, 81–82

runtime behavior altered with, 77

for slave process, 223

command line argument vector

building, 85–86

conversion to string, 85

processing, 78–82

command line options

arguments for, 79

defining, 79

long, 78

for naming context, 459

`operator()` for, 79

parsing, 78

+ or - in, 82

short, 78

command module

for command stream, 402–403

methods in, 403

retrieving, 410

socket pointer in, 400, 402–403, 409, 410
CommandModule, 402–403
Command object, 401–402
Command pattern, 315
command stream, 397–418, 397*f*
    Command object for, 401–402
    implementations of, 409–414
    initialization of, 415
    methods of, 399–401
    pointer to, in peer attribute, 415
    using, 414–418
CommandStream task, 398–399
CommandTask, 404–409
compiler(s)
    ACE build and, 29–30
    differences among
        data types in, 14, 15*t*
        in heap memory allocation, 18–19
        templates in, 11–14
    in portability, 9
    template applied in, 176
    template instantiation and, 11–12, 71
compiler macros, 10
compile time, service handler classes derived at,
        203–204
completion handler
    ACE_Handler and, 191
    cleanup of, 198
    deletion of, 194, 197
    handle passed to, 191
    in open(), 193
    registration of, 194
completion port, 201
Component Configurator pattern, 420
concrete design, reuse of, 7
concurrency
    in multithreaded I/O model, 188
    in self-adjusting binary trees, 111
condition variables
    in half-sync/half-async thread pool, 329
    in intertask communications, 257–260
    mutex reference in, 259
    semaphore *vs.*, 303
configuration, service. *See* service, configuration of
configuration files
    for ACE build, 28, 29*t*
    for logging client proxy, 66
    for logging server, 66

in Microsoft Visual C++, 34–35
    reading, for runtime behavior, 77
    service configuration without, 434
    for services, reprocessing, 431–432
    XML for, 432–433
configuration information, accessing, 83–85
connect()
    for client, result from, 131
    for socket connection, 126, 130
    vs. constructor, 130
connect() function, for client connection, 125
connection(s)
    accepting
        with ACE_Acceptor, 172–173, 172*f*
        with ACE_SOCK_Acceptor, 137, 143–149
        in bidirectional stream, 410
    ACE_SOCK_Connector for, 126
    ACE_SOCK_Stream and, 126
    address in, 126
    in Proactor framework, 198
    processing, 138–139, 143
    to Reactor-based server, 146–147
    service handler for (*See* service handler)
    in UDP, 208–213
connection-accepting handler. *See also* Clien-
        tAcceptor handler
    declaration of, 143
    handle association of, removing from reactor,
        143
    separation of, 144
connection requests
    accepting, 143
    accept() method for, 136
    connect() method for, 126, 130
    event handler for, 143
    timeout on, 130–131
connector. *See also* ACE_SOCK_Connector
    definition of, 123
    unicast mode and, 209
constructor
    of ACE_INET_Addr, 126, 129
    of ACE_SOCK_Acceptor, 135
    of ACE_SOCK_Connector, 130–132
    flexibility of, 129
    vs. connect(), 130
containers. *See also specific containers*
    ACE, *vs.* STL, 87
    ACE_Malloc for, 359–374
    allocator reference in, 359–360

associative, 104–112
C++ algorithms in, 90, 94
concepts for, 88–90
design methods for, 88–90
object-based, 89
position-independent pointers and, 360
subtype in, 88
template-based, 88–89
type in, 88
typeless, error protection in, 88
context object, in thread-specific storage, 310
context switch
    in half-sync/half-async thread pool, 327
    in leader/follower thread pool, 338
control block, position-independent, 357
cooperative cancellation, 285–286
copy(), for message blocks, 262
copy constructor, for hash maps, 109
counter, for buffer, 294
critical sections
    cancellation while executing, 285
    guarding, from signal interrupts, 245–247
C++ standard, compilers in, 11

D
DataElement, 90–91
data elements
    in bounded stack, 95
    deletion of
        in map, 107
        in self-adjusting binary trees, 112–114
        unbind() method for, 114
    in fixed stack, 97
    insertions of
        in maps, 104
        in self-adjusting binary trees, 111, 112–114
        in stack container, 98
    iteration of, in self-adjusting binary trees, 112–114
    locating
        in map, 105
        in self-adjusting binary trees, 112–114
    number of active, 94
    pointers to (See pointers)
datagrams, in UDP, vs. streams, 208
data order, in UDP, 208
data population, in containers, 93
data type
    in compilers, 14, 15t

in porting, 9
deactivate(), for worker thread pool shut-
    down, 332
deadlock
    detection of, 299–301
    on mutex, 254–257
    from mutex acquisition, 291
    prevention of, 301
debug statements
    enabling and disabling, 37–38
    usefulness of, 37
deferred cancelability, 285
deletion()
    for timer queue, 451
    for upcall handler, 453
design patterns, 5, 7. See also specific patterns
desired_threads(), 387
destroyList(), 94
developer forums, 22
directory tree, of ACE distribution, 26–27
disablecancel(), 285
disable_debug_messages(), 47
displayList(), 94
Distributed Object Computing group, 4
distribution, structure of, 26–27
DllMain() function, 18
DLLs, symbols in, 33–34
docs directory, 27
document type definition (DTD), for configuration
        files, 433
DONT_CALL mask type, 155, 184
Double-Checked Locking Optimization pattern, 16
doubly linked list, 90–94
    copying, 93–94
    data population in, 93
    element type in, 90–91
    testing, 92–93
    type definition for, 91–92
downstream tasks
    in command stream, 408
    definition of, 378
    message queue of, put() method in, 386
    in module, 383
    for PlayMessage, 412–413
    for RetrieveCallerID, 412
doWork(), for slave process, 224
Doxygen, for reference documentation, 21

DTD (document type definition), for configuration files, 433
duplicate(), for message blocks, 263
dynamic memory allocation
   from runtime heap, 18–19
   for service handler, 155, 182
dynamic stack, definition of, 94

E
elect_new_leader(), 340
empty_set() routine, 158
enable_debug_messages(), 47
EncodeMessage task, 395
end(), for maps, 106
EndTask, for special conditions, 391
environment variable, in parent process, 223
equal(), specializing, 107–108
equality operator
   in hash map, 109, 110–111
   in map manager, 105
   in sets, 101
errno, global, in thread-specific storage, 309
error checking, on acquire() and
       release(), 256
error handling
   acceptor and, 135
   in handle_input(), 152–153
error protection, in typeless containers, 88
event demultiplexer, 142. *See also* poll();
       select(); WaitForMultipleOb-
       jects()
event handle(s), 144, 204. *See also* handle(s); I/O
       handle
event handler. *See also* ACE_Event_Handler;
       completion handler
   ACE_SOCK_Acceptor wrapped in, 143
   in ACE_TP_Reactor implementation, 343
   in ACE_WFMO_Reactor implementation, 345
   for connection accepting (*See* connection-accept-
       ing handler)
   for connection processing, 143
   for connection requests, 143
   for connection servicing (*See* service handler)
   dynamically allocated, 184
   for I/O (*See* I/O event handlers)
   notifications for, 162–163
   reactor pointer in, 146
   removal of, 184

   for signals (*See* signal event handler)
   state data passed to, 163–166
   for timers (*See* timer event handler)
   XML, 433
event handling
   demultiplexer for, 142
   in process management, 229
   Reactor framework for, implementing, 141
Event Log
   in mixed environment, 65
   output to, 58
event loop
   ACE_Message_Queue in, 179
   in ACE_TP_Reactor implementation, 185
   active-timer dispatcher and, 449
   function of, 141
   proactor-based
       integrating with reactor, 204
       for I/O completion processing, 201
   reactor-based, 146
       integrating with proactor, 204
       stopping, 156–157
event notifications, intertask communication on,
       257
examples directory, 27
exception-handling, for pool growth handling, 369–
       374
execute(), for command stream, 400–401, 416
execution context, in ucontext_t, 245
exit functions
   cancellation and, 284
   Object Manager and, 17
   for threads
       number of, 277
       registration of, 277–278
expire()
   for timer dispatcher, 443
   for timer queue, 451, 453

F
façade pattern, 9
factory classes, in Proactor framework, 202–203.
       See also specific classes
failure code, from process(), in command
       stream, 406, 407–408
failure status, fetching, 467
FastLight reactor, 186
fetch()

for NODE_LOCAL context, 473
for PROC_LOCAL context, 462, 466, 467
FIFO scheduling policy, 271
FIFO sequences, 98, 213–214
FIFO thread order, tokens for, 297
file(s), direct operations on, in shared memeory, 349, 375–376
file(s), direct operations on, in shared memory, 349, 375–376
file I/O, for intrahost communication, 213, 214
fill_set() routine, 158
find() function
    allocator argument in, 369
    in shared memory, 363
fini() function
    Object Manager initialization with, 18
    for service removal, 431
    for static services, 421–424
fixed stack, 95–96, 97
Fix Kits, 26
follower thread. *See* leader/follower thread pool
fork() *vs.* spawn(), 220
format, for logging, 38, 41*t*–42*t*
forums, developer, 22
framework(s). *See also specific frameworks*
    in ACE, 5
    class libraries extended with, 7–8
    definition of, 6
    reuse by, 7
    at runtime, 8
    vs. patterns, 7
framework layer, 6
function tracing, macros for, 53–55
Future
    in Active Object pattern, 316, 322–323
    in half-sync/half-async thread pool, 333
Future Observer, 323–324
    in Active Object pattern, 316
    in half-sync/half-async thread pool, 333

G
get()
    for Future object, 323
    for return data, 401
    for stream tasks, 378
get_handle()
    ACE_Svc_Handler and, 172
    handle access through, 144–145, 150

get_message_destination(), 395
getopt(), *vs.* ACE_Get_Opt, 78–82
get_process_attribute(), for process ID, 226
getq()
    block with, 265
    for stream tasks, 378, 389–390
global errno, in thread-specific storage, 309
GNU Autotools, for build configuration, 28
GNU Make tool
    for application building, 31–33
    for compiling, 9
    options for, 30*t*
Graph, 474
Graphable_Element, 473–475
Graphable_Element_List, 474, 475–486
group ID, for thread pool, 275
grp_id() accessor, 275
guards
    for critical sections, 246–247
    for mutexes, 254–257
        classes of, 256, 256*t*
        macros for allocation of, 256
        vs. acquire and release, 255
GUI integrated reactors, 185–186

H
half-sync/half-async thread pool, 326–338
    ACE_Task queueing in, 330
    ACE_Task queuing in, 330
    advantages and disadvantages of, 326–327
    structure of, 326
handle(), 192, 193
handle(s). *See also* event handle(s); I/O handle
    from ACE_Asynch_Acceptor, 199
    in ACE_WFMO_Reactor implementation, 184
    in ACE_Win32_Proactor implementation, 201
    direct use of, 140, 144
    obtaining, 192, 199
    for Proactor factory classes, 202–203
    saving, 192
    signalable, 204
    for slave process, 223
    in Sockets API, 124
    stored in handler, 191–192
    value of, getting, 145, 150
handleCancel(), for upcall handler, 453, 454

handle_close()
in Acceptor-Connector framework, 175–176,
176*f*
in ACE_WFMO_Reactor implementation, 184
calling, 148–149
handle access through, 144
return value from, 154–155
handleClose(), for upcall handler, 453, 454
handleEvent(), for timer expiration, 453
handle_exception()
in ACE_WFMO_Reactor implementation, 184
control dispatched to, 159–160
handle_exit(), 230–231
handle_input()
in ACE_WFMO_Reactor implementation, 184
for Client handler, 179–180
error handling in, 152–153
handle access through, 144, 146–147
return value from, 148
for service handler, 150–152
in Acceptor-Connector framework, 173–175
handle_output()
in Acceptor-Connector framework, 175, 180–
181
in Reactor framework, 153–155
handler. *See* event handler
handle_read_stream(), 194, 195
handler threads
barrier and, 307–308
updating by, 253–254
handle_signal(), 156–157, 239–240
in ACE_WFMO_Reactor implementation, 184
parameters of (*See* siginfo_t;
ucontext_t)
signal state and, 158–159
for thread signaling, 279
handle_timeout()
for active-timer dispatcher, 448
for Client handler, 180
current time and, 162
for signal timer, 450
state data passed to, 163–166
for timer dispatcher, 443
for timer event handler, 444–445
for timer event listener, 441
handle_write_stream(), 195
HA_Proactive_Acceptor, 198–200
HA_Proactive_Service handler
deletion of, 194

handle passed to, 191
hashing function, 109, 110–111
hash map(s)
about, 109–111
allocator reference in, 366
record deletion from, 366–367
in shared memory, 361–369
head module
in command stream, 399
in one-way stream, 381
heap memory
allocation of
in compilers, 18–19
configuration information and, 83
queue on, 99
helper class, for self-adjusting binary trees, 111–
112
Hollywood Principle, 8
host name, in ACE_INET_Addr, 126

I
IBM mainframes, asynchronous I/O in, 188
implementations
of ACE_Proactor, 201–202
of ACE_Reactor, 182–186
of command stream, 409–414
reuse of, 7
include/makeinclude directory, 27
info(), for static services, 421
inheritance, in callbacks, 61
init()
Object Manager initialization with, 18
for static services, 421–423
initialization
of ACE_Acceptor, 423
of command stream, 415
of name options, 460
of Object Manager, 17–18
of reader object, in Proactor framework, 193
at runtime, platform and, 14–18
of semaphores, 307
of static service, 423, 425
of writer object, in Proactor framework, 193
input, handling, 149–153
instance(), for reactor instance, 146
instantiation
allocators passed during, 117
of Object Manager, 18

Institute for Software Integrated Systems (ISIS), 4
interface, iterators and, 95
interprocess communication (IPC)
    interhost, 207–213
    intrahost, 213–214
    shared memory for, 349
    in wrapper facades, 123
interval timer
    resetting, 441
    timer queue and, 438
int_value(), for PROC_LOCAL context, 464,
    467
inversion of control, in runtime architecture, 8
I/O
    completion of, 194–197
    initiation of, in Proactor framework, 193–194
I/O event handlers. *See also* completion handler;
        connection-accepting handler; service han-
        dler
    registration of, 144
        for multiple handles, 147
        at reactor shutdown, 155
        removing from reactor, 148–149, 155
I/O handle, association of
    in ACE_Event_Handler, 144
    removing from reactor, 148–149, 155
I/O operations, asynchronous, 196*f*
    completing, 194–195
    guidelines for, 195–197
    initiating, 191–194
    outstanding, 197
I/O sources. *See also* client; connection(s); input;
        output; server
    handling multiple, 142–155
iostream formatting, 38–39
iovec structures, 132–133
    receiving data with, 134–135
    sending data with, 133–134
ISIS (Institute for Software Integrated Systems), 4
is_member() routine, 158
iterator(s)
    about, 89–90
    in ACE_Malloc map interface, 351
    in array, 101
    in C++ algorithms, 90
    dereferencing, 106, 109
    in doubly linked list, 94–95
    in lazy map managers, 104

in maps, 105–107
in self-adjusting binary trees, 112–114
iterator APIs, in ACE, 89–90

K
kernel-level threads, 268–269
key(s)
    ACE_Less_Than functor specialization for,
        114–115
    in associative containers, 103
    comparability of, in map manager, 104, 107
    grouping, 457
    hashing function for, 110
    in hash maps, 108–109, 363
    in maps, 103
key/value pairs, in naming context, 457

L
layered architecture, of ACE toolkit, 6–7
leader/follower thread pool, 338–343
    in ACE_TP_Reactor, 343–345
    advantages and disadvantages of, 338
    becoming leader in, 340, 342
    follower created in, 341
    svc() for, 339–340, 342
less-than operator, in NODE_LOCAL context, 475
libraries
    flexibility from, 5
    linking, in application build, 32
    shared (*See* shared libraries)
licensing, for ACE, 4
LIFO sequences, stacks as, 94
linked list. *See also* doubly linked list
    ACE_Stream as, 385
list_name_entries(), for NODE_LOCAL
        context, 473
lock(s)
    in ACE_Malloc, 350
    in ACE_Svc_Handler, 172
    in guard classes, 255
    in hash map, 109
    in map manager, 108
    readers/writer, 292–293
log files, rotation of, 75
logger key, definition of, 66
logging. *See also* ACE_DEBUG macro;
        ACE_ERROR macro
    basic, 38–42
    format for, 38–39, 45

macros for, 43*t*–44*t*
  customizing, 47–55
  output of
    to output streams, 58–59
    redirecting, 55–60
    to standard error stream, 55–56
    to system logger, 56–58
  runtime configuration of, 73–75
  switching, with signals, 157–158
  thread-specific storage and, 309–310
logging client proxy, 65–70
  configuration files for, 66
  port value for, 66–67
logging server, 65–70
  configuration file for, 66
  direct communication with, 67–68
  starting, 66
logging strategy
  configuration options for, 75*t*
  definition of, 66
  for runtime configuration, 73–75
LogManager, 70–73
long command line options
  alternative specification for, 81
  definition of, 78
  long_only parameter for, 81
  without short options, 79–80

M
macro(s)
  for function tracing, 53–55
  for logging, 43*t*–44*t*
    customizing, 47–55
  for memory allocation, 19, 20*t*
  for mutex allocation, 256
  for service configuration, 424–425
  for thread priority, 272*t*
macro files, for ACE build, 29*t*
main()
  dynamic service configuration and, 429
  exit handler in, 278
  for NODE_LOCAL context, 469, 471–472
  Object Manager instantiation with, 18
  for one-way stream, 379–380
  process thread in, 250
  for PROC_LOCAL context, 465
  signal set in, 245
  vs. exit() function, 17
main thread, in process, 250

Makefile, for application building, 31–33
make_handler(), for
      ACE_Asynch_Acceptor, 199
map(s), 104–108
  bindings in, 105
  deletion from, 107
  insertions in, 104
  iterators in, 106–107
  lazy, 104
  locks in, 108
  operations on, 105
  retrievals from, 105
map interface, for ACE_Malloc, 351–352, 355
MapViewOfFileEx(), 375
master process
  dump by, 224–225
  environment variable in, 223
  mutex shared with, 231–232
  slave result and, 224
MB_HANGUP message type, 263, 264, 266
  checking for, 390, 406–407
  in stream task close, 389
memory, shared. *See* shared memory
memory allocation
  for ACE_WString pointer, 464
  configuration information and, 83
  pool growth and, 369
  position-independent, 356–359
  for record additions, 355
  for record deletions, 362
  resolve() method and, 463
  in timer queue, 439
memory allocation macros, 19, 20*t*
memory allocators. *See* allocators
memory-mapped files, 119, 458
memory ordering properties, 293
memory pool
  in ACE_Malloc, 350
  growth of, handling, 369–374
  insert values in, 351
  shared (*See* shared memory pool)
  types of, 351*t*
memory protection interface, for ACE_Malloc,
      352
message blocks, 262–263. *See also*
      ACE_Message_Block
  in command stream, 401
    downstream tasks and, 408

releasing, 409

read pointer from, 390

sending, in one-way stream, 391

svc() method for, in stream tasks, 389

type field in, 263

message passing, 257, 260–266

message processing, 273, 275

message queue

for message passing, 260–266, 266*t*

in one-way stream, 385, 387

priority in, 266

for thread pool, 275

in thread pool asynchronous layer, 329

types of, 266, 266*t*

using, 263–266

metadata, saving, 396

method. *See specific methods*

method, private, for processing code, 203–204

method request

in Active Object pattern, 315–316

creation of, 319–320

enqueueing, 321, 338

enqueuing, 321, 338

in half-sync/half-async thread pool, 333, 335

microarchitecture, reuse of, 7

Microsoft Visual C++, build configuration in, 34–35, 36*t*

middleware, flexibility from, 5

- (minus), in command line options, 82

mmap(), 375

mnemonic, for DLL porting, 34

module(), 410, 412

module(s), in Streams framework

in ACE_Stream, 383

for command stream, 399–400

instantiation of, 383

in one-way stream, 381

in open(), 382–383

ordering on stream, 400

overview of, 377–378

pushing onto one-way stream, 383–384

tasks in, 383

monitor()

for NET_LOCAL context, 477

for NODE_LOCAL context, 470, 472

for PROC_LOCAL context, 460, 466

msg_queue()

ACE_Message_Queue accessed with, 175

queue type specified with, 266

msg_type(), 263

multicast connection, in UDP, 208, 212–213

multicast groups, 208, 212–213

multiple threads

in ACE_POSIX_Proactor implementation, 202

in ACE_WFMO_Reactor implementation, 184

handlers in, registering and unregistering, 159

multithreaded I/O model, 187, 188

multithreaded programming, 249, 282–283

multithreaded server, 325

mutex

acquiring, 252, 255

automatic, 258

in hash map, 365

twice, 291

binary semaphore *vs.,* 303

condition variable in, 257–258

deadlock on, 254–257

named, ACE_Process_Mutex for, 231–232

recursive, 291–292

releasing, 252–254, 255

automatic, 258

in thread synchronization, 233

shared, 231–232

for thread safety, 252–254

type of, in ACE_Condition, 259

mutex(), lock reference obtained with, 108

N

Name_Binding

memory management for, 464

releasing, 464–465

resolve() result in, 463, 466

values extracted from, 474–475

named mutex, ACE_Process_Mutex for, 231–232

name options, 460

namespace, *vs.* class, 10

naming context. *See also*
        ACE_Naming_Context

binding in, 460–465

key/value pairs in, 457

shared, 469–476

reading data from, 471–476

saving data from, 469–471

types in, 457

types of, 458

uses of, 457
values stored in, 459–468
Naming_Context, 465
Naming Service
    about, 457
    API of, 459
    context types of, 458
    starting, 476–477
narrow character sets, *vs.* wide, 19–21
nested type definition, 106
NET_LOCAL context, 458–459, 476–478
netsvcs logging framework, 65–70
networked applications, difficulty in writing, 5
networked services layer, about, 6
network software, timers in, 437
next_step(), for stream tasks, 391
NODE_LOCAL context, 469–476
    access in, 458
    modifying, for NET_LOCAL context, 477
nonblocking connection operation, with
        ACE_SOCK_Connector, 132
notification
    for callback queueing, 159
    for callback queueing, 159
    control returned by, 238, 247
    in process event handling, 230
notification strategy, on ACE_Message_Queue,
        179
notify(), logging switching with, 159
NotifySomeone task, 396–397
Null Mutex, 16, 111

O
object, runtime initialization of, 14–18
object-based containers, 89
Object Manager
    about, 14–15
    initialization of, 17–18
    instantiation of, 18
    rules for, 17
    termination of, 17–18
object type, in containers, 88
one-way stream, 378–397
    initializing, 381–386
    main program for, 379–380
    modules in, 383
    stream in, 381–387
    tasks in, 386–397

open()
    for ACE_Asynch_Acceptor, 200
    for ACE_SOCK_Acceptor, 135
    for Client handler, 168–179
    for ClientService handler, in Acceptor-
        Connector framework, 172–173
    for command stream, 399
    for command task, 405
    for connection-accepting handler, 144–145, 146
    for HA_Proactive_Service, 192
    for logging service, 67
    for one-way stream, 380, 382–383
    for PROC_LOCAL context, 460
    service configuration with, 426
    for service handler, 148–149
    for stream tasks, 387
    for system logger output, 56–58
Open VMS, asynchronous I/O in, 187
operating system, OS adaptation layer in, 10
operating systems
    multiple, porting code to, 8–10
    priorities defined in, 271
    system loggers of, 58
operator(), for command line options, 79
operator->(), for thread-specific storage
        access, 310
op_status() methods, 47
ordering parameter, for argument ordering, 82
ordering properties, of memory, 293
OS adaptation layer, 6, 9, 10
OS methods, 9–10
output, handling, 154–155
output streams
    deleting, 60
    for logging, 58–59
    thread-specific, 309–310
owner(), for ACE_Select_Reactor, 183

P
parallel processing, in Streams framework, 378
parent(pid_t child), 226
parent process. *See* master process
parsing
    at arbitrary index, 80–81
    error reporting during, 81
pass_addresses argument, 200
peer()
    ACE_SOCK_Stream accessed with, 175

`ACE_Svc_Handler` and, 172
  for `ClientService`, 147
  for command module, 403, 409, 410
peer, in UDP unicast, 209, 210
`perform()`, method request enqueued by, 338
performance, in multithreaded I/O, 188
`PERMUTE_ARGS`, for argument ordering, 82
pipes, for intrahost communication, 213–214
Pipes and Filters pattern, in Streams framework, 377
platform. *See* operating systems
`PlayMessage`, 412–413
`play_message()`, 417
`PlayOutgoingMessage` task, 392–393
+ (plus), in command line options, 82
pointers. *See also specific pointers*
  in `ACE_Message_Block`, 154
  in `ClientService:open`, 173
  copying, in queues, 100
  data population with, 93
  in fixed stack, 97
  iterators and, 89
  position-independent, 358–359, 360
  in queue, 99–100
  to reactor, in `ACE_Acceptor`, 173
  in reference containers, 93
  in sets, 101, 103
  to shared memory, 354, 356–357
  typeless, in C, 88
`poll()`, for event handling, 142
port
  in `ACE_INET_Addr`, 126, 145
  choosing, 131
  for client, 131
  for server, 135, 145
  in UDP, 207, 209, 211
portability, standards and, 9
position-independent allocation, 356–359, 361
position-independent control block, 357
position-independent pointers, 358–359, 360
`POSIXLY_CORRECT` environment variable, 82
POSIX systems
  asynchronous I/O in, 188
  proactor implementation on, 202
  signals on, response to, 156
`prepare()`, for process spawning, 222–223
primitives
  for consistency, 289

for thread safety, 251
  types of, 290*t*
priorities, thread scheduling classes and, 271–274, 272*t*
`priority()`, in `ACE_Priority_Reactor` implementation, 185
private method, for code, 203–204
private thread of control. *See* thread of control
proactive I/O model. *See* asynchronous I/O model
`proactor` argument, 200
proactor event loop
  integrating with reactor, 204
  for I/O completion processing, 201
Proactor framework
  classes in, 189–191, 190*f*
  completion handling in, 201–202
  connection establishment in, 198–201
  I/O operations in, 191–197
  Reactor framework and, combining, 203–205
  UDP and, 208
`PROBLEM-REPORT-FORM` file, 26
process. *See also* `ACE_Process`; master process; slave process
  address space protection between, 349
  event handling with, demultiplexer for, 142
  logging severities of, 45–47
  main thread in, 250
  in shared memory, 365
  signaling, in multithreaded programs, 284–285
  spawning, 219–226
  spawning multiple, 226–231
  synchronization of, mutex for, 252
  terminating, 227, 229, 243–245
`process()`
  for command task, 406, 407–408, 410
  for stream tasks, 387, 390 391
`process_directive()`, for service configuration, 434
`process_file()`, for service configuration, 434
process ID
  in signal handling, displaying, 242
  for slave process, in process termination, 228
`process_message()`, priorities in, 273
process-per-connection model, 142
`processRecord()`, 372–373
`processWin32Record()`, 372–373
`PROC_LOCAL` context, 459–468

access in, 458
binding in, 460–465
protect(), for ACE_Malloc, 352
protection mode, for memory-mapped files, 376
protocols, for multicast group management, 212
Proxy
in Active Object pattern, 315–316
in method request creation, 319, 322
proxy, as Active Object, 313
Proxy pattern, in Active Object pattern, 315
put()
for command task, 405
for downstream task message queue, 386, 401
for stream tasks, 378, 385, 388
put_next(), for stream tasks, 378
bidirectional, 407
one-way, 391
putq()
for message enqueueing, 264
for message enqueueing, 264
for stream tasks, 388, 411

Q
Qt reactor, 186
quality-of-service parameters, with
ACE_SOCK_Connector, 132
queue(s), 98–100. *See also*
ACE_Message_Queue
for handle_input() errors, 152–153
for message passing (*See* message queue)
putq() method for, 175
shared memory allocator specified for, 371
as shared resource, 260
queueing layer, of half-sync/half-async thread pool, 326–327
queuing layer, of half-sync/half-async thread pool, 326–327

R
rd_ptr(), 154, 262
reactive I/O model, 142, 187–189
reactor. *See also* ACE_Reactor
in ACE_Acceptor, 171
handlers registered with, for state data, 166
I/O event handlers registered with, 144
removing, 148–149, 155
at shutdown, 155
notifications in, 159–160

control returned by, 238, 247
shared memory registered with, 214
signal handler registered with, 238
signal management with, 247
signal registered with, 157–158
timers handled by, 162–163
reactor(), for ACE_Event_Handler, 146
Reactor event, handlers for, from
ACE_Event_Handler, 144
reactor event loop, 146
service reconfiguration and, 431
stopping, 156–157
Reactor framework
ACE_Message_Block in, data handling with, 203–204
callbacks in, 141, 148
overview of, 142
Proactor framework and, combining, 203–205
process management and, 229
purpose of, 141
server based on, 145–149
signal-handling in, 235, 247
UDP classes in, 208
reactor pointer
in ACE_Acceptor, 173
in ACE_Connector, 179
read(), for ACE_Synch_Read_Stream, 192
reader object, initialization of, in Proactor framework, 193
readers/writer locks, 292–293
reader task, in Streams framework, 377
read operations
asynchronous, 194–195, 196
on memory-mapped files, 376
read pointer
in asynchronous write operation, 195
automatic update of, 196
in message block, in one-way stream, 390
readv(), 132–133
rebind(), in PROC_LOCAL context, 462, 466, 468
receive methods, in ACE_SOCK_Stream, 127
Receiver Implementation, in Active Object pattern, 315–316
reconfigure(), for services, 432
record(s)
adding, 355

binding, 355
copying to shared memory, 366
deletion of
  from hash map, 366–367
  memory pool growth and, 367
  inserting, into shared memory allocator, 352, 353–354
  memory allocation for, deletion of, 362
record(), for one-way stream, 384–385, 386
recorder(), for AnswerIncomingCall, 386–387
record_failure(), for PROC_LOCAL context, 467
record_history(), for NODE_LOCAL context, 470
RecordIncomingMessage task, 393–394
RecordingDevice
  for bidirectional stream, 398
  for one-way stream, 380, 386–387
RecordingStream, 380, 381–386
record-keeping information
  for dynamic services, 428, 429
  for static services, 424
RecordMessage, 413–414
record_message(), 417
record_temperature(), 466
  for NODE_LOCAL context, 470
recursive mutex, 16, 291–292. See also ACE_Recursive_Thread_Mutex
recv()
  for ACE_SOCK_Dgram, 210
  for ACE_SOCK_Dgram_Mcast, 213
  return value for, handle_input() method and, 152
recv_n(), buffer and, 127
recvv(), buffer allocation with, 134–135
Red Black Tree, 111
redirect* method, for output destination selection, 70
reference containers, pointers in, 93
reference documentation, for ACE, 21
register_action(), for callback registration, 238
register_handler()
  acceptor events monitored by, 145
  input events and, 148
  for signal event handler, 241
  for signals, 157–158
release()
  for message blocks, 262
  for mutex, 252–254, 258
  for readers/writer lock, 292
  semaphores and, 304
  for TextListener, 418
  vs. guard, 255
ReleaseDevice task, 394
release versions, 25
remap(), for pool growth handling, 369–374
remove(), for services, 434
remove_handler()
  in ACE_WFMO_Reactor implementation, 184
  handle_close() and, 148–149
REQUIRE_ORDER, for argument ordering, 82
reset_device(), for PROC_LOCAL context, 468
reset_interval(), for timer dispatcher, 441
resolve()
  for NODE_LOCAL context, 473
  for PROC_LOCAL context, 462–463, 466
resource sharing, coordination of, 231
Result
  for ACE_Asynch_Read_Stream, 195
  in Proactor framework, about, 191
  in Proactor framwork, about, 191
resume()
  for services, 432, 434
  thread management with, 276
  for thread schedule, 271
retrieve_callerID(), 392, 416
RetrieveCallerID module, 411–412
RETURN_IN_ORDER, for arguments, 82
reuse
  of addresses, 136, 145, 200
  of code, templates for, 11–12
  in frameworks, 7
  in patterns, 7
reuse_addr flag, 136, 145, 200
Riverace Corporation, 22, 26
root section, of configuration data, 84
round-robin scheduling policy, 271
runtime
  behavior at, altering with command lines, 77
  configuration at, 420
  debug statements at, 37–38
  frameworks at, 8

initialization at, 14–18
logging configuration at, 73–75
service configuration at, 419

S
SA_RESTART, 239
SaveMetaData task, 395–396
schedule()
  for timer dispatcher, 443
  timer ID returned by, 440
Scheduler
  in Active Object pattern, 315–316, 319
    thread of control in, 320
  aggregation of, with agent implementation, 321
schedule_timer(), return value of. *See* timer
    ID
schedule_wakeup(), 180
scheduling, of threads
  real-time, 271
  time-shared, 271
  user-level *vs.* kernel-level, 268–269
scheduling classes, priorities and, 271–274, 272*t*
scheduling state, thread, initial, 270–271
Schmidt, Douglas C., 3–4
Secure Sockets Layer (SSL) handshake, 199
security parameters, in process spawning, 225–226
SEH (structured exception handling), in pool
    remapping, 369–370
select()
  for event handling, 142
  vs. WaitForMultipleObjects() func-
    tion, 153
self(), thread ID from, 285
self-adjusting binary trees, 111–115
semaphores
  ACE_Process_Mutex with, 234
  acquiring, 302, 303
  conditional variables *vs.*, 303
  definition of, 302
  initialization of, 307
  releasing, 302
  for thread synchronization, 302–307
send methods, for ACE_SOCK_Stream, 127
send_n(), buffer and, 127
sendv(), 133
sensors, state data from, 163–166
sequence containers. *See* array; doubly linked list;
    queue(s); set(s); stack container

server. *See also* I/O sources
  communication with, 126
  connection to (*See* connection(s))
  constructing, 135–140
  message to, processing with threads, 250
  querying, 125, 129, 133–134
  Reactor-based, 145
  send and receive in, 137–138
  socket connection to, 126
service
  configuration of
    methods for, 434
    reprocessing, 431–432
    without configuration files, 434
    XML for, 432–433
  dynamic configuration of
    overview of, 420
    at runtime, 419
  reconfiguring, during execution, 431–432
  removal of, 431
  singletons and, 434–435
  specifications of, in stream configuration file,
    430
service, dynamic
  configuration of, 426–430
  declaration of, 428
  loading, 429
  runtime subsitution of, 426
  runtime substitution of, 426
  writing, 427
service, static
  cleanup of, 423–424
  configuration of, 420–426
  ignoring, 426
  initialization of, 423, 425
  instantiation of, 421
  in service configurator repository, 424
Service Configurator framework
  direct action on, 434
  for logging, 65–66
  for logging strategy, 74
  options in, 426, 427*t*
  overview of, 420
  repository in, 424
  XML event handlers for, 433
service handler. *See also* ClientService han-
    dler
  in ACE_Acceptor, 170
  allocation of, 155

`ACE_Svc_Handler` and, 182
creation of, 147
declaration of, 149–150
deriving at compile time, 203–204
`handle_input()` method for, 150–152
messages enqueued by, 264
messages received by, 263
in Proactor framework, 198
queueing in, 152–153
queueing in, 152–153
registration of, with reactor, 148
separation of, 144
set(s), 101–104. *See also* bounded set; unbounded
    set
  equality operator in, 101
  pointers in, 101, 103
  for signal registering, 158
  signals in, 238, 245
`set()` methods, 129–130
`set_process_attribute()`, for process ID,
    226
severities
  enabling and disabling, 44–47
  mapping to Event Log severties, 58, 59*t*
  mapping to Event Log severties, 58, 59*t*
  parameter for, 38, 39*t*
  at process level, 45–47
  in runtime logging configuration, 74–75
  at thread level, 45–47
severity mask, 45–47
shared libraries
  building, from multiple source files, 32–33
  naming, 430
  services loaded from, 426
  services resident in, 427
shared memory
  allocation in, 115
  hash map in, 362–363
  for interprocess communication, 349
  `Unbound_Queue` for, 370–371
shared memory allocator
  creation of, 365
  instantiation of, 353
  persistence with, 352–356
  remapping, 359
shared memory pool
  base address for, 356–357, 369
  growth of, 367, 369–374
  pointers to, 354, 356–357

shared memory stream, for intrahost communica-
    tion, 214
shared mutex, 231–232
shared resource
  coordinating, 232
  queue as, 260
sharing mode, for memory-mapped files, 376
short command line options, 78
short reads, `send_n()` and, 127
short writes, `recv_n()` and, 127
shutdown. *See also* MB_HANGUP message type
  reactor, I/O event handlers at, 155
  with semaphores, 306
  worker thread pool at, 332
`shutdown_barrier`, 307–308
`si_address`, 243
`si_code`, 243
`sigaction()`
  for action association, 236
  signal interruption and, 239
`sig_add()` routine, 158
SIGBUS, `si_address` and, 243
`sig_del()` routine, 158
SIGFPE, display details of, 243
SIGHUP, for service reconfiguration, 431
SIGILL, `si_address` and, 231
`siginfo_t`, 240, 241–245
SIGINT signal, catching, 155–157
SIGKILL, masking and, 246
signal(s), 156–158
  about, 235
  `accept()` method interrupted by, 136–137
  action associated with, 236, 239
  asynchronous, in multithreaded programs, 282
  callback registration for, 236–237
  display details of, 242
  interruption by, 239
  multiple callbacks for, 237, 245
  in multithreaded programs, 282
  passed to condition variable, 258
  on POSIX systems, response to, 156
  in process event handling, 230
  in process termination, 228
  for service reconfiguration, 431
  synchronous, in multithreaded programs, 282
  system calls and, 239
  in threaded applications, 279–283
signal context, control in, 247

signal event handler
    execution of, signal disabled during, 238–239
    registration of, 241
    for signals, 239–245
        multiple, 157–158
        single, 156–157
signal handler
    associating, 235, 279
    callback for, registration of, 238
    code for, 237
    creation of, 240–241
    in multithreaded programs, 282
    in pool remapping, 369–370
    registration of, 238, 281
    stacking, 245
    testing, 245
signal mask, for threads, 279
signal number
    character strings mapped to, 242
    passed to handle_signal(), 240
signal state, control in, 158–160, 246
signal timer dispatchers, 449–450
signal type, signal handler for, 279
SignitHandler
    timer cancelled with, 168–169
    timer reset with, 167
SIGSEGV
    display details of, 243
    pool remapping and, 370
    si_address and, 243
sigset_t argument, 236
SIGSTOP, masking and, 246
Singleton
    about, 15–16
    declaring, 71
    services and, 434–435
Singleton method, for cleanup, 16
Singleton template, in LogManager, 71
slave process
    code for, 223–224
    command line arguments for, 223
    handles for, 223, 224
    mutex shared with, 231–232
    options for, 220–222
sleep, in signal handlers, 237–238
sockaddr_in structure, in Sockets client, 124–125
socket() function, file descriptor from, 125

socket handle. *See* handle(s)
socket pointer, in command module, 400, 402–403, 409, 410
Sockets programming
    client program in, 127–128
    disadvantages of, 124
software development, complexity and cost of, 7
source code, multiplatform, difficulty of writing, 5
source files, multiple, building from, 32
spawn(), 46
    fork() compared to, 220
    for multiple processes, 227
    for processes, 221
    system() compared to, 220
spawn_n(), 46
    for multiple processes, 221
special conditions, in one-way stream, 381, 391
sprintf(), for PROC_LOCAL context, 462
SSL (Secure Sockets Layer) handshake, 199
stack container, 94–97. *See also* bounded stack; fixed stack; unbounded stack
    dynamic, 94
    insertions on, 98
    iterator in, 94
    static, 94
stack memory
    exit handler on, 278
    guard called on, 255
    queue on, 98
standard error stream (STDERR), output to, 55–56
standards, portability and, 9
standard template library (STL), support for, 87
start(), for start-up hooks, 283–284
startup_barrier, 307–308
start-up hooks, for threads, 283–284
state change, intertask communication on, 257
state data
    consistency of, 251
    consistency of, 251
    passing, to event handler, 163–166
    in thread-specific storage, 309
static service
    configuration of, 420–426
    ignoring, 426
    initialization of, 423, 425
    instantiation of, 421
    in service configurator repository, 424
static stack, definition of, 94

status server, querying, 133–134

STDERR (standard error stream), output to, 55–56

STL (standard template library), support for, 87

Strategy pattern
in ACE_Reactor_Notification_
Strategy, 178
wrapper facades and, 123

strdup(), 464

stream. *See also* ACE_SOCK_Stream;
ACE_Stream
bidirectional (*See* bidirectional stream; command stream)
configuration of
from file, 430
at runtime, 420
with XML, 432–433
definition of, 123
one-way (*See* one-way stream)
in Streams framework, 377, 379*f*
vs. datagram, 208

Streams framework, 377–378

string, argument vector conversion to, 85

structured exception handling (SEH), in pool remapping, 369–370

subtypes, in object containers, 89

suspend()
for services, 432, 434
thread management with, 276

svc()
for command task, 404, 406–407, 410–411
for leader/follower thread pool, 339–340, 342
for stream tasks, 389–390
thread started in, 250

switch(), 243

symbols, importing and exporting, in DLLs, 33–34

sync(), for ACE_Malloc, 352

synchronization classes, 231

synchronization complexity, in multithreaded I/O, 188

synchronization primitives, for threads, 302*t*

synchronous layer, of half-sync/half-async thread pool, 326–327

synchronous signals, handling, in multithreaded programs, 282

sync interface, for ACE_Malloc, 352

system logger, output to, 56–58

system() *vs.* spawn(), 220

System V shared memory, 119

System V STREAMS framework, 377

T

tail module
in command stream, 399
in one-way stream, 381

tasks, in Streams framework. *See also* downstream tasks; upstream tasks
base class for, 387–392
for command stream, 399–400, 402
message queue of, 385
methods in, 387–392
in modules, 383
in one-way stream, 386–397
in open(), 382–383
overview of, 389–390
shutting down, 387, 388
threads for, releasing, 394

Tcl/Tk reactor, 186

TCP connection, *vs.* UDP, 207–208

technical support services, 22

temperature graphing application, 471–476, 478
Graphable_Element in, 473–475
Graphable_Element_List in, 474, 475–476
Graph in, 474

temperature monitor application, 465–468

template(s),
compiler application of, 176
in compilers, difference among, 11–14
instantiation of, in compilers, 11–12, 71

template arguments classes, types defined in, 13–14

template-based containers, 88–89

template specialization
about, 89
for ACE_Less_Than functor, 114–115
for hashing function, 110–111
for key type comparability, 107–108

terminate(), for slave processes, 228

termination, of Object Manager, 17–18

testcancel(), 285

testing
in doubly linked list, 92–93
of signal handler, 245

tests directory, 27

TextListener, command stream used by, 414–418

`TextListenerAcceptor`, 410

THANKS file, 27

`THR_BOUND` flag, user-level thread bound by, 269

`THR_DETACHED` flag, 269

thread(s). *See also* thread of control

 in `ACE_Select_Reactor`, 183

 cancellation of, 284–288

 for command task, creation of, 405

 communication among, 257–266

 cooperation between, 313

 creation of, 250, 272

 data added to, 283

 detached, 269–270

 event handling with, demultiplexer for, 142

 execution of, ordering, 302

 exit functions for, number of, 277

 joinable, 269–270

 kernel-level *vs.* user-level, 268–269

 logging severities of, 45–47

 management of, 276–279

 multiple

  in `ACE_WFMO_Reactor` implementation, 184

  handlers in, registering and unregistering, 159

 number of, in barrier, 307

 owner, recording, 258

 priority in creation of, 272

 in proactive I/O, 189

 readers/writer lock on, 292–293

 scheduling, 268–269, 271

 scheduling classes for, 271–274

 scheduling state of, initial, 270–271

 shutdown of, barrier and, 307

 signaling, 279–281

 signal mask for, 279

 start-up hooks for, 283–284

 start-up of, barrier and, 307

 for stream tasks, 387, 394

 termination of, with cancellation, 284

 types of, 267–271

thread of control, 313, 320

thread creation flags, for thread attributes, 267–268, 268*t*

`thread_hook()`, 284

thread ID

 of leader thread, 338

 mutex and, 291

 obtaining, 285

 in thread-specific storage, 310

threading policy, in multithreaded I/O, 188

thread manager

 exit handler registered with, 277

 multiple, 279

 pointer to, 277

 signals sent with, 279

 as singleton, 279

thread-per-connection model, 142

 for multithreaded I/O, 188

 thread-specific storage with, 310

thread-per-request model, *vs.* thread pool model, 326

thread pool(s), 274–275

 about, 325–326

 in `ACE_TP_Reactor` implementation, 185

thread pool model, for multithreaded I/O, 188

thread-pool reactor, implementation of, 183

thread priority macros, 272*t*

thread safety

 basics of, 251–257

 in map manager, 108

 mutexes for, 252–254

thread-specific storage (TSS), 309–311, 327

thread synchronization, 301–309

 `ACE_Mutex` for, 252

 `ACE_Process_Mutex` for, 231–234

 in half-sync/half-async thread pool, 327

 semaphores for, 302–307

threat, callback in, 61

`THR_JOINABLE` flag, 269

`thr_mgr()`, 277

`THR_NEW_LWP` flag, user-level thread bound by, 269

`THR_SCHED_FIFO` flag, 272

`THR_SCHED_RR` flag, 272

`thr_self()`, 285

`THR_SUSPENDED` flag, 270

timed block, on condition variable, 258

timeout

 with `ACE_SOCK_Stream`, 132

 on connection request, 130–131

 on connection requests, 136

 in multiple process management, 229

 thread for handling, 345–346

 in timer queue, 438

`timeout()`, for upcall handler, 451, 453

timer(s), 160–169

 about, 437–438

block on, 443
cancellation of, 168–169, 441
expiration of, event handlers for, 439, 453
handling, with reactor, 162–163
hardware, 437
interval
  resetting, 441
  timer queue and, 438
in Proactor framework, 202
process-based, 162–164
resetting, 166–167
scheduling, 443
timer dispatcher, 441*f,* 442*f*
  parts of, 439–440
  prebuilt, 440, 447–450
  timer queue in, 455
timer driver, definition of, 440
timer event handler
  for active timer dispatcher, 448
  for cancellation, 444
  managing, 450–455
  registration of, 163
  specification of, 450
  for timeout, 444–445
  for timer expiration, 162, 439
timer event listener, 440–441
timer ID, 167–169, 440
timer queue
  about, 438
  characteristics of, 439
  class hierarchy for, 438*f*
  memory allocation in, 439
  template types in, 450, 451*f*
  in timer dispatcher, 455
timer queue event handler, 451–452
timer singleton, 441
timerTask() function, 160–162
time-shared schedulers, 271
token, 254, 299
Token framework, 297–301
token manager, 297
Trace, 51–55
TRACE_RETURN macro, 53–55
TRACE_RETURN_VOID macro, 53–54
tracing. *See also* ACE_TRACE macro
  about, 39–42, 44*t*
  of functions, macros for, 53–55
try and back-off strategy, for deadlock prevention,

301
TSS (thread-specific storage), 309–311, 327
type(s)
  in naming context, 457
  synchronization around, 293
  in template arguments classes, use of, 13–14
type awareness, allocators and, 116
type definition
  for doubly linked list, 91–92
  nested, in maps, 106
type information, in configuration information, 85

U
ucontext_t, 245–246
  passed to handle_signal(), 240
UCS (Universal Multiple Octet Coded Character
    Set), 19
UDP/IP
  for interhost communication, 207–213
  vs. TCP, 207–208
UDP sockets
  closing, 210
  vs. TCP, 126
unbind()
  allocator argument in, 369
  for element deletion, 114
  variables reset with, 467
unbounded set, 100, 102–103
unbounded stack, 94–97. *See also*
    ACE_Unbounded_Stack
Unbound_Queue, for shared memory, 370–371
unicast connection, in UDP, 208, 209–211
Unicode, 19
Universal Multiple Octet Coded Character Set
    (UCS), 19
UNIX/Linux syslog
  in mixed environment, 65
    output to, 58
upcall handler, 451–455, 452*f*
upcall manager, 451
update_device()
  with multiple threads, 298
  mutex acquisition in, 252–254
update_graph(), for NODE_LOCAL context,
    472–473
upstream tasks
  in command stream, 408
  definition of, 378

`putq()` method on, 411
  for `RecordMessage`, 411–414
  for `RetrieveCallerID`, 411–412
user ID
  in signal handling, 242
  for slave process, setting, 223, 225–226
user-level threads
  binding, 269
  vs. kernel-level threads, 268–269

V

`__VA_ARGS__`, 49, 50–51
`validate_connection()`, for
      `ACE_Asynch_Acceptor`, 198–199
`validate_new_connection` argument, 200
`value()`
  for `ACE_Atomic_Op`, 294
  for name binding, 466
value containers
  bounded stack as, 95
  vs. reference containers, 93
`VERSION` file, 26
Visual C++. *See* Microsoft Visual C++

W

`wait()`
  on barrier, 307
  on condition variable, 258
  on follower thread, 341
  for process termination, 228
  slave process and, 221–222
  for thread completion, 251
  for thread joining, 269–270
  thread management with, 276
  with thread manager, 278
  on timer, 443
`wait_for_activity()`
  for `RecordingDevice`, 380
  for `TextListenerAcceptor`, 414–415
`wait_for_event()`, for timer dispatcher, 441
`WaitForMultipleObjects()`
  in `ACE_WFMO_Reactor` implementation, 183
  for event handling, 142
  `select()` function *vs.*, 153

`while` loop, client connections and, 138–139
wide character sets
  macros for, 20*t*
  vs. narrow, 19–21
Windows
  asynchronous I/O in, 188
  Event Log of, 58, 65
  proactor implementation on, 201–202, 204–205
  reactor implementation on, 183
  registry of, configuration information in, 83, 84–85
  service DLL on, 430
  signals in, 235
  Sockets portability to, 125
`WinMain()` function, 18
worker thread pool
  in `ACE_Unbounded_Queue`, 329
  at shutdown, 332
wrapper
  for shared memory primitives, 375–376
  for signal handling, 236–239
wrapper facade layer
  about, 6
  interprocess communication (IPC) in, 123
wrapper facade patterns, in OS adaptation layer, 9
`write()`, noncontiguous buffers and, 133
write operations
  asynchronous, 195, 196
  on memory-mapped files, 376
write pointer
  in asynchronous read operations, 194
  automatic update of, 196
`writer` object, initialization of, in Proactor framework, 193
writer task, in Streams framework, 389
`writev()`, 132–134
`wr_ptr()`, 262, 264

X

X Toolkit reactor, 186
X Windows, reactor extensions for, 185–186

Also Available from Addison-Wesley

C++ Network Programming, Volume 1:
Mastering Complexity with ACE and Patterns
C++ In-Depth Series
By Douglas C. Schmidt and Stephen D. Huston
ISBN 0-201-60464-7
© 2002

As networks, devices, and systems continue to evolve, software engineers face the unique challenge of creating reliable distributed applications within frequently changing environments. ***C++ Network Programming, Volume 1,*** provides practical solutions for developing and optimizing complex distributed systems using the ADAPTIVE Communication Environment (ACE), a revolutionary open-source framework that runs on dozens of hardware platforms and operating systems.

C++ Network Programming, Volume 2:
Systematic Reuse with ACE and Frameworks
C++ In-Depth Series
By Douglas C. Schmidt and Stephen D. Huston
ISBN 0-201-79525-6
© 2003

C++ Network Programming, Volume 2, focuses on ACE frameworks, providing thorough coverage of the concepts, patterns, and usage rules that form their structure. This book is a practical guide to designing object-oriented frameworks and shows developers how to apply frameworks to concurrent networked applications. *C++ Networking, Volume 1,* introduced ACE and the wrapper facades, which are basic network computing ingredients. Volume 2 explains how frameworks build on wrapper facades to provide higher-level communication services.

For more information, please visit www.awprofessional.com.

CD-ROM Warranty

Addison-Wesley warrants the enclosed disc to be free of defects in materials and faulty workmanship under normal use for a period of ninety days after purchase. If a defect is discovered in the disc during this warranty period, a replacement disc can be obtained at no charge by sending the defective disc, postage prepaid, with proof of purchase to:

Editorial Department
Addison-Wesley Professional
Pearson Technology Group
75 Arlington Street, Suite 300
Boston, MA 02116
Email: AWPro@awl.com

Addison-Wesley makes no warranty or representation, either expressed or implied, with respect to this software, its quality, performance, merchantability, or fitness for a particular purpose. In no event will Addison-Wesley, its distributors, or dealers be liable for direct, indirect, special, incidental, or consequential damages arising out of the use or inability to use the software. The exclusion of implied warranties is not permitted in some states. Therefore, the above exclusion may not apply to you. This warranty provides you with specific legal rights. There may be other rights that you may have that vary from state to state. The contents of this CD-ROM are intended for personal use only.

More information and updates are available at:
http://www.awprofessional.com/